VOLUME TWO

The Joyous Path

THE LIFE OF AVATAR MEHER BABA'S SISTER, MANI

HEATHER NADEL

2015
SHERIAR FOUNDATION
MYRTLE BEACH, SOUTH CAROLINA

© Copyright 2015 Avatar Meher Baba Perpetual Public Charitable Trust,
Ahmednagar India.

All rights reserved. Published 2015.

Printed in the United States of America.

Credits for photographs, historical materials, and archival objects
used in *The Joyous Path* can be found in the
List of Illustrative Materials on pages 1087–1107.

Credits for excerpts from published works reproduced
in *The Joyous Path* can be found in the
List of Source Materials on pages 1109–1110.

No part of this book may be reproduced, stored in a retrieval system,
or transmitted in any form, or by any means, electronic, mechanical,
photocopy, recording or otherwise without prior written permission of
the publisher, except by a reviewer who wishes to quote brief passages in
connection with a review written for inclusion in a magazine, newspaper,
broadcast, or on the Internet.

For information contact Sheriar Foundation, 603 Briarwood Drive,
Myrtle Beach, SC 29572, USA, or visit www.sheriarbooks.org.

Library of Congress Cataloging-in-Publication Data

Nadel, Heather, 1950–
 The joyous path : the life of Avatar Meher Baba's sister / Mani Heather Nadel.
   p. cm.
 Includes bibliographical references and index.
 ISBN 978-1-880619-43-8 (pbk.) -- ISBN 978-1-880619-44-5 (hard cover)
 1. Irani, Manija Sheriar. I. Title.
 BP610.I732N33 2015
 299'.93--dc23
 [B]
                                       2015019473

TABLE OF CONTENTS

VOLUME ONE

	Foreword	*ix*
	Preface	*xi*
	Acknowledgements	*xiii*
	Introduction	*xvii*
PART I:	**GOD'S SISTER**	**1**
	Prologue	3
	God's Sister	5
PART II:	**TO BE WITH YOU ALWAYS**	**123**
	Into the Fire	125
	East-West	187
	The Blue Bus	258
	Traveling	382
	A New Life	453

TABLE OF CONTENTS (CONTINUED)

VOLUME TWO

PART II: TO BE WITH YOU ALWAYS (CONTINUED)

In The West	537
Fiery and Free	603
The Last Twelve Years	656
Eternal Beloved	802
The Great Darshan	857

PART III: CONTINUING ON — 877

Continuing On	879
Endnotes	1071
Glossary	1079
List of Illustrative Materials	1087
List of Source Materials	1109
Index of Mani's Stories	1111
Index	1119
About the Author	1145

IN THE WEST

ON THEIR WAY

Almost straight out of the New Life, Mehera, Mani, Goher, Meheru, Kitty, and Rano were plunged into a wholly different experience. They went to America, travelling to the West for the first time since Mehera and Mani's visit to Europe in 1937. They knew, of course, that Baba had sent Elizabeth and Norina to America to create a center for Him there that He would someday visit. Now it was ready.

Mani remembered:

> Elizabeth for us has always been an outstanding disciple and person. No matter what Baba asked her to do, it was always, "Yes, Baba dear, yes, Baba dear." And when Baba said, "Build Me a centre in America," it was "Yes, Baba dear." And she did it. She not only did it, she put her all into it to make it what it is for Baba. No wonder Baba told Norina and Elizabeth, "It is My home in the West."

Baba at Meher Center, 1952.

Later Elizabeth remarked to me with that endearing humour of hers, "Mani, you know, the place that Baba has chosen for His home in the West [Myrtle Beach, South Carolina] also has His initials, M.B. Someday it will become 'Meher Beach'!"

Isn't that lovely.

So in 1952, when it was complete for Baba, it is natural that Baba wanted to be there. He was the first to stay on the Center, along with some of us. Of course, Elizabeth arranged every detail for our going to America and to Myrtle Beach, and with such perfection! We went by plane on TWA [airlines] as first-class passengers, on our first plane ride and, so far, our last plane ride.

Baba had told them about His next life phase, the Free Life, and its three parts: "Complicated Free Life, Full Free Life, and Fiery Free Life." At the very beginning of the first part, the "Complicated Free Life," when "binding will dominate freedom," came this visit to America; Baba hadn't been there in fifteen years.

Baba was exhausted from His New Life and Manonash work, and "still in that New Life mood," as Meheru recalled, so He decided to go to Bombay for a peaceful rest before leaving India. He was disturbed by the outside noise in two places in the city before the mandali finally found a quiet house at Marve Beach, some distance away. Baba liked it very much, and the mandali stayed there for a week.

On April 18, 1952, Baba, Mehera, Mani, Meheru, Goher, Rano, and Kitty flew off to the West. They were followed two days later by the men mandali: Adi Sr., Sarosh, Meherjee, Gustadji, and Nilu. (Dr. Donkin had been sent by Baba earlier to help Elizabeth prepare for Baba's visit.)

Mani's interest in the view from the air is obvious in the first entry of a new diary:

18th April 1952 – take off 11 p.m. (lights of B'bay). Dahran [Dhahran, Saudi Arabia] – 4 a.m. (time back) Cross mountains – also Suez gulf – rough twice. Cairo 8. had tea at restaurant (police). Start 9 – over extensive quilt of fields in every shade of green and brown – canals, roads, villages, towns, cars on roads – above the clouds. Speed 285 m.p.h. 5 miles a minute. Keep putting back time all the time - Crossed much desert - + also marshy land.

Saw from above Capri, Mt. Ves [Mt. Vesuvius], Naples . . .

As Mani recalled:

Now, for us the flight was a real adventure, because of the contrast with our life in any case, and because we were going by plane to America. And the greatest thing about it was that Baba withdrew our diet restrictions while we were on the plane. We could have anything that was served to us, which was grand. I was quite happy about that. And the food was very interesting. After all, there was not much else to do on the flight except eat, and then wait, and then eat again.

I was seated by the window next to Meheru. Every mealtime the stewardess would come with a little cushion that she would place on your lap, and then she'd put the food tray on top of it. The thing that fascinated me right off was, when the first tray was put on our laps, there were these two big poached eggs, side by side, covered with a white film on top of the yolks. I said, "My God, they look like Eddie Cantor's eyes." You know, big. And so I just tipped the tray a little bit and wiggled it and the eyes would go round and round. And all of that was fun. Now just wait, now what will the next tray bring? It's not that we were hungry, but it was very interesting to see what would be on the tray.

And then, you wouldn't believe it, Baba says, "You can have whatever is served," and on the tray at lunchtime were little champagne bottles, one on my tray and one on Meheru's. Here at last, something I'd read about in so many books when I was reading out to Baba or to myself: champagne, which rich people gave at parties or when a son was born, and which, in France, the men drank out of the slippers of celebrated beauties. I was so excited about it. I was determined to make the most of whatever there was on the flight, not just the food, but in every way.

So I saw the champagne, and quickly had a swig at it. You don't say "swig" for champagne? OK, a sip at it. And horrors. I was so disappointed. It didn't taste like anything. I said, "I can't believe it. Maybe the slippers make a difference, I don't know. But it's certainly a 'sham' and it gives me a 'pain' of disappointment." I wished I hadn't had it, because I would always afterwards have a picture of champagne as it probably is.

But the martini made up for it, more than made up for it. I didn't know that was coming. Rano was sitting behind me. The stewardess was going up the aisle and she stopped by Rano and asked something. And Rano said, "Beer, please."

Now I couldn't stand beer. I've had it as a schoolgirl at home, when my brother Beheram won first prize in amateur photography. He gave a family party with the amount he received, and Adi, Jal, all the brothers, said "We can have beer." Of course I also put up my hand at that party and said, "Beer!" although I didn't know what it was all about as a young girl. Then when I drank it, it was so bitter it was all I could do to keep a straight face and not give myself away.

So when Rano said beer, I said to myself, "No how! Beer is out! Now what shall I ask for? There must be something I've never had, something I can boast about afterwards: 'I've had such-and-such, I know all about it.' Quick, quick, Mani, quick!" Then I realized that whenever I read these detective books to Baba, they were always having a martini. They were always [here Mani puts on a tough-guy voice] leaning against the door with a cigarette ordering a martini, you know?

So when the stewardess came to me, I looked quite blasé and said, "Er, martini please." And, to myself, "I wonder what it's like? What does it look like? What does it taste like? How much will there be?" After a while, she came with the martini. And I wasn't disappointed. It was in a beautiful clear glass that opened out like a bowl. And with a thin, long stem, like a crane's leg, that bird that stands on one leg. I was fascinated. And a lovely colour liquid inside. But what was that in the centre? A green beetle? I forgot to be blasé. "Oh, what's that?" She looked at me, surprised, and said, "That's an olive."
"Oh," I said, in my bored voice, "of course, an olive."

That martini was so delicious. I only wish the olive hadn't taken up room; if there was no olive there might have been more martini. It was wonderful; I just loved it, and I had it!

So things went along well for a while. However, Mani had no idea that people could get airsick. She wasn't, but Meheru obviously was because she kept refusing food. Kitty wasn't looking too good either. And the stewardess was getting concerned.

So the stewardess said to Meheru, "Are you sure you won't have anything?" At last Meheru said, "Yes." The stewardess brightened up, "What?" "Some hot water."

"Hot water!" said the stewardess. And then she pointed at me, "Look at her. She never refuses anything!" And I said to myself, "Why should I? Elizabeth has paid for it!" In fact, I'd tell Meheru, "Don't refuse the food. Get it. Then I can take my favourites from both the trays. Remember, Elizabeth has paid for it." But poor Meheru had all the trays that were coming to me passing under her nose, and she couldn't stand even the *smell* of food.

Both Mehera and Mani remembered children on the flight being attracted to Baba and coming right up to His seat on the aisle. Mani remembered "Johnny," a little boy who just couldn't keep away from Baba. He kept running up and standing next to Him, engaging Baba's attention.

Baba smiled and smiled over it all. But the boy's mother was very agitated. She kept calling, "Hurry up, Johnny, come back." Johnny wasn't coming. So she called again, "Johnny." Johnny went on touching Baba, smiling at Baba, while Baba was giving him a kiss, patting him, smiling, and so on. In the end, the mother came up, grabbed Johnny under his armpit, and dragged him away. Then she turned around and apologized to Baba, "I don't know what's happened to Johnny! He's never done that before, never!" Baba just smiled. And of course, after a while, Johnny came back.

ARRIVAL

As they travelled, Mani recorded some details of their long flight in her diary. On April 20, they finally reached America. As Mani recorded: "Passed Long Island (v. large) – fields of cucumber, string beans etc. Land at International air-drome – actually at Long Island – 10:30 a.m. 20th [April] – Saw E. [Elizabeth] waving frantically. . ."

And so they arrived in America. "We drove over to N.Y. [New York], on way going thru beautiful lighted tunnel (ivory-coloured, lighted + curved) <u>under</u> the East River. . . The taxi driver wished us 'Welcome to America'."

As you can guess, they were delighted with New York. Years later Mani described it to some young Baba-lovers:

> The Empire State Building at that time, I think, was supposed to be the tallest building in the world. Is that right? But what would you know, you probably weren't even born then! It was the tallest building then. We went up with Baba in the lift [elevator], which was marvelous: you feel butterflies in your stomach going up and coming down. Way up on top we stood next to Baba and looked down, and the people below were like little ants.
>
> But one of the things I loved best were the lights of Broadway, those neon, colourful, flickering, moving lights. The ads, the advertisements, were expressed through lights. I just couldn't move my eyes away from them.
>
> There was a kettle and a cup and saucer in neon lights, and the kettle kept pouring tea into the cup. And it kept pouring and it kept pouring. The cup never filled up and the tea-kettle never emptied. And then there was a sheep jumping over a stile, over and over. [Mani writes in her diary: ". . . lights on Broadway of man smoking, cats leaping, mickey mouse, tea pouring, etc. etc."] This forest of lights was so fascinating. Even on the plane, whenever we were coming down to land, it was as if the sky were upside down and all the stars were underneath us. This aspect of lights was so beautiful all throughout our trip there.

That very first evening, they had a tour of the town. There was only one hitch: a disastrous dinner at an Indian restaurant, the Ceylon India Inn:

> Elizabeth wanted to take us to a Chinese restaurant so that Baba could have rice. Look at her consideration for every detail of Baba's comfort and liking. But the Chinese restaurant was closed, I believe because it was Sunday. So she took us to an Indian restaurant, which she found hurriedly, because there also Baba could have rice.
>
> But that restaurant! You wouldn't believe it. I mean, that was an experience; we had never seen anything so Indian in India. It was like a museum. The carpet on the floor had pile six inches thick, so it was like walking through snow to walk to the table. Once you put your foot down, you couldn't lift the other one up; each step seemed like mountain climbing. And it was all a little dark, not bright at all. I guess that was supposed to be Indian, I don't know. We love it bright here in India.
>
> There was this dining table, and at the head of it, or was it the back of it, was a big oval mirror. On both sides of the mirror were these huge elephant tusks. Now Rano was a very strong-natured person, and if Baba wanted her to do something, she wouldn't be shy about it. She would be quite formidable, as a matter of fact. So just imagine Rano sitting there in front of that oval mirror, with two tusks around her. And Baba seated at the table, too.
>
> Now Baba was displeased about something. I never could find out what it was, but He was angry. I didn't know what was happening, Goher was just cross-eyed from the trip, and Meheru had just recovered from her fast, as it were, and was trying to keep up. (Goher had been feeling a bit wobbly ever since we got off the plane—she wasn't

air-sick, she was land-sick.) So Goher went to the bathroom, poor dear, because she was feeling sick.

I think to ease the situation, Rano went to the kitchen to tell them something. And just after that the waitress came in with a bowl of curry and tripped over the carpet. She almost dropped the whole curry bowl over our heads. It just missed me!

At that point, I became hysterical with laughter. But you see, we had learned to be very sensitive to Baba's moods. When Baba was happy, well, that's the time for jokes. If Baba was displeased with something, you didn't sit up and grin or say something you shouldn't be saying. So here with Baba angry, it was not the time for me to laugh. But I couldn't contain it; I didn't know what to do. So I bent down as if I'd dropped a spoon on the floor and I was bending down to pick it up. I put my head under the tablecloth and silently laughed and laughed. Took me a long time to get that spoon. At last I was all right, and my head emerged from under the tablecloth, and nobody knew what I'd been doing.

After their New York sightseeing, they boarded the train for Florence, South Carolina ("slept in most comfy Pullman compartments"), from where Elizabeth drove them to the Center.

AT THE CENTER

About her memorable stay at the Center, Mani once remarked in the Hall:

When we first got to this beautiful place that was created for Baba, an amazing thing happened. Baba was with us and yet, when we arrived, it was as if Baba was already there, welcoming us. Every nook and corner of that place was filled

Baba in front of the Guest House on the Center, May 1952.

>with Baba's Presence, even as we went in for the first time and discovered it. This was an experience I never expected.
>
>Isn't that amazing? It shows how much heart, how much love, how much labour, how much of herself Elizabeth had put into it, when Baba sent Norina and Elizabeth to America in 1948 to create a centre for Him.

Also about the Center, Mani observed:

>Every nook had so much of His Presence: on the bridge, under the trees, at the beach, in the Barn, by the lake . . . Naturally, as it is the one place in the West Baba had directed to be found. But He had already found it before He sent Elizabeth and Norina to look for it. He gave them conditions, which were like clues to that place where Baba already was. He had already planned it before He sent them out to look for it, so it was like a treasure hunt.

Boaters on the lake at the Center, 1956.

> And even now when we think of the Center and its beauty—Baba's beauty, that is reflected there at the Center—it is with a nostalgia, as if we had been there, oh, so long ago, and yet we are there right now in heart.

Kitty wrote of Baba and the women's first visit to Baba's house on the Center:

> When we were again assembled in the living room, Baba spelled out on His board, with Mani interpreting, how happy He was to be at the Center, and most of all how deeply touched He was with the love, devotion and work shown by both Elizabeth and Norina throughout the past years in preparing such a unique spot for His work and comfort. No detail, no expense had been spared to carry out His wishes, and all had been the labor of love—love direct from the heart, and as such He accepted the gift.

Long Lake at Meher Center seen through the trees.

After embracing Elizabeth and Norina He said, "I have had many homes this time. I have laid My head on the ground . . . in palaces and on concrete floors of humble homes." Then Baba gestured over all the Center and continued, "Of all the homes I have visited, this is the home that I love the best, because it was given to Me and built for Me with such love." After a bit He added, "I never leave. Remember, I do not leave because this is My home."[1]

Having just arrived at the Center, Mani wrote the following letter to the women mandali back in India:

No. 1
Meher Center "on the Lakes"
P.O. Box 487
Myrtle Beach, South Carolina.

23rd April '52

Dear Everybody,

Today is the second day of our arrival in Myrtle Beach. We have our sweaters on for it is quite coldish, but in a very pleasant way. Mehera is sitting beside me dictating this letter. From the window in front of me we can see the lake (which is our own private lake; freshwater lake in spite of its being so close to the blue sea, which we can also see in the horizon).

We had a very comfortable journey except cramped nights, with excellent service on board, and pretty hostesses serving dainty little trays every little interval. Meheru and Goher and Kitty were sea-sickish on the last day. (If you mention airoplane [airplane] to Goher just now, she looks ready to scream.) Our first stop in Cairo was quite cold and we got down to have a cup of tea. Second was Rome, and when we got down Baba had a brisk walk at the air-station. Of course Baba could not sleep at nights in the plane, though he had a very comfortable seat, with the seat in front facing towards him so he could stretch his legs. The crossing was rough and stormy over the Atlantic (with a gale of 180 miles an hour) and therefore our course was changed and we had to stop at Shannon and Gander. We got down at Gander at 4 in the morning, and it was piercingly cold, with ice everywhere on the ground. The funniest part on the plane was that they kept putting the clock back every now and then, and so the nights and day seemed doubly long, and we were tired and longing for N.Y. to come.

When our plane landed in New York (actually Long

Island), the first person we saw was dear Elizabeth waving frantically to us. We got thru the customs very easily, and the officials were very friendly and kept smiling at Baba. Now about Baba's health; He was looking very tired and weak on the plane up till N.Y. but the minute he got down, we noticed a marked change in Baba's appearance and he looked wonderfully better. The airodrome [airport] was actually at Long Island, from where we drove over to a hotel in N.Y. On the way we crossed a beautifully constructed tunnel which is actually under the river. This 1¼ mile long tunnel is the dividing line between Long Island and New York [City] proper. The taxi driver was a friendly soul and wished us "Welcome to America". New York at night was a most beautiful sight, with its towering skyscrapers and the gay lights of Broadway, and its lovely shop windows. We went up the Radio City building (65 floors up), and looked down on a very gorgeous sight of the lighted city. That night we also saw the ice-skating rink where couples were dancing to the music – it was a lovely sight. It was fascinating to find beautiful bits of garden and parks right in the midst of busy street corners, and as it happened to be a Sunday everybody were very gaily dressed. After seeing the lights we went to the station, and on the train slept most comfortably in Pullman compartments. We crossed beautiful scenery, trees in spring-time bloom amidst pine forests, and adorable little houses. We will tell you details when we meet. I forgot to mention one thing. The American people are the most friendly and warm-hearted people—everywhere. And the service is so efficient and willing, it is a perpetual pleasure.

We got down at the station of Florence (which is 70 miles from Myrtle Beach) and Elizabeth drove us over.

Delia, Ruano and Margaret are also with us. On the M.B. property we first went to see the house that is especially built for Baba (with a sound proof bedroom), and it was not only beautiful in structure and surroundings, but most conveniently furnished in minute details (with every modern fixture and convenience, including a Hollywood kitchen).

Norina was at the door to embrace Baba. We next went to see our little house (which is also newly built and it is a most dear little cottage made of pinewood and also with modern conveniences.) The situation is most inexpressibly beautiful. Mehera's little bedroom with pink furniture is facing the lake and there is acres and acres of ground for beautiful walks in the woods. There are also many other cottage-shacks all over the place. This morning Elizabeth drove us round the whole of the property, and Baba told Elinorina [Elizabeth and Norina] at the end of it, "I am not only extremely happy with all this, but also touched by your love which has made you do all this for me." Really they are a wonderful pair!

Goher, Mani, Mehera, and Meheru.

Norina is actually not at all well, in fact her condition according to the doctors, is quite bad; but Baba has chalked out a programme of medicine for her, and has ordered her complete rest.

The mandali have just arrived, and Baba has gone over to see them. That is why we have time now, and therefore Mehera made me sit down and type this letter to you. So don't eat sugar and expect long letters again. Read this letter also to Masi, Khorshed, our gang, and to those only whom you think best. I have been typing this in a terrific hurry, so tell Kaity not to turn up her nose at any mistypes. Baba has been very busy looking to details and so far has not had any of the rest that he needs so badly. He hasn't slept well as yet, and today is developing a cold. So from tomorrow he wants to take complete rest for ten days so as to be prepared for his work which is fast approaching.

Love to you all from us all,
Mani.

. . .

Elinorina had kept Baba's coming date a very guarded secret as Baba had told them to, and therefore we met no one else at the aerodrome, or else there might have been crowds of reporters etc. Pascall [Gabriel Pascal] had sent over an agent of the International Airways, and he was a great help to us. But the funny thing is he didn't know who Baba is, but he was looking for a Mr. Irani, and came over and shook hands with Baba and offered his card. Isn't it strange how the unexpected have a chance of meeting Baba.

This was meant to be posted yesterday but I'm just adding a line today before Elizabeth goes to town with it. This morning as I am typing it is very cloudy drizzly and chilly outside, Baba has not slept at all, last night – he has a bad cold; and we have all developed colds as well. Let us hope tomorrow will be a nice sunny day. Anyway the view from our windows is still lovely.

Mani.

IN THE WEST 553

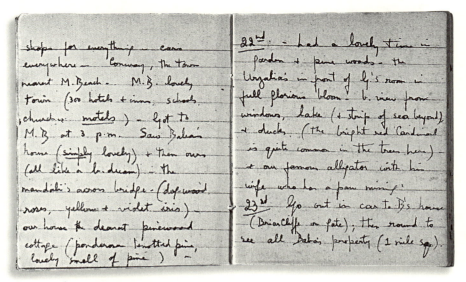

Two pages from Mani's diary, written at the Center.

From Mani's 1952 diary:

[21st April] ... Got to M.B. at 3 p.m. Saw Baba's house (<u>simply</u> lovely) + then ours (all like a b. [beautiful] dream) – the mandali's across bridge... our house the dearest pine-wood cottage (ponderosa knotted pine, lovely smell of pine) –

<u>22nd</u> [April] – had a lovely time in garden and pine woods ... b. [beautiful] view from windows, lake (+ strip of sea beyond), + ducks (the bright red Cardinal is quite common in the trees here) – + our famous alligator with his wife who has a paw missing.

<u>23rd</u> [April] Go out in car to B's house (Briarcliffe on gate); then round to see all Baba's property (1 mile sq.). our fresh water lake, the land bet. [between] lake + ocean, + the beach beyond... Saw the barn (the wheel; inside made of ponderosa knotted pine – cedar wood fireplace – outside barn brought over as it was) – then went to see Gater Lake – B. liked it v. Much ...

Mani and Mehera dressed up on the Center.

Mani loved the fragrance of the pinewood that came from the walls of the Guest House, and the view of the lake from inside the house ("We didn't have to go out to the lake to look at it"). They were very at home in the natural surroundings, yet there were so many new things to see; even the birds were different. So many aspects appealed to them. As she told pilgrims, "One of my favourites was the bridge. The kitchen, the cardinal, Elizabeth's love, and all the love that was there . . ."

Not to mention fruit juice:

> Elizabeth, you know, was so bountiful and so careful in every detail of looking after us. The first thing that she stocked for us in the Guest House, that absolutely beautiful fairy-doll house where we women stayed when we were in the Center, was fruit juice. There was this cupboard in the wall, and when we opened it, we found prune juice bottles! I love fruit juices. I found America was full of fruit juices. And I said, "If I were to draw a map of America I would draw

peaks of beautiful mountains, with waterfalls coming down each mountain, and one would be the prune juice waterfall, and one would be the orange juice waterfall, one would be an apple juice waterfall . . ."

Things on the food front were not as exciting. At the Center, their diet restrictions were back in place, and the women ate only vegetarian food:

> When we were at the Center, what used to amaze us was that the cooks would come to work in cars, posh cars with radio antennas. We couldn't get over it: cooks driving up to the kitchen in cars to cook for us. When we were at the Center, Ruano Bogislav made out the menu. But after all, how varied a menu can you get with vegetables? I mean, there'd be cabbages, there'd be corn-on-the-cob, there'd be something else, and then the sweet. The cooks would drive up to the kitchen in their posh cars, get down, roll up their sleeves and begin making breakfast for themselves. And what was their breakfast? Fried chicken! Oh, Ruano said, the smells that wafted to her from that. And after cooking their chicken breakfast, they would start cooking vegetables for our lunch.

Mehera and Mani's (and Goher and Meheru's) life of seclusion continued and they spent most of their days in their "fairy-doll house." Baba would come every day for breakfast to the Guest House, and later take the women on a walk through the woods to the beach, where they would gather shells. Mani had a life-long fondness for the ocean, so she must have loved this.

And that grand entertainment capital, downtown Myrtle Beach, had lots of novelty to offer. On some days Baba took them on outings there. One, Mani notes in her diary, was to a drive-in cinema: "There had popcorn – film Flaming Feather – lovely cartoon of mouse and hawk – Florida Oceanarium – parrots – chimps..." Another was to Brookgreen Gardens, a large park full of statues south of the Center: ("Beaut. view of live oaks + hanging Spanish moss – v.b. [very beautiful] statues..."), and a fair ("icecream cones + donuts – saw scenic railway – merry-go-round... the swinging airplanes, + the fishes in Kiddieland....").

They went out on the Center lake with their old swimming teacher, Margaret, who taught them rowing. "We go boating," Mani noted in the diary. And as always they had outdoor games, again with Margaret.

Kitty recalled the early evenings that they spent gathered around Baba at the Guest House: some would tell jokes; Mehera, Mani, and Meheru would tell early stories about Baba. Mani would read out passages from Hafiz or other Persian poets as Baba would explain the deeper spiritual meaning, or stories of the saints. And once Mani interpreted while Baba spoke to them all about His future plans for the Center.

Meanwhile, Baba began meeting His lovers: "9th [May] Mrs. Duce + Charmian + Sparky come. 10th Baba sees more people... 17th May: About 300 people come to see Baba at barn – most touching response to Baba – we are all touched by their love and devotion."

During the following week, Baba often sent some of the women followers to the Guest House to see Mehera, Mani, and all. One of them later wrote of "the little nuns": "so gay and bright and happy, living only for Baba, talking of Him with such love and showing us albums of photographs of Him...." This was Mani's chance to meet and become friendly with some of the Western women she had only heard about— important contacts, as it would turn out, when she became Baba's scribe to the Western world soon after. Her letter to their brother Jal of May 17 showed her attention to the people Baba was drawing in.

Mehera and Baba with Filis and Adele who were thrilled to stay in the Guest House with the women.

>Meher Center,
>Myrtle Beach.
>17th May 1952

Dear Jal,

This is the third letter I am writing to you. I hope you received my first two letters. Today is the 17th. Many people came to see Baba yesterday on the 16th. But today cars have been coming all day since early this morning and Baba has only just finished seeing them tonight. He has been seeing them at the big wood cabin called The Barn. I have a list of about 110 people who had written to say they were coming to see him today; but more and more people kept coming, till by now they have added up to about 300. They came from places far and near – from California (about 30 people of Mrs. Duce's sufi group), from Panama, from New York, from all over U.S., and even from Australia (Francis

Barbazone [Brabazon], a great Sufi leader in Australia; and he loves Baba very, very much). Most of the people put [up] at the Lafayette Manor hotel, and the Manageress (Mrs. Eustom [Houston]) also loves Baba, and came to see him yesterday. Some who could not afford to come by train have hitch-hiked here, and one woman (Evelyn Blackshaw) even took on a job at the hotel for a week, so she could stay in Myrtle Beach. Baba is not going to see anyone tomorrow, except four of Margaret's pupils who simply could not come today, and who are flying from N.Y. by a chartered plane for which they have been saving money for a long time. Really, the love of all these people here in America for Baba even before they saw him is very touching. Their love and devotion is so great that it isn't a wonder Baba came here in spite of all the difficulties. Some of the women [who] after seeing Baba were allowed to come and see us were Mrs. Shaw and her two daughters; and Mrs. Shaw remembers meeting you in California and asked me to remember her to you. Phylis and Adele [Filis Frederick and Adele Wolkin] are staying with us for a week (they are going tomorrow), and they are extremely devoted to Baba.

On the 20th we are leaving by car for California. [Gabriel] Pascal will see Baba there, and he is putting his two houses at Baba's disposal, so that when Baba goes to Hollywood for a day, he will see people there at his house.

After we come from California, Baba is going to plan out a spiritual universal centre on this property here (Myrtle Beach) for the future.

Norina's health got much worse, and she is at present in a hospital some 150 miles away [Duke Hospital in Durham, North Carolina]; she will not be able to come with us to

California, but we hope she will be well enough later to join us in New York.

Up till a few days ago nobody knew about Baba's presence in America (except a few intimate ones) as Elizabeth tried to avoid publicity. But now after Baba saw all these people these few days it might become more public, and if there is anything in the papers, etc. I will let you know.

Actually when Baba saw all these people he was not feeling well, and looking thin and tired to us, but it was wonderful the way all the people were emotionally touched and therefore it was very satisfactory.

The pamphlet (circular) 'BABA EXPLAINS' which was given to all who came to see Baba, I am enclosing a typed copy of as the printed one is too bulky for airmail posting. I am also sending a list of the names of some of the people who came to see Baba, but I haven't got them all.

Baba sends his love to you all; and give my love to all at home and special love to Perin and Gulnar.

MANI

Our address there [in California] is as follows:
Meher Mount, Route 1, P.O. Box 127
OJAI (CALIFORNIA)

Three days after this letter was written, Baba and the party set out in cars for California.

A PRECIOUS GIFT

A far-off ripple from this Center visit: in 1995, Mani sent a gift from India to the young Baba-lovers attending a Youth Sahavas at the Myrtle Beach Center. She loved this annual event, a time when teenagers come together at the Center for a week of activities focused on Baba. Every year as a gesture of love and encouragement, Mani would send the participants a gift of some kind related to Baba. In 1995, it was tiny seashells.

In a letter accompanying the shells, she explained:

> In 1952 Beloved Baba made His first visit to Myrtle Beach especially to inaugurate and grace the Meher Spiritual Center, His beautiful home in the West created by dear Elizabeth under Baba's detailed direction. He took along some of us women mandali with Him, and decided to stop over in Bombay for some days before flying to America. During that period we went with Him to Marve, a quiet beach in the suburbs of Bombay. That was forty-three years ago, but memories of the visit repose within us, to blossom now and then at the touch of some special reminder.
>
> This happened recently when I came across the dazzling assortment of little shells we had collected from that beach and brought home with us. What reminders could be more special than these bright little witnesses to that happy carefree time by the seaside with our Beloved. Just picture us wandering barefoot along the shore, hunting for shells, excited at every new find, rushing to show them to each other. Baba beamed at His own finds and admired Mehera's and ours as we poured them into His beautiful hands.
>
> The fact that Baba held in His hands these shells collected at Marve Beach just before He left with us for Myrtle Beach, surely carries a symbolic message. And now it so happens that the seashells thus blessed with His touch in 1952 are destined for His young ones coming together at Myrtle Beach Center for the 1995 Youth Sahavas! Placed in individual boxes (one box for each Sahavasee) these precious shells are as pearls from His Ocean of Love.

Greetings from our hearts to each participant in Baba's company, and a salute to all His dear staff whose loving hands and hearts serve to make the Beloved's Youth Sahavas a glorious Victory unto Him.

With a united "AVATAR MEHER BABA KI JAI" from all Meherazad family,

(signed) Mani

DRIVING ACROSS AMERICA

In a letter from Adi Sr. to Pappa Jessawala in Poona written on May 18, 1952, Adi writes:

> Tomorrow morning all the male members excepting Sarosh are leaving by car for a long 3000 miles journey to California. We are expected to reach there within a week. Donkin and I will drive the car alternatively. On 20th Baba and all the ladies are also leaving by two cars. Elizabeth will drive one car and Sarosh will drive another.
>
> After about one month's travelling and stay at Hollywood and San Francisco we are expected to come back here by car and stay here for one month. Then we will go to New York about the middle of July. Then we will go to Europe . . .

The men mandali left for their trip, and then, on May 20, so did Baba and the women—Baba, Mehera, Mani, and Meheru in one car with Elizabeth driving, and Goher, Rano, Kitty, and Delia in the other driven by Sarosh. In retrospect, Baba's serious mood the day of departure, His sending Elizabeth for the insurance papers just before their leaving, and His insistence that the second car keep up with His more powerful one, portended the terrible end to their westward crossing.

Meheru told us that His mood during their journey was unusually irritable. She recalled that He was very disturbed and put out of sorts by little things, which was unlike Him.

Some sense of trouble also pervades Mani's diary description of their first four days' drive, woven into her pleasure at the natural sights:

> [DIARY]
>
> 20th We leave 2.15 – in pouring rain – but sunshine in lit. [little] while + another pour. Cross Conway, Florence, Sunter [Sumpter] (biggish town) + then stop at Columbia (S.C.) in Forest Motor Court. lovely place . . . – have unsuccessful supper at eating-place (tough steak by candle-light – poor Baba could not eat anything). Slept badly because of sound of cars on roads all night.
>
> 21st Left Columbia 6.45 a.m. after some tea made by us . . . had brkfst at quick lunch place (nice waitress – had nickel [nickelodeon/jukebox] music). missed 2nd car – 32 m. to Laurens – still no car. 32 m. to Greensville [Greenville] – there met car after frantic time. We are crossing the lovely Blue Mountains [Blue Ridge Mountains] . . . – 20 m. away stop + see Caesar's head (lovely view of mountain, lake, mountain-laurels, etc.)
>
> Then starts North Carolina. Starts 200 miles of lovely scene + waterfalls – you do not pass it by train – only by car – had "drive-in" lunch by way-side of hot dogs, sandwiches, coffee + cakes . . . over mountains, furry pine-clad mountains, + many waterfalls . . . also lakes, + streams + fields of yellow + white flowers, + simply charming houses . . . 3.15 Franklyn [Franklin] (school bus and bad coffee). 5 stop Murphy – lovely houses – go round whole town looking for Motel – saw one quiet one of little cabins but it wasn't open – at last at Mooreland Heights Tourist Court – <u>cold.</u>
>
> 22nd Leave Murphy (N.C.) – . . . sign of "Welcome to Tennessee state border ["] – stop twice amidst most superb view of pine mountains + river. . . On rock written "Christ died

for the ungodly." Crossed Cleveland – one sign on stone cross. . . which said "Jesus is coming soon". . .[After a few miles they saw another sign that read "JESUS IS HERE", which Mani remarked was a secret that they knew. Mehera said, "It was so lovely to be in the car with Baba and see that sign."] At Chattanooga missed car – B. very upset – lost time – awful. 10:30 saw Rock City (see 7 states from Lookout mountain) – most fascinating sightseeing ever done – with picture card followed trail (needles eye, fat man squeeze, deers, pigeons, lover's leap, swing bridge, coral caves, fairytale tableaus, tiny train, etc.) – had Cococola outside . . . saw Ruby Waterfalls . . . in underground cave – down elevator.

Ruby Falls was a waterfall inside a huge cavern (hence the need for the elevator), which was lit by red spotlights. Here Mani had a sort of premonition, as she told pilgrims. She didn't like the falls at all; she felt uneasy there and was happy to leave; the red water falling down into the dark reminded her of blood. After Ruby Falls, Baba said, "This is our last sightseeing."

After a night in Waynesboro at Sims Tourist Court ("lovely little place"), they left at 5:30 a.m. "20 m. away Savannah [TN] (big worm ranch)" and into dark clouds and rain. In Memphis it was cool and cloudy: "Stop at Gas St. (drilling hole) then Cococola." Mani reported that they "couldn't get out of Memphis", but finally did, crossed over the Mississippi and into Arkansas.

[DIARY:]

At Surcy [Searcy] had sandwiches + tea (K. [Kitty] got onions raddish etc.) in pouring rain at White House Cafe (also Western Union) – bought raisins + B. had a Dr. Pepper drink – + gave ½ $ to old Negro woman. (at 5.15 B. asked about Norina – phone). Passed Clarksville + just before Ozark stopped at Pond

> Crest Motor Court – lovely place and lit. [little] cabins with red roses, mauve clematis, brook, green hills in front, hens at back.

Kitty wrote:

> On the night of May 23 we stayed at Pond Crest Motor Court in the Ozarks. Baba sent us out to a nearby small restaurant for a meal, but He with Mehera, Mani, Meheru and Goher remained in the motel and had just milk and bread. I recall Baba asked me to bring back some milk and bread for the morning.
>
> We were up early as usual. Sarosh, Delia, Rano and I were again sent out for breakfast, but the others stayed with Baba. I think of Baba, knowing what was to happen before the day was over, spending the last few hours with that small, close group whom He had known since they were children and who had loved Him for so many years; finding in their presence the comfort and love He so much needed in that fateful hour.

Before they left, Kitty recalled, Baba was withdrawn and sad, and unusually still.

Mani's diary continued:

> 24. Leave Ozark 5.30 – Fort Smith 6.45 – cross bridge of Arkansas River + come to Oklahoma state. (v. good roads – state of rich oil). Stop at Sallisaw for gas.
>
> 10.15 – the wretched accident
>
> •
> •
> •
>
> Prague

THE WRETCHED ACCIDENT

This cable was sent to the mandali in India on May 24, 1952:

> Class XF Code 1401
>
> R 36/25 PRAGUE Date 24 OCS CTF Words 20
>
> Sarosh Ahmednagar India
>
> BABA LADIES PARTY ELIZABETH DRIVING INJURED IN MOTOR ACCIDENT NOW AT PRAGUE HOSPITAL PRAGUE OKLAHOMA – DETAILS FOLLOW
>
> SAROSH

Sarosh described the terrible scene in a letter written the next day to Baba's close ones in India:

> ... We had done about 800 miles out of the 3,000 that we had to do for Hollywood, etc.
>
> Yesterday 24th, we were on our way to Oklahoma, Elizabeth's car was very powerful, so she could go very fast. We followed her in a small car – Nash station wagon. Oh, what should I write. Yesterday was a hellish day for us. We arrived nearly half an hour late after Elizabeth's car met with an accident. It was such a sight that we all those who saw it, would not forget it for [a] lifetime. It was a very serious accident and all the five occupants of the car including Baba were very seriously injured. On arrival, we saw Baba covered with blood on all the face on one side, Mehera, Meheru full of blood on the other side. Elizabeth got stuck in the seat with the steering wheel. You can imagine the condition of such a sight . . . I straight went to Baba and tried to help him.

Delia, who was in Sarosh's car, described their reaction:

> With lightning speed we jumped out of the car and

rushed forward. The anguish of that moment is unforgettable
. . . . Baba's face with blood pouring from His head, the
extraordinary expression on Baba's face, His eyes just
staring straight ahead as if into unfathomable distances.
He made no sound or sign . . . just lay there motionless . . . .
Elizabeth was in the car doubled over the wheel. Her first
question had been "Is He alive?" The only one not injured
was Mani.[2]

Sarosh wrote the day after to Jal:

This is U.S.A. so the police and the help arrived on the
scene very soon and the injured were removed to nearest
hospital Prague.

Elizabeth's car collided with another car. The injuries
are:

Baba has a fractured left foot at the ankle and the
fracture of the left arm and the face inside and outside
all bruised. Mehera has a fractured skull and forehead.
Elizabeth fractured both her arms [and her collarbone, and
also broke eleven ribs]. Mani has many scratches and small
bruises on foot, etc. It was Mani who helped all the rest until
we arrived to the spot, say after 20 mins. Baba says this is
for the good of the world. They are well fixed up and the
doctor is a very good man at heart. . . .

Adi wrote to Pappa Jessawala later, "The trip to America justly proves the truth of Baba's hesitation to come to America and the prediction of a personal disaster."

As the Baba-world knows, Elizabeth's car was hit by another car hurtling along the wrong side of the road towards them; the other driver, a double-amputee driving a specially altered car for the first time, was avoiding a mailtruck, and swerved into the opposite lane. Elizabeth's car was going over 90 miles an hour, at Baba's instruction.

About the accident, Mani remembered:

> Elizabeth was driving and Baba, Mehera, Meheru, and myself were in the car. I was at the back. At the point of the impact, I was sitting with my feet up and my head back, dozing. I heard the excitement [Mehera and Meheru, on seeing the approaching car, cried out, "Baba, Baba, oh it's coming!"] but I kept saying to myself, "Why are they excited? It's all right. Baba's right in the car." Like when we would see a goat coming along [in the path of the car in India], we would say "Baba, Baba, Baba." So I was lying back. Then it happened, and suddenly the picture in the car was so different. I still remember that beautiful little hat Elizabeth had on, with a small veil in front, full of blood. Everything was blood at the time.

In another account she recalled:

> I was dozing and had both my legs up on the seat when the accident occurred. I got severe whiplash. To this day, I sometimes suffer pains from it. When I came to, I saw Elizabeth slumped over in the front and thought she was dead. . . . I found myself alone in the back seat. Baba and Mehera were not there. . . . I remember before Sarosh's car came, being on my knees by Baba and Mehera. My dress was covered with mud and blood. Frantically, I asked Moucka [a man who lived near the accident site], "But when is the ambulance coming!" And him being so kind, saying, "It's coming . . . It's coming."[3]

She had gotten out and seen Baba and Mehera on the ground, Mehera crying out in terrible pain.

I can hardly imagine Mani standing, almost unhurt, at this scene.

She was strong by nature, but intensely sensitive, so sensitive that even flower remedies or homoeopathic treatment affected her more than most other people. Sheltered from the world, focused exclusively on her two beloveds—Baba and Mehera—wholehearted, loyal, "sensitive to atmosphere" as she used to say: what could she possibly have felt seeing her adored Brother and her beloved lifelong companion lying on the ground covered in blood?

Shock, certainly. Almost everyone who wrote about the accident at that time mentioned Mani's state of terrible mental shock. Meherjee—who was ahead with the other men mandali, except Sarosh, and came back to Prague—wrote in a letter that Mani fainted at the scene. That couldn't be so, judging from other accounts: Sarosh, who was there soon after, said it was Mani who helped all the rest until he arrived. But Meherjee's comment indicates how stunned she must have seemed to them. And gradually, as Mani later expressed, along with the shock came grief and torment that she alone was uninjured, that she had been spared the suffering that Baba, Mehera, and even Meheru carried. Her knee was injured and she had severe whiplash that bothered her through the years, but compared to them she felt she was not hurt. And that was a torture to her. Perhaps that was her share of the suffering.

A CUP OF COFFEE

Mani remembered being very strong immediately after the accident. When Goher started crying in disbelief, Mani shook her, saying, "Goher, don't cry! Don't cry! Things have to be done, you have so much to do!" Because of the accident involving Baba's car, it was clear why Baba had not allowed Goher to ride in the car with Him, despite her pleas. As their doctor, she was unhurt and so able to help oversee the care of Baba, Mehera, and Meheru.

After ensuring that the injured were being well attended to, Sarosh brought Mani and Delia to a small room some distance away from the hospital. "Before he could find a motel, he must have found this room. We never ask these things, you know, we're just taken there, and plonked down with the luggage. Sarosh said, 'Delia, Mani, stay here, I'll come back. I'll find a motel. I'll do the spadework, but in the meantime, just be here.'"

Mani told pilgrims:

> Now I can be very good in a crisis, till everything has been seen to. So I went through it so beautifully, so bravely, so strongly. The whole thing. Afterwards, the reaction comes. Delia, poor dear, was having her own problems and she was in another little room. I went into the room where Sarosh had put us, and just broke. And I cried and cried. I've never sobbed so much in my life, I think. I cried till I was just completely emptied out, like a bowl.
>
> After I'd finished, and cried myself out (well, nearly), I knew there were things to do, work to do. But I was feeling so weak after all this that had happened, I needed something hot, a hot drink. I needed a cup of coffee, because that's what they'd have in America, coffee.
>
> Now what was I to do? Sarosh wasn't there, and I was down and out. I had to have a hot drink.
>
> So I started out. Delia was in her room, lying down with a terrible headache. I thought, "I'll ask somebody for a cup of coffee. Surely I can knock on a door and say, 'Will you please give me a cup of coffee?'"
>
> But it was so different from India. As I walked down the street, I was amazed to see every house was shut up. All the doors were shut, and all the windows had the blinds down. I thought they must have gone on a holiday. I looked at the opposite side, but it was the same. In India life is so

much in the streets, every door is open with children going in and out, and hens and goats, and people screaming from the upstairs windows. But this was fantastic. I said to myself, "But they couldn't all have gone away at the same time?"

But there was no sign of life. Anyway, I thought I should try. So I gingerly knocked on one door. I heard a little shuffle. I knocked louder. Somebody came and opened the door a little bit, just a couple of inches. And an old, old man looked at me. He took one look and shut the door. I think I scared him. I said to myself, "Now what shall I do? I must have a cup of something hot!" It was a matter of life and death to me at that moment. I skipped a couple of doors and said, "Baba, whichever You want" and again knocked. Then I went to a third house and knocked again.

A woman opened the door this time, a young woman, again opening just a few inches. At first she was a bit suspicious, but she looked at me in the eyes, and then she was interested. So she opened the door and asked, "Yes, what do you want?"

"All I want is a cup of hot coffee, please."

"Well," she said, "I'm sorry. We have no coffee in the house. But I tell you what I'll do. I'll give you a nickel and you go and have a cup of coffee."

So she put some money in my hand. I hadn't seen American money, as we didn't handle money at any time. She gave me a nickel. I didn't know what it meant, or how much it was worth.

And I said, "E—excuse me. Where can I have coffee? I don't know any shops. I'm new to the place." She looked surprised, so I explained, "You know, we've just been in an accident and we're from India, and I need a hot drink, but I don't know where to go."

So she said, "Well, go straight like this and turn to the left and go to this place and there it is."

So I followed her directions and sure enough, I came to the place and just walked in. I couldn't believe I was doing it. It was like I was in the world all by myself, as if I walked in every day for a cup of coffee. I went and sat at this little table. A man came and said, "What?" and I said, "Cup of coffee," and plonked down the nickel. Inside I was just dead, and I said, "Baba please, I hope this money is right, whatever it is!"

It must have been because he seemed very natural, picked up the nickel, went and got me a cup of coffee. Nice hot coffee. Oh. Life surged into me after having that cup of coffee! Color came back into my face, I was able to walk a little better, and remembering the directions—I'm not very good at directions of roads and places—I went back to the room.

After a while Sarosh came. In fact, he took a long time in coming. But when he came, he immediately said, "Come on, come on! We have to go! Hurry up, I've got to find a good hotel!"

"No, no, Sarosh," I said, "wait a minute! First I want some money! I borrowed some money, I have to give it back."

"How much?"

"I don't know, just show me all the coins and I'll pick the one I mean. I can recognize it if I see it." So he brought out a lot of American change and put it in his hand, and I picked out the nickel.

I went back to the house and knocked. When the young woman opened the door, she was surprised to see me and asked, "What do you want now?"

I said, "Thank you so much! You'll never realize how much I appreciate your giving me this money for a cup of coffee. Now I want to return it."

She couldn't believe it. I think she never thought I'd come back; she had meant for me to have the nickel. "Oh, no, no!" she said. "Don't give me back the money! No, please! I didn't mean that! You please keep it!"

"Oh, but I must return it. What shall I do with it? You keep it as a souvenir of a girl from India who came and knocked on your door and asked for a cup of coffee."

That seemed to appeal to her. So she laughed and I laughed and she said thank you. And I came away.

You see, Baba had to give me a real hot cup of coffee, because the only thing I had complained about on the plane was the coffee: black, cold, no milk, no sugar. But this—this coffee was wonderful.

Straight from the helpless, hopeless New Life, Mani, who had never been alone in the world in all her adult years, was begging in the streets of America.

IN SHOCK

So after the coffee infusion, Mani "went to work," helping in the hospital in any way she could. Later, too, Mani realized that Baba had spared her from injury so that she could help Mehera, whose injuries made her so helpless.

But Mani was not herself. Ivy Duce, who was called to Prague to give them a hand, wrote in her journal:

> Mani was the least hurt, her feet and knees badly scratched, and limped with a cane. She did not eat for days

and was overcome with grief and tormented that God had not given her as much to bear as the others (although she had recently had a severe operation).[4]

Meheru told me that it took Mani the longest to recover from the shock of the accident because she had to keep going; she was never able to lie down or rest like the others had to. (Meheru, with two broken wrists, a deep head cut, and other injuries, was lying in the hospital's library.) In addition, it was very hot in Mani and Delia's small motel room and Delia was also terribly shaken. They were too upset even to eat—"we were not in the mood," Mani said—so they were surviving on soup.

The hospital in Prague, Oklahoma, in the 1950s.

Even when the others were well, she was still affected. She told pilgrims, "You see, I was the least hurt, physically I mean. But it hurt me most that Baba and Mehera should have so much of the suffering and I was left out, as it were . . . "

Remembering those days, Meheru told me that it was a great shock for all of them, a nightmare, and Baba was deeply affected by the crash, although He recovered very well and was able to walk afterwards as before. Mehera, too, was changed; her mood was subdued, she was much more sensitive to little things. Meheru wrote to a Baba-gathering in Oklahoma, convened on the 50th anniversary of the accident: "That He [Baba] allowed Mehera, the one closest to Him, to participate in this event and thus intensify many-fold His own suffering, shows how much He has done and has kept doing and giving to the world throughout His physical life here. . . . "

Thinking on this once, Meheru softly remarked to us, "What He did out of His Love!—you have no idea what His Love was."

IN THE BURLESONS' CARE

The doctor at the little hospital was Dr. Ned Burleson, and he lived just next door with his wife, Julia, and their two daughters, Margaret and Beth.

Some of those who treated Baba: Velma Davis (head nurse), Jess Dobs (lab technician), Dr. Ned Burleson.

Of course, it was natural that Mani, Miss Friendly, became friends with the doctor's wife and two little girls. "You know her nature," Meheru observed about Mani, "mixing with everyone, being friendly. She was so good with the Burlesons and their daughters, getting involved with them and their lives—of course she couldn't help that—she'd do that to her dying breath!"

Imagining Mani in that town, alone in a way she had never been alone, suffering in a way she had never suffered, it is easy to see how much Mrs. Burleson's warmth and support meant to her. And playing with the girls was a welcome distraction. Mani once told us that it was Mrs. Burleson who helped her out of her shock. When they had first gone to the hospital, and Mani was running from Mehera to the doctor, Mrs. Burleson took her aside and washed the mud off of her dress and clothes, as gently as if she were a little child.

When asked what Mani did during that time, Goher remembers that she would sit with Baba or Mehera or Elizabeth, but mostly with Baba. "And you know how Mani's nature is. She would become friends with everybody. The whole hospital knew her. She would even go out and talk to the doctor and his wife and be friendly with his children. . . . She would make friends with people walking on the street."

While the injured were resting and Mani was free, she would go visit the Burlesons at their home. Margaret Burleson (later known as Julia) remembered that she and Beth, her seven-year old sister, had a marvelous time playing with Mani, and that Mani was particularly fascinated with their automatic washing machine.

Mani gave both the girls nicknames. At the 50th anniversary commemoration of the accident, Julia said, "Mostly I remember Mani. She was beautiful. I thought she was about the nicest lady I had ever met. It seemed to me that Mani was at our house quite a lot. I wanted her there all the time." In the years that followed, she was always so excited when she saw that another letter from Mani had arrived. When asked to describe her, Julia responded, "Oh, she was *magical*."[5]

"Dr. Burleson's wife was such an angel," Mani said to pilgrims. "She need not have done all she did for us personally, she and her whole family. So when we left, it was really as very good friends. I still write to her every Christmas. And she tells me about her children, and her grandchildren now . . ."

In the 1970s and '80s, I remember Mani being very attentive to any correspondence she received from Mrs. Burleson. She would read and reread Mrs. Burleson's card, then choose a card with great care, and draft and redraft her response until it conveyed just what she wanted to send: a little news, a lot of affection. She was so excited when she heard that the now grown-up Margaret had gone to the Center in Myrtle Beach.

Dr. and Mrs. Burleson.

Mrs. Burleson called Mehera "the lady," and she said to Mani when they left, "Write to me sometimes. Let me know how the lady is doing."

"I will, Mrs. Burleson," Mani said, "but tell me, what is it that you expect to happen, that you tell me to do this?"

Mrs. Burleson said, "At the least, she will have terrible headaches." Mani later said in Mandali Hall:

> Well, she was so amazed when I wrote that Mehera doesn't have any headaches. As a matter of fact, I am the one who has the headaches. Mehera, by Baba's grace, doesn't. It's very, very rarely that she will even complain of a little tightness in her head, and even normally we all have headaches. So I wrote that to Mrs. Burleson, and she wrote back that it was really a miracle; she couldn't understand it.

Dr. Burleson's kindness can be seen in the cable he sent to Pappa Jessawala in response to worried cables from India:

PRAGUE 29.5.1952
[from] PRAGUE OKLAHOMA
  HOSPITAL
[to] "JESSAWALA" INDIA

IRANI FAMILY ALL DOING WELL NONE WILL DIE NONE WILL BE PERMANENTLY DISABLED; WE SHALL SEND THEM HOME TO YOU ULTIMATELY AS WELL AS WHEN THEY LEFT EXCEPT FOR THEIR UNHAPPY EXPERIENCE.
  DOCTOR

Dr. Burleson in later years.

THE KINDNESS OF AMERICA

In fact, the whole town was kind. Actually, Mani found the whole country kind. As she told pilgrims:

> When somebody asked me what I liked best about America, I said, "First and foremost were the people." I'm talking of strangers, people aside from Baba's lovers. The best thing we found in America, with all its very beautiful things, were the people. Amazingly friendly, wherever we went, perfect strangers. A dentist we had to go to. A writer in the road when we were walking. This I experienced right from the start, from the plane ride, from the very first. The friendliness, the reaching out of the people, was amazing.
>
> On the plane, an American couple were sitting behind me. The woman and I said something to each other, and they were so friendly. They didn't know I was with a whole party of other people, and they invited me to their home to stay, and they would show me around America. Then I came to my senses and said, "Oh that's very, very sweet of you, but, you know, I'm along with others." They didn't know; they thought I was alone. But going to that extent, inviting a stranger to stay with them so they could show me around America.
>
> I still remember when I would go and come from the motel to the hospital where Baba was. I'd go round this particular row of houses. And one day the children were waiting there with a basket. They'd obviously been waiting for over an hour, because somehow I was later that day coming from the hospital. They were waiting to show me that their doggie had a litter of puppies just that morning,

and they wanted me to be the first to see them; they wanted to share that with me. I mean, overwhelming things like that happened. And the parents, too, came out, and they were so happy. They would always ask, "How is the injured party?" Amazing.

As I would limp home (I hurt my knee and had a cane), people would stop on the road, perfect strangers, lift their hats in greeting, and ask if they could give me a lift to the hospital or wherever I wanted to go. Children would stop outside their homes just to greet me, or to give a flower "for the gentleman at the hospital." The proprietor of the motel would always come with a beautiful bunch of flowers, again for "the gentleman at the hospital." And other people would ask us, "Are you the people who were in the bash?"

"Yeah, we're the people in the bash."

"Oh," they'd say, "will you give this flower to the folks who were injured?"

Mani found this friendliness in the most unexpected places:

Americans are a very naturally friendly people, I'd say. We were in a hospital in New York—was it Johns Hopkins? [Goher piped in, "Cornell Medical Center"]—where Mehera had to have x-rays for her head injury. Charmian [Duce] had driven us there, and she left us in a room in the hospital while she went to park the car. She had to go a long distance away to park it, so it would take quite some time before she would come back. So we said, "Fine, Charmian" and we all sat down— Mehera, Goher, Meheru, and myself. We looked at each other, and I think we all at the same time realized something: we were so thirsty.

"Are you thirsty?" one of them asked.

"Yes, I'm parched." I said. "Wait a minute, I'll go out. After all, what can happen? I'll go and find out if there's something available to drink."

So I went out and I almost got lost. I saw corridors, miles and miles of corridors; I think you need skates for the corridors in those hospitals. I just walked and walked, wondering if I'd ever get back. Suddenly I saw someone in a uniform going by, not a nurse, but a sort-of nurse. And she was so friendly that I said, "Excuse me, where can I get some soft drinks, or a drink of water?"

Oh, she looked at me like she'd known me for ages. "I'll take you there, don't you worry!"

She put her arm around my shoulder and we went off walking and talking like long-lost buddies. She took me to a place where they sold Coca-Cola and Seven-Up and all that sort of thing, soft drinks, mind you, no martinis. She asked me which I would like. So I picked out some drinks and she said, "Can I help you carry them back?"

"No, no, no!"

Then she wouldn't even let me pay for them, even though I kept saying, "No, I must pay, no, you've already been so kind."

"Please," she said, "this is on me. You mustn't say no, you can't say no."

So she paid. And as I was walking back with the bottles, I suddenly realised, "Baba, it's good You sent her!" because actually, I didn't have any money. I forgot that. We never carried money. So it's good she didn't take me at my word when I said, "I'll pay!" What would I have paid with?

A LETTER HOME

Only after several weeks could Mani bring herself to write a description of the accident to the other women mandali in India.

> YUPON [YOUPON] DUNES
> P.O. Box 487
> South Carolina, U.S.A.
> 10th June, 1952

Dear Naja, Khorshed, Masi, Arnavaz, Kaity, Chicky [?], Naggu, Alu (and all dear ones of Baba's group),

I received your letter two days ago, and will try and write a short and concise account of the whole thing to you. We are at this moment at Youpon Dunes, Myrtle Beach (Elizabeth's house by the sea, not the Center)[;] we came here three days ago, and it is over a fortnight since the awful accident. First let me tell you that the critical period has passed, and now it is a matter of time only before everyone can be well again. The doctor (Dr. Burleson), his wife, other doctors, nurses and staff were all extremely kind and helpful and friendly, got very fond of Baba, and before we left the doctor wrote to Baba a beautiful letter (a copy of which [I] enclose inside). This was very lucky for we were completely helpless otherwise. When we started from M.B. we were in two cars. Baba, Mehera, Elizabeth, Meheru, and myself in one car, and Sarosh, Rano, Goher, Kitty and Delia in the other. The rest of the Mandali had gone on to California ahead of us, and were not able to come to us till two or three days after we had been in the hospital. We had the most hellish time for the first week, and it was Sarosh who managed to send off telegrams. We were without money,

and Elizabeth who had to sign the checks was helpless. It
was the complete 'Helplessness' and 'Hopelessness' of the
song of the new life, for a time. I will not be able to write to
you the details of it, for just to think of it makes me feel so
sick I could not go on writing at all. Baba, Mehera and
Elizabeth were the most injured. Meheru had a wound on
the forehead which was stitched up, and small fractures on
the wrists (one wrist is in a cast and the other is bandaged),
but otherwise she is alright. I will write about Baba and
Mehera last. Elizabeth was slumped over the wheel with
both her hands badly fractured, and seven broken ribs. One
arm had to be operated upon for the fractures endangered
a nerve which nearly paralyzed her arm. She is of course in
bed and very helpless at the moment, but seems cheerful
in spite of it. Mehera had a concussion and a bad wound on
the forehead which has been stitched up, a bruised ankle,
and her eyelids were so swollen she could not open them for
days, and even now she can only partly open them. But the
eyes have in no way been affected and as the swelling goes
slowly down, she will be able to open them wider and wider.
She is able to walk about, and yesterday Baba was brought in
a wheel-chair and Mehera sat beside him on the verandah.
Baba's left arm and left leg were fractured—the leg is in a
cast, and the arm is bandaged to his chest; they could not
put the arm in a cast for the fracture is below the shoulder
joint, and the angle is awkward. He is still sometimes in pain,
and spends bad nights. His face, which is almost normal now,
was badly bruised. In the hospital, on the second day of the
accident, his face was so badly swollen and distorted, that
not a feature of his face was recognizable as Baba's and he
could not eat or drink for two days. Very slowly the swelling

has been going down, till, as I said, his face is now almost normal. (But his face still hurts him from the bruises; X-rays of the face proved that there were no fractures of any kind thank God.) In a week or two the cast on his arm will be taken off, but his leg will take longer. He can be got onto a wheel-chair, but his position in bed is most uncomfortable as he cannot turn over on his side and can only lie on his back or sit up. He is looking thinner than ever, and said that this is the personal physical disaster that he had told us about.— That until July 10, weakness dominates over strength and that he has to suffer this. The world will benefit, said Baba to someone, but my God! how can one accept any good that comes at the cost of such a horrible experience, and such personal suffering to Baba and Mehera.

The doctors were amazed at Mehera having escaped any internal head injuries, and the specialist said that it was a miracle and he took down Mehera's name and address for his medical data.

Mehera has been a wonderful patient, and Baba sent word to her that she mustn't mind the doctors touching her. Elizabeth has been wonderful about the whole thing, and Goher, Rano, Kitty and the others have all been wonderful. The worst is now past of course, it is nice to be home again (away from the hospital), and our [men] mandali and doctors are with us, Donkin's knowledge of

Baba and Mehera (with forehead bandages).

orthopedic surgery helps a lot. The [men] mandali are looking after Baba and they all have duties. Margaret is with us and helps massage the patients. I was hardly hurt except for a sprained foot and a wounded knee but I suffered from shock. There isn't much else I can think of writing so I will end. Please forward copies to all you think will be anxious (Mansari, etc.). I received Kitty's [Katie's?] letter a few days ago, and reading it seemed like a dream from another world. Please understand that it was impossible to write before this; it was not a matter of time, it was just impossible. Baba has many telegrams from all over America and India and other places—your telegrams were received and read. I personally thanked Dr. Burleson for sending that long and understanding reply to Khorshed's telegram.

    The patients are gradually improving all the time, but bones take time to heal, and to see Baba confined to bed again is very sad. We cannot help him not suffer, and at the moment he has made himself so helpless that he cannot help himself; there is nothing for us to do but to pray for the period of 'Strength' to soon come, so that our beloved ones may be well soon.

Love to all
Mani

THE JOURNEY BACK

As Dr. Burleson predicted, Baba, Mehera, and the others recovered somewhat, and, as Adi wrote to Pappa, "After about twelve days stay at Prague the party was driven back to Myrtle Beach with great difficulty and under the trying conditions of heat and rain."

    Mani rode in a car driven by Adi. The first entry in her diary after "the wretched accident" was on June 4, when they left for the east coast. She wrote about their trip across half of America, about the decrepit places and fine places (where they had "good tea and Colonial cakes"), the cotton and tobacco, the peach farms and "road-side tables everywhere and water-melons to Memphis – also strawberries."

The sandwich place at Monteagle gets a mention (Loretta Young had something to do with the town? – she's in parenthesis there in the diary) and Bethea's Restaurant, a "very lovely and classic place." They were caught in a storm with rain, hail, and thunder, and then sunshine and some never-ending hills between Murphy and Franklin. Rivers, waterfalls, roses, pine trees; coke and "chok Ice" (chocolate ice on a stick)— until June 6, when they reached Youpon Dunes, Elizabeth's home in Myrtle Beach.

Mani recalled that journey back:

> I couldn't just *touch* on the subject of that most memorable stay at the Center and that unforgettable accident in Oklahoma. Either I talk for days or . . . So I will not speak on that. But I'll tell you some of the things that amused Baba, even though He only heard of it later from us.
>
> For instance, after the accident Baba had gone on ahead to Myrtle Beach with Mehera, Goher, Donkin, Rano, Nilu, and the rest of the party. Adi Sr., Delia, Gustadji, Meheru, and myself were told to come by van along with a lot of the luggage, much of it very blood-splattered.
>
> So we were following the ambulances that went ahead with Baba, Mehera, and the others, in a van carrying the luggage and ourselves. Twice we had to stop for the night at a motel, and we had to stop at little places to eat, to have a quick snack somewhere or the other. So there again came another first in my experience. I'd never seen a drugstore.

I'd read often about drugstores, but I thought all they gave was aspirin or something for your headache. But when we got there, we saw it was quite different. It even had books for sale, and counters where they served food, and oh, lots of things! [The diary tells us: "lunch at Columbia drug store."] There was this row of piano stools at the counter that turned all the way around, and we four went in and each sat on a piano stool. There was a lovely, motherly lady across the counter. Now we had decided we were going to order something we had never had before, and would probably never have again, and that was a hot dog. That nice big bun with a sausage inside. We'd known of it, but we'd never had it. So we all said, "Hot dog!" when it came time to order.

Or rather, Meheru, Adi, and Delia gave the order, so I was looking around because there was so much in there that interested me, the books, the people . . . Suddenly I heard the lady behind the counter, the mother, lean over and ask me [Mani imitated a drawling, nasal American accent here], "Do you want it all the way up?" Do I want it all the way up? I look at the rest of the piano stools with all the people sitting on them, and I thought she meant, am I standing the treat for all of them. "No, no, no," I said. "It's just for me."

But she was so patient. She leaned over and talked to me as if I were a deaf child, "Do you want it all the way up?" This was terrible—what was I supposed to do? In the meantime, Meheru, who was next to me, whispered in my ear, "She means do you want onions, mustard, this, and that?" I got the idea. "Yes," I said, "all the way up, as high as you can go!" And I had the biggest hot dog, with all kinds of things in it. Oh, it was just so lovely. Baba chuckled when we told him about it; He was quite amused.

At another place, Adi asked if they had tea. "Well," the lady said, "we do have some tea for truck drivers with ulcers." I said, "Well, we ain't truck drivers and we ain't got ulcers, but if you could give us a cup of tea . . ." So she did, but the tea was not satisfactory, certainly not up to the standard of Adi and Delia. They were so finicky, so particular about tea. Now we all like a good cup of tea; it's our beverage in India. But Adi and Delia were really what I would call fussy. Delia would say, "I can't understand it. Americans don't know how to make tea."

Oh, that tea we had there. They would plonk down a cup of hot water in front of each of us. It was brought from the kitchen, so by the time it got to your table it was lukewarm. There were teabags on the side. So you took a teabag and *blip, blip, blip, blip,* dunked it into the water, and by the time you've done five or six blips, it's cold and flat, and then by the time you put in the sugar and stir, well, it isn't tea.

So Adi had a bright idea. He told her, "Bring a teapot of only boiling water."

"Boiling water?"

"Yes."

So she brought it. She couldn't understand what it was for; she was positively wondering what we were going to do with it. After the pot of boiling water was on our table, he said, "Now bring twelve teabags." So there are the twelve teabags. And then I was supposed to lift the lid on the top and *blip, blip, blip* the teabags. It was delicious. After that we had no problem about tea. No problem at all.

Now, Mani would recall, Delia could be great company and lots of fun. But on this long drive back east in the car, out of shock and nervousness she commented on every single thing they saw, keeping up non-stop chatter. The others were still so shook up by the accident, especially Adi, who was driving, that it drove them crazy. Finally Meheru whispered to Mani, "Do something!"

What could she do? Well, Mani suddenly turned to Delia as she was chatting away and told her that they had to be very quiet with Adi at the wheel because whenever he was startled, his arm jerked, which would jerk the steering wheel and they could get into another accident. Delia just clammed right up, poor thing, and was too scared to say much of anything else all the way back.

Mani loved to recall how Gustadji, who was with them, was very taken with Delia's rosy cheeks; his aunt had rosy cheeks just like that, he gestured to Mani through his odd sign language. When Delia found out what he was saying, she was horrified. An aunt of Gustadji's must be a hundred years old! Then she giggled, took out a tissue, wiped off a bit of the rosiness, and showed the tissue to Gustadji. It was rouge. He was amazed.

YOUPON DUNES

On June 6, Mani wrote: "Reach Yupon Dunes 6:30 p.m." and on June 7: "Baba + Mehera + E. [Elizabeth] party come."

In Youpon Dunes, Mani was very down and depressed. As she remembered in the Hall:

> Baba and we all were accommodated in Youpon Dunes, that lovely house by the ocean that was Elizabeth's father's house, which she had given up just to be at the Center. Baba had a room upstairs, a very nice, smaller room. As I said, Baba and Mehera were the most hurt in the accident; Meheru was a little hurt. I was barely hurt at all, at least physically.

View of Youpon Dunes where Baba recuperated after His accident. His room was on the top left corner.

I just had a little knee injury and what I now understand is called whiplash, that gives me neck trouble now. But I was hurt very much in my feelings, as I said. Baba was having all this suffering, and Mehera, and why was I spared?

Anyway, when we were in Youpon Dunes, we would go into Baba's room whenever He called us. Otherwise we would be doing our duty. Rano and I were helping Elizabeth do her things. And I'd go down into the basement and wash clothes for Mehera and the others.

One day when we were in Baba's room, Baba suddenly looked at me and said, "What's the matter with you? Hmmm? Look at you!" So everybody looked at me. "Black circles under your eyes," Baba went on, and then He made a delightful gaunt face, "with your cheeks like that . . ." And He made all kinds of faces to show how dreadful I looked. (He had such a twinkle in His eye when He was making those faces.) "What is the matter with you?"

"Well," I kept saying, "I don't know. Nothing."

"You eat?"

"Yes, Baba."

So Baba sent the other women out and called Dr. Donkin.

Usually the men mandali wouldn't look directly at us, and we wouldn't look directly at them. But this was Baba, and He said, "Don, what are you doing standing there. Look at her!" So poor Don looked at me and back at Baba.

"Can't you see, she's got these black circles under the eyes, and the cheeks go 'mmmm,' like that [Mani sucked in her cheeks imitating Baba] and she's walking like this, and what are you doing about it?"

No answer.

[Mani imitated Baba snapping His fingers:] "Didn't you hear?"

And Don said, "Yes". Baba said, "Go on! Give her some nice strong vitamin tablets to make her strong, and tonic; build her up."

No answer.

"Didn't you hear what I said?"

"Well, Baba, I don't think vitamins or tonic will do her any good. What she needs is rest and change."

"Oh!" said Baba, "You're crazy!" Then He turned to the others and said, "Look at this man! I talk to him, I tell him to give her vitamins and tonic to make her strong, and he, he talks about irrelevant things like rest and change and all those silly things. Look, I said vitamins and tonic."

"All right, Baba, if You're saying it, I'll prescribe vitamins and tonic."

"That's it!"

So Don prescribed vitamins and tonic. With all that love and compassion and care, Baba called me when the bottles had arrived. And with the medicine came a lot of instructions from Baba, very particular instructions: that I was to have the vitamins at such and such a time, so many times a day, some just ten minutes before lunch. The tonic was to be so many minutes after meals, and that in between such a time and such a time. And following all that, my head was in a whirl. This wasn't helping me at all, let alone the rest and the change. The most difficult was the vitamin I had to take ten minutes before lunch. We never knew when lunch would be. But it kept me occupied. I would be down in the cellar washing clothes, and wonder, "What's the time?" And go running up and find out, no, no, still five minutes. So I'd go running down. Or I'd sit at the lunch table and twiddle about, fiddle with something or the other, trying to pass the interval between the vitamin and lunch. Which was more of a headache, and probably pulled me down more. At least, that's what I thought. As for rest? Change? I always say Baba forgot to include those in His dictionary!

So it came about that when she was so upset, Baba gave Mani a host of little problems to keep the big one away. Mosquitoes to keep the elephant at bay. About her focus on those vitamins, she once again spoke of Baba's "real meditations" that He gave them:

... those were meditations, the real meditation, constantly remembering Baba. The mind has to be occupied; it must have worries, things to work on. So it is good to have small problems, small things. We had a thousand little things to occupy our minds. "This Baba wants us to do." "At ten o'clock I must take my medicine." "At this time I must remind so and so to do this." I think blessed is the person who has many little problems or difficulties, little things, so the mind is never faced with a big one. Meditation was not sitting in a corner and taking His name. It was: "Oh, this time, He wants that done." "This is for Baba." "This I must finish in time." "This I have to do."

There was a blistering heat wave in Myrtle Beach at this time, and everyone, injured and uninjured alike, suffered terribly from the heat. Elizabeth had an air conditioner installed in Baba's room. One facet of life in Youpon Dunes that Mani remembered was how much they all longed to be called into Baba's room. She was most often the one taking messages from Baba to Elizabeth and she would linger in His room for as long as she could, making the most of every cool second, practically backing out when it came time to leave.

"Last week of June went to Durham 3 days – Duke's [Duke] Hospital. Baba's plaster changed twice + M. [Mehera] examined – O.K. Baba's hand plaster removed," says the diary.

Before they left for New York on July 14, Baba took Mehera and Mani to the Center for one more visit, which turned out to be the last time they saw His "home in the West."

NEW YORK

From Youpon Dunes to Florence by car, from Florence by train overnight to Penn Station, from Penn Station by limos and taxis to Scarsdale, by easy stages Baba and the mandali arrived at Mrs. Kate Ferris' house for their stay outside New York City.

Baba's arm was still not fully recovered and his leg was in a plaster cast. In spite of this, on July 18, 19, and 20, Mani wrote in the diary, "Baba saw about 500 people from all over the states, at Mrs. Duce's apartments – v. touching love of all for Baba."

Nilu described these darshan days in a letter to India:

> On the 18th, 19th and 20th hundreds of people of different walks of life came to see Baba. At the sight of Baba many were crying, many were sobbing, and many a one smiling. Their emotions and devotion for Baba reached them in this way. Baba at that time was a grand personality. He sat erect in the bed with his injured arm across his chest and his plaster leg

stretched out in the bed, his face, pink and radiant, his eyes flashing, dancing and twinkling everywhere, men, women and children standing all around him in the hushed silence with different emotions in their hearts, the whole scene was a grand spectacle of a great devotion for Baba and a play of many colourful emotions for the visitors. It had sort of a divine touch. Baba's interviews with the West were not only successful, but in a way they were unique.

Baba said of this darshan, "It made Me really happy to meet these people, wonderful souls."

They had a few days of visits to doctors for Mehera. However, Baba wanted Mehera and the ladies to enjoy the city. Mani wrote in her diary:

> 22nd We went (with Baba) to Radio City Music Hall + saw Where's Charlie? [Charley] v. beautiful theatre, saw the ballet . . . Stayed at Mrs. Ferris's . . . till the 29th. During that time saw among other things, the Empire State Bldng – had lunch at Junior League Club (Charmi's) with Ivy – 3 times dined at Ivy's – Saw a play at St. James's Theatre "The King + I" – drove across the [George] Washington Bridge – the Natural History Museum (simply beautiful – Baba came in wheel-chair + M. [Mehera] wheeled him round) – saw Planitarium [planetarium] (trip in rocket to moon) – had tea at Ella Winterfeldt's – Phyllis [Filis] and Adele came over for a day – saw exterior of [The] Cloisters – missed Acquacade [Aquacade].

However, in spite of everyone's efforts, they didn't enjoy these treats much; they were not in a sightseeing frame of mind.

LONDON

Nilu informed Pappa by letter: "We are all flying on the 30th to England where we will stay only for six days, then we will fly to Switzerland and

Baba at The Rubens Hotel, London; Mary Backett sitting on Baba's right.

stay there until August 20th. Afterwards we will go to Egypt and back to India by the end of August."

And on July 30, Mani wrote they "Left at 3 by tourist plane" for London. On the plane, "B. didn't sleep – at 1.30 a.m. was broad daylight – were informed it was 6.30 London time . . 31st London airport 10 a.m. Mary + Delia met us and stopped at The Rueben [Rubens] Hotel – Eve [evening] went to Vaudevill theatre to see comedy "Sweet Madness" – passed Buckingham Palace – changing of guards + Traf. [Trafalgar] Square." This last looked "lovely" at night with lighted fountains.

After the strain and rigors of the New Life, it's no wonder that Mehera and "the girls" had looked forward to the novelties of America, a country they had never seen but heard and read so much about. Of course, the horrors of the accident overshadowed everything there. Mehera remembered that after that, they just wanted to go home.

In England, Baba again wanted them to have the pleasure of seeing the sights, but this time the outings were more successful. England had a different appeal. As Mani recalled to pilgrims, "You see, we've had an English education, not only in the English language, but we were educated during the English regime. So our geography and history were very much of England."

Like Mehera, Mani loved India deeply, but she also had a special feeling for England. In their family home had hung pictures of King George and Queen Victoria, and in later years she continued to follow the doings of the royal family with interest. They read English books and magazines like many other educated Zoroastrians, and she was much more conversant with the places and persons of England than most of the young American pilgrims, who visited with her in later years. The things Mehera, Mani, and some of the other women mandali knew about England!—this was yet one more ingredient in the invigorating cultural stew of their twentieth-century Indian background. As Mani described in Mandali Hall:

> We were taken by Delia to so many places in England, which made us very happy. She went out of her way, conducted us everywhere and to everything that she thought we would like. I wanted very much to see the Queen, but of course we couldn't see the Queen. We couldn't see much of Buckingham Palace either because there's a big wall around it. But by the palace gate stood a guard in a beaver hat, a long thing with a gold chain strap under the chin. He was in a little wooden box, and I was just thrilled to see a palace guard in person, not just in a magazine. As we walked past him, I dawdled just to see if he was curious about these strange people going by. Not a bit. He looked straight ahead, as if carved out of granite. Very stolid. And I said to myself, "Hmmmm. . . ." I wanted to arouse his curiosity. I was sure he really was curious, but why was he not doing

Delia De Leon.

anything about it? I was the last one to walk by, and after I passed him I suddenly whirled around and looked back. Sure enough, his head had turned a little, and then snapped back to looking straight ahead. "Gotcha, my boy," I said to myself.

Mani had other English curiosities she wanted to see, too, including some odd ones:

> I'd always wanted to see a London bobby. When Minta was driving us to Stratford-on-Avon, Shakespeare's birthplace, she wanted to find out if we were taking the right turn, so she stopped and signaled to a policeman. He came over. I was on the side of the car by the window, and he came over and stood right outside by me. I couldn't believe it. I just looked at him: in person, at last, a living bobby.

Delia wrote in her book that although Baba was getting about with great difficulty, He insisted on going to all the evening entertainments that Delia had booked for them in advance (before the accident) so as not to disappoint Mehera and Mani. Mani wrote in her diary that they saw "South Pacific," starring Mary Martin, at the Theatre Royal, Drury Lane; saw an ice skating play; and, of all things, a rodeo, which delighted Mehera. (As the women would say, not in America, but in jolly old England they finally got to see a rodeo.) During the day they went to the Tower of London, Fleet Street, crossed the Thames and had a picnic, and visited Oxford. Being nature-lovers, they loved Kew Gardens and found in Richmond Park "simply lovely country—trees—many riding—children playing, people walking, sitting on broken tree trunks, giving their dogs a walk. Tame deer being fed." And Stratford and environs full of "picturesque thatched cottages" like Anne Hathaway's, rose vines and multi-colored flowers, and on the river, swans and people boating. And Mani noted a tramp they saw by a London river.

In England, Baba ordered Mani to keep silence, which was to last until they reached India. The only exception was that she could talk and read to Him.

Silence was a true restriction for chatty Mani. She later felt Baba's inner purpose in having her keep silence may have been to relieve Mehera of some of her own suffering, or to share it in some way. As she described it to pilgrims, Mani remembered people being very kind in England to this "dumb lady":

> When I'd go down to the dining room at The Rubens Hotel, I couldn't talk, but the headwaiter would conduct me to my place like I was a princess or something. He'd say, "I'll read out the menu, and anything you'd like, just nod." He knew I couldn't talk. I didn't know anything about the menu: there were all these long and wonderful names, but I didn't know what they were. So I thought I'll do it like tic-tac-toe: to the second thing he says, I'll say yes, the third thing I'll say no, and so on. So every now and then I'd nod, and he'd tic; then he'd read on and every now and then I'd nod again and he'd tic. Somehow I nodded at the right things, because everything that came was just wonderful. He'd call out to the waiters what to bring. I heard one of them say something like, "Coo, blimey, she's dumb but she ain't deaf!" I just glared at him, saying to myself, "Now, you wait, my boy, just wait. . .!"
>
> There was an Italian worker in the hotel who I always seemed to pass in the hall on the way to our rooms. He would come straight to me and talk, I think, in Italian, because he thought I was Italian. So he talked to me, and I

knew he was telling me all his woes. He'd make faces at the cold: everything was so shivery; he wanted to go to nice, sunny Italia. I couldn't reply, but I would look interested. He didn't have enough money to go back to Italy, that was the whole thing. But I didn't have any money either, so I couldn't help him.

Once, as I was going back to Baba's room, right at my feet I saw a big shiny gold coin. I picked it up and thought, "Hey, maybe if I go back and give this to my Italian friend it will help him get to Italy." But then I realized I didn't know how much the coin was worth. I'm glad I didn't take it back to him because I was told it was only a penny.

And the page boy, the page boy I loved. He was a young little thing, very smartly dressed in a uniform. He loved asking me which floor I was going to. "Which floor, Miss?" he'd say, "Which floor, Miss?" He knew darned well which floor, because he took me up every morning, afternoon, and evening for breakfast, lunch, and supper, but still, I could see the glint in his eyes: "Wait till I go home and tell the family about the lady who couldn't talk"—that kind of glint. So, "Which floor, Miss" and I'd hold up three fingers, and he'd be so happy.

In that day, a tourist's visit to London would be incomplete without a drop-in to Madame Tussauds Wax Museum, where they have wax effigies of famous people. Delia took Mehera and Mani there, as Mani remembered:

> At Madame Tussauds, you go up a staircase to reach the top where all the exhibitions are. On the landing before you turn into the museum is a wax statue of a bobby, an English policeman. I knew it was wax, and when I went up the steps

I reached out and shook his hand. Of course we were not supposed to touch men, and Delia was shocked. "Oh Mani, how could you?!" I suddenly realized she thought it was real, so I gestured, "Why not?" and defiantly put my hand out again to touch it. Poor Delia. When she finally saw it was wax, we had a good laugh.

What moves me in these stories is that despite the distressing outcome of their American visit, despite her shock and sadness, Mani continued to display so much spirit, so much willingness to continue: to play, to tease, to write down towns and sights in her diary. Deep down she had real grit. We saw it in Mani in the later years, too, the resilience that enabled her to always start again, to keep going for Baba, to tackle new obstacles full-on. It was part of her character not to give up.

SWITZERLAND

Baba recuperating in Hedi's home in Locarno, Switzerland.

A visit to France to stay with Anita [Vieillard] was one of the items on their itinerary that fell by the wayside because of the accident. However, Baba and party did go on to Switzerland, on a visit arranged by Irene Billo and Max Haefliger, a Baba lover from Switzerland. Hedi Mertens had offered her house for their use, and, as Delia recalled, "Although there were many visitors. . . it was still an intimate and wonderful two weeks."

Mani's diary takes us there:

> 6th Left by plane for Switzerl (London air-port cozy + nice) at 11.30 + reached Kloten Air Port [Zurich] at 2. Irene [Billo] met us. Customs were nice – opened only one bag – v. nice taxi driver. Crossed Zurich – + had lunch at Andermatt restaurant (v. nice food + waitress + proprietor thought us Prince + Princesses). all way most beautiful scenery.

Hedi's house was a "lovely little place" in the fashionable resort town of Locarno. In her diary Mani noted Locarno's Swiss charms: outdoor restaurants, colorful boats on the lake and red benches all around it, roadside flowers, quaint houses, chalets, etc. Over the days that followed they went on outings in the car, including some through the Alps into Italy. One evening they went out to see fireworks, with "lovely music (Italian + V. waltzes) drifting up to us from the waterside where little lighted boats dotted the lake."

In the evenings, when the group would sit with Baba, often Mani would read out spiritual poems or stories of the saints. There is a movie of Baba taken here at Hedi's, His leg in a cast, Donkin attending, and also shots of the women in the garden, with cameo appearances by Irene's huge white rabbit. Later Mani would speak of how she enjoyed playing with the Haefligers' children there despite keeping silence.

Meherjee and Adi Sr. helping Baba walk.

It was always a pleasure to watch Mani imitate Baba gesturing. Her supple fingers and expressive face mirrored His, a dimmer reflection, of course, but still suggestive of Baba. When she was keeping silence herself, naturally she gestured, too, and Meheru told us what a marvelous sight it was one day in Switzerland to see Baba and Mani, far across the garden from each other, carrying on a seamless, fluent conversation in gestures.

Anita came to see Baba and the women there. She recalled:

> I took them out in the streets of Locarno. But these outings didn't mean much to them – to go out to a cafe or to look at this or that. Their whole being was being with Baba, and they experienced everything by being with him. The outside world was unnecessary. Living with Baba and being in that kind of vital way of being with him – What is there to see outside in the world? They were not interested in curiosity, what for most people is a necessity. For them, their whole being was to feel the play of sensitivity between Baba and themselves. Since they knew and felt what Baba is, naturally everything was reflected in him. It was a reflection in him of all their needs and wants.
>
> They had led such a retired life, there was no such thing as pleasure any more.[6]

For those who enjoy the word-sketches in Mani's diary, here are their trips into Italy:

> 10th [August] Went for a lovely outing into the mountains as far as Maloja – where Irene's mother met us in the restaurant. Went thru Italy (had visas, etc). Stopped at the 2 borders – Gandrie [Gandria] + Castasegna – Italian + Swiss at both ends with a neutral space in bet. [in between]. When going the It. visawalas [Italian guards checking their passports] were v. excited but not so capable. We left 7.25 reached there 11.30. Most beautiful scenery + lovely day. Avenues of plane trees + Chr. [Christmas] trees + other trees – many waterfalls, church bells, lanes + lit. towns + most picturesque quaint houses (esp. [especially] Italy[)] + in It. more Cypress trees than others [here a tiny line to

illustrate a tall thin tree] + not [here a tiny sketch of a wide-branched tree], donkey carts + hay carts, bearded people + peasant women, wild flowers (purple) + little flower shops on wheels. lit. church + graveyard beneath a silky long waterfall – lit. towns suddenly projecting on the lake. Italian church spires against blue mountains – many cyclists with shirts off + hats on – many tiny cars here + also small-wheeled motor-bykes – sightseeing bus – churches on mountain tops – green water of the lakes – fort – paintings on outside of churches, holy statues every few miles – pictures in square lit. bits of inlaid stone – boating, swimming, diving on the lake. The beautiful Lake Como of Italy – famous – horse victorias with flat fringed tops – outdoor bazaar shops in Lugano. (Ristorante + Pensiones) Half hour before reaching Maloja, scenery changes suddenly – panoramic view of mountain peaks, + pine trees + some snow on [?] of the mountain – lovely place up there – had v. good food + had Cianti (red It. wine) + white wine + beer – met Irene's mother – returned home 5.15 eve . . . [The women are photographed at this restaurant – Mehera and Mani in stylish pants, Mehera with a small bandage on her forehead.]

 16th Went to Streza [Stresa] in Italy – all along the Lago Maggiore – only small part of the lake is in Swit. most of it in Italy (?) – + visas again on the 2 border, (a stone pillar marking the 2 division [here Mani drew a crest and a flower symbol]) – the Italian custom officials had the gray hats with the long feather + turned up at the back – lovely drive – Streza inn – big place – picturesque open-air eating places – yellow balcony with the *flower pots* + the chair facing each other. we had *kascerta* [cassata] (famous Italian ice-cream) in a tea-room by the lake. Baba came in in wheel-chair.

Lunch at Hotel Schweizerhaus in Maloja, Switzerland. Delia (seated at the table), Mani (arms crossed), Meheru, Mehera, Goher, and Irene Billo's mother.

After this refreshing visit, they had a beautiful drive to Geneva, had a terrible time getting tickets to India because of an Air India strike ("19th we're leaving but mess about the Air India line on strike – frantic efforts to book on some other plane"), but after two restless days in Geneva, they finally flew out on August 21 to Karachi and then back home.

FIERY AND FREE

Photo of Mani taken by her brother Beheram.

For the women mandali, Baba's Fiery Free Life opened a new world—on the other side of the New Life, their visit to the West, and the accident in Oklahoma. Between 1953 and 1956 Baba went on mass darshan tours—traveling across India, overwhelming hearts in Hamirpur and Andhra as He gave out key messages and prayers and publicly declared His Avatarhood—and also returned to the West. Through all this, the women went back to a retired life, "keeping house" for Baba.

We can glimpse the intensity of this period from the first entries in Mani's 1953 diary:

> Jan. B. returned on 30th from intense programme of South [darshan programs in south India] – in Andhra one day 60,000 mass darshan . . .
>
> Feb. 1st We break silence of 2 ½ months.

DEHRA DUN

On February 16, Mani wrote that they left Pimpalgaon for Poona and then Bombay, where they took a train to the foothills of the Himalayas, to Dehra Dun. The diary says, "end of Feb. still cold here + read about heat-wave in Nagar." It got colder still; after a few days they went to Mussoorie, a hill station above Dehra Dun, even closer to the mountains. From up there, Mani wrote, "When clear in couple of days see beaut. range of snow mountains behind the blue ones – lovely walks. roses everywhere – the tiny roses (bankay roses) climb richly to top of pine trees (yellow white and pink)."

As I picture that trip to Dehra Dun and Mussoorie in 1953, five things spring to mind: Peter, Sheba, and—at the end of their stay—*God Speaks*, the Master's Prayer, and Baba's message "The Highest of the High."

PETER

Here is Peter, toddling into the diary on one of those clear Mussoorie days: "Mrs. McLoyd + Cooper give us Peter – (Peter born on 10th Jan 1953)."

Peter was one of those Mani called "the four-footed mandali," a black cocker spaniel puppy who grew up to become one of Baba's favorite pets. When, years later, Mani wrote to someone who had lost a dog, "I know what it is to lose a beloved pet," I immediately thought, "She's thinking of Peter."

Peter hamming it up.

Mani with her dear Peter.

You see Peter in the films, following Baba around and, when he isn't following Baba, following Mani. He's the clown wearing a hat and spectacles, with a fake pipe coming out of his mouth.

In Mussoorie the women would go on long walks with Baba, and every day they'd pass a cottage with a huge rose bush in front. It turned out that Mrs. McLeod (Mani referred to her as Mrs. McLoyd) lived there, and her elderly sister Mrs. Cooper would come and stay for the summer. On their walks, Mani and the other women became friendly with Mrs. Cooper, who wished for company, and Mani and Goher would sometimes go and visit her. On one of these visits, they were offered one of the McLeod spaniel's puppies. There were only two left. Mehera came with Mani to see them, and picked the little black one, who drooled on her shoulder half the way home, and on Mani's the other half.

Peter started out shy, but that didn't last long. Baba gave him to

Mehera and Mani, and then, at Mehera's suggestion, because she felt it was best for a dog to have one owner, to Mani.

Among Mani's possessions is an extraordinary item: a handmade book all about dog training and care. There's a cut-out of a mournful-looking bassett hound on the cover. The basic form is that of a bound notebook into which Mani has inserted typed sections on dog training, diet, etc., and included typed tables with titles such as "Suggested Drugs" and "For Home Nursing & First Aid."

I can tell she typed these herself, as the typing is in blue ink, like much of her correspondence. When you first open it, there's a picture of a cocker spaniel looking at a petite hedgehog drinking milk. The subtitle is: "I wonder where it all goes." The next page displays the title in flowing script: "The Dog Book," followed by a curlicue, under which is typed: "(From Donkin's THE BOOK OF THE DOG)." Then the text begins, interspersed with dog pictures obviously cut from magazines. That the sister of the Avatar would have the time and interest to hand-make a dog training book. . . .

Mani once told me in all seriousness, "The trouble with me is, I do everything one hundred percent. I can't do anything by halves." So her care and training of Peter was one

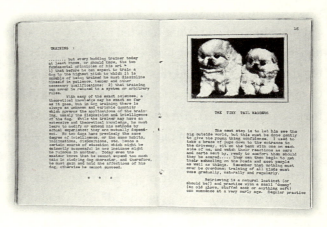

hundred percent. And I think her affection for him was, too. Even years later, she would brighten up when it came to talking about Peter. Over her desk on the verandah in Meherazad she kept a framed picture of Peter with chipmunks crawling on his legs. In her bedroom still is a statuette of two cocker spaniels facing Baba's picture.

Many of Mani's character traits showed up in her relationship with Peter. As we've seen, she made a book about taking care of him (as she made books about Mehera's activities). Of course he was put into costume quite often; the women said he loved it because he was a big show-off. He features prominently in the films of Baba that Mani took in Meherazad, and is captured a number of times by her still camera. In Dehra Dun, Mani learned to make baskets from a woman beside the lane, and she taught Mehera. Peter, naturally, was pressed into service as a basket-carrier: bringing in the mail or carrying flowers (he's in a movie doing this, gripping the basket handle carefully in his teeth) or other items as needed on walks. And he was a great source of entertainment: Meheru remembered that when he got excited he would run madly around, jumping on sofas, chairs, anything, making the women laugh.

Peter loved to show off.

He walked where they walked, and Mani proudly described how scrappy and brave he was, charging forth to challenge dogs even outside his own territory. He even peed on one, a much bigger dog, to show him who was boss. Goher says that when Peter went out on walks with Mani, the local people thought he was a bear.

Yet he could be very loving, even maternal. In later years, he helped to "raise" Mehera's dog Mastan, a much bigger dog, and they became very attached to each other.

This maternal side of Peter's nature was also revealed when the women found some tiny orphan chipmunks on the roof in Satara. After Peter saw the women putting them in a box and feeding them, he took them under his wing. Goher remembered how Peter doted on them, how he'd just sit and look at them, even forgetting his meals. He became so protective that he'd stay home from his evening walks with Mani to keep an eye on the chipmunks. They in turn regarded him as their surrogate mother, and played and climbed all over him without fear. He'd chase other chipmunks, but with these helpless ones, his tolerance and warm-heartedness came out in full force.

Peter was tricky, too. Once, when he was a puppy, he was going to be tied up outside. Knowing Peter wouldn't be happy about this, Mani took a few of his dog toys out and put them near Aloba, who was sitting outside as a watchman. Very quietly Peter came right after her, picked up the toys one at a time, and returned them to their place under the dining room table. Poor Mani, seeing what looked like the toys she'd just taken out back under the table, couldn't figure out how they kept transporting themselves.

It's an interesting coincidence that another of Baba's most memorable pets—Mehera's beautiful and spirited horse Sheba—came to them during the same stay in Dehra Dun. Also on Mani's desk, there is a photo of Sheba kissing Baba, a moment captured by Mani at Mehera's direction. Mani described Sheba as "a young Arabian filly. She is really a beauty—sorrel, with gold mane . . . "

Peter and Sheba became friends, which was good; Sheba ran free in the compound around their house, so the two met often. Once when Sheba was playfully galloping around the house, Peter ran behind her, very close to her hooves. Mehera called to him as they ran out of sight, afraid that he would be kicked. Sure enough, back came Peter, straggling into the house with a clump of mud on his head. He must

Mehera with Sheba and Peter.

have been kicked by Sheba—a catastrophe. Poor Peter! Mournful and subdued, he was gently carried to Mani's bed and placed on her pillow (an unheard-of luxury). Everyone gathered around to minister to him, and Goher determined he must be in shock. She came up with some brandy as a restorative, and Peter had a tablespoon full. They turned away to confer about the case, when suddenly someone noticed that Peter was sitting up happily, wagging his tail, delighted by the attention. "Naughty Peter." said Mani, and off the bed he went.

Mani often told the story of poor Peter's failed romance. In Mahabaleshwar, a man who owned a female cocker suggested Peter be introduced to his dog, who was in heat. Baba, Mehera, and Mani agreed. The female was brought to their place and left with Peter. Peter was very eager and attentive, but he didn't know how to go about the courtship. He only knew that if you wanted something, you sat up and begged for it. So he sat up in front of her and begged. The female gave him the cold shoulder. Peter went off his food, and the female not only ate all of her own food but Peter's, too

For two or three days Peter tried to approach her and each time he was rejected. Then, amazingly, he began to ignore her completely. Here was a female in heat, in close quarters, and Peter paid no attention to her at all. He acted as though she didn't exist. If she entered the room, he would turn away and look in the other direction.

Meanwhile Baba became concerned that Peter was getting thin; "What is this?" He wanted to know, and had the female sent away.

When I asked Goher, "Did Peter love Baba?" she replied, "Oh yes, he always wanted to sit by Baba's feet. Even here [in Meherazad] he always would go and sit by His feet in the Hall. Baba allowed him to do it." And sometimes, she said, he'd lie down, fall asleep, and snore there at Baba's feet.

Mani corresponded with Mrs. Cooper occasionally, and once, after some good rains at Meherazad, she wrote, "Peter takes advantage—(or disadvantage) of these showers and jumps into puddles at the least excuse, emerging like one of those Hollywood stars with the mud pack on—though I can't say it enhances his beauty but it does make him happy . . . not me though, for it means washing and drying him over again . . . He's fine and an important member of our family! . . . "

Peter died of an incurable illness in 1965, at Baba's feet, in Baba's bedroom at Meherazad. He was buried there in Meherazad, covered with a handkerchief that Baba had placed on his body, with the repeated direction that it should be buried with Peter exactly as it was.

Mani wrote in the next Family Letter, "Beloved Baba told us how immeasurably blessed Peter was, for it was the first instance in His present Advent that anyone had thus breathed his last in His physical presence!" Baba said Peter would come back as a human being, as a baby boy who would come to Baba and be cuddled by Him.

She continued:

> Knowing all this, yet he is greatly missed by us and by his much loved pal and "brother" Mastan. Baba says that even He, who is God and knows how truly blessed Peter is, misses Peter's presence as "Peter". Every day when we are with Baba, we find ourselves talking of this loyal little Baba-lover and are flooded with reminiscences of his gentle loving companionship, his clever playful pranks, his incredibly "human" understanding, and above all his devotion to Baba. In his fragrant memory a Champak tree has been planted on his grave, and Baba has ordered a headstone to be placed bearing the words: BABA'S PET, PETER. This epitaph of three words bespeaks Peter's great good fortune in his dog-life with Baba and in the human-lives to come. The most priceless tribute he received from his Master, was when Baba said: "Peter deserves the good fortune that he has received."

DAILY LIFE IN DEHRA DUN

Dear Goher; as I interrogated her yet again for this book, she tried to remember their daily schedule in long-ago Dehra Dun:

> We would get up very early about five, latest five-thirty, and keep ready for Baba to call us. First Mehera would enter, always, then Mani, then we would go into His room . . . If Baba didn't call us early, I would have my tea because I was a tea addict, and in the morning I wanted my tea. And Baba always permitted me to have my tea.
>
> *So would Mehera and Mani have tea?*
>
> No, they would have it later . . . Then Baba would wash up, have His breakfast and go to the [men] mandali's side.
>
> *And would you have breakfast with Him at that time? When Mehera would serve Him, you all would be around?*
>
> Yes . . . And then Baba would walk over to the mandali's side, and I would accompany Him—just see Him to the gate—and one of the mandali would come and receive Him, and I would return.
>
> *Do you remember what Mani would do in the morning? Sewing? Typing?*
>
> Sometimes she would be sewing. I don't remember her typing in Dehra Dun, no. Sew? Yes. She stitched a dress for me, such a pretty beautiful dress. I don't know where it's gone. Mehera would help her. Each of them would be doing their own work. Mehera would be looking after Sheba; I don't think there was any garden there. But there were lots of mango trees . . . Mani would go for a walk with Peter . . . and then she learned basket making from a basket maker on the street, and she came and taught Mehera, and both of them would make baskets of different

shapes and sizes. Mehera made some nice tablemats also, very delicate . . .

So Mani would go alone for a walk?

Yes, we were in a side-lane house. And she would go up the side lane to the main road. At that time there wasn't much traffic.

So if she were walking Peter, she could interact with someone on the road?

She would. She was free to do that. Mani wanted to talk! Then we would go out sometime for walks with Baba. There was a dry riverbed with pebbles and all, so we would go there and walk . . . in the mornings . . . Maybe eleven or eleven-thirty Baba would come and have lunch and then He would rest.

And you would have lunch together?

Yes.

Did you all rest?

We never rested. Mani would be reading stories to Baba. We didn't have *Time* magazine at that time, but some books we had brought with us, or I went to the library and got some.

At what time would you have tea?

In the afternoon, three or three-thirty.

Then you'd have tea together with Baba. Did you have a little dining table where you'd sit down?

Yes, there was a dining table . . . Baba would have tea, and again He would go back to the mandali.

Then, in the evening, when would Baba come?

Maybe five or five-thirty, and then we would sit in the hall, and Mani would read . . . And then Baba might have something to eat, and then He would retire.

Would you sit around the table when you ate with Baba in Dehra Dun?

Sometimes; if He ate very early, then we would wait on Him . . . in the dining room. We also used to have our supper very early.

And what time would you retire to go to bed?

By eight or eight-thirty.

ALOBA REMEMBERS

Although he was a veteran of the Meher Ashram of the 1920s, Aloba remembers first seeing Mani in Dehra Dun. When I asked him about it, he recalled:

Mani would come out for her walk in the evening. First I saw her there, and such a brilliant personality—all shining, all light, very beautiful. I had not seen such beauty in my life, ever. And immediately I felt that—the sister of the Avatar—it was befitting to be like this. Because God is very beautiful and so His sister must be beautiful.

Then he elucidated: "But at Dehra Dun I would not talk to her; I would just see her taking a walk and going back." Of course, the men and women were still very strictly separated from each other.

In later years, after Baba dropped His body, Mani would consult Aloba for lines or a fal* from Hafiz. He would be very excited to perform this service for her, and would jump up and do it immediately. Mani, who knew a little Persian (knowing Dari), and wanted to learn more, would go over the lines very carefully, and with great respect and attention.

---

* To "take a fal," a common practice among some Persian families, one opens the *Divan* of the 14th-century, Perfect Master poet Hafiz at random, with a question in mind. Traditionally, the first line upon which the reader's eyes fall provides a direct answer to the question, and the rest of the ghazal provides further clarification and guidance.

MANGOES!

Their compound in Dehra Dun was full of mango trees, and, as luck would have it, they were there in mango season. When Baba was away on one of His mass darshan tours, the women decided to simplify their meals. Naja would cook rice, and they would pluck mangoes, and have mangoes and rice for lunch. When Baba came back and saw what they were doing, that was the end of that. No vegetables? This is all you're eating? He ordered Naja to cook vegetables for lunch.

But in the meantime, Mani had gone mango-mad (she was actually mango-mad all her life). As she put it:

> No mango-lover would question "why this rhapsody over a mere mango?" Beloved Baba has referred to the mango as the king of fruits and when Margaret Craske had a mango in her hand she appeared to be in a blissful trance. This poem, penned in 1953, was inspired by the sumptuous season of mangoes in Dehra Dun, a land of plentiful fruits and vegetables, while the sensational news of the conquest of Mt. Everest and the coronation of Queen Elizabeth II filled the newspapers.

MANGOES!

> Everest news may rock the Nation,
> Headlines scream 'The Coronation',
> No matter how big the sensation
> Under your nose;
> To stir the heart and light the eye
> One needs to hear the lusty cry
> MANGOES!

They may be small they may be big
No one seems to care a fig,
They may be good they may be bad,
Babes in arms
Well-dressed marms
Every blinking fellow-me-lad
Cousins, sisters, mum and dad
One and all are Mango-Mad.

The river Ganges is in spate
The Delhi train is awful late.
There's flying saucers in the sky
The price of cups is soaring high;
The yogi squats a-mountain top
The rains have spoilt the bumper crop.
Egad sir, who cares to know
S'long as I have a MANGO!

== Mani

Another Mango poem—this time, a dramatic one—was inspired by an incident on the men mandali's side:

An episode In <u>Dehra Dun</u> 1953

NILU: The clock strikes 12 – it's midnight, Hark!
A figure's prowling in the dark –
He does not mind the raging storm,
His heart is glowing strangely warm,
As bending down towards the loot
He gathers up the King of Fruit!

GUSTADJI + BAIDUL:
There's others too
Oh quite a few!
As fondly dreaming
Lovingly scheming
Eyes a gleaming
They wait to hear
The 'thud' that says a Mango's here.

Then in a flash
They make a dash
With leaps and bounds
And hungry sounds
Feverishly scanning
The mangoless ground

A sudden halt –
What is this here,
Beneath a leaf, a mango's rear?

Alas, alack! A gasp a moan,
'Tis nothing but a leering stone!*

== Mani

READING TO BABA

Around this time, reading aloud to Baba became a more regular feature of their daily routine. As mentioned, in the early days Baba would read the newspaper or His favorite books—often Edgar Wallace detective stories—Himself. Now and then, Mani, Rano, and others would read

---

* The seed inside a mango is quite large and referred to as a "stone."

aloud to Him, but Meheru pointed out that this became a regular occurrence only from the time of the New Life.

In Dehra Dun, Mrs. McLeod, the bestower of Peter, was also custodian of a small, private library that she opened up to the women. Here, they found plenty of books to read to Baba (such as Ellery Queen and Agatha Christie detective novels, and the perennial dramatic favorite Edgar Wallace) and for themselves. Margaret Craske had a knack for picking books Baba would like (she later introduced Him to Rex Stout's Nero Wolfe, and J. R. R. Tolkien), and she would send them over. Rano also continued to read to Baba, particularly the newspaper, but Baba reserved certain characters for just Mani to read.

Mani recalled in the Hall:

> Margaret sent all the books for Baba, to be read to Him. In the early years she sent a book to Him by P.G. Wodehouse, in which he [Wodehouse] had inscribed, "To the Greatest Humanist in the world." He was one of those blessed authors who entertained Baba, who relaxed Baba, who lightened a bit of Baba's burden of work.

After speaking of her ability to imitate any tune she heard, Mani remembered:

> My talent for emulation had even greater scope for giving Baba pleasure when I would read books to Baba, stories of all kinds: spiritual stories, detective stories, adventure tales, fantasies, Wodehouse and other humourous novels—in short, endless varieties of stories. I used different voices for the different characters, and recall with pride that once when reading a Nero Wolfe story to Baba I used twelve distinct voices to match the assorted characters. To read to Him was my greatest

pleasure, and my highest award from Beloved Baba was when He turned around to Mehera and said, "I'm always happy when Mani's reading to Me because it makes Me feel like I'm watching a play."

In a letter from around this time, Mani wrote Kitty a clear picture of Baba relaxing as he listened:

> Yes, Margaret's books are welcome, and her last two came in time for Christmas and went into the Christmas stocking. With His fast and the concentrated and intensive working, they are useful as relaxation (I read them aloud as we used to do in Meherazad, and Baba sits relaxed often with eyes closed and His fingers moving rapidly as if He was "writing" or sending messages like they do in code [)] (I mean that is what it looks like)."[1]

One day in Meherazad in the 1980s, I came upon Mani reading *The Song Celestial*, a version of the Bhagavad Gita rendered into English by Sir Edwin Arnold. Seeing me, she read a few lines out loud in a lilting, lyrical voice:

> "Not comprehending Me in My true Self!
> Imperishable, viewless, undeclared,
> Hidden behind My magic veil of shows,
> I am not seen by all; I am not known—
> Unborn and changeless—to the idle world.
> But I, Arjuna! know all things which were,
> And all which are, and all which are to be,
> Albeit not one among them knoweth Me!"

Then she held out the book for me to see. It was the very book she had read out to Him, and that He had enjoyed. It was an old edition, from British times, well kept and beautifully illustrated, with old-fashioned fonts, and tracing paper in front of each illustration. It seemed a relic from another age.

Under the spell of that sublime passage, she was very reflective. She then said that she had to remember to tell Baba-lovers in the Hall that it wasn't just detective stories and novels that she read out to Baba, but spiritual books and poems, too, like *The Song Celestial*, or quotations from St. Francis, St. Teresa of Avila, the Perfect Master and poet Kabir, and others.

Those readings with Baba must have been unforgettable. Several times in her book *Love Alone Prevails*, Kitty described evenings when the women sat around Baba, listening to Mani or another companion read Him spiritual stories, with Baba interrupting from time to time to elucidate a point.

THE HIGHEST OF THE HIGH

Several memorable things happened in those Himalayan foothills. In August, still in Dehra Dun, Baba started dictating *God Speaks* to Eruch; on the 13th He composed the Master's Prayer, and on September 7, Baba gave out His message "The Highest of the High."

On Mani's dresser to this day, one can see a framed, postcard-sized picture of Baba. At the bottom, in Mani's handwriting, now faded, is written, "I am the Highest of the High" and underneath that, Baba's signature.

Mani's copy of the "Highest of the High" on her dressing table.

Mani once wrote out the story behind this picture:

> Beloved Baba's brother Beheram, gentle and artistic by nature, was adept with the camera and won several prizes in amateur photographic competitions. Because of his immense love for his God-Brother, it was natural for Beheram to channel his talent for photography into taking and making pictures of Baba whenever possible. Working with the barest equipment and under unimaginable inconvenience in an airless little room at home, Beheram produced pictures of much beauty acclaimed by brother-photographers in the Baba-world. Beheram's ambition to occupy himself solely with Baba-photos was fulfilled in an unexpected way and carried on to the end of his life.
>
> It was in the early 50s when Baba personally directed Beheram to make His pictures in sizeable numbers, and directed me to send them out to His lovers in the West. And, Baba said, His part would be to touch each picture before it was sent out. – He did this without fail every time before a batch was airmailed to the West.
>
> Prior to the Sahavas in 1954, Baba took a big stack of different pictures of Himself that Beheram had developed in postcard size, and signed every one of them. Before putting His signature, our beloved Avatar had me write (for Him) under each photograph the words "I am the Highest of the High". After sealing this ancient declaration with His signature Baba gave one picture each to the few who were with Him at the time, while the rest He put in His pockets and later gave them out to a number of His close ones. I do not know who all received them, but the one He gave to me is always in my room. The original writing and signature on it have faded over the years, but indelible is the memory of

> those timeless moments at the table with Beloved Baba, while I wrote out His dictated words "I am the Highest of the High" dozens of times on dozens of pictures, and He patiently put His signature on each one – symbolic surely, of His Signature on the many hearts destined to be blessed with the Love of the Highest of the High! Avatar Meher Baba ki Jai!*
>
> =Mani

A month after Baba gave out "The Highest of the High," Mani wrote in her diary:

> From 1st Oct. Baba does night work . . . We meditate few minutes midnight – wake up at midnight - We meditate evenings for 1 month. On 28th Oct. all in India meditate 12 to 1 p.m.
>
> Nov. 1st Baba gives pub. [public] darshan – D.D. [Dehra Dun]

You can see His serene yet fiery beauty in a film of this Dehra Dun darshan, given in the compound of their place on Rajpur Road.

A month after that, they left Dehra Dun and the mountains.

1954 DIARY

In twelve pages of Mani's small diary (from the end of 1953 to the end of 1955) is compressed a world of Baba's external work: mass darshans, mast work, fasts—and also some "time-outs" for the ladies.

Here are some excerpts, just to give a flavor of that time (Mani's shorthand and Gujerati entries are in italics):

> [Nov.] 29th [1953] We leave D. Dun
>
> *M'war [Mahabaleshwar] – Aga Khan Bung. [Florence Hall]*

---

* From Mani's personal papers.

In Mahabaleshwar: (seated from left) Manu, Khorshed Jessawala (Eruch's wife), Mehera, Meheru holding Peter, Gulnar; (standing) Rano, Mani.

Dec. + Jan. On the whole nice crisp winter – with fog + drizzle at times.

Jan. end [1954]. B. leaves for Hamirpur Mass Darshan. Ret. Feb 12

14th [February] *Meheryan Parab* [when, in the Gujerati calendar, the day named "Meher" and the month named

"Meher" both come together] we celebrate Baba's birthday – concert, cake, etc.

19th Baba and mandali leave for Andhra. Mass Darshan – tremendous programme – his *birthday celebrated* there on 25th. fire-works in sky - Baba's name -

6th March. Return

19th March we all go Gaimai's [Eruch's mother's place in Poona] . . . B. goes Sakori Mass Darshan. 21st we all return M'war – rain + cold (inexplicable weather).

. . .

Apr. 10th our party of girls [including some close Baba-lovers from Bombay] come picnic Aurther Seat [Arthur's Seat], boating, pick jambuls [astringent berries] – orchids – + [the Bombayites] leave 18th –

The v. good Kohlapur mast (one sitting in cave) was brought for a day with great difficulty. Later v. good Rishikesh mast (Nilkanth) comes + stays M'war few day[s]. B. very happy. Mast cooks sometimes for all – v. tasty.

May 2nd We leave M'war for Satara.

. . .

On 10th July to 11th all fast + silence at <u>same</u> time in all countries. B. fasts longer.

Aug. B. not well. preparing for big Meeting. 23 coming from abroad.

. . .

12th Sept. Mass Darshan at Ahmednagar – 16 Westerners from, U.S.A., *England, Switzerland, Australia.* We go too.

[Here Mani leaves a large gap.]

30th 31st [Sept.] the Great Meeting – [which occurred on the 30th]

1st [Oct.] Westerners leave.

Pages from Mani's diary during this period.

5th return to Satara

. . .

7th [Oct.] B. gives up alphabet board + communications – no darshan –

Nov. 6th B. leaves for Pandharpur keeping promise to Gadge Maharaj – gave darshan on great pilgrimage day – Return 7th.

. . .

Jan. 1955

We go Bombay 25th see Gone With the Wind – Republic day – saw lights – lovely day at Arnavaz [Arnavaz's home] -

High [that is, spiritually advanced] mast from Kolhapur brought for a day – B. very happy. tall – lives in stone niche

[Jan.] All B.lovers (West + East) fast 24 hours on water only from 8 p.m. on 12th to 8 p.m. on 13th.

. . .

May 1st – B. in seclusion at Jal Villa. M. + I go to see Him every five days . . .

Mehera with Bhooti in front of the house verandah steps at Meherazad (Pimpalgaon) circa 1954–1956.

22nd vigil till midnight.
23rd Baba comes. 7 days with us at Grafton.
. . .
Aug. 13th B. goes Bombay – Darshan to over 700 . . .
17th B. works 12 hours with K [Kaikobad] from 7 a.m. also fast 12 hrs. (we also).
40 inches rain in Nagar this year! Awful floods in north, + Punjab – people on trees for days (2 women delivered babies on trees) – hundreds of thousands homeless –

Oct. 27 we left for Pipp. [Pimpalgaon] Sa[ha]vas month in Nov. from 3rd - 4 groups of 250 each staying with Baba one week. 1st Guj. [Gujerati] group, 2nd Andhra (came in chartered bogeys) - *wonderful time* had by all. Third Hindi Group – 4th Marathi.

Wonderful *arrangements*. Baba gave *wonderful* discourses. F. Brabazon was there for whole month. Don Stevens for first week and part of 2nd.

went to M'abad (for 2 days) also saw lower M'abad tents etc. + the boards with:

> Whoever loses his all in Me
> Shall find his all in Me ever after.

11th Dec. we returned Satara . . .

25th Xmas + M's [Mehera's] birthday. Wonderful celebration . . .

The year 1956 began with more darshans—in Poona, Sakori, and other places. Baba returned to Satara on January 31, "happy but tired," as Mani reported.

LOVELY SATARA

"One day Baba commented, 'How nice Satara is; how lovely the climate'. We loved it there, and we thought we were going to live with Baba at our bungalow, Grafton, for the rest of our days. It was a very quiet place at that time, even though we lived on a road that led from a village to the main market in Satara. The villagers, on market day, came walking by laden with vegetables, and Naja would buy these very fresh vegetables for our kitchen. The rainfall and the soil were good, so I had a thriving garden. I liked to be very active, and I loved to dig in the soil and tend to the garden myself."[2]

Baba on the verandah at Grafton, the house where the women lived in Satara.

So Mehera remembered their home of two-and-a-half years—from June 1954 to December 1956—Grafton, in Satara. In retrospect, that quiet, homey, happy time for the women was the lull before the storm of Baba's second accident, one that would cripple Him. It would be the last time He could walk freely, the last time concern for His suffering did not dominate every aspect of their lives.

I often heard them refer to Satara as a quiet locality, and Mehera would describe how much they enjoyed their walks here, down tree-lined streets with few people and lovely gardens and homes, all spaced well apart. Goher remembered that it drizzled a lot, so it was most often green and beautiful, with fields of grass all around them. They got books to read to Baba—and for themselves—from a library in an English club just across the way. Mehera took care of Sheba, and Mani of Peter. Peter would accompany them on walks, swim in a nearby well, and follow Baba the half-mile to the mandali's house every morning. Mani wrote Kitty that Peter "from early morning is like a house detective, following Baba wherever He goes."

Mani wrote that their house, Grafton, "although smallish—has a lovely situation and a lovely verandah where we work and read." The women were few, just Mehera, Mani, Meheru, Goher, Naja and Rano. (Irene Conybeare came and stayed with their landlady, Mrs. Cooper, in another house.) Interestingly enough, it was these six who were to be the resident women with Baba in His last twelve, secluded years at Meherazad.

Baba and Sheba enjoying each other at Grafton.

I bet Mani compiled her dog training book in Satara. Although she is reputed to have always had a typewriter before her for correspondence at Grafton, it's possible that she did some knitting, too, following the elaborate instructions and patterns she had copied out into a tiny notepad. We know for a fact that in Satara she wrote a story for the *Illustrated Weekly of India* that was accepted by that magazine.

Baba relaxing in Grafton.

Mani was very busy. When Murshida Duce wrote at that time, urging Mani to set down her impressions of the New Life, Mani wrote back:

> There is a very practical obstacle. Believe it or not, I haven't a minute's time that does not have to be calculated, juggled, cut out and pasted to fit the pattern of our daily life and duties. Now that Baba is in retirement for the time being, I have been trying to get on with some of my sewing and mending that I have been neglecting disgracefully these days. We make all of our clothes, including underwear. We never know when Baba may change his plans—the seclusion and so forth—and then there is even less of that spare half-hour.[3]

The women had an unusual experience there. In Satara's grassy fields, among the leafy trees, grew mushrooms. Wild mushrooms were a dubious edible, according to Goher, but Mehera and Mani couldn't resist gathering them up on their walks, putting them in buckets and bringing them home. "Now look," Goher told them, "if you get poisoned, I'm going to put a stomach tube in you." They retorted, "No, we know exactly what is edible and what is not."

Well, mushrooms can be edible and still have unexpected effects. One day, after eating their day's mushroom collection (sautéed in butter and poured over toast), Mani felt "funny in the head." Woozy. Wonky. She figured it out about twenty years later, after hearing ex-hippie Baba-lovers tell stories about their psychedelic experiences; then she used to joke with pilgrims at Meherazad about her "trip" on Satara mushrooms. Of course, the butter-sautéed-and-poured-over-toast mushroom concoction eventually tempted even the doctor, and Goher ended up eating some, too (though not the psychedelic kind). That was a triumph for Mehera and Mani.

FIERY AND FREE

CORRESPONDENCE FROM SATARA

I think of Mani in the years 1953–56, and realize that she came into her own as a correspondent during this time. From 1954, it was Mani who wrote to Elizabeth and Kitty about the Center and Baba's visits there, Mani who began sending photographs of Baba touched by Him to lovers in the West, Mani who began corresponding more widely, particularly with the women she had met and become friendly with in the West.

And how wonderfully Mani could correspond. She could pour so much into a letter. I pick up Bili Eaton's book (or Kitty's or Ivy's or Jane Haynes') and there is Mani, writing letters full of warmth, personal interest, and intimate, friendly details. Her letters show so much care and affection for the individual person. She is full of gentle advice and understanding. Above all, she demonstrates a keen empathy for people's feelings of separation from Baba and their longing for news of Him, and she tries to share as much of His activities and atmosphere as possible.

Look at this letter she wrote to Bili in 1955:

> Dear Bili:
>
> I loved reading your "mad" letter. It strikes a most familiar chord in me who would rather have that than any old depressing "sanity." I suppose that's where the expression "madly happy" or "madly in love" comes from. Baba must love the mad, too, or He wouldn't have picked some of us. Besides, of all the advanced "saints" and "*saliks*," He loves the *masts* the most, the *mast* whose salient characteristic differs from the conscious seeker of the Path in that he experiences sheer, uttermost, overwhelming love for God. Long live such madness!
>
> I'm ever so glad you send Baba news to

Typewriter doodle by Mani.

the Shaws as well. We have very fond remembrances of Jeanne and her girls. Please send our love as well.

Baba's feet, as He relaxed on the carved sofa in Satara. (Flowers probably put by Mehera for the picture).

I wrote the latest Baba news in my letter of yesterday to Beryl [Williams]. Whenever we went over to Baba, I could not help thinking of you all. This is not meant for a figure of speech but that's what happened. As I would lower myself gingerly into the rickety chair (the one extra chair) and gaze up at Him "talking" to Mehera, you would all file past in my thoughts, perhaps because I had just written you letters or just read your letters, or perhaps for just no reason at all—except your love.[4]

I date Mani's growing relationship with the West from Satara. She had lived with (and been friends with) her "Western sisters" in the ashram since the 1930s. Then she'd made new friends and connections on their trip to the West in 1952. But in Satara, keeping these people in touch with their Beloved became much more a part of her work.

On the one hand, she was reading to Baba, picking up His new gestures, being with Mehera at home, in the library, or on walks, dressing up Peter and helping Naja get into a new costume every day (something Baba ordered Naja to do). On the other hand she was reaching out beyond their world, sitting at the ever-present typewriter writing "the latest Baba news" to Beryl Williams or Bili or Filis or Adele, packing up and sending the photographs, conveying Baba's instructions for His next Center visit. Bili began circulating these newsy Baba letters to others, and a wider circle of people began to read Mani's descriptions of how Baba looked, what He was saying and doing, what life with Him was like, along with helpful advice on living their lives with the focus on Him.

Baba posing on the carved sofa to show His hands for the photo at Mani's request.

It went both ways. In her own, considerate fashion, Mani also brought up to Baba things that her correspondents wanted Him to know or wanted to ask Him. For example, she wrote to Kitty:

> We have had the promised explanation about the Circle from Baba and in a few days I will type it out and send to Filis for *The Awakener* so all can read it. Darling Baba—it was so slow and tedious explaining without His board, but when I told Him how pleased everyone would be, He smiled.[5]

And Kitty wrote to her, "Mani dear, how can I ever convey to you what your letters mean to Baba lovers here. On all sides they are deeply appreciated—their whole atmosphere of Baba that goes with them. Never think you are just writing a letter—you are doing something far beyond the scope of a letter."

CHATTING WITH ELIZABETH AND KITTY

In Mani's letters to Elizabeth, Kitty, and Norina ("Elinorkit"), there are odds and ends about her life with Baba that make those days come alive. I think of her in Satara, writing to these dear old ashram-pals with whom she was so comfortable, so familiar, and so linked in work for Baba, and I imagine her at her relaxed, chatty best—or so her letters show.

For example, for Baba's birthday in 1955:

> I made an orange chiffon cake (recipe from an American magazine) with white and pink icing and seven blue candles on it.... At the stroke of five we shouted His Jai and I gave a seven "gun" salute (from those little firework pellets that give out such a resounding bang when hammered upon), and then the birthday song was sung... We ended the day with an amusing little performance (only a 20-minute affair) which as you can guess Baba enjoyed very much. Oh Kitty, I did miss you then! Shall I give the cast? Rano was Mr. Reeder—the favorite detective of Baba's favorite author, Edgar Wallace. I was a detective inspector of Scotland Yard, Meheru was an Italian taxicab driver (and didn't she look it!), Naja was an American woman singer with bangs on her forehead, who loved jitterbugs. There was "Honey" or "Sugar" in almost every sentence of her speech, and Goher was her Egyptian husband who looked like Robinson Crusoe in a fez cap. The trouble as usual was to get everybody to rehearse at the same time when Baba was away at the mandali's and on bath days almost impossible. You of course can imagine all that![6]

In the same letter she wrote:

> ... of course however big the trouble, bigger is our

love for Baba, and bigger still His Love for us. No wonder Baba says, "Don't worry. Just love Me and obey Me." When one thinks of the number of people who haven't Baba's Love to guide and sustain them it can seem to us—who know it so well—appalling. Also how wonderful to think, no matter what the worries, cares, disappointments one goes through, they are all stepping stones—always a going forward—nothing useless, all a purpose of "experiencing," part of a special design to the Goal.

In these letters, too, one sees Mani "at work":

> I sent you a cable this morning about the silence to be observed by all on July 10th: "Inform All Observe Silence on Tenth."
>
> . . .
>
> [About His upcoming visit to the Center in 1956] Mehera says not to forget to tell you to always put before Him yogurt for lunch and some fresh butter. We think Baba will also like thick cream soup (no peas). . . . About Baba having His meals at the Guesthouse—fine. Asparagus—couldn't get a response from Baba either way, but I'm sure He will like it. Anyway try it and see and then you will be able to find out if He likes it again or not. About breakfast, the men will take what is normally served but Baba won't be taking toast, marmalade, eggs, etc. For fruit at meals I suggest perhaps a little prune juice or a peach, etc.
>
> . . .
>
> I'm taking the opportunity of letting you know well in advance about the February fast that Baba wishes all those who love Him (and if possible all those even just

interested in Baba) to observe the 15th of February, the day He emerges from His present Seclusion. Do, Elizabeth dear, see that as usual it reaches *all concerned in the U.S.A.*

Baba wishes all to fast for 24 hours on 15th February, 1957, i.e., beginning from midnight of the 14th and ending on midnight of the 15th. During this fast all participants should think of Baba as much as possible, and repeat His name as often as one conveniently can.

Baba has observed so many of these strict fasts of 24 hours without water during His present Seclusion, and here at last we're allowed to share one with Him.

And then there were reflections of her outer occupations:

We will be leaving for Meherazad soon and it seems Baba is giving me a holiday from typing there (which will mean confidentially a lot of "reading", [aloud to Baba] as Baba thinks of "relaxing and resting" while there—outwardly at least).

. . .

Kitty dear—please inform Margaret she can send books again, and not to forget to include the "short story" ones—Ellery Queen Murder Mysteries or The Saint ones are good and much needed when Baba wants reading for just a half-hour or so.

. . .

I just feel like a little chat this morning. I know I don't write often enough these days to you or any of the others, but it just isn't possible to always write promptly, and I know you all understand, so if a letter is long in coming it's not from lack of remembrance or love—just lack of time.

Besides, as I know I'm keeping all supplied with Beloved's news (through the help of you dear ones) with a letter to either one or the other of you, that leaves me happy.

. . .

As you know, we don't give news of "information" to Baba on our own since May 1st but sometimes Baba will ask in general or particular and then of course we can speak accordingly. Hence I always keep the main points and bits of news in my head to be prepared to give it in that second . . .

The letters reveal some of her other interests:

Baba gave one [of the pencil sharpeners Elizabeth sent] to the "Ghorawalla [horseman]," the boy I teach Hindi to; you should have seen his face.

. . .

I bagged a lovely picture of [Mehera] and Baba on His birthday—will send it some time.

And, rarely, she wrote of her inner feelings:

You know, Kitty, it's funny—for all my talks and advice (our Filis calls me affectionately "Granny Long Ears," as I listen to all "complaints," etc.) my spirit sometimes drops (like the continental barometer this winter) so low I can scarcely see it. At times like that do you know what "kisses the place to make it well"? Your gift to me I treasure—*Theologia Germanica*, which says on the fly leaf "To Kitty with love from Herbert". I know I'm "down" at those times only when there is more of "myself" than of "Him" and the bit I love to reread most from the book is the bit that says: "When that which is perfect is come, then that which is in part (i.e., I-hood, creature-nature, desires) will be rejected and counted for naught."

BABA'S GESTURES

"I miss His gestures the most."

So Mani once said to us in the 1980s. She loved His gestures, and she could imitate them beautifully. Just as, among the women, Mani was the one who read Baba's alphabet board fluently, when Baba gave up using the board in Satara in 1954, she became His primary gesture-reader along with Eruch.

She wrote to Elinorkit on November 27, 1954, "Although since the 7th of October Baba has stopped using the alphabet board, we scarcely miss it. It is like His silence that has never needed words."[7]

As the women explained, even when Baba had the alphabet board He always used elementary gestures when conversing, especially for simple communications in the household. I asked Goher to describe how Baba "spoke" with them:

> If it was among the women, then Mani would be the one who would read the board. If it concerned me, if Baba was talking about something medical, then I would read the board.
>
> *So, she would read it out loud?*
>
> Yes. You always had to read it out loud so that Baba knew that we were understanding Him right.
>
> *So even you, if you were reading out the board with just Baba there, you would say it out loud?*
>
> Yes.
>
> *And when you were there in a group, Mani would read out.*
>
> Yes.
>
> *And Mehera would be looking at Baba.*
>
> Sometimes, if there was something private, Baba would spell it out very slowly for Mehera.

Goher, when it came time to learn the gestures, Mani picked up the gestures pretty quickly?

Yes, very quickly.

. . . So, gradually you all learned the gestures.

Yes.

In Satara, Mani entered more deeply into His gestures. If you have ever seen her on video, imitating His gestures to the words of the song "Welcome to My World," you know how well she could do it. It was more than an imitation; it was an echo. It shows how intently and deeply she must have watched Him, caught the gist of His expressions and meaning, and conveyed it to the others. After all, Baba said of Mani, "in reading My [hand] signs, Mani is matchless; after her is Eruch."

Many years after Baba dropped His body, Mani participated in something informally called the "gesture project." It seemed to give her real pleasure. In a small room in the Trust Compound, she sat through a number of Baba-films and, while being videotaped, interpreted what He was conveying on the board or through gestures.

In those years after Baba dropped His body, the mandali would sit in Meherazad Hall with pilgrims every Sunday, and listen to songs or poems and watch Baba movies. During the movies, Mani and Eruch would often speak aloud what Baba was gesturing. Pilgrims in the audience would find out the most unexpected things.

For example, in the East-West Gathering film you see Eruch saying something to Baba. It turns out Eruch is telling Him that the darshan line stretches beyond the gate—or something to the effect that it is still very long. He is nagging Baba to give darshan faster. Baba gestures, "So long?" and then, "What's the time?" Eruch doesn't see this last gesture, and so Baba asks again, "What's the time?" When Eruch tells Him, Baba brings His hand to His forehead in the timeless motion for "good grief."

And then there is the sequence in the same darshan when Eruch wants Baba to have something to drink. Baba indicates it will make Him pee, and then points to the crowd and gestures, "What about them? Where will they pee?"

BABA'S WORK

In November 1954, Mani wrote to Elizabeth & Co: "Though nowadays Baba often seems preoccupied and sometimes profoundly sad and tired, His sparkling flashes of humour are irrepressible as ever, though less frequent."

And to Kitty, about Christmas that year:

> Owing to Baba's 40 days programme of three stages of fasting we do not feel we had the heart to celebrate at all, but as you know, Baba loves gaiety, and what with Mehera's birthday on the same day [as Christmas] we were hectically busy the last few days making paper caps and a huge Cracker* (in which to put them with the jokes), an enormous Christmas stocking for Baba (with books), a

Christmas celebration in Grafton.

---

* A "cracker" makes a loud burst of noise when pulled apart.

lovely little Christmas tree, etc. On 24th evening Naja dressed up as Santa Claus and my Peter came in dressed up as the reindeer, with horns and all (he doesn't mind being dressed up, in fact he really enjoys it for he loves to show off).

"Baba loves gaiety," Mani wrote. And of His wonderful sense of humor, taste for jokes, for wit, for turns of phrase and funny stories and humorous books, Mani said to pilgrims, "Baba's humour has been so, so much a part of His life with us, and so, so much a part of our life with Him."

As He put it, "Thank God I have a sense of humour."

. . .

. . . and Mehera's celebration on the same Christmas. Both photos by Mani.

In the Hall in 1980, Mani told a story from Satara while reflecting on the intensity of Baba's work:

> Even what we do now, anything concerning Baba that is happening now, which apparently is a result of what we are doing, He has worked for. He has already done the work for it in His seclusion periods, those times when He would say, "I have to be in seclusion, this work is very serious. You have no idea how important and serious My work is." We would say, "Yes, Baba," but we never knew what that work was.
>
> But some of the results we see today, and much more is yet to come. Last night I dreamt of a big tree, a very bright tree with shiny leaves. It was just a tree, but that tree had so much feeling, as if it were a person. It's like when you relate to a person, and a feeling comes from that exchange—I felt so much love for that tree, and so much love came out of that tree. It was a being, not just a tree that you walk by.
>
> It reminded me of a time when we were in Satara, and Baba was in seclusion in Jal Villa, a very dilapidated little house that was found for Him, that Baba selected as the right one. It didn't depend on how nice the house was. The men mandali might find a particular house that Baba would not like. As I used to say at the time, this house He selected was just like us broken-down furniture. But that was right for His work. Like we happened to be.
>
> So, anyway, Baba was in seclusion there, and Mehera and I were allowed, I think twice a week, to go and see Him for just half an hour and then come back to our place, Grafton. One day, when Baba's work there was finished— I think He was to come out of His seclusion shortly after that—we came out after seeing Baba and started walking down the road. It was one of those nice, quiet Satara roads,

and as we walked we passed a tree just outside of Jal Villa. The tree had snapped in two. There were still green leaves on it, and the branches were green, but the trunk had broken in two from the top. The other part of it was lying on the ground. Through a hole in the trunk we could see a flame burning. We were amazed that a green tree could catch fire. And how was it that the big top branch had fallen down from the part where it was charred out? Through this big hole inside the trunk you could see that flame, actually a flame burning, like a light inside a pumpkin on Halloween day. We were amazed by this phenomenon of nature. Then looking back, we could see that it could have been a symbol, a glimpse of the work that Baba was doing there.

That work must have been done with such love. In our thoughts, that fire is ever connected with Baba's love. Baba is love. This morning after my tree dream, I thought of one of Baba's favorite songs, a ghazal [here Mani sang a few lines in Urdu]. It speaks of a lover who writes a letter to the beloved, putting his love onto that piece of paper. The force of that love is carried along with the paper to the beloved by a pigeon. And the lover says, "The pigeon who carried my letter to you has burnt up with the fire of the love enclosed in this letter." If that can happen from the love of a lover, how much more from the love of the Beloved?

The tree I saw in my dream reminded me of that tree in Satara, a tree selected to receive something of what Baba was giving out in His seclusion work. Something which is given out in silence, given out unseen, but which is being heard today, which is being seen today. This all that you see now is still only a part, a point, and from that point so much more will come out and grow. Baba very casually has said, and not just once, "The whole world will come to know I am God in human form."

But you see, He is compassion itself, and He knows that if the whole world were to become His lovers now, what would happen to His broken-down furniture, the poor mandali?

Seeing you all at Meherazad, seeing everyone helping at Meherabad, all of you coming, makes us realise that this wave will one day become such a tidal wave that it will cover the whole ocean.

GOD SPEAKS

Mani's in-depth understanding of editing, publishing, obtaining copyrights, and so on was a mystery to me until she revealed that Baba had her work with Ramjoo during the 1950s on copyrights for His books. Then, in Murshida Duce's book *How a Master Works*, I found this little clue: "During the interchange of many letters between Manija and me regarding the Supplement to *God Speaks* . . ."[8]

Baba signing God Speaks title pages in Satara on March 18, 1955.

It turns out that Mani was very involved in Baba's corrections of the *God Speaks* supplement, and typed out the corrected manuscript. She also, from what Murshida wrote, reviewed the entire book before it was published: "Baba's sister Manija wrote me in late December [1954] when she returned the manuscript [of *God Speaks*] that she was completely satisfied with the whole job except that she wanted two more commas. . . . "

One of the most important messages Baba gave to Murshida about *God Speaks* was written by Mani. When Murshida was working on raising some money to publish it, Mani wrote to her: " . . . because Baba wants you to know that in the future when people see, understand the enormous importance of the words in this book, they will realize that they [the words] come direct from God Himself."[9]

Mani readily grasped the beauty of His themes, as Murshida writes:

> Mani's comments on the book [*God Speaks*] are well worth recording: "I'm basking in the profound depths of our Beloved's book—the explanations he gives to make us see a glimmer (if only intellectually) of the immeasurably vast pattern of Creation which is but a shadow of his glory . . . But most of all it increases our external gratitude to him for awakening our hearts with the divine breath of his love.[10]

Mani herself wrote Elizabeth in August 1956:

> I am writing Ivy today and sending her a wonderful coloured drawing (crayon water-colour) that she had asked Rano to make of Evolution and Reincarnation, etc., and which she had just completed—Baba directed her often (which was unexpected—but her table was out and Baba would stop now and then during His walks on the verandah and correct and direct her). Isn't it wonderful how He notices the tiniest details.[11]

A year or two later, in her 1956–57 correspondence, there are waves of letters going back and forth between her and Don Stevens.

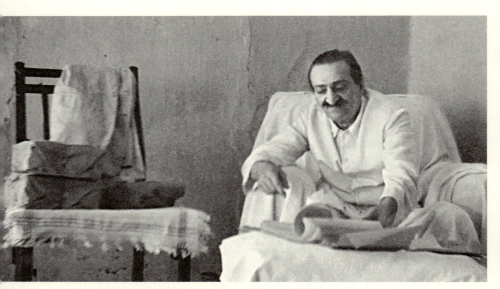

Baba looking through some bound papers on February 7, 1955, in Satara.

Most involve points—compiled by both Mani and Ramjoo—on the discourses Baba gave to Don to be published in *Listen, Humanity*. From 1955, Mani was also very involved in correspondence about Baba's corrections to the *Discourses*. Around 1966, Mani wrote and received many letters to and from Don Stevens and Ivy Duce regarding the reediting of the *Discourses* into a 6th edition, which was eventually published in 1967.

When I would talk with Mani, I couldn't help but notice her intelligence, but she was too charming and funny to convey the impression that she was an "intellectual." Yet how interesting it is that Baba used that word when talking about her to a gathering of some close men lovers:

> Mani is very intellectual. You all say so, but even Eruch, who is himself very clever, says so. Even in reading my [hand] signs, Mani is matchless; after her is Eruch. She writes for Filis Frederick's American magazine *The*

Awakener. The Americans, too, say Mani is really very bright.[12]

And, again, He "bragged" about her:

. . . Baba commented to Moorty, who had a doctorate in philosophy, "Deshmukh can put you in his pocket. He is so intelligent."

Then to Deshmukh, he remarked, "You are intelligent, but at the same time a first-rate idiot! Mani can put you both in her pocket! She corresponds with the West and spends the whole day typing." (A joking comment, this meant that Mani appeared more intelligent than Deshmukh and Moorty put together. Both Deshmukh and Moorty had doctorate degrees in Philosophy.)

By His wish, she worked on His books—an invaluable task in which she certainly showed her intelligence.

THE SECOND ACCIDENT

In mid-July 1956, Baba left for a one-month trip with four men mandali to Europe, the United States, and Australia. When He returned to Satara, their life continued in the usual pattern. But as Mani had written to Murshida Duce, "We never know when Baba may change his plans."

The huge change which "shot them out of Satara like a cannonball," as she later said, was right around the corner: Baba's second car accident, in December 1956. Unlike the 1952 accident from which Baba recovered well (you can see His free-flowing stride in movies from 1954 and 1956), the second accident was the beginning of a decline in Baba's health that continued for twelve years. He had ups and downs, but He never walked freely again, and the women date the period of His final, unremitting suffering from this time.

Meheru recalled to a few of us how, after the first accident but before the second, Baba often would walk up and down the veranda as well as up and down the road in Satara "He loved to walk, and would ask us, 'How do I walk now?' 'You're walking beautifully, Baba. There's not a trace of a limp.'" It was an outlet for Him, she said; when He was restless from His work, He would walk—and one can only imagine that His suffering was all the more when that outlet was gone.

In her diary Mani recorded a somber portent that occurred when Baba and the men were on a mast tour. On September 10, 1956, ". . . they had a narrow shave from bad car accident – mandali call it a 'miracle'! Baba of course says, 'I don't know anything about it.'"

On December 2, 1956, there was no such "narrow shave." In what was to become the very first of a series of circular letters to Baba-lovers in the West, the Family Letters, Mani described the horrible car accident that He met with that day while traveling with some of the men mandali:

> Satara, India
> 5th December 1956.
>
> Dear Family:
>
> The first impact on the minds of Baba-lovers as they read the following news, or have already heard of it, must naturally be the recollection of Baba's recent words given in "The Circular Message from Baba, in His Seclusion" circulated in July 1956, to all concerned in the U.S.A. referring to the personal tragedy that was to occur again. To those at Grafton [the women mandali], Baba said, as recently as three days before the accident, that the month or so before the termination of His Seclusion on the 15th February 1957 would hold greater and concentrated suffering for Himself in which a number of His close ones would also share.
>
> In the course of His present seclusion, Baba has traveled for His work over 10,000 miles (in India) by car,

Entry in Mani's diary about the accident.

driven by Eruch who has proved himself to be an excellent and careful driver. Baba's recent mast tour to the north of India was another trip of particular significance in connection with His seclusion, from which He returned to Satara on the 23rd of November. On Sunday, the 2nd of December, Baba went to Poona for a day accompanied by Eruch, Pendu, Vishnu and Dr. Nilkanth (better known as Nilu). At around 4.45 of the same evening, while returning to Satara, the accident occurred – about 12 miles outside Satara. The car was running normally and at moderate speed, when it seemed suddenly and inexplicably to go completely out of control and dashed against a stone culvert, landing eventually in the ditch on the other side of it. Baba and the men were heavily injured, the most serious being Nilu. The road was deserted of traffic and pedestrians, until three minutes later a man going to Poona sighted the wreckage and lifted Baba (and Vishnu who was the least one hurt of the occupants) into his car, retracing his journey to leave them at Grafton. A truck not long after picked up the remaining ones and brought them to Rosewood, the mandali's place. They were badly injured and immediately hospitalized, except Nilu who died without regaining consciousness. The condition of the others is not serious."[13]

Mani was at the stable at Grafton when she heard a car drive up. It was after six in the evening, and they were all listening for Baba's car since He had said He would return at six. Meheru remembered that they had eaten dinner early so that when Baba came, they would be finished and could attend to Him. The car drove up, and the others held back so that Mehera would be the first to greet Baba. Usually, when the men drove Baba back to Grafton, the car would stop at the gate, and Baba would get out. But this time the car came into the compound. Vishnu called out for Goher, so Goher went out first, and immediately started crying. Mehera and the other women rushed out, and they were aghast to see Baba lying in a strange car, bleeding. They ran to get Him an armchair. Meheru remembers that at first Baba tried to stand, then when He was seated in the chair, the women with their servants, Sev and Rakma, carried Baba inside the house. Mehera was weeping but the other women encouraged her to help. Goher recalls that Vishnu was in a state of shock, and at first couldn't even tell them what had happened. In the end, he managed to say that they had been in an accident and Baba had broken His hip or something.

Mani, who had been at the stable with Peter, described her reaction:

> As I was hurrying towards the house, the driver of the car, a curly-headed boy, got down, and as I looked up at him,

I stopped in my tracks, struck by the strangest feeling. . . . As I looked at the boy, my thought was, "Why, he looks like an angel." And he did. I had the impression somehow of wings and a halo, yet could not for the life of me describe what the boy actually looked like.

Mehera recalled:

> Only we women were there. I remember that when we helped Baba out of the car onto a chair, Baba with great difficulty got into the chair. From the car, we carried the chair up the stairs, inside through the dining room, to Baba's bedroom. . . . Before we reached the bedroom, just for a fraction of a second, Baba looked up into my face with such a look in his eyes that I can't express. A very sad look, full of pain. He glanced up into my eyes only for one second, but I still remember that look. I didn't know what Baba meant then. Now I know that it was because he knew he would not be able to walk again. Though he did walk, his leg never healed completely so that he could walk as normally as before. So much pain and sadness filled his expression; he knew he would not be able to walk as before.[14]

Mani ran and got a bicycle (they had a lady's bicycle at Grafton), and rushed over to Rosewood, about half a mile away, to call Dr. Donkin.

When Goher and the others saw poor Baba in that terrible condition, they started crying, but Goher recalled Mani saying, "No! This is the time you have to be strong!" and giving them instructions, and "guiding the whole thing."

Meanwhile, Baba was on His bed. After Donkin came, he arranged for an ambulance that took Baba late at night—with His two doctors, Donkin and Goher—to the Civil Hospital in the town.

When Baba came back in a cast, the women took care of Him at Grafton for several days, but neither doctor was at all happy with His care in Satara, and Donkin went to Poona to find an orthopedic surgeon.

So, shot out of the cannon, the women packed a few things and went with Baba to Poona, never returning to Satara. Their idyllic life there disappeared overnight. Rano and Naja came back to Grafton, packed up everything, and took it all back to Ahmednagar.

From Mani's first Family Letter:

> Baba's silence is rarely felt in His abstention from vocal speech which He has observed these last 31 years, but the deep silence in His suffering is a profoundly felt experience. The morning after the accident, in the midst of tremendous pain He was undergoing from His injuries, Baba said something that revealed a fresh glimpse of the depth of His compassion. He said (with gestures of course), purely from the point of man's suffering and irrespective of political or world situations: "The Hungarians suffered much in their recent struggle. Many were lying wounded and helpless on the roads, away from their loved ones and from care or relief from pain; at least I am lying on a bed, with the care of good doctors and the love of all my lovers present and absent." A few days before He said, "Nobody suffers in vain, for true freedom is spiritual freedom and suffering is a ladder towards it. Men unknowingly suffer for God, and God* knowingly suffers for man." We cannot need a better explanation of why the Avatar allows suffering to His human body that He assumes, from time to time, for our truth-blinded sakes. He loves us as He ought to be loved by us

---

* God as the God-Man.

– our only question is are we worthy of it? – and may our only prayer be that we too may love Him as He ought to be loved.[15]

In a letter, dated December 6, to Elizabeth and Kitty accompanying a circular that was sent to them for distribution, Mani wrote:

Dear Elizabeth and Kitty,

The enclosed circular is for all concerned in the U.S.A. and heaven knows it speaks for itself. Please send it out immediately to all as usual. Baba and the men have been in a car accident, but I hasten to add that Baba's condition is all right even through the injuries were bad. Two of the men (Pendu and Eruch) are in the hospital, and dear Nilu died. Baba is at Grafton under every care, though in much pain, particularly from leg injury. Enclosed circular explains in more detail. Baba did not wish me to send a cable about it, so this letter and circular are going off to you for the U.S.A. and to others for England, Europe, and Australia as soon as it was possible to do so. We are so helpless when Baba makes Himself helpless and suffers like this. He will not help Himself and God knows we cannot help Him. By the time you get this He will (please God) have improved much and will be in much less pain. There is so much to say and nothing to say.

Don't know how the writing of this circular was managed, for the mind is numb and there's lead where the heart should be. But it cannot help Baba if we cannot be brave and He has helped us to be that, even dearest Mehera. I must stop being incoherent—please inform all concerned that I will not be able to write personal letters for some time. Any further news of improvement, etc., will send in weekly letter.

. . .

Can't think of anything else—enough that one can think at all.

> Love,
> Mani[16]

In a special circular dated December 17, 1956, sent out from Satara to Baba-lovers, Mani wrote, "Baba, whom we know by nature to be infinitely active and restless, is now confined to a bed, lying on His back in one position all the time and virtually unable to move. Combined with His long-standing vocal silence, His retirement could not be more absolute, more imaginably complete."[17]

As Baba told them, "The accident has been a blessing for the universe and a curse for Baba!"[18] And later, drawing a circle around the spot of the fracture, "The suffering of the whole universe is concentrated on this little spot. This is a tangible expression of the universal suffering I bear." But despite His terrible suffering, He said, "I am happy. It is as I wanted it."[19]

IN SILVER OAKS

After leaving Satara, they stayed in Poona for two months with Baba (in a house called "Silver Oaks"). During this tense time—as the accident's long-term impact on Baba was becoming apparent—Goher recalled that she received an unwelcome message from the Tex toothbrush company.

Some time before, Mani had composed a slogan for a Tex toothbrush advertising contest that she'd read about in the paper. The line she submitted, "Your smile will prove your choice was right," won the contest. Normally this would have been a source of pleasure for them (and I could see, as she told the story years later, that Mani was proud of her win).

But, as Mani explained to pilgrims, the problem was that she submitted her entry in Goher's name (Goher being a doctor—why not?). So the company thought Goher was the winner. The prize was a Rolex watch, and the toothbrush company wanted Goher to go to the very fancy Taj Mahal Hotel in Bombay for a ceremony to receive it. Goher wanted nothing to do with all this, being terribly shy to begin with, and very busy with Baba's health as well. But Mehera, with an eye to their economy, insisted that they not pass up a free watch. Goher finally agreed to go, but, she said, "I said no to everything they wanted." (Donkin, who had tobacco-stained teeth from smoking, told Mani, "You should have put it in my name.")

The company finally agreed to have the award ceremony in a shop in Poona, and there was a picture of Goher in the paper, in a sari, smiling, claiming the Rolex. Goher recalled to me that on her return, Baba gestured, "What does Goher need a watch for? I need the money!" And it was immediately sold off to Nariman for Rs. 1,000.

THE LAST TWELVE YEARS

Baba and Mehera after the accident.

Baba's severe accident in December 1956 marked the beginning of a gradual decline in His health over the last years of His life, described in the Family Letters sent out by Mani.

After His lovers received her first Family Letter, about His car accident, three more arrived soon after with the details of His slow recovery. In Poona on January 23, 1957, Mani began the fourth letter: "Am sitting down to this family letter with a curious expectant feeling of what's going to come out on the paper, for we're all feeling rather light-headed since the evening of the 20th when Baba, the Beloved, was able to leave the bed for a few minutes on to His wonderful new wheelchair, a gift from Don (Dr. Donkin)."[1]

With this upswing in Baba's health, they soon returned to Meherazad. Mani wrote from there on February 20:

> Meherazad,
> Pippalgaon (India)
>
> Dear Family,
>
> We're back at good old Pippelgaon, in 'Meherazad' where the peace and stillness is a tangible presence, particularly in the evenings when the sun sets in a motley of pinks. The familiar garden bespeaks the loving care Kaka has given it in our long absences; and as of old the wind plays its raucous whispering among the trees, broken by the distant cooing of the doves, the morning song of birds, and the barking of the dogs. But it all cannot be the same while we miss the beloved familiar sight of Baba striding back and forth to the mandali's as He used to, or go with us for quick morning walks to the lake accompanied by His dog Bhooti which He brought as a pup during one of His treks in the Himalayas and which is Kaka's faithful companion and 'guardian' of Meherazad.

After Baba dropped His body in early 1969, the mandali often talked to pilgrims in Meherazad Mandali Hall about their memories of Baba's last twelve years. Perhaps this was because these years with Him were still so fresh in their minds and hearts. Or perhaps it was because He suffered so much and worked so hard, and they felt helpless in the face of His suffering. Baba was often in seclusion for His Universal Work at this time, and their obedience to His orders and sensitivity to His wishes was of paramount importance.

As Baba no longer went on mast tours or—after 1958—darshan tours, it was the one period when the women mandali were with Him day in and day out. His health was precarious, His work crucial, and His suffering visible; they had to be more responsive to His mood than ever.

In the twelve years after the accident, they stayed in Meherazad most of each year. But it became increasingly difficult for Baba there during the Indian summer months of April, May, and June. Mani writes in the Family Letter of April 11, 1957: "It is already very hot here, but this is usual for mid April. It is more trying for darling Baba, who has to lie in bed for many hours. We are hoping He will agree to move for a time to some other place where it is cooler, as May and June are the apex of the hot weather here."

Mehera often spoke to pilgrims of how much Baba suffered in the heat after the second accident, because He could not move around freely. He had to spend most of the time sitting in one place, which, when it was very hot, was difficult. She also felt very deeply that His silence was even more of a restriction on Him when He was injured. He could not call out for assistance, but had to clap, and He could not sing or laugh or talk as a diversion from the pain, the heat, and the confinement.

So, with a lot of persuasion from the mandali, Baba began spending the summers in Poona. First He stayed at Ganeshkhind, a government garden estate where Dadi Kerawala, a close Baba-lover, was supervisor and could arrange accommodations for them. Then in 1958, for a short stay, and from 1959 onwards for the full summer, Baba stayed at Guruprasad, a palatial part-time residence of the Maharani of Baroda. The mandali had first stayed at Guruprasad with Baba in 1951, during the New Life, and Meheru remembered that the women talked Baba into returning seven years later. It was to become their "summer home," and the site of many memorable darshans.

"We're once again at Guruprasad," Mani wrote in January of 1959, "the place often graced with the Beloved's presence, and once again offered with love by the Rani [Maharani] for His stay in Poona. It seems odd that we should feel so at home in this palatial house with its spacious rooms, high ceilings in white and gold, its marble statues and fountain—but perhaps that is because of the singularly light and bright atmosphere of this house where we continue to live our simple ashram life with astonishing ease."

In June of that same year, when they were back in Guruprasad for the summer, Mani wrote, "That same [darshan] Sunday had another special visitor sitting throughout the program at Beloved's feet—it was our lovely Rani, owner of Guruprasad. Baba has often mentioned how pleased He is with Guruprasad, which apart from its right atmosphere seems made to order for many of our ashram requirements, and specially prized is its marathon verandah which affords comfortable walking facility for Baba. But perhaps the biggest reason is the love with which the Rani has offered it for His use. . . ."

Mani at home in Meherazad.

But most of the year, they were in Meherazad, which Mani described eloquently in a Family Letter: "Set in a rural landscape, it is an 'oasis' in the midst of nowhere, conveying a unique atmosphere of peace; a place where Baba has been in Seclusion for long periods—a place blessed most with the physical presence of God."

It was their home in the deepest sense. As Mani wrote in August 1962:

> Returning to the quiet atmosphere of Meherazad after a spell in Poona, is like kicking off one's shoes in the privacy of one's room after a late evening out with friends. We put by our good clothes and pretty saris for the next trip to Guruprasad, and slip back into our comfortable rags—for here we almost never go out anywhere and seldom is a visitor allowed.

The big windows, open verandahs, surrounding garden, and vistas on every side brought nature into every aspect of their lives. Mani often mentioned the weather in her letters, as she painted a picture of Meherazad life: "One afternoon the clouds broke down, and it poured so profusely that within half an hour Meherazad was looking like a duck pond. With beloved Baba we watched from the window of His room the saturated fields, and the *nullahs* overflowing with the torrent of water rushing down them."

Or another year:

> After the first refreshing plunge into Meherazad's quiet life we cease to gasp in renewed wonder at all the little things that make Meherazad what it is, but we can never completely take its blessings for granted. In the moonlight, when the jasmine bushes look like leafy nets that have caught a shower of fallen stars, we still gaze fascinated. And when at dawn these fragrant little flowers cover the garden paths like white carpets, we still find time to stand and stare .... more than once we've picked up a bewildered and bedraggled young bird from one of the water tanks in the garden. Whenever this happens, after the bird is thoroughly dried by the log fire until its feathers are fluffy and it has regained its aplomb and lung-power, before setting it free we invariably take it to Baba. The Beloved gently caresses

Baba in Meherazad garden.

its sleek head, and sometimes blesses it with a kiss. That is as far as we see of the blessing – how can we fathom its unseen depths? How can we stand the silent miracle of His presence that wipes out hordes of sanskaras, the alchemy of His touch that turns the consciousness of a bird or animal into that of a human being in its next life? As Kabir has said: "One moment, half a moment, even half of half a moment spent in the company of a Perfect Master, cuts away crores [tens of millions] of one's sanskaras."

During these years at Meherazad, Mani read to Baba and played music on the gramophone (phonograph) and the radio for Him more often. (In 1965, she mentioned their radio in a Family Letter: "Among the few luxuries that have a part in life at Meherazad is our transistor radio .") She also attended to His everyday needs, along with Mehera and the others. While it was an increasingly intimate time with Him in seclusion, and quiet (few visitors, fewer outings), she shared Baba's activities more and more with people around the world through the Family Letters and through home movies of Him that she took at Meherazad and Guruprasad.

A DAY AT MEHERAZAD

After Baba's last visit to the West, in 1958, the daily pattern of life changed only in the details until 1969. To set the scene, here's the schedule of a usual day with Baba in the 1960s at Meherazad, as recalled by Dr. Goher.

The women would get up around 5:00 or 5:30 a.m., and when Baba rang the bell from His bedroom around 6:00 or 6:30 a.m. (after dismissing His night watchman), Mehera would go into His room and greet Him first, followed by Mani. Then the others would go in and sit down. Some days they would sit around His bed and massage Him, if He wanted it—one person massaging Baba's neck, someone else His back, and so on, for about fifteen or twenty minutes. Then He would get up and walk on Mehera's arm to the dining room, where Mehera would turn His chair to face toward Mandali Hall. Mehera would have the hot water and everything else ready at the table and, as she held the mirror, Baba would shave Himself and then wash His face. It was quite a procedure.

Meherazad gates.

The dining room in Baba's house.

As Goher recalled, first a stool would be placed between Baba's legs, and Mehera would tie a bib or towel around His neck. Then from two buckets of water, she would pour water onto His hands, which He held over a basin on the stool, and Baba would splash His face and hands with the water, and then dry off.

Goher said that Baba used to do all this by Himself in earlier days, but after the second accident, He could not stand for a long period, so they helped Him while He sat down. After that, Mehera would turn His chair toward the table, and Baba would sit down again and tea would be served. They would all sit around the table with Him, and Mani—or, in her absence, Goher—would play the radio for Him. (At a quarter past eight some good Pakistani qawwali music came on, which Baba liked.) Mehera would have broken up little bits of chappati for the birds who came to the open window, and Baba would ask if the birds had come and if they were eating. He even would motion for the women to be still when a shy bird flew in, so that it would not be frightened off. (He once asked them how many different kinds of birds they had in the garden, and they enumerated several.) Baba would call His dog Mastan and pet him and, after breakfast, walk out to the porch and sit in the lift chair to be carried over to Mandali Hall by two of the men mandali and two of the garden boys. (Mani's dog Peter would usually go along.) Baba would stay in the Hall with the men until lunchtime.

The women with Mastan in Meherazad.

The Hall began as a roomy garage for Elizabeth's car and then became a stable for the horse Sheba. In the later years it was, as Mani described it in the Family Letters, "a 'sitting room,' with a tin roof and crude flooring, unfurnished except for a chair for Baba and a bench and strip of carpet for the mandali to sit on, where Baba spends most of the mornings and afternoons with them." Almost all the small darshans and singing programs that Baba allowed at Meherazad in these years were held in the Hall.

Baba would eat lunch back in the house around 11:00 or 11:30 a.m. For some years He would eat lunch in the sitting room, seated on the gaadi. Naja would bring His food there, and Mehera would serve Him on a tray. Some years He had lunch at the dining table. (In the very last years—*'67 and '68 were very heavy years,* Goher said—He would eat in His room, as He was very tired when He came in from the Hall after doing His seclusion work. Goher remembered, "He always looked very

The sitting room with Baba's gaadi today, remaining as it was in His time.

sad and depressed and, you know, burdened. And we could do little to help Him in any way. We used to sit around and be very quiet—not disturb Him.")

Goher recalled that after lunch, Baba would go to His room and sit or rest on His bed while Mani read out loud from a book, or Rano read to them from, say, *Time* magazine or the newspaper. The others would sit around Him, until He told Mani to stop the reading. At that point the women would go out of the room, or else sit there very quietly while Baba rested. He would have tea about 3:30 or 4:00 p.m., in His room or sometimes at the dining table.

"Teatime at Meherazad is a happy hour for us women," Mani wrote to the Family, "when we sit together at the dining table with the Beloved; and mingling with snatches of conversation and the tinkle of teaspoons in cups, is the music from our transistor radio—occasionally accompanied by heavy snores from our old Cocker-spaniel [Peter]

Baba reclining on His gaadi in the 1950s.

fast asleep in his corner by Baba's chair. . . . This would find Baba drumming briskly on the table in rhythm with the music, the response from our brass tea-kettle being a jerky little dance as it would bob up and down with the vibration of the table. Sometimes there is a kavvali [qawwali] program on the air... and this at times puts Baba in the mood to discourse to us on matters that matter."

After tea, Baba would go over to the men's side and stay there for an hour or so, then come back to the house. During that time, the women would see to their own work, Mehera attending to Baba's things, Mani typing, and so on.

Goher remembered that Baba would have His supper in His bedroom. Mehera would make sure He washed His hands ("You know how particular Mehera was!"), and they would put a table in front of Him. He'd ask Naja what she had cooked for Him, and then Naja would bring it from the kitchen. The women all sat with Baba while He ate, and Mani (or sometimes Rano) read out loud to Him. This was a longer reading session than in the morning.

They would then leave the room around 6:00 or 6:30 p.m., depending on how long Baba listened to the reading. Mehera and Mani were the last to leave. As they did, Baba would embrace Mani, and then, last, He would embrace Mehera—"none of us," Goher added, "except on our birthday or His birthday. We were asked to just kiss Him very gently. So we would do it on the cheek. He'd point up to His cheek."

Then Goher would go and call the watchman, one of the mandali, who was waiting on the small cottage verandah where Mani typed. Whoever it was would then come in and sit with Baba.

After Baba retired, "we would do our own little things," Goher remembered, or they would read in the sitting room, around an Aladdin wick oil lamp, as Meherazad had no electricity. Mani gives a picture of a typical evening there in a letter to Kitty:

> I'm writing this by the Aladdin lamp in our little sitting

room, a beetle is buzzing noisily around it, and outside it is raining, while Mehera, Goher, Naja and Meheru are also gathered about the lamp reading some magazine or other; and soon we will be dispersing, one by one, for bed (Mehera and I being the first to do so). Baba has retired to His room, and Bhau is with Him, for he is the first of the three paharawalas [watchmen] who sit up in the night in Baba's room, taking care not to make the least sound and that's some job when one of them gets a sudden cough!

Mehera would peruse *Reader's Digest* or something like that, Mani would read "anything, some novel or something," as would Meheru and the others, and Goher would read her medical books and articles. Or Mehera might go to the back garden and putter there, or play with Mastan or Peter.

Sometimes Baba called them in the evening around 7:00 or 8:00 p.m., saying He was hungry and asking what there was to eat. The watchman rang the bell, and Goher went in and brought back the message. Then the watchman left so that Mehera, Mani, and the other women could enter and attend to Baba. (Goher herself might be called by a light knock at any hour of the night to check on His health and comfort.)

The women would go to bed by 8:30 or 9:00 p.m.

THE FAMILY LETTERS

In her book, *Love Alone Prevails,* Kitty wrote:

> In 1960, we see the beginning of the gradual shift from Mani's personal letters to us to emphasis on the Family Letters and circulars as the predominant means of correspondence. I am sure nothing has contributed more to keeping the various members of the various groups knit

together than Baba's love which permeates the Family Letters from Mani, reminding us again and again that love, as Baba shows us, includes tolerance, understanding, and a harmony in diversity. These Family Letters became even more precious in the 1960s, as they became the main link between East and West.[2]

Elizabeth Patterson, in her introduction to the published collection of Mani's 82 Family Letters, described how the letters came to be:

By 1956 the Meher Baba groups had grown and spread throughout the U.S.A. and Europe. A great many people met Meher Baba during His six visits to the United States which included stays at Meher Spiritual Center in South Carolina in 1952, 1956 and 1958. Baba then called all those who loved Him, His family. The men and women disciples who lived with Him throughout the years, were called the resident mandali. His sister Mani was one of them and in 1956 Baba directed her to be His scribe to the West. The eighty-two Family Letters began at that time.

These unique and loving letters by Mani continued over a span of thirteen years until 1969, and reached His family in the United States, England, Europe, Australia, and later encircling other parts of the world.

Mani would send these letters to us (Elizabeth Patterson, Norina Matchabelli and Kitty Davy) at Meher Spiritual Center, Myrtle Beach, South Carolina. Immediately photocopies were made and dispatched to all the Meher Baba group-heads in the various cities of the U.S.A. The group heads knew all the individuals who attended their group meetings or who in their area were otherwise drawn to Meher Baba. With remarkable speed,

the group-heads and their helpers distributed the Family
Letters. Thus the individual felt always in personal contact
with Meher Baba.

The letters to His Family were not only approved by
Meher Baba, they were written at His wish; and often Baba
would remind Mani that it was time for another letter.
Every letter was read out to Baba. At times He directed
some portion of it to be deleted, and often He had some
message or information added to the letter. And so these
letters were, in effect, from Baba.[3]

The back cover of the paperback collection of the Family Letters
describes the intimate picture Mani managed to paint of life with Baba
from 1956 to 1969:

With camera-like clarity, Mani describes the
touching stories of devotees' first meetings with Meher
Baba; the great outpourings of love that flowed continually
to the thousands who contacted him over those years; his
radiance during even the most strenuous darshans; the
unforgettable sight of Baba bowing down to the feet of the
"untouchable" poor and the lepers; the tales of unwavering
faith in Baba's name; the routines of daily life for Meher
Baba and his *mandali*; and the wonderful humor, the
stirring power of the unique individual who touched and
changed so many lives around the world.

Mani typed those eighty-two letters sitting at her desk in her "open-
air office," whether a small cottage verandah at Meherazad or the palatial
balcony of Guruprasad.

Seated at her typewriter, she might have specific messages from Baba
to write. Also, she would have notes from Eruch (Baba had told her to

Mani typing at her desk in her "open-air office."

ask Eruch for any news of Baba's activities that she might not know firsthand).

In the months since she had sent the most recent Family Letter, she would have collected many other things to include: excerpts from letters from Baba-lovers, reports on Baba-work in their areas—plus her own reflections, reminders, and word-pictures of Meherazad or Guruprasad, to make the readers feel they were there.

Sometimes Baba did not allow news of His activities to be given out, so these tidbits of other material came in handy. "Here comes the news-letter that cannot give news," she started in September 1960. "On the other hand, the silence of Seclusion will afford space for those tidbits that couldn't manage to elbow their way into previous letters, and which were tucked away in memory's attic for future use."

She once described to me how she would type out a draft, then cut and paste the pieces of it together with other notes and scraps and quotes until it looked like a long paper patchwork. And then she'd retype it and read it to Baba. After incorporating His corrections or additions, she'd type multiple carbon copies of the final letter (and heaven help you if you made a typing error.), and finally send it off to Elizabeth and Kitty. She was a very fast and accurate typist, but this, she said, was quite a job. And she was a perfectionist, which must have made it harder.

Then, she said, just when the relief of having it all done was beginning to seep in, Baba would suddenly gesture, "What about another Family Letter? Isn't it time?" And Mani's eyes would get wide, and she'd have to start all over again.

If you read the Family Letters straight through, as I did a while ago, they give you a moving picture of the growing intensity and importance of Baba's work in the last phase of His Advent. Nothing quite compares with this collection of letters in affording a glimpse of that time. Mani is innocent of what is coming, but we know.

After the shocking news of Baba's accident, the letters settle down for a while, to report on Baba's health, His activities in Meherazad and Guruprasad, the atmosphere there, things Baba said or did or wished His lovers to know, things Baba-groups around the world were up to, and so on. Baba's health takes a slight upturn; there is a feeling that things are "back to normal" (if you can say such a thing about life with the Avatar!). Baba's wonderful humor continues, as always, and His interest, curiosity, and particular involvement with all His lovers remains.

But about midway through, Mani's tone takes a turn and begins to grow more serious. How could it not when what she had to report, and what she was living with, were Baba's seclusions and their effects on His body, His withdrawal from people and outward activity, His continuing health problems and pain from the accident, His repeated emphasis to the mandali and His lovers on pleasing and obeying Him, His "infinite tiredness."

Of course, here's where knowing the "end" of the story changes your reading: how perfectly Baba orchestrated everything; how much He suffered for us; how much Mehera, Mani, and all of His close ones suffered with Him; and how totally He sacrificed Himself and those He loved for His creation.

༄

WORK AND SUFFERING

In reading through the stories that the mandali would tell about these last years, you can sense an underlying constant—Baba's final, intensive work and the suffering it caused Him. It was the backdrop to every day they spent with Him.

"As we have seen through the years," Mani wrote in a Family Letter, "doctors and health, as everything else concerned with Baba, serve as a smoke-screen for the real purpose of His work not revealed to us."

Here are a few excerpts from the Family Letters that give a glimpse of this, and of the mandali's intensifying focus on Him over those last years.

From September 1957:

> The bone union [of the hip joint fractured in Baba's second accident] is firm, but the pain does not allow Him to walk for more than a short distance (though with the aid of sticks).
>
> This is as far as we can outwardly see and through it all Baba seems to sit back serenely, that as we hear Him in His Silence we may see Him through the veil of outward suffering. And the glimpse is sometimes startling – one feels through this present "physical helplessness" of Baba more than ever an immeasurable strength that I think sometimes one could almost touch! At times, when suddenly called into Baba's presence one feels like a person squinting his eyes on coming out from a dark room into the bright light of sun.

From the same letter:

> Baba told the Mandali the other day, "There is no compromise—either you please yourself, or you please Me in the littlest thing". And so His lovers try on, Baba guiding our efforts, wanting not 99% but a 100%, giving the strength that He knows we are capable of in His love if we tried one-pointedly.

Baba once explained to the mandali, as quoted in a letter of June 1959:

> These days "maya", the principle of ignorance, is in full play and tries to oppose my work. So, particularly those who live near me must remain very watchful. Knowing my love for you, maya awaits the opportunity to use your weaknesses. The moment you neglect my instructions, maya's purpose is served. I have to put up a big fight with Maya – not to destroy it but to make you aware of its nothingness. The moment you fail to obey me implicitly, it tightens its grip over you and you fail to carry out the duties as assigned to you. This adds to my present suffering.

Mani wrote, "And so we tread each day as 'cats on hot bricks', lest we are caught off our guard and trip unintentionally. . . ."

In May and June of 1958, Baba traveled to the United States and Australia to give His sahavas to His lovers. In movies of that trip, you can see what Mani meant when she wrote (in February of that year), "These days it seems not so much the physical suffering as the inner pressure of work one can see Him bearing." But you also see Baba giving His Love without restraint or thought of Himself.

Mani and the other women did not accompany Baba this time, but He spoke of

Baba with Elizabeth in 1958 at the Meher Center in Myrtle Beach.

them. At a meeting in the United States with His women followers, Baba remarked, "In My love, first comes Mehera, and then Mani. Mehera is My Beloved. Mani is My true sister in work. She loves Me and works for Me from morning to late at night with correspondence and other details, even though she is not in good health at present. She loves Me and has surrendered to Me one hundred percent."[4] Later, in Australia, He said to a group of women, "Mehera is the purest of women, and she has sent her love to you all. She has sent some gifts to give to each of you. After Mehera is Mani, My sister. She has no thought of herself and does all for Me."[5]

On August 25, 1958, Mani wrote:

Dear Family,

Have been sitting at the typewriter for the last quarter hour, doodling all over the blotter, wondering how to begin this and just what to say. Over a month has gone by since the last letter, but there seems little to report in the way of news. The outer circle of activities appears to be almost at a standstill, while inwardly there seems to be constantly a sense of tension, anticipation and urgency. If a simile can express it, I can only say it is like sitting quietly on a volcano. . . . The insight into His present working is gleaned at rare moments from Baba's remarks, as for instance (over a domestic problem one morning): "Why do you worry over a trivial thing like that, when the whole world is at stake!"

She refers to this again, in a December 1958 letter:

This again brings to mind the August circular . . . and how in His love and compassion He warns and prepares us, alerts us that we are not "caught napping" when the time comes . . . And then I hear the words of Jigar (poet-mystic) that Beloved quoted to us three consecutive evenings in

Satara after the Seclusion there:
> *"Understand well,*
> *this love is not easy.*
> *It is as an Ocean of fire*
> *and you have to drown in it."*

While the mandali saw Baba's suffering, often people who did not live with Him saw the opposite. In June 1967, Mani quoted Dr. Ginde, for whom Baba had demonstrated His ability to walk, at Guruprasad:

> Beloved Baba looked a picture of radiant health with bright shining eyes, rosy cheeks, exuding joy and happiness. He did not seem to have much pain in His neck and His movements were relatively free and spontaneous. His gait was strong. I have never seen Him walk like that before; one stretch and back along the verandah was enough to make me breathe heavily. It was really a unique and thrilling experience.

Mani continued:

> If Beloved Baba appeared in such glowing health and radiance to Dr. Ginde, that's how He appeared to us. But that is not to say we see Him always in this light, as we do when His radiance is turned on full for those whom He calls for a while. For us who see Him all the time, He often keeps the shade down or we could be dazzled into forgetfulness of His humanity. Baba made a statement on this one morning recently in Meherazad when He was seated with His mandali. Baba said: "I am both divine and human. Those who live with me feel more of my humanity than my divinity. Those whom I permit to come and see me for a while see more of my divinity than my humanity. All my intimate lovers whether living

with me or away from me will, in the end, experience my divinity."

. . .

In Mandali Hall in later years, Mani spoke to pilgrims about the God-Man's suffering:

> In order to free us, His creation, Baba bound Himself in so many ways, coil after coil, knot after knot. First of all, His being in human form was the biggest binding, His coming as man. Then there was His silence all those years; He participated in everything, and directed everything so actively, yet He was totally silent. Then He gave up writing, then reading. Then walking, when He suffered Himself to have an accident which led to terrible injuries to His body. After that, He bound Himself with so much pain. So He was binding Himself through each stage, each phase of His life.
>
> And our suffering was our helplessness as we watched Him. We couldn't lessen His pain, although He allowed us to do little things for Him. But He said the only thing that would help Him was our obedience, because this was suffering which He had taken upon Himself. Sometimes when He was seated here in the Hall wearing a cervical collar around His neck, we've heard Him say, "There is nothing you can do. It's My work. It's the burden of the world around My neck." And that helplessness was our suffering.
>
> His silence was not just silence of the tongue, not just of speech. His silence was also His silent giving to the world, doing all that He did silently. If you were behind the scenes, you might get a tiny glimpse of that, if He so allowed. He used to say, "As Jesus Christ, I was crucified only once. But in this Advent, I am crucified daily."

Stories From Meherazad

Sitting in Mandali Hall on a weekend in Meherazad in the 1970s, '80s, and early '90s, you would often find Mani telling Baba-stories. Some of Mani's favorite anecdotes reveal how, despite His suffering, those last twelve years with Him were full of lively, humorous moments as well as deep lessons.

DRAB, DRY, DUSTY

In Mandali Hall, Mani reminisced:

> We love to remember Baba best as our "household Baba." Not dressed in His pink coat, as He was when He was before His lovers on occasions when He "opened the door of His heart a little bit," as He would say. We loved to have Him in His white silk coat, or the grey cotton coat, a little frayed at the edges (but His favourite, so He wanted it kept that way)—when He would come into the dining room and have breakfast or lunch with us, and the little things that happened at that time.
>
> Or when He would be with us in the garden. There He would put up with us when we would plead with Him, "Please, Baba, we're going to take some pictures of You. Please sit here under the bougainvillea arch; it's in beautiful, glorious bloom." Or someone would say, "What about by the yellow sunflower patch?" So Mehera would make Baba put on His blue coat that would go with the yellow sunflowers, and then we'd all get into the picture.
>
> One morning, we were at the dining table. Baba was seated in His chair, Mehera and I seated on both sides of Him, and the others all around the table. Now Mehera always felt bad that the garden had such poor soil, and there was

never enough rain, and so much wind in certain months, and strong sun all the time. All of which makes it hard to create a garden, especially a garden like the one you see here. It's all that love and care that has been put into it, like into a nursery of children, that makes it as beautiful as it is.

We used to call Ahmednagar DDD, meaning drab, dry, and dusty. Now, we could even add another D and make it "dirty." But it was DDD then.

We'd been to so many places with Baba, all over India in the Blue Bus and on other travels. So that morning in the dining room, Mehera said to Baba, "Baba, the whole world is Yours. Then why of all places do You go and choose Ahmednagar to settle down in?" And you know, Baba practically looked guilty. He scratched His chin, and said, "Yes, I made a mistake. I made the same mistake as Jesus. I made the same mistake when I was Mohammed. Same mistake when I was Lord Krishna. And now again."

Then Mehera, because she loved everything green, flourishing, and in plenty, said, "And next time?"

"Next time, sure enough, I promise," said Baba, and put His hand over Mehera's hand. "Next time, plenty!" And Mehera was joyous and delighted.

Then Baba left the dining room to be brought over to the Hall on the lift chair. Suddenly, Mehera thought of something and turned to me, "But how will we know next time?"

"Don't ask me!" I said.

Yeah, DDD.

Then afterwards, I realized that apart from all that Baba was saying about the garden, He was also saying, "I was that one [Jesus], I was that one [Mohammed], I was that one [Krishna]."

When I was relating this incident in the Mandali Hall a few years ago, Amrit's father, Kumar [Shatrughan Kumar, one of Baba's close lovers], was here. He said to me afterwards, "You know, in the old Hindu scriptures there is a verse that says, speaking to Lord Krishna, 'Oh Lord, now and again, You also make a mistake. In Kabul, You gave such orchards and such fruits.'" Kabul is way up in the mountains in the north, where you get beautiful fruit. "'And the place of Your birth has nothing but babul!'" Babul are those thorny, dry trees you see around here. "'So what is this! Sometimes, You also slip up!'"

You know, it is so true that the place of Krishna's birth [childhood], Gokul, does not need fruit, because it has the Lord Himself. Why does it need anything else? Other places need it, but He is the All.

I always say that Baba is number ten. Baba is number ten because He's the One, the One and Only, and then there's the zero after Him. Now, number 10 includes every number—3, 5, 7, 0, them all. He's all-inclusive. You'll find all in Him. He's complete. Whereas number 5 would not have number 7 in it. Number 4 would not have 9 in it. But Baba is the number 10. All you ever worship, whatever it is, all goes to Him, all reaches Him, because He's all-inclusive.

QUESTIONS

For the mandali, Baba's humanity was uppermost. As Mani described it:

> So much of His Godness came through His humanness. We would witness it all the time. We had the household side of Him; Baba was our "household Baba," as I say. And for us that meant everything. We women participated in the big darshans for His lovers that took place in Guruprasad only from behind the scenes.
>
> And we would just wait for the darshan to be over. For Baba to walk back in, with the support of Mehera's arm. Mehera would have put out a fresh sadra for Him, and of course He'd wash His face, and Naja would bring His food, Goher and Meheru would be doing something for Him, and I would be ready with my book to read out to Him. You know, just a family; that was the best time for us. A bit selfish, but . . . !
>
> Now that we have His promised children with us, now that we're going through being with Baba in another form, in another way, now we wish that we had asked Baba questions. When people ask, "What did Baba say about such and such?" we have nothing to tell because, no, we didn't ask Baba that. So then we say, "Oh, how I wish I'd asked Baba!"
>
> But at that time when Baba was present with us physically, with us all the time, He left no room for questions in our minds, in our hearts. Baba is so vast, so complete; He fulfilled our lives and days so totally, there was no room for questions. It's not that we didn't ask because we couldn't ask or didn't want to ask. Questions never came up. There wasn't, as I say, room for a question.
>
> But sometimes there would be a question in our minds,

and I'll give you an example of the kind of questions we had.

We'd be seated in Baba's room in Meherazad, and He would be sitting on His bed. Now His room was not just His bedroom, it was His sitting room, too, where we sat around Him when reading a detective story, as He had His meals or washed His face. And what He called His "television" was the window in front, the one facing the bed. He said, "I can look out and see the flowers and the changes [in nature and the seasons]."

Baba's bed in His bedroom at Meherazad.

So when He was seated on His bed, with us around Him, sometimes His sadra, that soft, old, favourite sadra of His, would slip off His shoulder a bit. Baba had such beautiful shoulders. And naturally, seated around Him, we'd be looking at Him. And sometimes a fly would come and rest for a moment on His shoulder.

The immediate question in my mind would be, "Why this fly, out of all the billions of flies in the whole world, especially in India, and most especially in Ahmednagar; why does this particular fly have this fantastic good fortune to rest on His person? Is there such a thing as God-chance, God-luck? Or maybe this is His whim, His grace; is this what is called His grace?" So questions like that would come up in the mind.

But we never asked Him such things.

PURITY

Mani remembered:

> So, we didn't ask questions, and when we were around Baba, we didn't touch Him or go up to Him or embrace Him whenever we felt like it, either. That wasn't the pattern, ever. Only if Baba called you over—you'd pleased Him or something—and He gave you an embrace or His cheek for you to kiss or a hand for you to kiss, would you touch Him.
>
> But sometimes, when He was lying on His bed and resting in the afternoon, He would tell us we could press His feet and legs. So some of us would do one side, some would do His other side, pressing His legs, not massaging, but pressing, which He liked, up to the foot. At those times we women would sit on our little stools, three of us here, three of us there, however many we were, and press Baba's legs. Mehera usually had the privilege of pressing His arm, which was a privilege Baba gave her, one of her many privileges.
>
> One afternoon Baba was resting in His room. He had body aches and He looked tired. He was lying on His back, eyes closed, and gestured to us to press His hands and legs. We arranged ourselves on both sides of His bed, sitting on our little wooden seats. We began pressing His hands and legs. Massaging the elder of a household is not an unusual practice among Indian families. After a while, Baba, His eyes still closed, snapped His fingers and gestured to us to stop. We withdrew our hands to our laps, but did not get up in case we might disturb Him.
>
> While sitting there, looking at Beloved Baba's form in silence, I felt wave upon wave of purity emanating from Him.

I recognized this purity just as a blind man sitting in front of an ocean senses, by the fresh tang of the salt air reaching him, that he is facing the ocean. I was overwhelmed and awed by the experience, and heard myself say inwardly, "So, God is not only supreme Love but also supreme Purity."

GOING FORWARD

As always, Mani was concerned about Baba's lovers:

> Once I did ask Baba a question, and I'm very glad I did. Because the question applies to the ones who were His lovers, who are His lovers, and who will be His lovers. I was a bit concerned about what happens to someone who loves Baba when they die and are born again. What happens then? If they come back, is it to begin to look for Him all over again?
>
> So I asked, "Baba, what happens when someone who loves You dies and takes another birth, another form? Will they know You, will they recognize You, or will they miss You?" When I said, "Will they miss you?" I meant, miss coming to You.
>
> Baba made a very intimate expression, a confidential expression. "No," He said. "You pick up from where you leave off. It is always a going forward, never a going backward."
>
> So to pick up from where you leave off, means where you leave off in the present life. The present is so important. How far can you get away from yourself and how much closer can you get to Him in this life? Because you're going to pick up

from there and go on another mile of a lifetime each time towards Him. So the present is all-important, not what's past, or what your past lives were, or what the past meant, or the future. He's the Future. But the present is an all-time, all-life job, and that job is to love Him more, to remember Him more, to come closer to Him more and more.

֍

NICE FLOWER

Even the simplest things Baba did would often reveal something about Him—revelations that stayed with Mani long after:

Now, I've told you about our early times in Meherazad garden: Baba's walking and playing there with us, the longer walks we had with Him in the fields around Meherazad, and the rocks we used to collect, and the Seclusion Hill we used to climb.

But it was quite different in the 1960s, after the second accident, when Baba's movements were confined. He could not walk as He did before. He walked with the support of Mehera's arm, or sometimes mine or one of the men's. He went over to the men's side carried on a lift chair. How we missed that easy stride of His! He loved to walk and He used to love

Mehera, Naja, and Mani with Baba.

sitting up on His gaadi with His leg up, which He also couldn't do anymore.

But still, at that time I had some revelations in the garden that have remained with me like perennial flowers.

I'll have to give you some background. In the morning after Baba had dismissed the night watchman (whichever of the men mandali He had with Him at the time), He would ring a little battery-powered bell. It would go *tring, tring* and Baba's favourite music on the bell was, *tring, tring, tringtringtring, tring, tring, tringtringtring*—nonstop! No matter what you were doing, you would drop your toothbrush or whatever you had in hand and run. Mehera, of course, would go into His room first and we all would follow.

Then Baba would come to the dining room, walking with the support of Mehera's arm, and we would come along with Him. He'd sit at His place in His chair, wash His face, have His tea, and then Mehera, standing behind His chair, would comb His hair. I would be playing the radio, qawwali songs from Pakistan or All India Radio, or very often, the Voice of America program. Baba liked it, specially one commentator, Phillip Irving [Phil Irwin], and when that particular man came on He used to call, "Where's Mehera? Come on! Listen, listen! He's on again." He liked a nice voice. I also kept, by my side, letters—and also notes and jokes and interesting clippings from the newspapers—to regale Him, if He wanted.

Just before He went over to the men's side, Goher would arrange for the lift chair to be on Mehera's porch. You've seen the lift chair that's now here in the Mandali Hall, right? Baba used to go from the women's side, the house, to what we used to always call "the other side"—which meant the men's side—to Mandali Hall every morning to be with the men. He would go on the lift chair, which would be carried by either four of the men mandali or four of the staff: the driver, the garden boys, the household cleaning boys, or someone like that.

Sometimes through the dining room window we would see Kaka Baria standing by the Mandali Hall gate, impatiently waiting for Baba to come. Baba, from His dining chair, would turn round and gesture, "See, Mehera, Kaka looking for Me, keeping an eye out for Me, when will I come, eagerly awaiting!" So then Baba would come with Mehera to the porch to sit on the lift chair. The moment He came on the porch, Goher would signal for the men mandali or the boys to come, which is when Mehera would go back inside the house.

At that time I would go over to my little "open-air office" on the verandah of the small cottage between the house and the Hall. I'd quickly gather up any papers or a book I had to have ready for Baba as soon as He got to Mandali Hall, so I could finish the work with Him there before Baba started listening to Eruch read out the correspondence. So I'd come away from the house a couple of minutes before Baba, as soon as Baba came onto the porch.

Now Baba, when going to the Mandali Hall from the women's porch on the lift chair, would hold His scarf over His nose and mouth, because He was allergic to cold air ever since the 1952 accident, which injured His face. So He would sit on the chair with a scarf held over His mouth and nose to keep out the draft.

As He would be carried across the garden, He would pass what we call the "oval." There's an oval area, a part of the garden, which is bordered by a short, green, herbaceous

Baba sitting in the garden's "oval."

border with flower beds inside. We change the flowers each season. On the morning I'm talking about, I had come over to the cottage a minute earlier, as usual, but before I could reach my office, I saw Baba pass by the oval on His way to the Mandali Hall, carried on the lift chair by the four men.

And so I stopped and looked, waiting with the pages in my hand. Baba went by at a pretty brisk pace towards the men's side, past the oval, with the scarf over His mouth and nose. And as He passed me, He just removed the scarf, looked to the side at the oval for a split second, and then gestured to me, "Nice flower."

Nice flower? Where was the flower? I knew there were no flowers; the beds were green with leaves that had just come up and it was the time for the flowers to appear, but not a single one was visible. And Baba goes by at a quick pace and simply gives a glance to this green expanse and says, "Nice flower."

Then He continued along the path and into the Hall. But I was stuck where I was, bewildered: as you all say, it "blew my mind"! Where was the flower??!! Definitely Baba's gesture was "nice flower," so I went to the oval, bent down and looked for it. No flower. I squatted; looking for that flower was like looking for a needle in a haystack. I was practically kneeling, looking for the flower.

And then I saw it. One lone little flower in that whole green expanse, barely visible, just coming up. And I had to search for it on my knees almost, sniff it out like a dog looking for a bone, till I could find it. And here was Baba, high up on the lift chair, just breezing by, and just a glance, a look, and He greeted that flower.

I just stood there; I couldn't move. And I said to myself, "If Baba could notice a little, humble flower that was not visible to the eyes of others, how then can we ever think that He would neglect the littlest thing about His lovers? That He would forget a single one of His followers! That His eye, that His sight, was not on all who were connected with Him!"

It gave me such a feeling of fullness: Ah! He has His sight on all who are His, in His garden. All the flowers, all the humans, all life under His view. And it was something that I carried not just for a moment, but it seemed for hours, for days; in fact, it seems like I'm still carrying that feeling.

As if that one wasn't big enough, something else then happened that was another revelation of Baba's Love, of what we take for granted, of what we don't understand.

The situation was the same as the one I've just described. The only difference was it was perhaps a week or two weeks later. I had left the house a few minutes before

Baba could reach the Mandali Hall in His lift chair, quickly rushing because I knew there were some photographs of Baba that I was to take to Him to touch, and then send to His lovers in the West.

I had them ready and wanted to be in the Hall as soon as Baba got there, so I went straight to the verandah of the small cottage. But before I could get the box of photos, I saw this simple village woman we knew standing there, her face glowing with innocence, with joy, with love like a child would have for its mother. That's what I mean by innocence.

She said to me, "Oh, Baba, my Baba." I said, "Yes, yes."

Then she said, "I want to see my Baba. I just want to see my Baba!"

"Dhondi," I replied, "you can't see Baba, you know that. Baba is in strict seclusion. Even His own very close lovers can't come and see Him. You know, they can't even come from Ahmednagar. Adi's not coming. It's not possible, Dhondi; you can't see Baba."

"Oh, but I don't want to see; I only want a glimpse, even if it's from far, just a quiet glimpse I want of my Baba."

So I said to myself, "Oh, God, what am I to do?" And yet I could feel her longing, a live, vibrating longing and I didn't have the heart to say flatly, "No."

But suddenly, when I said to myself, "Oh, Baba, what am I to do?" a brilliant thought came to me. "Look, Dhondi, let us both stand here behind the wall of the cottage. Baba is going to pass by on the way to the Mandali Hall, and you'll get your glimpse. It'll be just a glimpse through the opening in front of us. When Baba passes by through that open passage going to the Hall, for that distance we will be able to glimpse Him." That would be quite a few seconds that she would be able to see Him.

So I said, "Dhondi, just stand here. Now Baba's going to pass by. As soon as He passes before us, we'll see Him."

"Yes! My Baba! Oh, my Baba!"

So we both stood there. But I was curious as to when He was coming, so I peeked out around the passage, expecting to see Him coming as usual with His scarf held to His nose. But I was horrified. That morning Baba wasn't just holding the scarf to His nose and mouth, He had taken the scarf and covered His whole head and face with it like a veil! So there goes Dhondi's glimpse of Baba. I said to myself, "Oh, no, how will Dhondi see Him? There goes her glimpse." Just one glimpse, one little glimpse, but no.

But you wouldn't believe it. Just when Baba came up to the passage where He would be visible to that simple villager, that lady with the great longing for just a glimpse of Him, just as He came within her visibility, He very swiftly flung the scarf up. And as soon as He had passed by her, when she could no longer see Him, He covered His face again. And I witnessed this. She never knew. He hadn't turned once; He didn't show He knew she was there.

This was a revelation to me not only of His love, but of the fruit of one's longing, if it is for Him. No longing is denied. He really is the Filler, He really is the Fulfiller. He filled her heart with joy. He fulfilled the longing of her heart.

So, in little ways, in casual moments, in unrehearsed times, we would catch glimpses of His glory, glimpses of His love, just like you catch the sunlight hitting a hidden leaf or a little stone that suddenly sparkles like a diamond. And you go in close up to it and pick it up, and you find it's nothing but a tiny chip of a pebble.

So these moments filled our days in so many ways. Nothing that you could write or talk about. But something you held within yourself, something that filled you. Just like what I call His "simple sermons," when He made these casual remarks at unexpected moments that were not discourses that were published, but little crumbs of grace dropped from His bountiful table of love. Which are feasts to us "ants," feasts to our hearts, feasts to the longing of those who have the good fortune to love Him.

That is why I say the greatest good fortune is that we have settled for nothing less than the Highest of the High. Nothing else, no one else will do.

TEASING

Sitting at the Meherazad dining table, Mani would often remember Baba's teasing:

> When Baba would joke or tease someone, even the person concerned would not mind; it would be something of delight, and He'd do it with such a twinkle in His eye. It was a life-giving joke; it had so much life in it, bubbling and sparkling. For instance, when He would tease Rano . . .
>
> Usually we women had breakfast and lunch with Baba at the dining table. So one day, we were at the dining table and Baba was being served His food: Naja was bringing food in from the kitchen for Baba, Mehera serving Him, Goher

bringing a glass of water, Meheru bringing a basin for Him to wash in. I was sitting next to Him, to His left (Mehera would sit on His right), and Rano was at the end of the table. After Baba was served, Rano started eating. Baba looked a bit bored, you see, and He looked around and then saw Rano. He looked at me and gave me a light wink, sort of as if to say, "watch this," that kind of thing.

He snapped His fingers, "Rano?" She looked up. "Why do you talk through the nose?"

It was like pressing a button. Rano immediately started in, "Oh, Baba, but I don't talk through the nose. You should hear how people talk through the nose in this certain state in America. This is not talking through the nose . . . " and so on. Baba was very happy and He went on eating with a real twinkle in His eye. He was bored and He wanted something to happen, so He did it just to get a rise out of her, just to have fun. A little thing like that, Baba would enjoy.

We once asked Mani if Baba would "needle" her, as He would most of the other mandali. Of course He wouldn't needle Mehera, and Mani told us that He didn't needle her in that way either. But it was not hard to gather that He didn't let His closest ones off the hook. Baba was very exacting with Mani.

Mani once told us about one day when Baba had been upset or strong with her about something—she didn't say what. She went off very disturbed about it, but said to herself, "Just concentrate on your work; think about the work," and applied herself to some task. Not long after, Baba came in with one of the mandali. With the most innocent face in the world, He asked her, "Would you say I'm *bola*?" Now bola is a wonderful word in Gujerati that means "guileless" or "innocent," as a child is innocent. Mani paused for a moment. "He was bola," she sighed later on, "but I just couldn't give it to Him at that moment." So, instead, she said, "Well, Baba, Mother always said so."

Baba smiled delightedly, and turning to the other disciple, gestured, "See! There you have it!"

HURRY!

So many memorable things happened around the Meherazad dining table. Mani reminisced:

> Baba would want everything fast. I remember one morning we were having breakfast, and I'd just poured the tea into my cup. I also had the radio on, which I played for Baba in the mornings. Anyway, we were just about to begin when Baba turned to me and said, "After you finish breakfast, go and tell Eruch . . ." whatever it was, I forget now. I began pushing back my chair to get up, and Baba said, "Sit down! Sit down! Where's the hurry. Finish the breakfast. Then!" So fine. I sat back down and tried to resume my breakfast.
>
> Baba looked at me and after a few seconds said, "Do you think it will take you a long time to finish?" I said, "Well, no, I can get up . . !"
>
> "Finish. Sit down."
>
> So, now I'm eating in a hurry, trying to finish, and Baba says, "Where's the hurry? Lots of time."
>
> This goes on: I push the chair back, sit down, eat fast, then slow, get up, yes, no . . .
>
> I tell you, it ended up with Baba gesturing, "Hurry up,

hurry up," and "Slowly, slowly" at the same time. One hand was saying, "Hurry up," and the other hand was saying, "Slow, slow, slowly. Where's the hurry?" I didn't know which hand to look at, or what I ate and what I swallowed, and how I went!

Mani said Baba liked everything fast, even the mechanisms that served Him:

> There is a clock in Baba's room in Meherazad, and Rano is the one who sees to all the clocks: puts them to the right time, see that they're wound. She is very correct and particular in everything she does. Very conscientious. So when we were sitting with Baba, she would suddenly look at the clock in Baba's room, and go out and compare the time with the other clocks. Suppose she found that it was fast. Then, while Baba was seated on His bed, Rano would go to the clock on the wall and open it. Seeing this, Baba would snap His fingers, "What are you doing?"
>
> "Well, Baba, this clock is one minute fast."
>
> "Leave it. Leave it alone. You always want to interfere with the clock. Leave it alone."
>
> But if it was one minute slow, and she said, "Baba, it's one minute slow," He'd say, "Yes, yes, put it up. Forward, forward." He wanted it fast, not slow.
>
> That's what's happening now. Fast, forward, forward. After all, didn't Baba say, "It's always a going forward. Always." And now it's going forward fast, fast!

So how appropriate when, into His world of fast-fast, came Flubber:

> Sometimes Baba amazed us by remembering something at a time when we would never have thought of it, when we had completely forgotten about it.

THE LAST TWELVE YEARS   695

The last movie Baba saw, and we were with Him, was "The Absent-Minded Professor". Frank [Fred] MacMurray was an absent-minded professor in the film, and he invents something called Flubber [flying rubber]. He was so absent-minded that while he was in his laboratory working on an experiment, his landlady held a big sign up in front of him that said "YOU ARE GETTING MARRIED TODAY. YOU ARE TO BE AT CHURCH AT 10:00," or something like that.

Flubber was an accidental discovery. He rolled up this substance he'd made that was like rubber, and dropped it. When he dropped it, it started bouncing and his little terrier dog started playing with it. Thus he discovered what he named Flubber. Not rubber, but Flubber.

The story goes on: there were two teams of net ball [basketball] players; one side had players who were all small in stature and the other side had players who were tall. The little ones were helped by putting Flubber under their feet so they could bounce. Every time they jumped, they bounced higher and higher, until they practically put the ball right into the net. It was very funny.

Anyway, a long time had gone by since we'd seen the movie. Then one day we were here in Meherazad and Baba was in His room. He wanted Goher to convey a message to some of the men mandali, so He called for her, and when Goher came, He said, "Now go, go and tell Eruch"—or Kaka or Pendu or whoever she had to go to—a certain message. So she started walking over

Mani with her pal Goher.

to the men's side (she didn't have her little bicycle then), and she'd barely gotten halfway through the garden when Baba said to us, "What's the matter? Goher taking so long?"

"But, Baba, she's only just gone."

"All right."

Then, when she must have reached the Hall, Baba said, "Goher hasn't come yet? Just a little message to give and come back?"

"But, Baba, I mean, she . . ." But we went out and looked. No Goher yet.

At last Goher came back, and when she did, Baba said, "Whatever made you take so long?"

"But, Baba, I did nothing. I just went straight to the mandali, gave your message, and came back. It takes time to walk."

And then Baba said, "What you should have, what you need, is Flubber!"

At first we couldn't catch what He meant because He had no specific sign for the letter "F." It could have been "J," so we first said, "J?"

"No, no." And then we guessed "F, F." then He went on spelling it out, "L, U, B, B, . . ."

"Flubber? . . . Oh, Flubber!"

Then Baba said to Goher, "All you'd need to do is take one jump from here to the men mandali and one jump back."

A TREAT

Mani loved to talk about Baba's ways of detaching them from their desires. He would do it so subtly, so masterfully.

For example, sometimes Baba would tell them days in advance that they were going to be given a treat by someone, a feast. He would keep mentioning it as the day drew nearer, until everyone was totally focused on the delights to come. The day itself would arrive and everyone's thoughts by then were totally on the food. When would it come, what would it be, when would lunchtime ever arrive?

They were all ready, primed. But there was no guarantee that they would get to enjoy it.

Once a Baba-lover wished to treat Baba and them all with *pulao* (a rice dish cooked with spices and meat or vegetables). As usual, Baba got them all eager and excited about it. The day came, and at lunchtime the women sat with Baba at the table waiting for the pulao. Almost at once, Baba started in, "Why hasn't it come? Why is it taking so long?" So, a little tension crept into the atmosphere. At last the treat arrived, and after Baba had been served by Mehera, everyone dished it out onto their plates, where it sat, fragrant and steaming hot. But of course, no one would start eating until Baba did, and He wasn't starting. Instead, He started questioning Naja about whether she had kept some aside for this one and that one; had she kept enough for the servants? Naja said yes, she'd done it all, but Baba kept on asking about it until she brought the pulao vessel in from the kitchen so He could see for Himself what was left.

Meanwhile, that steamy pulao was cooling off—until Baba finally started, at which point it was cold and flat and all the fragrance and special taste was gone. And that was their treat!

DHUN

Baba had several close disciples who, Mani remembered, would offer Him the gift of laughter:

> Baba would call these people to be with Him for a few days, so that they could regale Him with their jokes, their stories, their humour. And that lessened—a little bit—the burden of His work.
>
> There's one person whose gift of laughter to Baba was the most touching. And that was Dhun. Do you all know Dhun, in Ahmednagar? She has a crippled body from progressive muscular dystrophy, which means the disease is always progressing and she's getting worse and worse and worse and worse. The last bit of embroidery she did was a cushion for Baba. She would paint, with her own hand, greeting cards for Baba and Mehera. Once, she sent a card with a rose that she had painted, and that rose was so realistic, I couldn't help marveling at it.
>
> But now she's more and more confined to her chair. She has to lean on a table in order to prop herself up in a sitting position. But she always says, "I have Baba! You don't know what Baba has given me."
>
> And I say, "Dhun, you're really lucky, because you can only depend on Baba."
>
> "Yes, if I were hale and hearty, who knows how far away from Baba I might have been inside."
>
> She's the kind of person who loves pretty things. Even now she chooses what dress to wear, what kerchief to wear to match the dress, which scent to put on, as if she were a young dancer. And yet she can't even sit up by herself. She has to be lifted from her wheelchair onto her bed. She even has to be turned over on her bed when she's lying down. She can barely talk nowadays, because her lips don't meet.

Yet no matter how handicapped she was, she would make these cards and write these humorous letters to Baba. And see how something like that, made with so much effort and love, is accepted by the Lord of Love.

On Baba's Birthday each year, there would be a pile of greetings from His lovers all over the world, India and abroad, placed on His dining table in the morning. There would be telegrams, cables, greeting cards, and letters.

On His Birthday, we would go into Baba's room to meet Him at five minutes before five in the morning, as we were told. There with Baba, we would sing out seven times at the top of our voices, according to His directions, "Avatar Meher Baba ki Jai!" Then with the support of Mehera's arm, wearing a new pink coat (He always had new clothes on His Birthday), Baba would walk to the dining room.

As He came from His room across the hall to the dining room, I would quickly slip into the sitting room, where the gramophone [portable] was ready with a record all set to play, and as Baba was walking by with Mehera and the others, the strains of "Happy Birthday" would follow Him: "Happy Birthday to You, Happy Birthday to You, Happy Birthday my Darling, Happy Birthday to You. From old friends and new, from good friends and true, may good luck be with You, and happiness too." We still play this song on His Birthday.

There on the table would be all these greeting cards and the decorations we had done overnight. First He would have me read out who each card was from. Then later on, either Eruch or I would read out all of the greetings to Baba. He would hear every greeting, every word, whatever His lovers had written to Him with their love.

But at the dining table, He would just say, "All right, call out!" And I would say, "This is from so-and-so, this is from Myrtle Beach Center, here is something from Avatar's Abode, this is from Bill Le Page . . . " You know, like that. And when it came to Dhun's card and I said, "This is from Dhun," Baba would say, "Read, read, read it!" Dhun's letter was read out at the dining table on the Birthday morning itself; it didn't wait for later. He would chuckle and really enjoy it, because Dhun is really very witty. And she would make the whole morning just sparkle with humour and joy.

She has even sung for Baba. Up till two years ago, she would still make these beautiful greeting cards. And now, if she has to write a note, it takes her three days. She says at the bottom, "This took me three days," because she can't move her hand, even with the support of the other arm, as she used to. But how blessed she is. That is when a suffering becomes a blessing.

Which makes me wonder, what is it? What is it that makes her feel that she has received—it's Baba, Baba's love.

MUSIC

Baba loved live music, and especially ghazals sung by good qawwali singers. Mani, another music devotee, was almost as enthusiastic about music as He was. So she well understood His exquisite attention to musical performances, of which they had many in the halls at Meherazad and Guruprasad:

Jaipuri Qawwal entertaining Baba in Mandali Hall, October 1963.

When a good singer would be singing before Baba, the expression and the movement of Baba's body and hands would express the rhythm of the song. And only Baba could explain the true depth of the meaning of a ghazal. He would give us just a tiny glimpse of the depth of those words, and that gave a different shape to the song, a different fire to the song. Which is what ghazals and qawwali singing is all about. The music would come alive in the words.

Jaipuri qawwalis were some of His favourite ghazal singers. Knowing this, Gadjwani [Kishinchand Gajwani], a Baba-lover from Bombay, would arrange for them to come and sing before Baba. First of all, playing just the harmonium and a very few other instruments, they would create that atmosphere of music that just carries you away. It can't be described; it's wonderful.

At such programmes, the men mandali would all be here in the Hall with Baba and the singers, and we women would be sitting out in the lane by this other gate. From there we would look at Baba through the outside window, sitting so that we could just see Baba now and then, and also hear the music.

They would always begin with one song, [and here Mani would sing] "Allah Hu, Allah Hu, Allah Hu . . ." accompanied by the harmonium and other instruments. They would go on repeating that same phrase and yet you never wanted it to stop; it never seemed like repetition.

They were masters at it. And then of course, the Master of masters was seated before them. At times Baba would ask for particular ghazals: "Sing something by Jigar," "Now something by Simab," "Now by Ghalib". . . Their faces would light up because not everywhere are such songs appreciated or commonly understood. Then sometimes Baba would ask for a poet who was rarely heard of, and they would look at each other. This was a challenge. And then they would bring out the song and sing it.

While the qawwali singing was going on, Baba might just clap. And Baba's clap was such that no matter how much sound or music or whatever else was happening, it all stopped when He clapped. You could always hear it. When He clapped, the qawwals wouldn't stop slowly, wind down. They would stop like the clap, suddenly. And then there would be silence, utter silence. And Baba would point out a particular word of the song or just some nuance of pronunciation: "It is not this, it is not *'chala'*, it is *'chali'*." Or something like that.

And the singers would beam. They knew He was right; here was someone who knew, naturally, the one who created the music. Then they would start again with added gusto, with added fervour and fire, and the whole performance would go on. To watch a qawwali sing before Baba was something.

At another time, speaking of singing for Him, Mani mentioned the other side of the story:

Then again there were the best of singers, ones who were very popular all over India; even now you hear them on the radio, they're so good. But they were not Baba's type. If they were brought by someone to sing before Him, He would just tolerate them, just manage to get through part of the programme. One song, now two more, then finished. Yet they were paid to sing for hours.

There's an Irani word, *yakh,* which literally means "ice". When something is yakh, it means it's a joke that has gone wrong, say, when you try to be funny but you're not really. It leaves people cold. Then you're being yakh. Baba's gesture for yakh was His gesture for ice, which was [Mani gestures] something from the heavens, from the sky. The Parsis are Zoroastrians like the Iranis, but they don't know the Irani language, so yakh would mean nothing to them, which is why Baba would use it even in public with us, to let us know exactly how He was feeling at the time.

And so for a certain type of music and singer, Baba would listen lovingly as it went on and on, and look at us and gesture, "Yakh!"

Or if someone's voice wasn't good or not to His liking, He'd gesture, "She seems like she had castor oil." And that person, not knowing, may have nodded, "Yes, yes, Baba!"

That's something that my mother would do. She'd say, very nicely, an Irani word that would fit, that we would understand, but that the person standing before Baba wouldn't know. It would be so hard to keep a straight face. Oh, she'd say it nicely, you know, very nicely!

Speaking of Baba's appreciation, Mani recalled Baba's childlike delight in little things—a story, a flower, a toy—exclaiming in wonder and admiration, "Look at that!" or "Isn't this great!" It reminded Mani of a poem by Francis Brabazon in which he called Baba "The Beautiful Stranger." How true it is in a way, Mani would say, because each Advent when the Ancient One takes form, He meets His earth anew after 700–1,400 years. And, moreover, when God the Reality takes form as Man, He *is* a stranger to illusion, just as light is a stranger to darkness.

Mani was fascinated by certain subjects, subjects that meant something special to her. For instance, we heard quite a bit about sound, a natural topic of interest for someone so musical:

> I've heard Baba speak about sound. One day He suddenly asked us, "Where does all the sound go?"
>
> We looked at each other blankly.
>
> "Where does all this old sound go? It cannot go anywhere. It collects," Baba said.
>
> See how compassionate God is! Even the sounds that we are careless with, like something we say to hurt each other, or the sound of guns booming, or a baby crying, laughter, prayers, any uttered sound, sound that we are so heedless with, cannot go anywhere. Baba says it all collects. It's a force; sound is a force. And there comes a time when all this collected force of sound, Baba said, is used for the destruction of illusion, used constructively for destroying the darkness of illusion.
>
> That is why when we had to say the Parvardigar Prayer, both on the men's side and on the women's side, one of us would read the prayer out and Baba Himself would stand up to participate, as we all did. Baba would say, "Say it aloud. All this that is said will be of benefit to all after I drop My body." He said this in 1968, when we were saying the Prayer.
>
> So even when we sometimes think, "Oh, this praying is so automatic; we're just saying the prayers but our hearts

aren't in it; we're not meaning it," it doesn't matter. The sound of Baba's word, the sound of Baba's Name, the sound itself is of a tremendous importance. In the age-old Hindu tradition which still continues, when a mother is pregnant, they read aloud the Upanishads from the Vedas, from the scriptures, reading out God's Name, because even the child-to-be absorbs it. Sound is a much greater force than we realize. But we just use it as carelessly as we use our lives as human beings.

It is written that in olden times when a particular singer would sing a particular raga, lights would come on where there were no lights. Of course there was no electricity then; the lights were oil lamps. But if the singer was very good, the oil lamps would ignite by themselves. Or when the singer sang another kind of raga, rain would fall. I once asked Baba if such stories were true. He made a face and gestured to convey, "What is so phenomenal about that? That is nothing!" Because sound can do even that when it reaches the heights of expression. But the song must be sung from the heart.

Then Baba told us about a seventh-plane majzoob in Bombay who was completely absorbed in God. Now God arranges and ordains everything so naturally that such great beings, who are divorced from their own gross consciousness, have others around them who maintain and protect their bodies, as a majzoob would automatically drop his body if it was not taken care of.

So this majzoob had such people revolving around him who loved him and took care of him. He would be lying down, apparently unconscious, apparently asleep, because he was not conscious of his gross surroundings. His eyes would be closed and he would lie inert. Now how can you look after an inert person? You have to feed him, wash him, and so on.

Well, in that same place there was a fakir who used to walk up and down that same street. These fakirs usually sing for their alms; they don't beg. They have bowls with them and as you pass by, you can put something in the bowl if you like. They sing a lot, and usually very beautifully.

I still remember one who used to go down our alley in Poona when I was a child, singing in a very, very warm and beautiful voice.

So these people looking after the majzoob would call the fakir and ask him to sing before the majzoob. In that lovely voice of his, he would sing, sing, sing and sing, and as he kept on singing, the majzoob would open his eyes and sit up. His caretakers had everything ready for his care: water and soap for a bath, milk and food, and so on. And as he sat up—quick, quick, each one would tend to him, like mechanics working on a car: one would wash him, one would brush his hair, one would feed him. And all the while the fakir would keep on singing.

When they had washed and fed him, they would give a sign and the fakir would gradually slow down the song, and the majzoob would slowly slowly sink back into his apparent sleep.

Baba said that sound could do that. If it can affect a majzoob, what about life's dream?

But, Baba said, it was not only the voice that mattered; you had to sing from the heart. He again stressed this to us when He asked us to repeat the Seven Names of God: "Sing from the heart!"

HIS ACCEPTANCE

Mani remembered:

> When Baba tells you to do something, then it's very easy to do. But when Baba tells you to do it for somebody else . . . ! For instance, we have seen those who have come to see Baba with a gift for Him, a beautiful shawl, money, whatever. They're very happy; they've got something for Baba. And Baba accepts the gift by saying, "I'm very happy. It's your love and I accept it with love." Then sometimes He would say, "I accept it, and you keep it. You use it." Or "You keep it for My work; you will know what to do with it."
>
> But sometimes He would say, "I'm very happy, I accept it, now give it to so-and-so, the person sitting there." You haven't gotten it for that person. And, if it's money, maybe you even know that that person doesn't need this money and will just squander it! You have really saved, and brought your savings with all love for Baba, and Baba's telling you to give it to someone else.
>
> We've seen that face that was offering something to Baba with such joy suddenly turn flat. "Oh, give it to him? Give it to Barry? OK." But you see, the real thing was: he wasn't giving it to Barry. Baba was giving it, because Baba had already accepted it. It is no longer yours when you have given it to Baba. There should be no strings, absolutely nothing attached to a gift for Him. Now it was for Baba to do what He liked. He is Lord, He is Master, He can give it to a scoundrel, He can

give it to a worthy person, He can give it to a needy person; that is no one's business, because HE is giving it.

And the very fact that Baba has accepted the gift is a big thing. Because Baba didn't always accept things offered to Him. I still remember one day we women were at lunch with Baba and Mehera had made Him a glass of orange juice. Now nothing could be gotten from the bazaar without Baba's permission. Everything went through Him, and only what had gone through Him could be bought. Well, we were a bit devious this time; Goher had got some oranges for Baba, and Mehera had made the orange juice with her own hands. She made it very lovingly; it was sort of a surprise.

Now the glass of orange juice is put before Baba. And Baba says, "What is this?"

"Oh," Mehera says, "Baba, this is some orange juice. You know Goher [as His doctor] says it's good for You. And I made it."

"Goher? Call her."

So Goher comes. "What is this orange juice thing?"

Goher says, "Oh, Baba, it's really . . . well, You need it and Mehera. . . ." So Goher says Mehera said it, and Mehera says Goher said it. And Baba says, "How much did it cost?"

She says, so much a dozen for the oranges, I don't know what the price was at that time, but, say, five rupees a dozen.

"Five rupees a dozen? You people have no idea about economy! You don't know where the money comes from, you have no appreciation of how expensive everything is, how hard all this is; it's running not just on air, it all costs . . ." and this and that. Oh, Baba makes such an issue out of it! And we sit there listening and then Baba says, "Today I will have it because Mehera has made that orange juice for Me. But this is not to happen again!"

"Oh, no, never, never!"

We make up our minds, never are we going to give a surprise like that to Baba again. And then the whole issue blows over and everything is fine.

Then later in the morning, Baba goes over to be with the men mandali as usual. In the afternoon I go over there for some work. Standing there, I see that some Eastern Baba-lovers have come, close followers. They are seated in the Hall along with the mandali. Baba is asking them with concern: how is the family, how is your work getting on, how about this, how are you doing that . . . Because Baba is asking, it comes out that a man is really in need of financial help. Having gotten that out of him, Baba turns around and says, "Ring the bell. Call Goher." Goher is called. Baba says, "Bring five hundred rupees and give to him."

And I'm watching this drama. I've watched the morning drama and now I'm watching this afternoon drama. Five rupees was too much for a glass of orange juice for Baba, and now five hundred rupees—just like that [Mani snaps her fingers], "Give it to him."

Baba meeting with a family in the Hall.

Baba's ways are so different. So many purposes are served with every act of His. On the one hand it is the shaping and molding that mattered. On the other, it is something else.

So I said to myself, "Oh, five hundred rupees was

nothing, but five rupees was too much." [And here Mani laughed.]

On another occasion, a lady came from Nagpur, who had seen a vision of Baba, maybe it was a dream, I don't remember. But it was so clear: Baba was before her and she lost her heart to Him. And now she wanted to surrender to Him, to give everything to Him.

So she came here and Baba received her with much love, and gave her of Himself. Then she said, "And I have brought everything to give to you."

Baba said, "What is it?"

"Seventy thousand rupees."

Once again I happened to be in the Hall, and hearing this I said to myself, "Boy, all our monetary troubles are over now!" You know, now we can have orange juice, anything!

Baba looked with such love at her and said, "You've touched My heart. I've accepted it. But you keep it, you take it back."

I couldn't believe it!

She said, "But what shall I do with it?" And Baba replied, "You will know. You will know what to do with it. Take it with you. But I have accepted it."

But He didn't take it.

On the other hand, with His very close ones, those who had money, He would just say, "You put in so much for this work. So-and-so wants to publish a book of Mine. You, you give him the money for it." That's it, flat!

This reminded Mani of a story about Sai Baba, one of Baba's Perfect Masters:

When Sai Baba asked for money from His close ones—

"What have you got in your pocket?"—you might bring out everything but, say, one rupee, thinking that it might be useful later on. But Sai Baba would sit and wait till that rupee also came out and your whole pocket was bare! He'd take money from you and then give it to this one particular person who was serving Him. That person didn't really need money, he had so much already, but he just kept accepting it (and was probably there for that reason—just a thought).

One day, someone remonstrated, "Why do you take from them all and give to this man?"

Sai Baba replied, "What do you do when you sweep a room and collect all the dust? You put it in the garbage box, right? Well, he's my garbage box. I take away all this dirt from others and I put it in the garbage box."

Mani laughed at that, "Their ways are unfathomable!"

Speaking of Baba's acceptance of offerings, Mani would say that Baba forgets our faults, He forgets our weaknesses, but He never forgets our little efforts of love:

We've seen Him make such big issues out of people who have done something so little, that we've been amazed.

There was a lady who was helped quite a lot materially by Baba through His disciples. One morning, she came to Baba with a pot of curry for Baba's lunch that she had made with her own hands. All right, so had others! We looking on felt this was nothing to give to Baba, knowing how much Baba had helped this person on the material side. But Baba made a big thing out of it for her efforts, for her love, saying, "Oh, curry for Me! You made it with your own hands!"

"Yes, Baba."

"Mmmm! Mehera, look, she brought this curry, and she

made it with her own hands! What time did you get up, because you have come here early morning."

"Oh, Baba, at half past four . . ."

"Look! She got up so early in the morning to make this curry for Me!"

And here I am, knowing the other side, and it's blowing my mind to watch Baba make so much of it, "Oh, she's made this curry, she's made this curry . . !" And I kept saying to myself, "So what!"

But then Baba alone can see right through the action to the love with which she must have prepared that curry. That none of us could see. For example, Baba, who had, as a person, the highest of tastes for music and for everything, would sit and listen attentively to His lovers singing songs in cracked voices, or to somebody who had no ear for music and sang the notes all wrong.

Or someone who couldn't compose would say, "Baba, I've made this song for You, shall I sing it?" Baba would say yes, and we would groan inside, "Aw, she's going to start that again!" And Baba would show not only utmost patience, but He would turn around to us and say, "Isn't that good! Isn't that lovely!" And we'd say to ourselves, "Oh no, that's going to encourage her all the more to sing another song!"

And yet, when there would be that wonderful qawwali music sung before Baba, with the highest of words from poets like Hafiz and poets of other times, that music with a tempo and rhythm that's quite its own, Baba would be so discriminating, so all-knowing. But when His lovers offer something that's so broken, so discoloured, but from the heart—well, the deeper from the heart, the more He accepts it.

Or somebody would send in reams of poetry that he had

written in one hour, pages and pages of it. You can't write poetry just like that, in one hour! But he would write, "Baba, it's for You!" And poor Eruch would sit and read it all out to Baba, and as he read the poems out, Baba would say, "Oh, so good! Isn't that wonderful, eh? Just look at it! Just see!"

To my ears it was junk. I'd groan inwardly, "Baba says it's so good and He'll probably have Eruch write and tell the man Baba liked it very much, and the guy will print the poems, and everywhere people will ask, 'This is poetry?!'"

You see, I would think, "See how Baba overlooks our faults; He has such patience." But Baba doesn't just overlook. He looks through. We always see the surface. It was no good as poetry—there's no getting away from the fact—but that was the outward, the surface of the Ocean. Baba was seeing through and through, deep down, as only He could see. And He must have seen the love with which those verses were written.

MEHERA'S SPECIAL ROLE

Soon after Mehera's passing, Mani wrote to a Baba-lover about something that happened in these later years at Meherazad, an incident that reemphasized Mehera's unique role among them, the role of "number one" among the women with Baba:

> Awareness of Mehera's most special place in His Heart and work was given to His disciples by Baba from the earliest years. Hence, veneration for Mehera is not a newborn sentiment since she has gone to Baba. It is a continuation of the

A happy portrait of Baba and Mehera in Meherazad garden.

love and reverence accorded to Mehera over the years by her companions and the world of Baba-followers.

Moreover, her very role in this Avataric Age entitles Mehera to worldwide recognition in time to come. Clues to the fulfillment of this destiny have been given to us by Beloved Baba now and then, in a natural manner, on some occasion or another. When telling Gulmai (as far back as the '20s) that Mehera was His Radha, Baba was in fact declaring Mehera's ordained role as His chosen counterpart: same as Radha, Sita, Mary, and others in previous Advents.

Baba gave indications of the stature and dimension of Mehera's role in simple ways and through natural situations apparently created by Him for the purpose. The star role in one such instance was played by Baba's favourite pet dog, Mastan, a huge gentle giant looked after by Mehera. Just the sight of him was enough to scare the neighbouring villagers and shepherds, and therefore Mastan was usually tied up.

One morning Mehera took Mastan on his leash for a little stroll in the adjoining field, while some distance away a villager was grazing his cattle. Mastan started barking and the frightened villager picked up a rock, threatening Mastan, who had gotten free of his leash with a single jerk. Mehera ran to Mastan's defense just as the villager's rock came flying at Mastan, narrowly missing Mehera. There was a great commotion as we ran out to Mehera: our gardener and Meheru grabbed the man, and Mastan was brought indoors. The culprit, who happened to be a cousin to one of our servants, was brought before Baba in Mandali Hall. Baba heard his version, and Meheru was also called to give her account. The culprit received a slap from his cousin at Baba's command, and rubbed his nose at Baba's feet. Thus Baba brought the young man's guilt home to him, and then pardoned him—as was His way. Before the final curtain, while the repentant young man stood in tears in front of Baba, Eruch's ringing voice was heard interpreting Baba's gestures as Baba looked very sadly at this young man, who in his ignorance had lifted a hand against one whom he should have knelt down to. Baba said to him, "Have you any idea what you did? You flung a stone towards this lady whom all the world will worship some day!"

MANI IN AND OUT OF FAVOR

While gathered in the Hall, someone once asked Mani if the favor Baba showed her as a child, as His little sister, diminished as she grew up:

> No, it didn't diminish, but I've had it very strict. I've had to do very difficult things all my life. Personally, I haven't had a scolding from Baba except once in a while, not as I've seen with some of the others, no. But as I said, it's been very hard. Tough. Yes, very.
>
> But you know, there are many instances that Rano talks about, or Meheru or Khorshed or Naja, when Baba would do something to get a rise out of them. Somehow, I haven't had that from Baba, except on certain occasions. But sometimes when I've slipped and done something, even inadvertently, that's made Baba even a little displeased, just that was more than enough for me, more than enough. To see Baba displeased with you was punishment for any of us. To see Baba pleased with you, with anything that you did, was like heaven.

Then someone asked Mani for an example of an incident when she did something that displeased Him ("Just a small example; we know you were a good girl most of the time, Mani!"), and she replied:

I'll tell you an instance when it was something Baba wanted done to please Mehera. Now, I was very quick on the uptake where Baba was concerned; as I say, we grew to be very sensitive to Baba's pleasure and what He wanted. In this instance, someone had painted a picture of Baba that Baba showed to Mehera in His bedroom. Mehera was there first with Him, as usual, and Baba wanted to see how she liked the painting. If she would say, "Very nice," then Baba would be all praise for it.

You see, Baba would very often see to one's own inclination—say, if someone asked Him what career he or she should take up. And just like we would be sensitive to Baba's pleasure or likes, so Baba would see to Mehera's. At least in the latter years; before that, in the earlier times, she went through the rough, too, very much so! But this incident I'm talking about took place later on.

Mehera obviously liked the painting, so Baba said, "Very good. Now Mehera, isn't it nice?" "Oh, yes," said Mehera, but she indicated that others would not feel the same way about it as Baba and she did.

"Oh, yes," said Baba, "Mani? Oh, she'll like it. You just watch."

So I'm called and I come in from the outer door. Baba's sitting with Mehera on His right, and with His left eye Baba gives me a very light wink. I'm immediately aware that I have to be on my toes about something. I'd better be quick.

Baba says, "Look at this painting. Eh? How do you like it?" And I know what Baba wants me to say, so I say, "Baba, it's good. Mehera, who did that painting?"

So she says, "Well, it says here," and I read the signature. Then Baba says, "Mehera, didn't I tell you? Didn't I tell you she'd like it so much?"

I'm very pleased with myself. Now it's over and I'm off-guard, mind you. In the meantime Rano comes in. Mehera had mentioned that Rano wouldn't like the painting either. "Oh," says Baba. "Wait."

Now either Rano didn't catch His wink, or Baba didn't give her a sign; I don't know. But Rano comes in and she's looking at the painting. Now that I see my part is over, I'm relaxed and I'm looking with interest at the painting.

"Well . . ." says Rano. She puts on her specs and looks closely. "Well, the eyes . . ."

I jump right in, "That's it! It's the eyes that are not right. It's the eyes . . ." And the moment I say that, oh, I wish the floor would open up and swallow me!

Baba just looks at me. He doesn't say a thing. He doesn't berate me; that look is enough.

Ah, fool that I was.

Mani and Mehera posing together.

Mani would sometimes talk of Mehera trimming Baba's mustache. He was talked into trimming His long mustache of the early years by the Westerners when He first went to the West, to make it more "fashionable." So, Mehera would trim it after that. As with every little thing she ever did for Baba, she put great attention and care into the task. But the results would vary; getting the length of the two sides even was not easy. So when the first trim was done, Baba would turn to Mani: how did it look? Then it would start: Mani would look very closely at Mehera's handiwork and then point out that the left side needed to be just a shade shorter. Mehera would cut it. Again Baba would turn to Mani—oops—now the right side needed to be a little shorter. After a few more passes at the mustache, Baba would throw up His hands, "Enough, or between you two I'll have no mustache left!"

WITH BABA IN THE HALL

There were many of what Mani spoke of as Baba's "simple sermons" in Meherazad:

> At times some profound message was given by Baba in a very casual, light-hearted way, that reached our understanding later on. This was so in the case of our cocker spaniel, Peter.
>
> So this is the story of a little dog, one of the lucky dogs that were with Baba. Among all His dogs, Baba would say Mastan, a beautiful Tibetan mastiff mix, was number one, and Peter, a saucy, wise cocker spaniel, all black with curly hair and long, floppy ears, was number two.
>
> Peter and Mastan both spent their life with Baba. You see, there were also dogs in Baba's mandali, four-legged mandali, who had all the strict rules and everything like His two-legged mandali did. Mastan was Mehera's, and Peter was

Mastan with his beloved Master.

in my care. They were both with Baba over twelve years. In India, twelve years is a spiritual length of time, to be in exile, or with a master, or undergoing penance. That's how long these two four-legged mandali were with Him.

Mastan was usually tied up, but Peter was free to wander around, so wherever Baba went, Peter would go along with Him. When Baba went over to the men mandali in Mandali Hall, Peter would trot along behind Baba's lift chair, or in front of Him rather. He would be so impatient to get there; he'd look back at Baba as if to say, "When are you coming over? Come on, come on!" And then he'd trot a little way ahead and look back again, "Are you following? Are you coming?" And he'd go right inside the Hall along with Baba, happily panting, to be with Him there.

Now, when Baba went to the Hall, we knew He'd be

back, say, in a couple of hours, so we had better get everything done in the meantime—quick quick quick—before Baba returned. You had to do all those little things that Baba had designated to you, plus your personal things if there was a chance. So we women would be doing our little duties and chores, a constant meditation always with one eye on the clock, "Oh, I must do this; Baba will be coming back and that isn't finished," and so on. In the midst of all this, Goher and I would also be listening for a bell, which meant that Baba was calling either her or me.

There were two brass hand bells that were kept at the entrance of the Hall. One was a little bigger and the sound of that bell meant, Baba wants Goher. The sound of the little bell meant, Baba wants Mani. The bigger bell would go *TONONG, TONONG, TONONG, TONONG,* and Goher would go. Or the little bell—*teneng, teneng, teneng, teneng*—and I would drop whatever I was doing and rush over.

Mehera might be preparing soup for Baba at those times when He was not taking meals as He should, and Goher's bell might mean, "Is the soup ready? Goher, bring the soup." Then Goher would cycle over to the Hall on her little bicycle, her "circular legs," with the soup in one hand (quite a circus trick) that Mehera had prepared with such care. She would cycle right up to Baba's chair with the soup, or whatever.

Now I used to be typing the Family Letters, or letter writing, or doing something at my table in my little "open-air office," the small verandah of the cottage near the Hall. My bell was littler because I was nearer.

One day as I was sitting at my desk writing—*teneng, teneng, teneng*— the bell rang, my bell. "Oh, Baba wants me!" so I dropped whatever I was doing and came over to the Hall.

There was Baba seated in His chair, as usual, with the men around him. Eruch was reading out letters, someone else had the "bogus news" (the newspaper) ready to be read out, and there was Peter lying at Baba's feet, snoring away.

Peter was a big showoff, a real ham. (He loved to be photographed; he would have loved this videoing session more than anything!) And he was very human in many ways. One of those ways was, when he slept, he snored! Just like a person!

I used to read aloud to Baba in His bedroom, a Rex Stout book or an Edgar Wallace or an Agatha Christie, or a Wodehouse, or any of Baba's favourite books sent to us by Margaret Craske. (She supplied all the reading material over these years for Baba from America.) In the middle of the reading to Baba one day, suddenly I heard somebody snoring. I couldn't believe it. Who's snoring? Nobody would dare snore in front of Baba! I covertly looked around. Was it Naja? No, it wasn't Naja. Everybody's eyes were wide open. Then who? Tracing the sound in my mind, I suddenly saw Peter under a chair, snoring away.

So, that morning, Baba called me to the Hall and, pointing to Peter snoring, said with mock exasperation and a twinkle in His eyes, "Look! Look at him!" I looked, and we all chuckled. I didn't know what Baba wanted, so I asked, "Baba, shall I bring the leash and take him away?"

"No, no," said Baba. "Leave him, leave him. But look what I have to put up with. Here is Eruch trying to read letters to Me and here is Peter snoring his head off! Leave him alone. And go." So there was a laugh, and I went.

Two or three days later again the bell went *teneng, teneng, teneng,* and I came over to the Hall. This time

Francis was reading his beautiful ghazals for Baba, and Baba was listening. And the same scene: Peter sleeping at Baba's feet. "Look at Peter," said Baba. "Look at that!" Again we looked. But this time Peter wasn't snoring. He was fast asleep, but he was dreaming. And his legs were going very, very fast, and he was wagging his paws very fast and hard. Now Peter would make a squeaky sound when he was terribly excited, when he used to chase a squirrel or something, and he was making that squeak.

And he was so excited that he was frowning. Now when he frowned, he couldn't put up his ears, a cocker can't, so he would bring them straight forward and they'd hide his eyes, like that famous old-time actress Carole Lombard, who always had her hair over one eye. I was watching and Baba was saying, "Look at him!" and Peter was going *squeak squeak squeak*, and moving his legs like a machine.

"He thinks," said Baba, "that he's running fast. He thinks that somebody's chasing him, some wild animal, or he thinks he's chasing some wild animal. It's like he's going up mountains, crossing mountains, crossing deserts, always traveling and he's chasing, and he's so excited, and yet," said Baba, "he's not doing any of those things. He is lying safe and sound at My feet.

"But what he experiences in the dream now, he thinks he's doing all those things, he's running, chasing, frightened. He's not, he's not doing anything. And all this he's going through, so much action, so much emotion, and yet all the time he's lying safe and sound at My feet. All this movement, all that he's doing is just a dream. He's safe and sound at My feet."

Then Baba sent me off. At the moment, I thought it was Baba's humour. But when I recollected His words and reflected on them, I thought, Baba has just given me the most beautiful discourse about all the dreaming that we are doing. We think it is so real. We should always remember that we're safe and sound at His feet, that we're so secure, and that is why He tells us, "Don't worry. Be happy." He knows that we are safe and sound at His feet. And He tells us, "Don't worry," not like a doctor giving us advice or a parent giving us consolation. He's telling us that from His Knowledge, His infinite Knowledge, His knowing. He knows that there's nothing to worry about.

He could get into Peter's dream and tell him again and again, "Peter, don't worry. It's all right." But Peter wouldn't know that until he awoke and found he was safe and sound at Baba's feet.

From the first, Peter was safe and sound with Baba; when the women first got him as a little puppy, once or twice he crawled up onto Baba's gaadi during a reading session and fell fast asleep in Baba's lap, indeed safe and sound. Now *that* is a lucky dog!

༶

TOUCHED PHOTOS

Baba would call Mani to Mandali Hall for a number of things. One had to do with her task as photo-distribution walli:

One reason for my being present before Baba in Mandali Hall was that I would bring Baba packets of His photos to be individually touched by Him and then, as directed by Him, sent to His lovers in the West: America, England, Australia, and Europe.

At that time, Baba-lovers in the West used to order Baba's pictures, which Baba had my brother Beheram make in his little darkroom in Poona, and send to me. Each would be touched by Baba and then I would post them by mail to different people who would distribute them.

At first in America I sent them to Beryl Williams, and later on, after she passed away, to other Baba-lovers. So Beryl would write me, "So-and-so wants this picture of Baba, this size . . ." and Beheram would make the picture accordingly. Then Baba would want me to show the pictures to Him, and He would touch them.

See the contact. No matter how casually you might think Baba was doing something, it had a universal effect, which we can see now more than ever. Look at the connection that was being made through those touched pictures: even though His lovers could not come and see Baba at that time, He laid cables to them in this way.

So the procedure for His touching the photos was: the photos would arrive and when the chance came, I would bring them to Baba in the Hall. Baba would look up and see me coming and ask, "What is it?" I would reply, "Photos, Baba."

"Bring them over."

And then, going up to Him, I would take out each picture, read out the name of the person who it was for, and Baba would take it, hold it, and look at it.

Sometimes He would hold up His own photo and say to the men, "I look so good! Eh, Francis, Eruch, Bhau, see? See? Francis, isn't that a good picture? Isn't that nice? Do you like it?" and they'd reply, "Yes, Baba. Very nice."

Baba in His chair in Mandali Hall.

Once there was a picture of Babajan in the batch. Knowing the love with which Baba would speak of Babajan, I was not surprised when He bowed to Her picture. Sometimes He even bowed to one of His own pictures, to the Godhood in there.

Later on [in the late 1960s], when Baba was not well, you could feel the burden He was under, the burden of the world, of His work. One day when He was not feeling well and seated here in the Hall with the men mandali, I came over with a whole box full of beautiful photos. But seeing His condition, I didn't have the heart to bother Him with touching them. Now I realise that He wanted them touched, because it was something from Him to His lovers. When I entered He immediately turned and asked, "Yes, what is it?"

"Baba," I said, "it's quite all right. I've come with some pictures to touch but it's . . ."

"Bring."

So I brought them over. I just opened the cover of the box, and Baba put His hand on the top photo and touched it.

I said, "Fine" and turned to go. Halfway out of the Hall, a thought came to me. In my mind, He had touched one picture. But what about the others? I turned back and said, "Baba, it's all right, isn't it, for me to write that You have touched every picture?" Because that's what I would usually write to Beryl and the others. "It's all right if I say that You have touched all the pictures although You only touched the top one?"

Baba looked at me and very empathically nodded, "Yes, yes," and He called me back. So I held out the box to Him. Then He said something I've never forgotten. He said, "If I touch this pile of photos with just one finger," and He did that, "not only are all the photos touched, but all the space between the photos and the floor, and all the space beneath the ground..." And maybe down on through to the other side of the world!

And it gave me a glimpse of a horizon that's beyond us. The feeling I had was of magnificent majesty: just His one finger covering all. His grace, His bounty, His Love is so vast, so big it more than covers everything. We, with our little ants' eyes, all we can see is the surface.

In the same way, if that bounty is so unlimited, then when Baba has placed His feet in the ocean at Myrtle Beach, or Baba has washed His hands in the river in Jabalpur, or Baba has dipped into that bay that Eruch tells you about near Bombay, then that water is forever touched. His bounty is never limited, never bounded; it covers everything.

Mani would tell another story, an amusing one, about Baba's touch. One time Max Haefliger from Switzerland sent a 2"x 2" picture to Baba of a mountain there called Fallenfluh, where Baba had sat in seclusion for His Work in 1934. Max had said to Mani in his accompanying letter, "Could you show this to Baba and find out the exact spot where He sat and let me know?" as Baba had gone off alone to the spot where He had secluded Himself.

These kind of things would be attended to through letters in those days. We were sitting for breakfast at the dining table with Baba as He was finishing His tea. Mehera was standing behind His chair, preparing to comb His hair, which she would do so gently and lovingly that each beautiful strand seemed to receive her personal attention. I opened the mail. Max's letter was in it, so I said, "Baba, Max wants to know on which spot You sat in seclusion on Fallenfluh."

Baba seemed pleased to comply with the request. He looked at the photo of Fallenfluh as I showed it to Him. "Very nice. Yes, yes."

I went on, "But Baba, he wants to know where You sat.

"Yes," Baba said, and He just put His thumb on the picture, covering the whole mountain! It was a small picture, you see.

"Oh, but Baba," I said, thinking maybe He hadn't heard me right, "Where? Where did You sit?"

He looked at me, surprised and said, "I just showed it to you. I just did it." And again He put His thumb on the picture. And then I realised that the whole mountain is where Baba sat. His presence is unlimited. How we limit it;

we say, "Just on this little spot." But it was very very beautiful the way Baba indicated, "I showed you: all over."

So Mani wrote to Max, "Baba was sitting all over Fallenfluh."

Here is another Mandali Hall memory of Mani's:

> Once I came over to the Hall with some work and saw Baba seated in His chair, looking bowed down, weary, and tired. You could see He was suffering. He said to the men, "I'm going earlier today, to retire to My room. I'm feeling very weak."
>
> As He said that, Eruch and Francis both hurried forward to help Baba up from His chair. As they came, one on each side of Baba, Baba put His hands in their hands. And then, I swear, all Baba did was just move a finger of each hand with a little jerk.
>
> Before you knew it, these strong men, Francis and Eruch, were almost falling over! It was so funny to watch their efforts not to fall on Baba! I couldn't believe I was in time to see it.
>
> Then they recovered, and Francis looked at Baba, amazed. "Oh Baba! You're strong!"
>
> And Baba said, "Don't you forget it!"
>
> Then the next minute, "Help Me up."
>
> In that way, in those moments when we were so at home with Him, say in the middle of a game, when we felt His humanness so much that we had forgotten His Godness, He would remind us, "Remember, I'm God."
>
> On the other hand sometimes when we were very serious and aware of His Godness, maybe after a discourse or a statement that He had made, He would remind us that He is man.
>
> In this instance of Francis and Eruch, He did both! He first reminded them, "I'm man, I'm so weak." And when

they went to help Him up, they realized it was they who were weak and He who was strong: "Don't you forget it!"

That's one of my most delightful stories.

We realized at the time that all these chances were the little opportunities He gave us. He would say, "My health is not good, very weak, I don't know how I'll manage this or that," and that was an opportunity for us to help Him. We put out our hands, so Baba held them so that we could lift Him up from the chair, so we could serve Him. We would think, "We can do this for Him, we can do that for Him," but really it was He giving us those precious opportunities.

FAST TYPING

Once, in the Hall, Mani described a small event that gave her a big lesson in service:

> Another little thing that happened here in Meherazad shows how, when you are working for Him, He is working on you. As I always say, His work is each one of us: you, us, all His lovers. We are His real work. But while He allows us to work for Him, He is working on us.
>
> Now what happened was, one morning I was called to

the Hall. The little hand bell for Mani rang and I came over. Baba had been dictating something to Eruch, who had written it out very fast and furiously on his letter board [a type of clipboard]. And I understood at once that there was some typing that I had to do.

So Baba says, "How quickly will you be able to do it [the typing]?" Well I feel very happy. Baba has called me over to give me some special work, saying, "I need it fast." And I know I'm a fast typist. Baba Himself had shown off about me to others, "My sister, so fast!" So here is something that is needed instantly, and I can do it! So I'm very happy. I take the writing and say, "Baba, in a very short time I'll bring it back."

Now even as I'm taking this circular to the little cottage where my desk is, I'm thinking furiously, "Now I'll get the typewriter out, and use such-and-such paper, the carbon paper is there, all I have to do is one-one-one copy, remember to put the shiny side this way . . . " and so on. All this is going on inside my mind, so that no time is wasted. I go to the desk, and in a split second the typewriter is on the table and the paper is out. I'm just putting the carbon in and getting it straight so the wind doesn't blow it . . .

Mani working on her fast typing.

And suddenly the bell rings. [Here Mani imitates the sound of a bell ringing.] I put the paper away and run to the Hall. "Yes, Baba?" And yet I'm like a race horse, just champing at the bit to start typing. Baba then speaks of something totally irrelevant to the subject, something that would seem trivial, you know, maybe He asks about something that has nothing to do with what happened a few minutes ago, or with anything really important at all, as far as I can see. So I listen, and then Baba says, "Now you can go."

So I go. I'm still on the up and up. So I say to myself, "Never mind, now I'll do this and this . . ." and I get the paper out, I put it into the typewriter, turn the platen roll, space the line and am about to begin, just ready to race away . . .

The bell rings. I can't believe it! So I stop, and now I'm a little bit agitated, but I come to the Hall, "Yes, Baba?" Again it's something not applicable, something trivial from my angle. And I can't believe it. I say, "Yes, Baba, yes." Now I'm a little impatient. "Yes."

"You heard Me?"

"Yes, Baba."

"Go, go type."

So I go back. And then it happens a third time: the bell rings. Now I haven't got that fizz anymore about the typing work. I'm like flat beer. But inside I'm quite stirred up. So I go to the Hall and again the same thing: Baba brings up something seemingly irrelevant. But this time when He says, "Go," and I turn to go, He asks, "Have you finished the typing?"

That's when I explode! "How can I finish the typing, You haven't even given me a chance, I haven't even started. . . !"

"It's all right, all right, all right, don't get excited. All right. Do it as fast as you can. Now go!" And I go. And then I'm at my normal temperature when I begin to type.

I realised later that He was getting a rise out of me. He was doing it purposefully. As He said, "All right, all right! What's all the excitement about? Don't get angry! Calm!"

And the marvelous part is that I really finished pretty quickly after that, without all that steam [here Mani imitates panting]. And without a mistake, too! So He helps in that way also.

I thought afterwards, look what Baba's telling me: that we mustn't even put His work above Him. He comes first, above everything. Everything else follows. He must be above His own work. Because we can get so involved in the work that we lose sight of Him.

Remembering Baba is so important, Mani used to say:

Baba wants you to think of Him. He doesn't mind which way you do it. I still remember an incident with Dr. Ben Hayman's daughter, who had recognized Baba. I corresponded with her and she once wrote something that I read out to Baba, "Every time something happens, I call out to Baba. I keep calling out to Baba, and afterwards I feel so guilty because I'm—I'm bothering Him."

When I read this out to Baba, He said, "Hmmm. Very good. Tell her, tell her to keep calling. Doesn't matter when it is. Keep calling. Doesn't bother Me at all. I like it."

GIVING AND ACCEPTING

In later years, after a Baba-film was shown in Mandali Hall—in which one could see Baba giving alms to the poor, or darshan to thousands—Mani would reminisce:

> When God works as Man, He releases the spiritual through the material. Baba's every action had a spiritual import, a far-reaching import hidden from us. We could only see the material side of His working.
>
> Like when Baba helped the poor with His own hands. When the poor programmes were arranged, as wished and directed by Him a number of poor people would be brought to Baba. And Baba, with His own hands, would give them grain, blankets, and/or clothes.
>
> That is what we could see Him giving. And these were not lasting things. They would finish, would wear out after a time. After all, there are many organizations and missionary societies that give outer help, which is limited only to the material. But what would never finish, what would never wear off, is what Baba gave through that outer help on a spiritual level. That blessing was unseen, wrapped up in these outer actions that we could see.
>
> For example, Baba would wash the feet of the poor people that He had brought to Him, those gnarled feet, those young feet, so that these poor would receive His inner help. What was He washing away? It was not just the feet He washed, not just the dust He washed away.
>
> And not only did He give the benefit of His help and spiritual blessing to them, but also through them. A grain of rice given by Him specifically to a person would not just be for that person; it would benefit millions of others

THE LAST TWELVE YEARS 735

in time to come as He had planned. Looking on during these darshan programmes, we got a feeling of majesty and unboundedness. But we could not see what was given, where it reached, how it will flower, how it will benefit. So Baba, when He gave, was not just giving the thing we saw Him giving. Silently hidden in that gift is the Real Giving.

You must have seen in Baba-films how during the darshans, when thousands came to offer their homage, offer their love, they would file past Him and bow down to His feet one by one. And He would make this gesture of acceptance. He would be doing this: bowing and then accepting. There's another gesture that you only see in particular films—I marked it the other day—that you think is the same gesture but this time He's doing this [Mani demonstates a slightly different gesture]. This is the gesture for giving.

Baba's unique gesture of acceptance.

So when He is receiving, accepting, it's not just the people's homage and love He's taking on Himself. That acceptance means He's taking on their burdens, everything they are. So He's taking upon Himself, unto Himself, with this gesture, and then giving of Himself, giving of His Love with the other.

. . .

On another occasion, Mani elaborated on the theme of Baba's work:

When Baba would have poor programmes for those from the village of Pimpalgaon or those from Arangaon, if He was in Meherabad, or wherever He was, there was a pattern to the programme. He would specify a certain number. Then He would say, only the very poor, the beggars; another time He would say only boys. Another time He would say only the very old. And He would specify what He would give them: blankets and grain, money and clothes, and so on. The men mandali would make the arrangements and Baba would wash the feet of each one, bow down to each one, and give the items He had specified.

But was it really giving just a blanket and grain and a shirt? How long would that blanket last? Is He here to do what missionaries and organizations all over the world are doing? And not even making a dent in the poverty that they think they're really seeing to? Is Baba here for that? No. Baba, by giving those things, is giving so much! The items are a covering, a means, a box, a wrapping through which He is giving something that we cannot see. And that something is not only going to the person who is taking it in his hand, but through that person representing His work, to so many. His is such a wide, unlimited, unbounded scope.

That is why Baba says, "Do what I say, don't do what I do!" You understand? You might think, "Ah, Baba gave blankets to the village, now tomorrow I'll give blankets to the village." But it's not going to do anything. As I say, at this time there are more organizations, more kindheartedness than ever being organized into establishments to help the poor. Have they made even a dent in poverty? Is poverty any less today than it was before? It would seem like it's more. So that is not what people received from Baba. Baba has not come for that.

There is a poverty that cannot be seen, that is not wept over, the poverty in which there are people who obviously have everything, but they're terribly, terribly poor in spirit, in heart, in the spiritual. Which is why some leave their affluence behind and go out seeking something higher. That poverty nobody weeps over. That poverty nobody cares for. We are so busy seeing to the poverty of the body, we forget that other, wretched poverty which really needs, if not our help, our tears. That is the poverty Baba is concerned with, not this. But He sees to the outer poverty also, because He is Father and Mother, God and Brother in one.

I had a special glimpse of Baba's tremendous giving one morning in the mid-1960s in Baba's room. You see, in the mornings when Baba would sound the all-clear bell, we women would then go into His room. From the time Baba retired late in the evening until the time in the morning when He rang the bell for us, we never entered His room. There was always one of the men mandali there with Him, in turns as allotted by Him. So one of the men was with Him all the time in the night.

So in the morning, the bell would ring and I always love recalling that little electric bell sound—*tring tring tringtringtring tring tring tringtringtring*—going nonstop until we just dropped everything and went inside. Even as we were going, we would still hear it.

Now when we went into Baba's room on the morning I'm telling you about, Baba was still reclining and Mehera reminded Him to do His exercises. Very simple exercises, to be done while you're lying down, contracting the muscles of the feet, the calves, the thighs, the stomach, the arms, the hands and so on. Baba would do them, but hurriedly and each one just a few times, *1-2-3-4-5-6, 1-2-3-4-5-6.* But when it came to the arm exercises, when He would open both arms out wide and then bring them into His chest, He just went on and on, as if He loved doing them. Mehera told me recently that at one time she counted up to a hundred—Baba had done that exercise a hundred times, at a time!

So on this morning I'm speaking of, I was there along with Mehera and the other women in Baba's room while He was doing these, His favourite arm exercises. I kept looking at Him, and then I suddenly realized, "Hey, what is this!" Because this is how He did them [and here Mani gestured, both arms outstretched and then coming in toward the chest and then going out again]: giving from the heart! Taking from the heart and giving, giving, giving. And it suddenly struck me very forcibly, as if the significance was revealed to me, "This is not exercise! He is just giving unlimitedly, giving out, giving out from His heart." I sat there watching for a while bathed in this feeling, this unbelievable feeling.

And just as I had this absolute conviction, I looked up at His face, and saw He was looking at me. Our eyes met, and He had such a twinkle in His eye! And at the same time an understanding look, sort of, "Hmm! So now you know!" And that was all.

Every time afterwards when I would see this unseen giving of His, this Love that He was giving out of Himself, it seemed not limited to the room, it seemed like it was covering the world. It seemed like streams of His Love were forming rivers and the rivers were flowing everywhere from His Ocean into His Ocean. It gave me that majestic, mighty vision of what He was giving. He used material means for His *real* work, for the spiritual which is the lasting thing that He has come to give. So in each little thing Baba did, you could see His Love, love for His creation, love for His world, love for all His loved ones, love for His smallest circle of lovers. Nothing but love.

BEGIN THE BEGUINE

Mani and Eruch, who were such great partners in Baba's service when we came along in the 1970s, didn't even speak to each other until 1958. And not even really then! As Mani tells it:

Do you know that I didn't talk to Eruch till 1958? I really didn't talk to him then either: I sang to him.

We were staying in Bombay, in Ashiana—Nariman and Arnavaz Dadachanji's place. Arnavaz also had to keep the men mandali who were with Baba there as well. Baba would be with the men, Baba would be with the women, but the women would not see the men or talk to them, and the men wouldn't see the women. To arrange all that in a flat [apartment]: when they will eat, when we will eat, when they will go out, when we will come in, when we will be here, when they will be there—well, it was really a jigsaw puzzle!

But Arnavaz would manage that. She would herd us into the dining room so the men could come up the stairs and go into the sitting room, and then shut the door so they could be with Baba. And then we would go into the other bedroom, and they would come to eat, and so on.

One day, Baba was in the hall with the men. We were at the dining table and had just finished eating the sumptuous lunch that Arnavaz had arranged for us. Suddenly Baba came in and said to me (by snapping His fingers), "Come here, come here." So I got up and He took me to the hall. There was a man sitting there like a rock, looking sidewise.

Baba said, "You see that?"

I said, "Yes."

"It's Eruch."

I said, "Yes."

"Now go and sing to him 'Begin the Beguine'".

"Yes." And I said to myself, "My God."

And Eruch just sat there impassive, looking like he didn't care for music or what it was all about. It was the first time I'd approached Eruch that closely. We'd seen each other at a distance a couple of times when some work had to be done, but we had never talked with each other directly.

So he just sat there. I didn't even know whether he heard or didn't hear or whether he could think or not, I mean, he just sat there! Baba placed a chair in front of him and said, "Sing," and Baba left.

I was a bit nervous about it, you know. But I sang to his ear, "When they Begin the Beguine, it brings back the sound of music so . . ."

Once before the end of the song, Baba came in and saw

that I was still in the middle of the song, and He went out. He came in again and when I'd stopped, He said, "Finished?"

I said, "Yes."

"Good. You can go. Finish your lunch."

I went. Never asked, never questioned why.

Years later, after Baba dropped His body, when this story came up right here in this Meherazad hall, Eruch said to me, "Do you know why you were asked to sing that song to me?"

I said, "No." Then I said, "I didn't talk to you first. I sang to you. Do you remember?"

"Yes, but do you know why?"

"No."

He then said that Baba had told him when they were going to the West or somewhere, that when He dropped His body, the body was to be carried to Meherabad and put in the tomb, in the place He had kept for it. And when He dropped His body, the record of the song "Begin the Beguine" was to be played by His side seven times. Eruch said, "Yes."

Then Baba said, "Do you know what song it is?"

Eruch said, "No, never heard it."

"All right, you'll hear it."

So then Baba called me to sing the song so that Eruch would know which song Baba was talking about, what "Begin the Beguine" was. So I came to know years and years later why Baba told me to sing "Begin the Beguine" to Eruch's ear. Because I'm sure it didn't reach anywhere else!

. . .

Of course, Mani never had contact with any of the men in the early years, but after Baba had her teach Eruch "Begin the Beguine," occasionally He would have her work with Eruch on something, initially in His presence and in later years on her own but at His indication. They were the two among the mandali most familiar with Baba's gestures, so when dictating a circular, Baba would occasionally have Mani interpret what He gestured while Eruch wrote it down. At the time the following incident took place, Mani was not very familiar with Eruch, and in later years they would often tell this story in the Hall in tandem, with a lot of teasing in between the lines.

> [MANI:] It's always tickled me how much there was to say about Baba's silence! You know, correspondence would be read out to Baba from lovers who wrote, "Baba, I toured all over India and lectured at every place I went about Your silence." I would say to myself, "My God! How can you speak so much about silence?"
>
> And of course, Baba would encourage them. Every now and then He would bring out a circular saying, "I'm going to break My silence." "Send it out everywhere," Baba would tell us; "No one should miss it." Then, of course, nothing would happen in the time intimated by Him, so then the lovers would forget about it. But He would not let His lovers forget His silence.
>
> I believed it every time, and then when it didn't happen, it didn't bother me, or any of us. None of us was really concerned about Baba's breaking of His silence. We simply went along with it all because that was what Baba wanted. That's all. For us, Baba was never silent because His silence was so eloquent. When we kept silence on 10th July every year, we realized the difference. We were dumb! It was

always the most difficult day of the year for Baba, having a pack of women and men around Him not talking and doing this [here Mani mimics their clumsy gestures and facial expressions]. But *His* gestures, *His* expressions, *His* very face talked without a sound.

Speaking of those circulars, one day Baba called me and took me along with Him to Eruch's room, that Manonash cabin. Baba sat on Eruch's bed and made me sit next to Him. Eruch then stood in front of Baba with a pad taking down what I began interpreting of Baba's gestures. It was all about Baba's silence, "I'm going to break My silence in nine months" or something like that.

So I'm interpreting Baba's gestures in words, and Eruch is writing them all down. And in the middle of it [here Mani laughs], Baba turns to me and says, "Look at him! [indicating Eruch] He doesn't believe that I'm going to break My silence. He doesn't believe it." So Eruch says, "Baba, what has that got to do with it? Please continue, because I'm taking down the dictation. I'm going to send out the circular." Baba's still talking to me, "No, no, see, see, he doesn't believe it!"

"But Baba," says Eruch, "why are we wasting our time? What has my belief or not belief got to do with it? Please, I am doing what You want; it's all right."

"See," Baba says. "He doesn't."

Then Baba tells me, "If I were not to break My silence, why would I observe it?" Exactly! I'm glaring at Eruch anyway throughout it all. How could this guy not believe! But when Baba said this, I said, "See! Now what can you answer to that?"

But it didn't touch this guy.

Anyway, that's one of the incidents with Baba that I remember very endearingly. Because at the same time, although you might think Baba was serious about the silence circular and complaining about this guy who wouldn't believe it, He's drawing a doodle on an old piece of paper, a doodle of a fish. I still have that paper; I put the date on it, and I've laminated it.

At this point in the Hall, Eruch started sharing another, similar story.

[ERUCH:] So often He would point at me as to why I didn't believe in the breaking of His silence.

[MANI:] Yeah.

[ERUCH:] It was not just the first time there.

[MANI:] No?

[ERUCH:] No. What had happened was that . . .

[MANI:] Maybe I wasn't there.

[ERUCH:] Yeah. Well, time and again He would come over here, also after the circular had been circulated and all that, and complain to the mandali, "Look, this fellow, he doesn't believe that I'll break My silence." And naturally people, the elders who were around us like Kaikobad, would pounce upon me. Kaikobad would say, "How dare you don't believe!" And I would say, "I have nothing to do with it! I am just hearing and carrying out what He wants us to do. If He breaks His silence, well and good. If He doesn't break His silence, well and good. To me it is just the same." So time and again He would put the blame on me. But this here, in front of all these people now, it's a great humiliation for me that I have been stamped as an unbeliever, you know! [Laughter]

[ERUCH:] Well I believe in Him . . .

[MANI:] . . . it's true . . .

[ERUCH:] . . . so let alone whether I believe in His silence, breaking of His silence, or not!

In this same vein, one day, after agreeing with Eruch that it didn't matter to the mandali whether Baba broke His silence or not, Mani remembered this incident:

> There was a family that had been allowed to come and be with Baba here in Meherazad. Baba was seated in His chair and they were to come into the Mandali Hall. I met them on the verandah outside the Hall, because I'd gone over to that side to get a telegram form. I noticed that the woman, an Irani lady, looked very nervous. She embraced me and said, "Baba doesn't talk, does He? How will I understand what He is going to say? He doesn't talk!"
>
> "It's all right," I assured her, "it's all right. Somebody will be there to interpret. Don't be nervous! Everything will be all right."
>
> Truly speaking, I really wanted to get away. But after half an hour when I came back again to the verandah I saw the same scene; the lady and her family were there. On seeing me, the woman remembered, "Oh! Meher Baba doesn't talk, does He?" I said, "No."
>
> "You know," she said, "I forgot all about it. I didn't realize He didn't talk when I was with Him. I didn't know!"
>
> "Exactly!"
>
> You don't realize He's silent because His silence talks more than our speech does.

One afternoon in the Hall, Mani told another story involving Eruch:

> You know, I was saying this morning how Baba would

play a part in order to give us a lesson, to reveal a lesson to us. When He plays the part of a worrier, for instance, He would do that so that we would realize, "Yes! What is there to worry about? Why is Baba making such a big thing out of this little thing? Why is He worried?" But Baba would show us what it was that we were doing. It would be a mirror reflection for us.

To give you a little idea of this, Baba had said and it was given out in a circular or a Family Letter, I forget which, that something great will happen that has never happened before and will not happen again for a billion years. Or some large amount of time like that.

Soon after that one day Baba was sitting here in the Hall looking worried and frowning, with all looking up at Him. He said, "You know, I have said that this great thing which is going to happen will happen in May."

"Yes, Baba."

"But now, supposing it doesn't happen in May! Supposing it happens before May, or supposing it happens after May? Will everybody know that it is what Meher Baba has said, that it is from Me?"

And we said, "Oh, don't worry, Baba, of course it won't be like that, it's all right, Baba, don't worry . . ."

But no, Baba persisted in worrying about it. After a while He brought it up again. Then in the afternoon, He brought up the same thing all over again! "But supposing it happens before May, or happens after May. Then will everybody know that it's from Me?"

At this point, when Baba said it for a third time, this guy [here Mani pointed to Eruch] couldn't help himself and said, "Don't worry, Baba, don't worry. It won't happen, I'm telling

You; it won't happen before May, it won't happen in May, and it won't happen after May!"

And you wouldn't believe it! Baba sort of gave him a look, a very intimate look, as if to say, "Hmmm! So you, how do you know?" And He never referred to that again. [Mani laughs!]

DIVINITY

Mani often described the difficulty Baba had in hiding His Divinity:

When the Avatar puts on the clothes of a human, it's a very tight fit. An Indian Baba-lover once asked Baba, pleaded with Him actually, "Baba, You must manifest Yourself. When are You going to release Your Divinity?"

And Baba said, "It's very easy for Me to release My Divinity. It is holding it in that is so difficult."

To reveal Himself is easy; what's difficult is not to reveal Himself. And then He gave the most delightful illustration to that man. He said, "Just like when you have wind in the stomach it's so easy to release it. It's so difficult to hold it in till it's the right time and the right place. So at the right time and the right place I will manifest . . . That's very easy to do. It's this that's not easy."

Baba would give very apt similes sometimes. This was so simple an explanation. Because the real things are simple. That's why when Baba said something to us, explained something, it was simplicity itself. It's we who cannot always recognize it or take it. Because we like the trimmings. We like the icing. We like the bows. We like, in fact, to make it more complicated.

It's like how the village women coming to the clinic here used to love medicine that was colored pink or blue. They didn't like the plain, simple little pills or tablets. "No, no, it's the pink medicine that always made me well!" And so it took a long time for the people here to accept that the little homeopathic pills, such little things, could be effective at all.

On another day, she spoke about God-Realization:

We talk so glibly about a God-Realized person and God-Realization. And yet I remember what Baba said when someone asked Him what a God-Realized person would be like. I'm not sure whether it was the same gentleman that pleaded with Him to manifest; I may be doing him an injustice. He's just fixed in my mind as that kind of person, the character of the questioning mind. He loved Baba, of course, very much, that follower.

I had just come into the Hall, but he must have said something to Baba about God-Realization; I only heard what Baba said to him.

In those years, there were no carpets here on the floor of the Hall. It's only these eighteen years since 1969 that we have placed carpets on the floor for His lovers, for our royal guests. These Persian carpets are for you all. We had just plain flooring then.

So as I came in, Baba was pointing to the stone floor and looking at that man, "You see the stone?"

"Yes. Yes, Baba."

"What is the difference between you and that stone?" Baba asked.

The man laughed. Ha ha! Of course he knew the difference between himself and a stone. It was a rhetorical question, as it were, and he replied, "Of course I know the difference."

"Tremendous difference," Baba said, "the difference between you and a stone. You know what it is?"

"Oh yes, Baba."

"Exactly!" Baba said. "That is the difference between you and a God-Realized Being."

That said everything. I mean, if that wasn't a discourse!

To me these little instances, these explanations from Baba, were real discourses, real sermons, given in the simplest way in the most casual moments.

Mani shared another of Baba's "simple sermons" in Mandali Hall:

Baba's illustration of knowing by experience was so perfect (which is not to say I'm experiencing anything; I'm just giving similes!).

Somebody who had never experienced a headache asked someone else, "What is a headache? Can you tell me what a headache is?" How can you tell somebody what a headache is? So the other person picked up a rock and bonk! on the man's head. Then that guy knew what a headache was!

Baba gives words and explanations because we still need them for our minds. And He felt compassionate so He explained to our satisfaction in words so that we could receive through the mind that which is beyond the mind, which the mind cannot touch. But still He explains, giving

Baba conversing with Adi Sr. during an intimate darshan program in Mandali Hall.

us the food our minds need. What we are able to filter through the heart is different.

Baba gave an illustration for that too that was so perfect, like everything He did. He told a lover, one with the questioning mind, "You expect Me to tell you through the mind that which is beyond the mind." And then He explained. Supposing a little child comes and asks you, "Tell me, tell me about marriage." What would you do? How can you tell a child about marriage? The child has to grow up himself and know from experience what marriage is, know what it is to be married, to live with your partner, about sex and everything. You can't tell the child all that. But the child, when he grows up, he won't need to ask, because he will know. But because the child has asked and you love the child, you don't want to disappoint him, you want to give something in answer, you tell about the wedding.

The child will understand, Baba said. You talk about

what the bride wore. You talk about the flowers she carried; you could talk about the cake that was cut. You talk about the priest, the ring, the clothes, ad infinitum. There is just no end to the detail. You can tell all that but he still would not know about marriage. When you understand about marriage, there is nothing to talk about. So in the same way, Baba said, "Whatever is given out in words is still about the wedding. When experience comes, the divine, real experience comes, then that one [the experiencer] is silent. Then there's nothing to say."

COCA-COLA ORANGE

Mani often used to talk with pilgrims in Meherazad garden. One day, she shared:

> Sitting here in the garden, you all can imagine how pleasant it was for me to have my office on the verandah of the little cottage there. My "open-air office," where I would type the Family Letters and do other typing that Baba wanted, where while I was typing and working, I could watch the birds having their baths in the earthenware birdbaths on the ground. And watch the chameleons going up and down the trees. And see the flowers. In just open air, just natural light.
>
> So can you imagine then, me now working in the Trust Office [by the time she was telling this story, Mani was

chairman of Baba's trust and went four days a week to the Trust Office in Ahmednagar], within four walls, with two glowing [flourescent] tube lights on top of my head, and you look out and see nothing but cars, scooters, and cycles! Look at the difference!

But for years I had the joy of working in the garden, with my office in the garden. There was a very tame bird —a redstart—that used to come close to us when we would feed it biscuits. Because of the biscuits, we named it "Biki."

So even when there was a lot of work, some of the inspiration for what you see in the Family Letters really comes from the garden, from the birds, from the view. And best of all, I could keep an eye on Baba's door of the Mandali Hall so I would know when He was coming out. That way I could drop everything and go to be with Mehera when He came to the house.

Here in the garden, Baba gave His last darshan in physical form. It was Mehera's birthday, and Baba's nephew Dara and Amrit's wedding reception. Baba entrusted the wedding preparations to Villoo and Sarosh to attend to in Ahmednagar, and also to see to the food arrangements for the reception at Meherazad. We—Naja, Katie, and all of us together—were going to set the table and do all that, but they had to set the menu and see to the food. So there were numerous conferences about it.

Baba had given them a limit to their budget for the reception. Dara's father, Baba's and my brother Adi, had invested some money for his son, and this amount had come through just at that time. There were many coincidences like that. And Baba said, "This is what you must spend, not a penny more, not a penny less." So it all had to be talked over and arranged accordingly.

Villoo and Sarosh would sometimes come for meetings in Mandali Hall. Now when Villoo and Sarosh talk, it's more than a talk! It's an argument, it's a declaration of independence, it's all kinds of things. And sometimes Baba would come over and sit and listen. "All right," He'd say, "go on, continue, continue!"

One day Villoo and Sarosh were in the Hall here talking about the buffet. Somehow they had climbed the hill, with every clash they had gone a step forward, and now they had come to the last stage, which was what drinks to have. Soft drinks, of course. Now, Coca-Cola is much more expensive than orange, and Sarosh wanted "Coca-Cola!" and Villoo wanted "Orange, orange, orange!" So they were both at it.

Just when Baba came in, Villoo was saying, "Orange!" and Sarosh was saying "Coca-Cola!" "Orange!" "Coca-Cola!" "Orange!" And Baba came and said, "Hm? Hm? What is it?"

"Oh Baba!" Villoo said, and turned round to Sarosh, "Sarosh, don't talk about something you don't know anything about! Don't poke your big nose in everything . . . Just let me handle everything because I know what I'm doing!"

And Sarosh said, "Coca-Cola!"

And Baba said, "What is it?"

So Villoo sat there with her head in her hands. "Baba, I am fed up! I am really fed up! I have done so many parties and so many weddings, and so much arrangement I have made, but never . . . This is such a small thing, Baba, this is nothing, and this is giving me such a headache! Why only the other day there was a function that I arranged for five hundred people, and it was nothing; I arranged it just like that!"

Baba was listening and playing along, "Really? Really?"

"Oh yes, Baba, and there was my friend's anniversary, hundreds of people came, hundreds! And I just did everything!"

"Really!" Baba said.

Then He said, "It's true, Villoo, you did all that?"

"Yeah!"

"But tell Me, Villoo, was any of all this that you did, which you describe, was any of it for Me?"

And Villoo's face went down like a deflated balloon. "No, Baba, nothing of that was for You. It was not for You."

"Exactly!" said Baba. "This, Villoo, is for Me! So go on!" Meaning, it won't be as easy as that, but go on trying.

So Sarosh got into the spirit of it, and started up, "Coca-Cola!"

"Orange!" came back Villoo.

"Coca-Cola!"

Then Baba gestured, "Stop!" He was chuckling and getting pink in the face. "This hurts now! Enough!" Because He was laughing so much silently, it hurt!

Then He said, "What is all this? So simple! Simple, half Coca-Cola, half orange!"

"Oh, but Baba, if it is like that, everybody will rush for Coca-Cola!"

So Baba said, "So what! When Coca-Cola is finished, then everybody will rush for orange."

"Ah, yes."

So Baba solved the problem, and the solution was simple and delightful. But the lesson was that when you are doing something for Baba, it doesn't mean it's going to be easier. It can be much more difficult than when you are just doing it for yourself or your friends. When you're doing something for Baba, there's a weight, an importance. So you wouldn't want it to be light, or airy, or easy.

Mani often remembered an incident from that same gathering—a small incident that made a big impression:

> On that occasion Baba was seated on the Meherazad house verandah with His lovers before Him in the garden. It was a "little darshan"; the lovers were allowed to file past Baba to have His darshan from a distance, and then go and sit before Him. Baba was very occupied with each lover, making each one feel what he or she was receiving from Him; it was very personal, very individual. And those who wanted to express their love in songs and other entertainments were allowed to do so at the same time.
>
> Yet Baba was so occupied with the lovers filing past that those singing did not think He was really listening; He was asking someone something, telling someone else such-and-such, and so on. He was very much with His lovers.
>
> Then one girl with a very nice voice began singing a song. It was not a "Baba song" in the sense that it was composed for Baba, but there are many such songs you hear out in the world that seem as if they really were composed for Him. The one she was singing was a very lovely song, and the last line was: ". . . waiting for you, but in vain."
>
> Now Baba was busy with the lover in front of Him, but when she sang that line, He turned right round and snapped His fingers: "Stop! Sing that line again!" and He pointed to Himself, ". . .waiting for Me, not in vain!" So she sang the line again, ". . . waiting for You, *not* in vain" And to this day she sings it that way.

So there's never any doubt about it: He will come, He will give. It's now up to us: how deeply we long, what we long for, and to what measure we long. And that is what Eruch meant yesterday about separation and longing: that longing for Baba always bears fruit, because it's longing for Him.

Stories From Guruprasad

Mani had a number of stories from the times they spent with Baba in Guruprasad over the years, too. Here are some of her favorites, as she told them in Mandali Hall at Meherazad.

THE TAILOR'S DILEMMA

We know that it couldn't be chance that the Maharani of Baroda had this palatial house which she offered to Baba for His use, that Baba accepted and used it for our summer stays in Poona, that it happened to be called Guruprasad, that it would be so perfectly built for Baba's work and purpose.

Mehera with Pegu on Guruprasad verandah.

In Guruprasad, the women and men could stay in the same bungalow, the same place, and yet be completely and easily secluded from each other. The women's wing could be separate, the men's wing could be separate, and yet Baba could go over to both sides. Baba's bedroom was perfectly situated, where the men could easily

Baba in front of Guruprasad.

come in (from the verandah) and yet the women could be secluded from them. And in between was a huge hall where Baba could give darshan to so many. In every way it was the most adjustable place you could imagine, just as if made to order for our stay with Baba there and for His work.

A darshan in Guruprasad is something you remember; it was really an experience. On the days when Baba was giving darshan, the doors would be open so that all could come in, see Him, and attend the session. The hall would be full, overfull, so much so that the side rooms were also full with people, all peeking out to see Baba. Even the verandah was full, and the approach road right from the gate to the palace was always teeming with people coming and going.

And there would be Baba, sitting on His chair in the main hall, looking so radiant, so fragile, and yet so strong at the same time. As He sat there would be a time for the men to come for darshan; they would queue up and pass by Him, receiving from Baba either a caress, a pat on the back, or a question of concern, "How are you?" or "What are you doing now?" Like a river, the line flowed right past Baba, and after a while it would be the women's turn.

Now this is the story of a tailor: I'll tell it in short because I think you all know it. Among the many who had come for Baba's darshan in Guruprasad one day, among the tinkers and the tailors and the soldiers and the sailors and the doctors and the businessmen and the carpenters—people of every vocation, every kind of profession—among them was this tailor.

He was seeing Baba for the first time, and he just completely went overboard; he fell for Baba. So after the

Baba smiling in Guruprasad, with Adi Sr. and Eruch behind Him.

darshan, he hung around the verandah where Eruch has a little corner for writing and correspondence.

He comes to Eruch and says, "I am Tailor So-and-So." And Eruch knows him; he was a tailor of repute. So Eruch says, "Yes, I know. I'm told you're one of the best in Poona."

Then the man says, "Oh, it's His grace. But all I want to know is: can I stitch something for the God-Man? Can I make something for Baba? My whole life's vocation, my whole life's purpose, would be served if only I could sew something for Baba."

Eruch says, "Yes, why not? Baba would be happy. Why not make a coat?"

"Could I? Would you allow me to do it?"

"Yes," Eruch says. "Would you want us to give the material?"

"No, no, nothing. I'll do everything. I just want permission."

"But you'll want measurements?"

"Measurements?" he says. "I can give just one look, and I know what His measurements are. And you ask me to take measurements?" and his gesture says, "I'm THAT type of tailor."

"All right," says Eruch. "You express your love in your own way. Wonderful. Baba wouldn't mind at all. In fact, He'll accept happily. It's love that Baba wants," and all that kind of thing.

So the tailor went away. He immediately got to work and stitched day and night, so that in two days he brought the coat over to Guruprasad. The coat was brought inside by Goher and given to Mehera, and Mehera had Baba try it on right away because it had been made with such love.

But that coat! It was so big! The sleeves were down to here, the coat was down to here, the pockets were somewhere on the knees, the shoulders were way down here. And Baba waved His hands—you've seen the movie with Dopey [a reference to one of the dwarfs in the 1937 Disney film "Snow White and the Seven Dwarfs"]? His sleeves were always longer than his hands and he would flap them all the time. So Baba was flapping the sleeves, and the expression on His face said, "Look what I have to do for Love's sake. Even this!"

It was very funny. Nobody knew what had happened.

Then Baba went to the men's side and showed the men, gesturing "Look at this."

Eruch was surprised. "Oh, no, Baba, but I know the

man. How could he have made such a blunder? He has a good name and a good reputation for . . ."

"Well," Baba gestured, "look, look at Me!" And Baba stood there with a very merry glint in His eye.

When the tailor was told to come, he came promptly to Eruch. "Is it all right?"

"Well . . ." Eruch said.

"Ah, I know! It's too snug!"

"It's too snug?" said Eruch. "What are you talking about? It's too loose!"

So the tailor had the chance to see Baba again, this time in the coat. He couldn't believe it. "But when I first saw Baba, He looked so big! And I was afraid the coat would be snug. I didn't want it to be snug on Him so I made it like that."

Rano and I were talking about it the other day: it happened to us too. I have a recollection of Baba walking from the Guruprasad door, and in it, Baba is so big. Yet I have a recollection of Baba sitting in a chair, in the dining room maybe, and in that recollection Baba is so delicate, so fragile, so small.

And also the weight of Him would change, right, Eruch?

[ERUCH:] He would be light in weight, and then all of a sudden, when carrying Him on His lift chair, both Francis and myself would feel as if the chair were overburdened with some big weight.

[MANI:] Or He would be heavy as they were lifting Him and then suddenly light. When Baba walked [in the later years after His second accident] with us, He usually leaned on Mehera's arm or shoulder, but sometimes He would put His hands on my arm, just to go in the room from there to there. And I would indicate, "Baba, put Your weight, put Your weight, it's all right." Because His weight would be like a feather, a butterfly. You wouldn't even know it was there. Baba would put both hands on my arm, and I could still feel no weight.

The very next day, it could be that when Baba did that, it was all I could do to keep on holding my arm up.

Baba once explained this, saying it depended on the burden of His work. The weight of the burden at such times when He was working was heavy and at other times it was light.

THE EAST-WEST GATHERING

The East-West Gathering was a radiant darshan for Baba-lovers both from the East and from the West. Mani had some memorable stories about that great gathering:

> For those who have had Baba's company [on specific occasions], His sahavas, His darshan, that memory is like a photographic remembrance. Whereas with us, our life with Him has been like the flowing of a river, one day into another, one November into another. It's very difficult to look back and pin down a particular occasion. But we love reminiscing with and hearing from those who had been with Baba just for a certain time, because then we are reminded of many little details that for us had just flowed by.

The East-West Gathering was in November 1962 and it really was an East-West gathering. It's supposed to be a very pleasant time in Poona at the end of October and November, but how it showered that year! Can you remember, Eruch? It showered like mad before the darshan. The very first darshan day the Baba-lovers seated before Baba under the shamiana, which is a beautiful, decorated tent, all got sopping wet. They were just drenched, as if they had literally been in a shower.

So the Western women were all sent inside the bungalow [Guruprasad palace] to the women's side.

They had to wipe their hair, dry themselves, and change into our clothes. And how Baba provided! We're still sometimes amazed how we got out so many towels from goodness knows where. It was difficult to give them clothes because they were all sizes and the clothes didn't always fit. But saris were very useful; we simply wrapped saris round some. Even if you have no blouse, you can really wrap yourself round with a sari and look very elegant. And many of the clothes were Mehera's. I still remember Jane wore a beautiful dress that Mehera had. All our clothes were out and being exchanged.

And somehow the supply was sufficient. It was like they'd come in to change from West to East, because when they went back to be seated again before Baba, they were not in the same clothes.

An amusing thing we often remember is that we didn't know what to give to Elizabeth to change into. Then Rano suddenly remembered that she had Elizabeth's old silk dressing gown that Elizabeth had given her. Rano said she didn't know why she took that dressing gown to Guruprasad with her, but she had just in case she might need it sometime. Well, you know how neatly Rano keeps her things; she had used it and darned it and ironed it and kept it with her, and now she brought it out for Elizabeth.

Those who were at the sahavas were given a paper rosette kind of badge as a token of identity. When Elizabeth pinned that badge on her silk robe, she looked just wonderful, really regal.

At that time, the yogi Shuddhananda Bharati was sitting next to Baba on the dais, wearing the yellow ochre robe usual to him. He was very keen to meet Elizabeth, the head of the Myrtle Beach Center, Baba's Center in America. So when Elizabeth came before Baba on the dais, He introduced her to the yogi, "Mrs. Elizabeth Patterson." It was lovely the way Elizabeth stood there in her dressing gown and very regally bowed. She later remarked that the yogi probably thought these were her ceremonial robes! It would not have been half as effective if Elizabeth had stood there in just her usual dress to be introduced as the head of the Myrtle Beach Center! But here she was in that silk dressing gown, with the rosette. Perfect, the way it happened!

[And here, someone said, "That rain caused a mixing of the East and West."]

Yes, exactly. Baba's touch, Baba's humour, was seen in the most profound things too. The yogi I was speaking

Baba enjoying ghazals during the East-West Gathering.

of was devoted to Baba; he was a Baba-lover. But before knowing of Baba, he was very well known as a yogi in Japan and other Eastern places. He was a fine person. When he came for the Gathering, he had written beforehand, and Baba wanted arrangements to be made for his comfort. So the yogi wrote that he only ate fruits, nuts, and milk. G.S.N Moorty, a Baba-lover from the North, was given the charge of looking after the yogi and seeing to his diet needs and other things in his hotel.

The yogi would sit on the dais on one side of Baba's feet, and the Maharani Shantadevi, who owned Guruprasad, would sit on the other side. When darshan time came, Baba's lovers just thronged in, bursting through the enormous pandal [a term referring to both the cloth awning and the space underneath it] that stretched out before Him. Then Baba turned and said to the yogi, "When any of My lovers offer oranges or fruits, be sure to swipe them immediately

Yogi Shuddhananda Bharati and Maharani Shantadevi sitting on either side of Baba during the Gathering.

and put them in your satchel so that you can have them for lunch. You won't have to spend for lunch." Because, you know, it's the Indian way to offer flowers, fruits, something from your heart as an expression of your love to the Master when you come for darshan. Often Baba would touch the offering and give it back to the person.

But He said to the yogi and to Moorty, who was taking care of him, "Now if it's oranges and fruits, you be sure to take it." So they said, "Well, yes Baba, very happy . . ." Of course, it was Baba who would remind them. They would be so engrossed in the darshan and the lovers and this overwhelming occasion, and somebody would place a couple of oranges at Baba's Feet. Immediately, Baba would turn round in an aside, as it were, and wink at the yogi, "What's the matter? Didn't you swipe that? Didn't I tell you. . . ?"

"Yes . . ."

"Come on, hurry up, put it in your bag!"

So the poor yogi would fumble, pick up the oranges, and before you knew it, he and Moorty were not paying attention to the darshan, or able to really go along with the sahavas—they had all their eyes and minds on, "Oh, what did this one bring? Is it oranges? No, it's not oranges. Where are the oranges?"

I'm sure the yogi was sick of the sight of an orange after that!

But you see, they weren't doing it for themselves anymore. They were doing it because of Baba's order. That's really the point to this story: how it was from Baba.

THE IGNORED MAN

There were times when Baba would show indifference to you. That was the one thing that would really get your back up and make you go off in a huff. It would happen when you were determined that nothing would shake you up, nothing would make you feel or show unhappiness. Then Baba would show indifference.

Of course we realized later that He took pains to be indifferent to you. So He was really paying more attention to you, because it was difficult for Him to be indifferent; He is all Love. So when He was being indifferent to you, it was for a purpose. But it would make you feel, "Baba doesn't care for me. Baba doesn't love me. Why should I care?" Then He would make up for it and really give you twice as much special attention because of having been indifferent.

It's like that old story which I've told, I think, a hundred times. But I'll tell it again. Would you like to hear it?

Well, we were in Guruprasad and Baba was giving darshan. And His lovers had gathered from all over India in the Guruprasad Hall.

There was such a feeling when Baba gave darshan; He turned something on. It was that love, that joy, that radiance, among all this colourful gathering. Everybody would be gaily dressed and happy, joyously greeting each other and talking, and there Baba would be silently sitting at the end of the hall, a frail, silent figure in a white sadra looking beautiful, so lovely, delicate, sitting there. Yet He was like the center, the Sun; the radiance and the force of light and love that came from Him held everything

Baba showering His pleasure on some young dancers.

together. All attention, all one's focus would be on Him, on that silent, tiny figure at the far end of the room.

There would be music going on, qawwali singing as was usual at darshan time, and all the lovers would be sitting before Him, and Baba would be giving love to them all, with Eruch standing beside Him.

Every, say, fifteen minutes, people would be told to stand up and form a queue for darshan. When it was time for the men to have their moment with Baba, many from the men's side would stand up and form a line, and the line would move forward towards where Baba was seated. After fifteen minutes, the men's line would be stopped, and after a while, the women would have their turn. Everything was done in an orderly way.

One by one, each lover would come along in front of Him and have their moment with Baba. They might garland Baba, or offer Him some expression of the heart. It could be in the form of a garland, it could be in the form of sweets, it could be in the form of a coconut. Baba would sometimes just touch the offering and it would be kept by His side; or He would touch it and give it back to the lover. When something is done with love, it's no longer a ritual. A ritual is when it's a dead thing, when it's done from habit. But that same ritual, when you put your love in it, is different. Sometimes when some Baba-lover could not reach Baba with a garland, maybe it was a child or a woman who was tiny, Baba would be so gracious; He would help them by bending over a little. It was not for the garland itself, but because it was offered with love. And when the garlands piled up too high around Baba's neck, Eruch would remove the whole lot and wipe His brow with a kerchief (the darshan would be in summertime so it was hot). Baba would go on giving of Himself, regardless of anything, sometimes saying something to the Baba-lover before Him, sometimes caressing the lover or giving him a pat on the back.

Now this is the story of one lover. He was sitting somewhere near the end of the hall by the big palatial doors, and he was watching the lovers going one by one to have their moment with God. He could see Baba sometimes caress somebody's cheek, or pat someone else on the back, or ask, "How's your health?" Or say, "What about your family, how are they? How are your children, wife?" Something that meant something very special to each one, very intimate and personal.

And he watched and then when the lovers around him stood up to go to Baba, he thought, "Which will Baba do to me? Will He caress my cheek? Or will He pat me on the back? Or will He ask me 'How is your health?' Or will He ask after my family?"

For him, nothing existed in that hall absolutely brimful of lovers. He was oblivious to everyone else. He only saw his

Beloved; he only saw Baba there. And he knew that with each step he came closer to Baba, and he kept wondering, "Which will Baba do to me?" Only Baba existed. All his longing, all his one-pointed attention, was to receive from Him.

So at last the moment came, and he reached Baba. And just at that moment, Baba turned His face away, looked up at Eruch and gestured, "Eruch, what about Saigal? Is he going by train? Is he going by car?" Looking concerned, He put His hand on His chin. "What about his ticket?"

Eruch said, "Everything is all right, Baba. Yes, his ticket is reserved. Yes, I'm sure it will be all right."

But Baba went on and on talking with Eruch about something or the other and meanwhile this lover couldn't even get a look from Baba, let alone anything else. Now he was just wondering, "Oh, will Baba turn His head? Will Baba look at me?"

So he tried to make the moment last as long as possible. But it was very difficult to stretch it out, because others were standing behind him, waiting for their turn. Each one was to finish his or her darshan in a minute. He wanted just a glimpse from Baba, but Baba was talking away.

In the end, it wasn't possible to stand there any longer. So he turned away with a heavy heart. Then he had to go out through the Rani's room, circle right around and go back to his seat.

The moment he turned his back to go, Baba turned away from Eruch and was ready for the next person. A caress, a slap on the back, a question, some love expression; just for that man He had turned His face away. But that man didn't see this; he just slumped, went back to his seat by the entrance, and sat.

These darshans are something you cannot describe. An hour could go by and seem like a minute, or a minute could seem like an eternity. So the darshan went on as only darshan can with Baba.

Sometimes Baba would be tricky at the end of a session. The lovers didn't want to leave; nobody wanted to move; they all wanted to just sit there for eternity. But Baba had one eye on the clock. They couldn't see the clock but Baba could. So in His love and humour, Baba might suddenly say something about obedience, how obedience is greater than love. And you could see the lovers just preening their feathers; everybody sat up straighter. Everybody was ready to obey. Baba had only to say, "Get on the top of the mountain and jump down that cliff" and they were ready to do it. You could feel that.

So when they were ready for obedience, Baba would say, "Now, in three minutes flat, I want this whole Guruprasad Hall empty of My lovers."

Oh they would groan and moan. He had tricked them

Baba alone on His couch in Guruprasad.

once again! There would be a twinkle in Baba's eye and they would laugh. And then they would all get up, each one trying to leave last by having something to do.

As this was going on that particular day, in the midst of it, Baba says to Eruch, "I want that man."

"Which man?" Nobody knew. Baba's mandali were interspersed among the gathering, one here, one by the door, one on the verandah. So Eruch says, "Vishnu, Vishnu. Baba wants that man by the door. He's pointing."

And Vishnu says, "Aloba, there?" And Pendu looks and each one passes on the message. Meanwhile there's the commotion of everyone going, and talking, and trying to see Baba or greet each other. So you can't even hear another person in all that noise.

At last one of the mandali by the door goes to each man at the entrance and says, "This one?"

And Baba says from His seat, "No."

"This one?" He pats another man and Baba says, "No."

In the end somebody puts his hand on the head of that man, "This one?" Baba says, "Yes." So the mandali grab him like a prisoner, and that man is told, "Baba wants you."

"Baba? Wants me?"

"Yes."

So they hold his hand as if he might get away, because they've gotten him with such difficulty, and escort him all the way around through the Rani's room to where Baba is seated.

Now the man can't believe it. He's absolutely dazed. He's looking at Baba. And Baba caresses his cheek, and then pats him on the back, and then says, "How's your health?" And then He says, "What about your family?" And the man just bursts out crying, and drops at Baba's feet.

Then Baba says, "Go." And he is led away. But then he doesn't go all the way out. He waits till he gets a chance to come back to where Eruch is in the corner. And then he tells Eruch this story.

So that indifference was shown just to give more in the end. You see, God, Baba, is such a businessman that He never gives short on any measure, not even by a fraction. Baba gives to the full measure of one's longing. That man wasn't just allowed to go. His longing was special. The measure of it was more, so he received all the four things he wanted: Baba caressed him, patted him, asked after his health and his family. So it all depends on one's self, depends on the measure of one's longing, depends on the measure of how much you want, and what you want. He will never not give, and He will never short-change you. Never.

Waiting for Him, longing for Him, wanting from Him is never in vain, because you will get it! So what you ask for, what you want, is what matters.

THE CHILDREN'S PLAY

Sometimes spontaneous things would tickle Baba. For instance, there were these two Indian schoolgirls who would visit us in Guruprasad, children of Baba-lovers.

One summer, the children of the Poona Baba-lovers arranged a play for Baba at the Poona Centre. They'd all been involved, and different forms of the Avatar in many of the Avataric Advents were depicted in the play. I knew that.

So one day, I came upon these two young girls sitting down, one maybe about ten and the other about fourteen. "Well, Meherangiz," I said, "so you're in the play?"

"Yes."

"What are you?"

She stood up, to be polite like she was in a classroom, and said, "I am Jesus Christ."

"Oh!" I said, and she sat down.

Then I asked the other one, "And Dernavaz, what are you?"

She stood up and said, "I am Mary McDonald."

Mary Magdalene had become Mary McDonald! I thought to myself, "Just wait till I get inside and tell this to Baba and Mehera!"

And Baba chuckled, He was so tickled about it!

BABY CARRIAGE

Yesterday I remembered something very funny. Delightful, rather.

After Baba's second accident, when we were in Guruprasad, Dr. [S.C.] Chatterji said that Baba should exercise by walking with a support. So a secondhand baby carriage was found somewhere. We called it the "Baba-carriage." It's now with Dhun at Akbar Press, because she is disabled and can use it whenever she goes out.

So that carriage was wheeled by Baba from one side of Guruprasad's spacious verandah to the other. But it needed weight in it because Baba was supposed to push it for exercise. So on the first day when the mandali didn't know what to put in it for a weight, Baba pointed to Jal—His and my brother—and Jal sat in the baby carriage, and Baba wheeled him around. The next day onwards we put a big rock in the carriage for Baba to push, which was good exercise for His muscles.

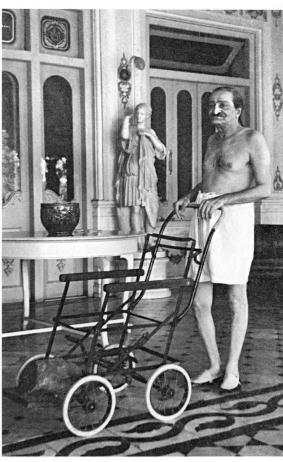

Baba wheeling the "Baba-carriage" on the verandah.

[Someone in the Hall said, "I think there's a picture of Baba doing that."]

Yes, you see the carriage but not the rock.

A child's pram in India is called a *baba gari* (baby vehicle) because *baba* means "baby." *Baba* also means "brother," "father," "friend." In fact, Baba is all so His name, too, encompasses all.

⌇

BEST FRIEND

Once there was a darshan in the big hall in Guruprasad. Two American ladies had come to Guruprasad during that time, friends of someone who had met someone, and they were taking part in the darshan as witnesses. They were very happy to be there; you could see from their faces. They were glowing as they looked at Baba and watched all that was going on.

But they were not Baba-lovers—as somebody said, not "registered" Baba-lovers!

Baba was very occupied giving so much of Himself to each of His lovers, that you'd think He would have no time for two individuals. But suddenly He turned and, referring to the American ladies, asked one of the mandali, "Are they comfortable? Have they got chairs? Are they comfortable?"

The women had been given chairs, and they sensed what He was saying and looked at Baba and nodded.

Sometimes it was very difficult for people to talk to Baba if they were not Baba-lovers. They'd think, "He doesn't talk so we mustn't talk either." But otherwise, you wouldn't even realize Baba was silent.

So when it was time for all to leave, Baba again turned to these ladies and asked, "Is there anything you have to say? Do you want to ask something? Is there anything you want to say?"

They were very sweet old ladies, and they said, "No, Baba. No, Baba, thank you, it's all right."

Then Baba again turned to His lovers; some babies had been placed in His lap and He was fondling them, at the same time blessing another person, smiling, giving of His Love. But again He turned to the Americans and said, "Is there anything you want to ask? Is there anything you want to say?"

Then one of them said, "Well, Baba, there's just one thing."

"Speak," Baba said. "Speak out."

She said, "I feel so bad that I cannot take You as God. But is it all right if I take You as my friend, Baba? Is that all right?"

Baba replied, "Why not?" He was all aglow. "Remember, I'm the best friend ever. You won't find a better friend. I am that. Take Me as your friend, take Me as your brother, take Me as your father, take Me as mother, take Me as your child. Take Me as anything. I am whatever you take Me to be. Take me as God; I am that. Or take Me as any of these things."

But then His eyes flashed and He looked stern. "But don't take Me for anything in between. Don't take Me as mahatma, guru, saint."

And they said, "No, Baba."

They were so happy. One of these women was an artist. They wrote to Baba afterwards.

JIM REEVES

One day in the later years, Mani brought the portable record player and some old records into Mandali Hall:

> I think we'll play some records today, especially the Jim Reeves records. Baba was sitting right here in this chair when He first heard Jim Reeves. In 1967 my brother Adi from London had sent a record of Jim Reeves, singing on both sides. When I played it here, Baba liked it so much; He kept saying it touched His heart. Later Baba said that Jim Reeves' voice touched His heart in English [Western] music, just as Begum Aktar's voice touched His heart in Indian music. Begum Aktar's songs were ghazals, with their words of spiritual poetry. Baba liked the words of certain Jim Reeves' songs very much, but others He liked only for his voice.
>
> When we were in Guruprasad in 1968, Baba wanted us to buy up all the Jim Reeves records we could find in Poona, so they were brought and would be played for Baba. This singing of Jim Reeves served to give relaxation to Baba

during that intense period of seclusion work He did in Guruprasad at that time. That period was unbelievable; when we look back, we can still feel the intensity of His work at that time.

So when Baba would eat His meals or His breakfast, with Mehera and others of the women serving Him, I would be sitting with the gramophone playing these records one after another. Baba would listen and then say, "Umm. So good. Mehera, listen, listen. Put that plate down. Listen. See? See this one we haven't heard. This one is the new one."

"There's a Heartache Following Me" was His favourite. He would want that record played first while He was having breakfast or lunch or supper, and when it was played, He'd put His hand on His heart and sway. Then I'd put on other Jim Reeves records. At the end, again He would want the same song. So the music session at the dining table began and ended with "There's a Heartache Following Me" sung by Jim Reeves.

When we were at Meherazad, the [men] mandali of course were on the other side also (the men were always divided from the women), and when Eruch heard "Heartache" played the second time, He knew that it was time for Baba to come over to the men. We'd hear Eruch say, "Francis, so-and-so, Baba's coming. Be ready." And Baba would go over to the men.

One day in Guruprasad in 1968 I played a new record by Jim Reeves for the first time, called "Welcome to My World." Baba liked it so much. He told me, "Bring it over. Bring it over to the men's side. We'll play it there."

I said, "Right."

After lunch, Baba walked towards the men's side, in His white sadra and with His hand resting on Mehera's arm. Goher went ahead to open the dividing doors so that Baba could go in, and then Mehera would step away and Goher would shut the door from the men's side. This time as Baba was walking along, I walked behind Him with the [portable] gramophone in my hands playing "There's a Heartache Following Me" as the song had not finished when Baba got up. So here I was following Him and that song was playing, following Him, as it were! Baba went in and sat in His chair on the men's side, looking radiant.

Just a few of the mandali were there. Because nobody was allowed to come in (not even barbers) and none of the household mandali around Baba were allowed to go out at that time, they were beginning to look like hippies! When Baba's work was finished, they would be allowed out, and people could come in, but not till then. So there were just the few sitting there—Francis, Eruch of course, Pendu, Aloba, I think Bal Natu or not, I don't know.

Anyway, the few who were staying with Him were there. Baba sat in the chair and I played "Welcome to My World". Baba would always make things appear as if they happened naturally, but now I can see that Baba wanted the message in the song to get across: "Knock and the door will open; seek and you will find. Ask and you'll be given the key to this world of mine. I'll be waiting here, with my arms unfurled, waiting just for you. Welcome to My World".

So He said, "Francis, now listen carefully. Listen carefully to the words . . ."

So Francis said, "Yes, yes." [Francis didn't like Jim Reeves' singing one bit!]

I sat at Baba's feet, as I'm sitting now [by Baba's chair in

Mandali Hall] and played that record, and while the song was being played Baba mimed gestures for each word, right through the song, as if to say, "See, see . . . See Francis?," as if to give the message of the song. It was conveyed so beautifully.

༢༽

DR. GOHER AND DR. GRANT

Baba's health was, of course, a huge concern to them all, particularly in the late 1960s. Poor Goher was especially distressed about it, having so much responsibility for His physical care. In the beginning, Baba had made her forget she was a doctor by having her take care of ducks, and according to Mani, when all her enthusiasm and excitement and pride in coming to serve Him as a doctor was razed by this, Baba then kept her continuously busy and on tenterhooks taking care of His health and the health of the mandali.

Mani used to love to tell the following story of Goher's dilemma as the God-Man's doctor:

> Goher was Baba's personal physician. Baba kept Goher very busy, not only as a doctor, but also as the link between the men mandali and the women mandali, busy in so many ways as only Baba can make you. You can't at the end of it all say what you've been doing or what you've done, but He can keep you very busy.
>
> One of the things that is most remindful of Baba's presence even now is interruptions. You could never do a single thing without a thousand interruptions. So even if you happened to open a book, someone would come, "Baba

wants you," or "Baba wants you to do such-and-such." This applied to all of us, but also to Goher.

So Goher had no time to brush up on her medical knowledge, or keep up to date with all the new medicines and techniques and advances going on elsewhere. Baba never gave her time to study.

And yet Baba would tell her, "Now Goher, what are you going to do? I have this," or "I'm feeling like that." And she'd find that no matter what she did medically, it didn't always work. So she was very anxious, wondering, "Am I doing the right thing? After all, it's Baba's person I'm treating. Am I doing everything that should be done?" or "What I'm prescribing for His diet, is this really all right?" "Here we are in the jungle, and what can I do for Baba?" and so on. So she wanted confirmation that she was giving Baba the correct treatment.

She felt helpless. That is the thing with Baba; you are helpless. You come to that point where, no matter how much of a doctor you may be, or how much of a cook you may be, or a painter or a writer, you feel that helplessness which makes you wholly dependent on His grace. So by His grace things get done.

During that time, we used to go stay at Guruprasad in Poona with Baba for the three months of summer.

So Goher determined that when we were in Poona, she would consult a top doctor just to confirm her treatment and assure her that what she was doing for Baba was right (which as a matter of fact he eventually did.) At Meherazad it was very very difficult for her as we had no electricity and were nine miles from the nearest hospitals. So in Poona she looked forward to having tests done, x-rays taken; whatever had to be done could be done easily there.

So when we were in Guruprasad, and Baba was again saying, "My health is bad and I don't know how I'll be able to do this or that . . ." Goher said, "Baba, I want to call this very good doctor, a top doctor, and . . ."

"Doctor?" said Baba. "What's a doctor going to do for My health? This is for My work! I don't want a doctor! I want *you* to treat Me."

"Yes, yes, Baba, that's all very well, but I don't know if what I'm doing is right, and it doesn't seem to work, because I've tried so many things. I feel so helpless. I'm not up on the latest things. I want someone to consult. For my sake, Baba, so that I feel reassured."

This discussion went on, and finally Baba said, "All right. Call a doctor."

So Goher called Dr. Grant. Dr. Grant was and still is a very famous doctor in Poona. He's a Parsi, a Zoroastrian. [Dr. K. B. Grant has since passed away.]

Now to call a doctor, Goher had to use the phone. We who lived with her had found out that Goher, who is such a soft-spoken, gentle person, has three voices. One is the ordinary voice you hear every day; one is the voice she uses when she gets mad about something, fast and angry; and then there's her voice for other doctors, very sweet and polite, "Yes, Doctor, no, Doctor, of course, Doctor . . ."

We had a phone in Guruprasad in what is known as the Rani's room. The Rani's room was like a bridge between the men's side and the women's side of the place. It was not used or occupied by anybody, but was sort of a neutral room. The phone was there. But when Naja, for instance, had to go over to the men's side for kitchen work, or when I had to go over to ask Eruch for some address or a telegraph form, we'd have to cross through the Rani's room. So there were two doors to open and close on the way through.

Now Goher goes to the Rani's room to call Dr. Grant for an appointment for Baba. I come in and hear her on the phone, using her doctor's voice, "Yes, Doctor, of course, Doctor, whatever you like, Doctor, I agree, Doctor . . ." But as I come in, somehow the door slips from my hand and makes a slight bang, and without even covering the phone with her hand, here comes Goher's other voice, "Whydoyouallmakeso-muchnoisecan'tyouseethisisaveryimportantmatterthisisfor-Baba'shealthandwhatdoyoupeopleunderstand . . ."

So I tiptoe to the other side of the room. Without a break she turns back to the phone and continues in her saccharine doctor voice, "Why of course, Doctor, I wouldn't mind at all. Yes, yes."

In the meantime, Naja comes from the other side, galumphing along because she has something very important to do in the kitchen—*taMUCK taMUCK taMUCK taMUCK*—right across the room, and the door rattles. Goher says into the phone, "Yes, Doctor, thank you, Doctor," and to Naja, "Can'tyoupeoplekeepquietevenforafewminutesbecauseI'm makingtheseveryimportantphonecalls??? . . . Of course, Doctor, I entirely agree with you. Thank you, Doctor."

We just couldn't believe it.

Now that the appointment is made, the next step for Goher is to dress up right, which means in a sari. At home she'd just wear a dress, but doctor-to-doctor, there's a certain etiquette to be observed, all these things only another doctor would understand. In the ashram looking after Baba she had none of that, but now she had a chance to be a doctor. She barely has time, but she goes and dresses very nicely. But she's very nervous and tense.

Baba is also all ready as a patient to receive the doctor. Baba's standing at the end of the hall, and Goher's standing by Him. Just before the car comes, Baba turns to Goher and says, "You know, Goher, My health is so bad!" "Yes, Baba, he's coming, the doctor's coming."

The doctor's car drives in under the portico outside, which is a distance away. Eruch receives the doctor and conducts him to Baba. Dr. Grant had met Baba before, and as he approaches Baba, he notices that Baba's looking so radiant! So blooming in health, just shining! He comes forward, Baba looks up at him and says, "I'm so happy to see you. Sit down." So Baba makes the doctor comfortable.

This doctor himself happens to be a very emaciated little person to look at. After they both sit, Baba asks, "How's your health?"

"Well, Baba, it's fine, it's all right."

"You don't look so well," says Baba. "So thin! Do you sleep well?"

"No, Baba, that's the trouble. It's the night watches, I'm always called at night, and I have so many cases . . ."

"Is that so? Well then, you should sleep in the daytime sometimes."

"I tried that, Baba."

"Do you eat well?"

"Well Baba, sometimes I just have to snatch a bite here and there, but then . . ."

"But what do you eat in the morning?" Baba asks.

So now the tables are turned. Baba is the doctor, and the doctor is the patient, with Baba asking all the questions and the doctor answering. Yes, he ate this, but he couldn't eat that . . . So Baba says, "No, no, you listen to Me," and Baba gives him a diet and timing for sleep and rest and all those kinds of things.

He says, "Yes, Baba," to everything, and Baba says, "Now, mind you, you do this!" "Yes, Baba." "Now don't forget." "No, Baba, I won't forget."

Now poor Goher is shifting her weight from one foot to the other, waiting for the chance to get a word in edgewise because she wants to ask him about Baba. As soon as all Baba's prescribing is over, Baba gives the doctor a beautiful discourse. Eruch said it was so good, he wishes he remembered every word of it. The doctor hears it through, and while giving the discourse, Baba also tells him, "I'm going to break My silence in nine months."

"Yes, Baba." This doesn't mean much to Dr. Grant, I guess, but he listens with respect. He is not a Baba-lover, but he has great respect for Baba.

So when all that is done, Baba dismisses him, saying, "All right, I am very happy you came, now you can go."

Poor Goher can't believe it! The doctor and Eruch walk away, and Goher follows to see if she can catch him at least on the way out, "Doctor Grant, I wanted to ask you . . ."

Dr. Grant turns his head, looks at Baba, and then turns to Dr. Goher and says, "You know, doctor, there's absolutely nothing wrong with the patient."

"Yes, but Doctor, I . . ."

CLAP! Baba's calling Goher back to Him very urgently. She knows that now Dr. Grant is escaping, he's slipping away from her, but Baba's calling, and . . . *CLAP! CLAP!* Baba's insistent, frowning. "I called you and you're coming immediately!"

So she goes to Baba. And Baba says, "Look, now that he's leaving, run, go and catch him in time before the car starts, before he goes away. Tell him I'm going to break My silence in nine months."

"But Baba . . . !"

In the meantime, the car starts. You can hear it. "Catch him before he leaves!" says Baba. "Hurry up!"

So poor Goher abandons all etiquette, clutches her petticoat and pulls it up along with her sari, and gallops across the hall, shouting, "Stop, stop!" in her second, loud, voice. Eruch, seeing this, halts the car and says, "Doctor, just a minute. Dr. Irani wants to say something."

So Dr. Grant stops and puts his head out of the window, waiting for Dr. Goher Irani who is looking very unceremonial now, with the sari clutched way up her legs like Charley's aunt, running down the marble stairs—*galumph! galumph! galumph! galumph! galumph!*—up to the car. The consultant says, "Yes, Doctor?" and Goher says, panting, "Doctor, Baba's going to break His silence in nine months!"

Dr. Grant can't believe it. He looks and very solemnly says, "Yes, I know. He told me that." And then he puts his hand on her shoulder, gives a gentle tap, and says, "Take it easy, Doctor, take it easy."

The car drives off. And now Goher's coming back up those steps, a bent figure, slowly walking right across the hall towards Baba. And she sees Baba bowed over in His chair, hunched, looking absolutely unwell, and then Baba looks up at Goher and says, "Goher, you know, My health is so bad and I'm feeling so weak. What are you going to do about it?"

And Goher replies, "As soon as I change my sari, Baba, I'll look in the medical book." That's when Baba becomes the patient!

1968–1969

In a Family Letter dated January 25, 1968, Meherazad, Mani writes:

> With the stepping in of the new year, we find a quick stepping up of Baba's seclusion work, not so much by what we can perceive as by what we can dare to conceive. Baba says "You can only see what you see me doing outwardly, but I am continually working on all planes of consciousness at the same time. As my manifestation time is closing in, the pressure of my work is tremendous. You cannot have an iota of an idea of it." We can, however, faintly imagine it from what His infinite tiredness reveals to us; watch it in the cauldron of world chaos that is boiling over; see it in the dawn of His Love rising gloriously over new horizons every day. But all that is happening is nothing compared to what will happen, Beloved Baba tells us. To help us imagine the measure of difference between the "is" and "will", Baba compared the small height of the Seclusion Hill at Meherazad to the awesome stature of Mount Everest!

Knowing what we know now—that in only a year and six days from the writing of this letter, their darling Beloved would drop His body—the Family Letters of 1968 strike me as specially poignant. With hindsight, it is so clear that His Universal Work was reaching its crescendo, and the 1968 Letters record many outward manifestations of it.

"Baba is awakening the Americans to Him on all fronts. The 'minor miracles' (of newly turned hearts) are daily occurrences," writes a Baba-lover, and other letters that Mani quotes tell of Baba's work in Bombay, Australia, and Iran, as well as many new Baba groups in America.

> Unquestionably, Baba's tempo in the U.S. is speeding up spectacularly – word of the Beloved has quickened the hearts of many who have been yearning for they knew not what. He seems

to be reaping a harvest of ripe souls with the ancient tools of love and inspiration . . . [And she writes later:] To the 'old' lovers the quick response of the 'new' ones often appears amazing.

Elsewhere she writes:

And so the Beloved's minstrels in many lands, East and West, in different tongues and in different tunes, sing of Him. His Love is their music, their hearts His instrument.

In January 1968, Baba directed that a circular be sent to the East (by Adi) and West (by Mani in a Family Letter), announcing the extension of His intense seclusion for one month, from February 25 to March 25:

Baba wants His lovers to know that by this date the phase of His universal work in Seclusion will end, and that there will be no further Seclusions.

Baba wants all His lovers to realize what He has said before, that the fate of the universe hangs on His Seclusion and the redemption of mankind depends on His Manifestation. He says that His having prolonged His universal work in Seclusion is an act of His divine Compassion and Love preceding His Manifestation.

Baba then directed His lovers to recite the Master's Prayer and Prayer of Repentance daily until March 25, and to observe complete silence for twenty-four hours from midnight March 16 to midnight March 17.

In another letter, Mani shared a glimpse of this intense time:

While I'm writing this Beloved Baba is sitting in the Hall, alone, for the special work He does every morning and afternoon, when we must not make the least noise. During these hours of utter quiet it is startling to hear a crow caw, or the sudden rattling of a window when the wind comes up. To walk on the gravel paths by the Hall is like walking on eggshells; and as a sneeze from dear old Baidul is a threat to the sound barrier at any time, he is made to sit a good distance away under the mango tree. While we go about our daily chores 'fast fast' as usual, we are constantly reminding one another "softly, softly". And when these soundless sessions are over and we are again with Baba, another kind of quiet is maintained: no correspondence can be read to Him, no questions asked, no argument or excuses offered in carrying out the smallest of His day to day orders, no cause given for the least disturbance—so fragile is the container of His momentous seclusion. But strong is the love and obedience of His lovers helping to keep it intact, for Beloved Baba informs us from time to time: 'My work is being done very satisfactorily'.

The women remembered how tense it was during the time of His daily sessions, as they tried to do their chores without making a sound. Occasionally Baba would call Mehera and Mani—and sometimes all the women—in the night, when He was restless. And Goher, who tended to Him all day, and whose bed was just outside the inner door to Baba's room, was often called in the night. Bhau remembers that the lightest knock would wake her, despite the fact that she had been up caring for Baba all day. Baba wanted the watchmen to knock on that door very lightly, as He didn't want Mehera and Mani disturbed.

Mani once told us, as we sat in the Meherazad dining room with her, how Baba was at the table in that last period when Naja came into the dining room. As the cook, naturally enough she was saying something about the food as she entered. But Baba stopped her and said that now was the time to focus on Him and to pay attention to Him in His presence. It was a "head's up" for all of them.

In the Family Letter dated March 1, 1968, Baba announced another extension of His Seclusion, this time to May 21. On the day in February that He decided this, a large stray monkey appeared in a tree at Meherazad. After all efforts to coax it down failed and everyone decided to ignore it, the monkey suddenly went wild, leapt from roof to roof—sending tiles flying—and ended up leaping from the topmost point of the house on to the roof of Baba's room "with a tremendous crash and impact." The mandali with Baba at the time thought the ceiling would cave in from that impact. After the monkey jumped down from the roof, it was vigorously chased all around Meherazad. It stayed out of reach, high up on roofs and trees, as the chasers pursued below with brooms, sticks, and branches—until, around sunset, it finally left. (It ended up staying in the nearby village for almost a month!) Mani reported, "Baba said that the havoc played by the monkey on the roof of His room on the day He decided to lengthen the Seclusion, was deeply significant to His work and that which is to happen after 21st May."

About His seclusion, Baba remarked:

> None can have the least idea of the immensity of the work that I am doing in this seclusion. The only hint I can give is that compared with the work I do in seclusion all the important work of the world put together is completely insignificant. Although for me the burden of my work is crushing, the result of my work will be intensely felt by all people in the world. . . . I repeat, something great will happen that has never happened before. . . . I also repeat that the fate of the universe hangs on my Seclusion and the redemption of mankind depends upon my Manifestation.

Mani added to this momentous message that Baba would be in Guruprasad from April to the end of June, but that His seclusion would continue there and that He wanted to remain completely undisturbed during His stay.

And so His seclusion went on. Mani said about their Guruprasad stay that year, "... except for the change of environment, we are still at Meherazad!" The seclusion atmosphere prevailed in both places:

> As I sit typing on the palatial verandah of Guruprasad, I can see a fraction of the city's life coursing along the Bund Road a little distance from where we are. There is the ceaseless criss-cross of pedestrians, cyclists, buses, cars, taxis, scooters, jingling horse carriages, rumbling bullock carts, peddlers' hand carts, droning auto-rickshaws (which we call bumble-bees), back-firing motorcycles, and trucks and lorries that thunder by them all. This current of movement and sound sweeping past us all day, is a storm when compared with the stillness which abides within Guruprasad: no visitor steps in, none of us who are with Baba step out; absolute quiet is maintained during the hours when Baba does His work in the solitude of His room, so that we practically speak in whispers and move about on tiptoe. No matter how loud the cacophony of traffic from the road, the roar of a plane overhead, the piercing cheep-cheep of sparrows right at His door, the least sound from any of us near His room would disturb Baba in His work.

Approach road to Guruprasad, which was completely empty during His strict seclusion in 1968.

In one of the most moving messages of this intense period, Baba said to His lovers (in the Letter dated May 12), "I know how you feel. I know your love. I know the agony of your longing to see me. I know what I am doing and what I have to do. I know when the time will be right for you to see me, and at that time I will call you."

Mani often opened and/or closed a Family Letter with a message from Baba. Always practical, she explained, "For the lazy ones, however few, who might glide across the central expanse of this letter, the messages of utmost importance are placed at both ends of the letter where none can miss them."

As soon as Baba stepped out of His seclusion on May 21, He entered a period of "exclusion," when His lovers were excluded from seeing Him. Mani wrote, "And, we understand from Him, this period of exclusion is the threshold leading to Inclusion, the time that will include all to His darshan!"

Much of the September 9, 1968, Letter is devoted to describing Baba's seclusion, and Baba's work that went on until the end of July. "How I kept it going over the last stretch to its completion, I alone know!" Baba told them. "You cannot have a seed of an idea how crushing the pressure was, for it is beyond human understanding. On the final day my body felt as though it had been through a wringer."

This, the mandali could see, Mani said, as He looked so infinitely tired after the work. Just to keep the link with His physical body required great labor. Once when the women begged Him to be less neglectful of His health and to take more rest, Baba said, "That would mean once again prolonging the Work and postponing the date of its conclusion. If now I allow that to happen, it will indefinitely postpone the result and set it on a different course."

"And so He kept working on," Mani wrote, "while we were in Poona and for weeks after we returned on 1st July to Meherazad."

On the evening of Tuesday, July 30, 1968, Baba declared:

> MY WORK IS DONE. IT IS COMPLETED 100% TO MY SATISFACTION. THE RESULT OF THIS WORK WILL ALSO BE 100% AND WILL MANIFEST FROM THE END OF SEPTEMBER.

Meanwhile the longing of His lovers to see Him was increasing, especially, Mani noted in the Letter, among "the Western sea of His young lovers whose eyes thirst for their first glimpse of Him."

> The greatest event for Baba-lovers is being with Baba. In their heart-scales no event can weigh more. Knowing their longing, as only the Beloved can who suffers His separation in them, Baba says: "I know that they are impatient to see me. And what about me? I also am impatient for them to see me. But the time has yet not come—so my lovers and I, we must wait a while longer."

"If the longing of His lovers is mounting," Mani wrote, "so is their number. In East and West, the number has grown to such an extent that we cannot imagine the next Darshan being arranged on the lines of any gathering or sahavas held in the past."

At the end of this September Letter, Mani included something Baba spelt out, "Coming, Coming, Coming—CAME!" And then what He added a few days later:

> COMING, COMING, COMING – CAME!
> I AM TIRED OF THE ILLUSION GAME.

Then on November 1, 1968, she wrote from Meherazad, "This unexpected letter following on the heels of the last one, is a momentous messenger carrying momentous tidings: the announcement from Beloved Baba for which His lovers have been waiting, waiting, waiting."

The Letter carried His Life Circular No. 70, announcing that Baba would give darshan, under certain conditions, from April 10 to June 10, 1969, for a fixed number of hours each day in Guruprasad. The darshan would be strictly for His lovers from the East and West, not an open darshan for the general public. Baba-lovers at the most could come for a week only, or a shorter time depending on where they were from. No more than five hundred lovers could attend each darshan week.

"This is the time for my lovers," Baba said. "The time for the world's crowds to come to me will be when I break my Silence and Manifest my Divinity. The 1962 East-West Gathering was nothing compared with what this Gathering will be."

At the end of this dazzling announcement, Mani quoted Baba:

> I have been saying: the Time is near,
> it is fast approaching, it is close at hand.
> Today I say: <u>the Time has come.</u> Remember this!

At the end of December 1968, Mehera's birthday was celebrated in Meherazad, and Baba's nephew Dara was married to Amrit, the daughter of Shatrughan and Subdhara Kumar. Beloved Baba called many of His closest ones from Bombay, Poona, and Ahmednagar, and sat on the porch of the Meherazad house to greet them. His lovers presented Him with some light entertainment. In the film of this occasion, although Baba is lovingly greeting His guests and laughing at funny songs, you can see how utterly exhausted and weak He looks. For most of those who attended the celebration, it was the last time they saw Baba before He dropped His body.

On January 14, 1969, Baba stopped going to Mandali Hall. The men mandali began coming to be with Him in His room in the house, entering by the outside door, as usual. The inner door would be closed and, inside the house, the women would hurry up with their chores to be ready when Baba called them. Mani said that she had much less time

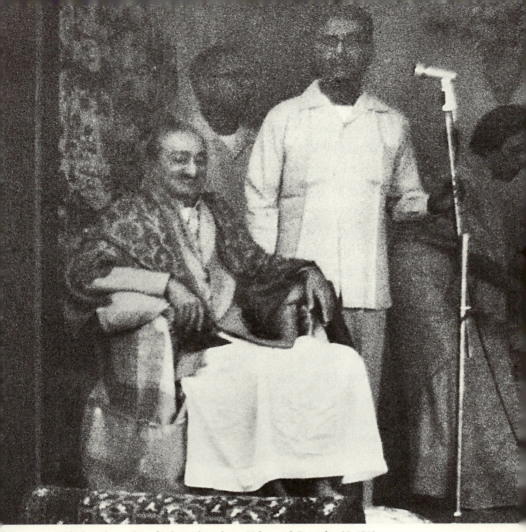

The last photo taken of Baba in this Advent. Meherazad, December 23, 1968.

for correspondence because they spent more time with Baba, massaging Him to ease the pain, or sitting with Him as she or Rano read aloud.

JANUARY 26, 1969

Paging through the Family Letters, it seems incredible that one of the last ones is dated the January 26, 1969, only five days before Beloved Baba dropped His body. Mani said in later years that although the women mandali—and especially Dr. Goher—had some glimpses of how bad Baba's health was after His seclusion work, He hid it from Mehera. And they themselves never dreamt that they would one day be living without Baba's physical presence. You can sense Mani's deep concern and worry for His health in this late January Letter, but also her innocence of what was to come within that very week. The Letter begins: "A prosperous 1969 to all of us—prosperous in the wealth of Baba's Love which thrives on poverty of the lover's self!"

A few paragraphs down, she touched on Baba's poor health:

> Although 1969 begins with clouded skies—the clouds of personal trials and tribulations in the lives of a number of His close ones, the clouds of world-wide disunity and violence—for His lovers there is the resplendent silver lining promising fulfillment of the long longed-for darshan of their Beloved. Even through the great cloud of Baba's health, there is a small soft light shining. I wrote to Fredella some days ago: "Beloved Baba's health has not been at all good for some time, from the tremendous strain of His Seclusion work. And although the extreme anaemia (which a recent routine test showed) has been promptly remedied, His physical condition is very weak. Goher and the other doctors strongly feel there should be a thorough check-up done. As this is not possible at Meherazad–Ahmednagar, we're trying to persuade Baba to make an early move to have it done in Poona. We are hoping He will agree."
>
> Baba did NOT agree. He refuses moving to Poona before the usual date, which is about the end of March, in time for the Darshan beginning 10th April. . . .
>
> Baba tells us that He is both God and Man. Seeing Him undergo sickness and accidents and suffering, are stark reminders that He is Man, that He has said: "I have taken on

the form of Man to take on the suffering of man." And when, tending to His body to the utmost of our ability we feel over-anxious or worried, He reminds us: "Don't forget I am God. I know all. Simply do as I say." We bow to His Will.

Mani then gave the text of the Life Circular No. 71, issued by Adi, for all of His Western family:

> Beloved Avatar Meher Baba wishes all His lovers to know that His three years of intense work has shattered His health.
> In spite of this He has invited His lovers from all over the world to come to Him for His darshan next summer, for it is the time for them to come to Him and receive His Love.
> It is the time; and the place, Guruprasad, Poona has been fixed.
> But with the present condition of His health, how beloved Baba will give His darshan to the thousands who will come, yet remains to be determined; but it will be. He will give His darshan.
> This darshan, Baba says, will be the last given in Silence – the last before He speaks His world-renewing Word of words.

Mani went on: Baba had told them that this was not only to be His last darshan given in Silence, but that it would be "unparalleled." Certainly unparalleled was the number of Westerners who had signed up to come—250 for the first week alone, which was the limit laid down. "It is astonishing but not surprising, for His Family has grown massively in the last few years. His children have waited long for this homecoming, and now that the way is open they are toiling towards the means."

At the end of this Letter, Mani wrote, "I don't know when the next letter will be going out, but at least I know it cannot be before the Darshan in Guruprasad—unless of course another Circular causes a premature delivery like this one!"

She ended the Letter with Baba's Birthday message for His 75th Birthday, February 25, 1969:

> TO LOVE ME FOR WHAT I MAY GIVE YOU IS NOT LOVING ME AT ALL. TO SACRIFICE ANYTHING IN MY CAUSE TO GAIN SOMETHING FOR YOURSELF IS LIKE A BLIND MAN SACRIFICING HIS EYES FOR SIGHT. I AM THE DIVINE BELOVED WORTHY OF BEING LOVED BECAUSE I AM LOVE. HE WHO LOVES ME BECAUSE OF THIS WILL BE BLESSED WITH UNLIMITED SIGHT AND WILL SEE ME AS I AM.

ETERNAL BELOVED

After the Family Letter dated January 26, 1969, there was no Letter until March 14, 1969. This silence spoke, of course, of the most momentous event in Mani's life: her beloved Brother dropped His body on January 31, 1969. From the moment He had first held her in His arms, her life had been continually focused on Baba in His physical form.

The mid-March Letter is heart-rending in places. Mani could not describe what we cannot begin to imagine: what January 31 and the days that followed were like for the mandali. Mani doesn't write about how, trying to hide her grief from Mehera, she would go to Eruch's cabin and weep her heart out, or how lightly she slept at night, some part of her always listening so that she would be awake to comfort Mehera if she cried too long. There are photos of Mehera and Mani (and Meheru) on walks in the fields around Meherazad in those early days after Baba was gone. Mehera's pale, grief-stricken face, so full of sorrow, gives some glimpse of what His physical absence was for her. In a movie of the entombment of Baba's body at Meherabad, you see heartbreaking scenes of Mehera, distraught and weeping, entering to bow down to Baba in the crypt, and Mani and the women, all completely focused on her, comforting her, taking the briefest of darshans and then turning back to Mehera, putting their own grief aside. Mani was next to her always, stroking her arm, talking to her all the while, smiling, calming, soothing, encouraging, literally holding Mehera up at some points. How could Mani describe all this? There are no words for such loss.

JANUARY 31, 1969

As Baba-lovers knew, Baba's health had gone steadily downhill from December. On the night of January 30, Baba had violent spasms all night. He then told Goher to awaken Mehera and Mani at 4:00 a.m. on January 31. Mehera stood outside the door of Baba's room as He told the men mandali (who were inside), "Whatever Goher has done, she has given Me the right treatment. She is not to be blamed for anything that happens to Me. She is not responsible."

After that, Mehera and Mani stayed up to be available if Baba should call them again. At 7:00 a.m., Mehera and the women went in to be with Baba, and Mehera washed His face and shaved Him. As He was having trouble breathing easily, Mani asked if they should call another doctor, and Baba asked what the date was. When Mani told Him it was the 31st, Baba said, "Thirty-first. Today is the day of my crucifixion. How I suffer nobody knows, and yet I have to suffer for seven days more."

Mehera persuaded Him to shorten the days by one day, which He agreed to. After an hour, the women went out and the men mandali came in. It was at this time that Baba sent a message to Mehera, through Mani, to be brave and not to worry. Mehera was called in again at 11:00 a.m., and left soon after when the men were called.

At 12:15 p.m., Beloved Baba dropped His body. As Mani told it, "I just stepped out of the room for a moment, for a split second, when I heard the men call, 'BABA'. I knew that He had dropped His body. I was opening the door and bringing something when I heard the men. For some reason, I was shouting at the top of my voice, 'BABA, YOU ARE GOD [*TAMO KHODAI SHEV*]. YOU CAN'T DO THIS, DON'T GO! MEHERA, YOU TELL BABA. YOU TELL BABA, AND HE WILL COME BACK. PLEASE COME BACK, DON'T LEAVE US! PLEASE COME BACK.'

"Mehera then started saying it. Later, I realized, I should not have said, 'You are God,' because God Himself was doing it; I should have said, 'You are the Avatar.' "[1]

Mani went on calling out, "Baba, you are God. For Mehera's sake, come back!"

The men and the women, in different ways, tried to revive Baba, but it was no use.

As they were wrapping Baba's body, Mani remembered something that had happened twenty-five years before:

> Anything that happens around Baba is never by chance; nothing is insignificant, even though it appears so. Sometimes Baba is providing seeds, which must always bear fruit for some effect in the future. On the day Baba dropped His body, it came back to me in His room.
>
> It happened years before in Dehra Dun, when Baba had made us shut our eyes and count to 20, as He quietly snuck out of the room. We enjoyed it at the time and completely forgot about it. One little incident of life with Baba. Years went by. On 31 January, when we were in the room, after we had realized Baba had left His form, this incident came back to me. And I put it in my heart. "You've done it again. You made us close our eyes and then You slipped away. Just like that."

There is an absolutely heart-wrenching chapter in the book *Mehera-Meher* about Baba's dropping of His body and the days that

Mehera with Mani and the women mandali inside Baba's Samadhi shortly after He dropped His body.

followed. It gives just a glimpse of what it must have been like for the mandali to lose Him, and lose Him so suddenly.

But in the March 14 Family Letter,[2] Mani's strength in Baba is again displayed. Every sentence seems to uphold Him in light of this devastating event. She started with His message:

"Although I am present everywhere eternally in my formless Infinite state, from time to time I take form. This taking of the form and leaving it is termed my physical birth and death. In this sense I am born and (in this sense) I die when my universal work is finished."

Then she reminded her readers, "On 30th July 1968, Baba said: 'My work is done. It is completed 100% to my satisfaction.'" And on 30th January, "Baba reminded us, saying to a visiting doctor: 'My Time has come.'"

She repeated the telegram that had announced His passing to the world, and included the resident mandali's "true account" of Baba's dropping His body, written by Francis. She wrote of how they took His form to Meherabad on the evening of January 31:

> Of the Meherazad men and women mandali who accompanied His body on that unbelievable journey to Meherabad, the role of Baba's beloved Mehera was the hardest. But she played it supremely, surrendering the anguish of her heart to the wish of her Beloved who had asked her to "Keep courage". And even now, through her overwhelming pain of separation from Him, He helps her to keep courage.

At sunset, they placed Baba's body in the Tomb on the Hill, in fulfillment of His order:

> Although we started out from Meherazad on that Friday evening with hearts numbed and empty, our hands had been kept occupied in doing the things that the Beloved would want us to do. In the midst of many practical details that Eruch was seeing to, he reminded me to take along our gramophone and the record of "Begin the Beguine". Eruch said that Baba had told him, many times over the years, to play this song by His side when He dropped His body. And

so on that night of 31st January, and the next day, seven times I played the song of "Begin the Beguine" by His side—at first in the Cabin where His body rested for a while and later in the Tomb. And while the song played, it seemed to convey to us His message that this was not an end but the beginning—the beginning of His completed work bearing fruit. A day before dropping the body, even while the movement of His fingers brought on a renewed spasm, Baba told us, "All this, all that I have been through all along, has been a preparation for the Word—for just the One Word!" And with a quizzical smile He added "Just imagine!"

As Mani mentioned, in the hours before the crypt was prepared, Baba's body was kept in the Cabin next to the Samadhi. Years after, when visiting the Cabin, Mani would recall how Mehera and the close women—Mani, Goher, Naja, Meheru, and Rano—sat around Baba's form in the Cabin as it rested on the stretcher that had brought His body from Meherazad. It was, Mani said, their last intimate time with Him, before giving Him up to the world.

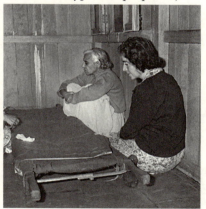

Goher and Mani by the stretcher.

Later in the night, seeing that Mehera and the others were in deep shock, Eruch called Mani and Goher aside and absolutely insisted that they take Mehera back to Meherazad. Eruch later said that he just knew they had to leave in order to break the downward spiral of their shock and grief. In her distress, Mehera couldn't bear the thought of leaving Baba's body; the only way they could persuade her to go was to remind her that there was no light burning by Baba's bed in His bedroom. So they went back to Meherazad to light the lamp and gather up some clothes and rest a little, and then returned to spend the next days at Meherabad in their old room there. Once away, riding in the car under a full moon, the others realized that it had been essential to take Mehera away, back to Meherazad, even if for a night.

Long after, Mani recalled in the Hall at Meherazad:

> In the last so many years [of Baba's lifetime], we went to Meherabad once a year, just to see to the things of Baba's that we had stored on the Hill in the East Room, precious things, some of which you now see in the Museum. When we came, Baba would stay down the Hill and send us women up. When we would drop Him off down below, we would say, "Baba, why don't You come up?"
>
> He'd reply, "No. Now, only My coat [His body] will come here. And that's for the whole world."
>
> And when His precious form, His "coat," was lying in the crypt, we saw the world of Baba-lovers come from every direction. It seemed like a line of ants climbing up the Hill, there were so many people! Then Mehera and we understood that now He was for everybody. So we only

went at certain times of the day to be with Baba in the Tomb.

And whenever we went, I found each one of His lovers had a different experience to relate. Baba's face even in the crypt was radiant and some of us found that His face had a different expression each time we went in. (Afterwards, of course, we compared notes.) That was the beginning; the dam had broken and the floods had started.

LAST GOODBYE

Of the week following January 31, Mani wrote, "Meherabad has no electricity, but there was enough light. There was God's lantern lighting the way for His pilgrims—the full moon shone in a clear sky during the entire Week." She talked of the pilgrims who came: "The singing and music went on from evening till four in the morning, and we thought of the smiling remark the Beloved had made on His return from His Andhra tour years ago: 'My lovers sang outside my window all night while I rested.' They were doing the same thing now."

As for when He was to be interred, there was much debate. The mandali kept on extending the interment date as Baba-lovers continued to travel to Meherabad for a final glimpse of Baba in the crypt.

Mani in discussion with Eruch, Dr. Ginde, and Dr. Donkin.

FACING PAGE: *Crowds gathered at Baba's Samadhi after He dropped His body.*

Mani wrote:

> Mehera and I felt that the Beloved Himself would give an indication of when it should be done, that as long as His dear body remained fresh and lovely we would not have it covered up. Even after a week it was not found necessary to place the covering! But as Baba had told us on the last day, the morning of 31st January, that after seven days He would be 100% free (from suffering, as we interpreted His hand gestures to mean), we took that as an indication. And so, seven days after the Event, at 12.15 noon on Friday the 7th of February 1969, the interment took place amid thousands of voices singing His glorious Name and resonant cries of AVATAR MEHER BABA KI JAI!!!

Soon afterwards, Mehera and Mani remembered something else. For many years, Baba's close ones celebrated His Birthday by the Zoroastrian calendar, so the date moved up a day every four years. Then, at some point, Baba declared that His Birthday should be celebrated only on the date of His birth by the Western calendar, February 25.

Naturally, when Baba was very ill in the last week of January 1969, Mehera was terribly distressed and concerned. One day she asked Him, "Baba, when will You get strong again?" Baba comforted her by saying that after His Birthday He would become very strong. Mehera and Mani naturally assumed that He meant by February 25, which seemed a long way away.

Of course as it came to pass, Baba dropped His body on January 31, and His beautiful form was covered seven days later, on February 7—which Mehera and Mani came to realize was His Birthday by the Zoroastrian calendar that year!

The fact that Baba had said He would be very strong after His Birthday comforted Mehera. And indeed, they came to see His strength in the great, overpowering force of His Love that was felt soon after by so many all over the world.

Mehera saying good-bye to her Beloved.

In the Trust Deed that had been executed by Baba ten years earlier, Baba indicated that Mehera should be present when His body was interred in the Tomb, and so, after her final darshan and tearful good-bye, Mehera and the women stood at the north window looking in as Baba's form was covered. Every year thereafter, Mehera would come to the Samadhi on February 7, and the poignancy of His interment and her good-bye always seemed to be evoked on that day.

TAKING CARE OF MEHERA

One day, about fifteen years before Baba dropped His body, Baba came into a room where Mani was alone. As she told the story in Mandali Hall:

With a charming smile, sort of taking me into His confidence, He said, "Say yes! I'm going to ask you for something—say yes!" And I was on the point of saying yes, we had always said yes, when something in the look on His face made me wait till I heard what He would say next.

He said, "If I pass away, when I pass away, will you look after Mehera?"

And I said, "No." For the first time in my life, I was flatly saying no to Baba! "How can You ask that of me? How can You do this to us, to Mehera and me and all of us? How can we live without You? You know You promised that we'd all be together, all go together. How can You do that?!"

"Of course it won't be like that!" said Baba. "You all will die long before I pass away." And I accepted that totally, literally. "But just say yes! Say yes to Me! Say yes to the request I have asked. Answer yes."

And, of course, after what He had said, I said, "Yes!"

And by His Grace, it was possible to do that, right from 31st January, 1969. It had gone, was rubbed out over the passage of years, sailed away. But it came back and confronted me in Baba's room on 31st January.

So when the unthinkable happened and Baba dropped His body, Mani hid her own great grief and turned her whole being toward Mehera. Mani said to some of us that for two years after Baba passed away,

FACING PAGE: Men lowering a three-sided, wooden box over Meher Baba's form on February 7, 1969. The box was covered by additional earth, and eventually by a marble tombstone.

she woke at the slightest sound in the room they shared: Was Mehera crying? What was Mehera doing? Was Mehera all right?

To encourage and console her, Mani used to tell Mehera that for her, Baba's Radha, this separation from Baba, her Lord Krishna, was but another tune played on His divine flute, for her life to dance to as perfectly as it had to the sweet music of His physical presence.

Mani told us that she herself would never cry in front of Mehera and she would upbraid those who did.

Yet when she was sure that Mehera was all right, Mani would slip off to Eruch's room to cry. Eruch told me once that Mani was very affected by the dropping of Baba's body, that this grief was very "deep-rooted" in her. She was in a kind of shock; he could see it—she was distracted, struggling to cope with Mehera's loss and her own, and with the need to adjust to the whole, unknown, wide-open, unprotected world they suddenly found themselves in, fighting fires right and left.

Eruch was worried about her. As he shared in the Hall:

> Well, the simple thing is that those days were days of great pain, despite what Baba had said, that, "I am not this body that you see, that this is not what I am, it is just My coat I put on reality to veil reality." But we were so used to the coat that we forgot the reality. So when the coat was dropped, well, we started missing the coat, you see. We didn't care for the substance that was being veiled by the coat. Well, it is a human frailty; what can you say? That's how we are, all of us, until we are blessed by Him. We began to miss His presence, the so-called presence of the coat. But we carried on, we had to do our duty, our responsibilities were there, we had to face them, we had to stand and face them, not to shirk because Baba wouldn't like it, we knew that, so we continued with our day-to-day chores.
>
> Soon after we returned from Meherabad after Baba's

interment, I felt somehow or other that it is not good if the women mandali were to carry on like that in their grief. It was telling too much on their mind, heart and body. I had experienced their grief when we were there on the Hill; we were all there with His body. We were there for more than ten days I think, twelve days all together. So I noticed how it was telling upon them in all respects. When we returned here to Meherazad, the only contact I had was with Mani, Goher, Rano, and sometimes Meheru would come. I found Mani was being affected, literally, and I thought, this is not good, so much responsibility is on her now. I was thinking something must be done, should we take them out for a change or something like that? Go on an outing? Something . . . something should be done now.

Then one evening, after they had returned to Meherazad after the 1969 Darshan at Guruprasad, Mani suddenly remembered some documents that Eruch had asked her for. As Mani tells it:

> So I hurriedly looked for the documents, found them, and walked briskly over towards Eruch's room. I found him outside his room, and I could hear from the splashing of water that he was washing his face. "Oh, Eruch," I said, "I brought the documents you wanted."
>
> He didn't say a word. He stood up, wiped his face with the towel hanging outside his cabin, and then, instead of coming towards me to take the documents, turned away and walked towards the field adjoining Meherazad.
>
> And he said, "Follow me."
>
> Now what's this queer thing Eruch is doing? Follow him? So I followed him, wondering what was the matter. He came to the field and stood facing it, and I stood beside him.

"Can you hear?" he said. I haven't very sharp hearing, but I heard.

What I heard was a sound of sheep, restlessly calling out, "Baa-baa, baa-baa . . ." I realized that the shepherds had done what they often do. They leave their sheep for the night on a field, which is allowed because the sheep provide manure for the farmer who owns the land. But to protect the sheep for the night, the shepherds put a little cordon of thorny branches around them.

"Yes, yes, I can hear," I said.

"Can you see?" And I looked hard. I could see a bit of white here and there, because the sheep were moving about, so I said, "Yes, I can see the sheep, they're moving around."

"No, to the left! Can you see?"

To the left? What was there to see? It's a field!

Then suddenly, my eyes made out a form darker than the darkness of the evening. And I said to myself, "What's that big rock doing in the field?" The contour of the shape was like a rock.

Eruch said, "Now can you see?"

I said yes, and then suddenly I realized. It was not a rock. It was a person. It was the shepherd sitting there, huddled with his homespun blanket over him, settled for the night, unmoving, looking straight at the sheep.

Eruch said, "You see, the sheep think their shepherd has deserted them. The flock think the shepherd has gone. Because it is dark, and they can't see him. So they call out to him, and they're looking for him. And they are confused, and stirring about. But he has his eyes on them. He sits there without moving, looking at them, looking after them. His whole attention is on them. And he will be like that through the night of darkness. When the dawn comes, they will know that their shepherd had never left them, that he was with them all the time."

And that! That was such a help, such a healing, such a comfort. I'll never forget it. That, too, Baba provided. It made such a difference. And I said, "Yes, Baba, I know You are here. And because it is dark and we cannot see You, we may feel that You have left, but You haven't. You're right here. And when the dawn comes, we will know that You have always been here."

So even when we cannot see Him, He is here.

A MESSAGE FROM THE TREE

For Mehera, too, Baba gave a heart-healing message. Some Baba-lovers know that there is a tree outside Mehera-Mani's room on which Baba's face suddenly appeared in the bark as beautifully clear as if it had been sculpted. As Mehera told the story:

> One day, it must have been in July 1969, I was standing at a window in the bedroom that I share with Mani at Meherazad, looking out at a little flower garden that Baba would also see from His bedroom. I had planted it for Him to enjoy, and I was missing darling Baba's physical presence and feeling very sad and lonely.
>
> Very close to my window is a large tree of the wild fig family. We call it an umar. It had always been there, so I never really noticed it. But this morning I felt my eyes being drawn to that tree. I looked at its trunk, and I could not believe what I saw. On the trunk of the tree was exactly the image of Baba's face looking so very beautiful.
>
> "Oh Baba," I said. I was so excited. How sad I had

The tree with Baba's image, just outside of Mehera's window.

been feeling without Him, and there was His lovely face with a crown on His head on a tree in His garden. And He was looking in my bedroom window. I knew that Baba was showing me that He had not forgotten us; that He is always here with us; that He is in the tree, inside the house, in every heart; that He is God, and He is everywhere. Baba was giving us proof that He is with us all the time, and so I felt a little consoled and comforted.

I quickly called Mani to see Baba's lovely image, and Mani called all the girls. . . . Then we had the idea of taking a photo in case the bark which formed the image changed. Mani took the photos, and she sent them to the West for His lovers there to see.[3]

The image remained for about ten years, after which time it naturally faded away as the tree grew and changed.

Baba's image in the tree carried a message for Mani also. After Baba dropped His body, she felt deeply, as did Eruch and the other mandali, that Baba would want Mehera to go on living at Meherazad, in Baba's home, in the house she had designed for Him, near His room, in the unique atmosphere and serenity of the garden she loved. Meherabad was now open to the public; it was the Trust estate, on the verge of great development and activity. Mehera, of course, longed to be near Baba's body and wanted to care for His tomb, but she listened to Mani and the others, and although they went to Meherabad often for darshan, they stayed on at Meherazad.

But every once in a while, Mani would ask herself, "Are we doing the right thing? Is this really what Baba wants for Mehera?" When His face appeared on the tree in Meherazad, she got her answer.

Mani told an amusing story about the photo of Baba's face in the tree:

At first, the image on the tree looked like someone had

done a sketch and started to begin a sculpture. It was not so three-dimensional as it was afterwards. A few days later when we looked there was actually contour. Of course all of us looked then, not just Mehera and me, and we were all amazed: it was not anybody's face, it was Baba. Even the size was Baba's.

Then I said, "Yes, maybe I'll try to take a picture." So with my silly little camera, I took a picture and sent it to Adi to develop in Nagar.

When he sent back the picture, we cut out a little circle in a piece of white paper and placed it over the picture . . . "Oh," they'd say, "I haven't seen that picture of Baba!" We didn't think about making a big thing out of it. But that, to me, was the answer; it was as if Baba were saying, "But I am here."

And, of course, Mehera said, "I know this is the answer, that He wants us to be here."

It was so much Baba's face that one day when Adi came, I asked him, "You saw the pictures? Did you like them? Do you like that tree?"

"Yes, yes," he said. "You've done it very nicely."

"Done it? Done what?"

Mehera talking about Baba's image into a microphone held by Mani.

"Didn't you sculpt Baba's face on the tree?"

I said, "Adi, we haven't touched the tree!"

"What!" Adi got so excited then. When he next gave a talk at the Ahmednagar Centre, he told everybody. The news spread and buses and buses of not only Baba-lovers, but villagers and everyone in the Lions Club, all the lions and lionesses, came. School children came by the hundreds. So much dust was raised here by so many little children with so many little feet, shouting "Avatar Meher Baba ki Jai!"

Every rafter was ringing with Baba's Jai. In fact, some of these little ones did not even know it was "Meher Baba" they were shouting for, they just followed by sound what the others were saying. They said, "Avatar Neher Baba ki Jai." I corrected one little child, "Not Neher Baba, but Meher Baba." But then "neher" means running water, and it was like a neher: the crowds and the veneration just flowed and flowed, for a long time.

You know why there was so much enthusiasm in the villagers' minds about Baba's image on the tree? Because the type of tree that His image came on is an umar tree, which in the Hindu tradition is believed to be the seat of the Dattatreya, the three aspects of God. When you see a god with three heads, it represents the three attributes of God, the Creator, Sustainer, and Dissolver. And whenever you see a Dattatreya temple, you always see it built next to an umar tree. And Baba's image appeared on an umar tree! Well, with that, they just kept pouring in.

Now after seven years there are changes in the bark, naturally, because it's a growing tree. We still have some of the fair bark from the very first time it fell off the tree.

So now in the daytime you can barely see the image. When people want to know where it is, all we can show is the spot. But at night it comes up. It's so beautiful. So I tell people, "Well, Baba's in seclusion in the daytime now." When that little electric bulb on the top is on, you even see the moustache, there is some shadow in that shape, and so warm and so lovely. But in the daytime it goes to rest.

Long before the image on the tree appeared, in 1959, an American Baba-lover named Joanna Smith came here. Baba was walking around in the garden, showing this lady around. The men mandali were there with them.

Mehera would always be inside when Baba would be out in the garden with the men, going from room to room watching Baba from a distance, just to see what He was admiring most, interested in most, showing most in the garden. We would be tagging along behind her.

But at one point on this occasion, Mehera saw Baba stop at this tree by her window, turn to the Baba-lover and place His hand like this, on the tree. And, as Mehera saw, the hand was obviously where the image appeared later. He placed His hand on the tree and said to Joanna Smith, "This tree I like. I like."

Mehera said to me, "You know what Baba said?"

"What?"

"He said this tree He likes."

"This tree? Hmm." Because there's another umar tree in the garden that is much more beautiful; that one is really something to show. We were puzzled: of all the trees in the garden Baba touches this tree? And says to the American lady, "This tree I like"?

He was telling her, but actually He was telling us. You see how deviously He would do it? He was telling her, but the message was to us, for the future.

. . .

Mani would add a little sequel to the image-tree story. One evening when she was walking in the garden, she noticed to her horror that a piece of the bark that formed Baba's nose had come loose and was about to drop off. She worried about it all night, knowing that it would distress Mehera, and finally came up with a plan. First thing in the morning she would tiptoe out with a small container of Fevicol (a kind of glue) and stick the bark back on the tree.

In the morning she got to the tree, and what did she find? A little spider had come in the night and spun the stickiest, strongest little web imaginable between the loose bark piece and the tree, cementing them together in places glue could never reach.

Mani used to say that when Baba would ask something of you, all you had to do was say "yes," and He would give you the help you needed when the time came to do it. You just had to be willing. So it was with Mehera. When Baba asked Mani to take care of Mehera, she had said yes, and Baba helped her (and the others) to help Mehera in the way He wanted. Time went by, Mehera came out of her desolation, and began participating happily in life again.

So much so that one day, twenty years after Baba passed away, when Mani in a moment of exhaustion said, "Mehera, isn't twenty years enough? How much longer do we have to keep doing this?" Mehera instantly replied that every moment of their lives was precious because they had memories of being with Baba in His physical form, of loving Him, seeing Him, serving Him. Mehera said that they had to make the most of their time here remembering Him.

When Mani related Mehera's words to us, she laughed, "In the beginning, it was I who was encouraging Mehera to keep going, and in the end, it was Mehera who was encouraging me!"

"... in the end, it was Mehera who was encouraging me!"

MORE MESSAGES

Mani wrote that they were "completely unprepared, taken entirely unaware" by Baba's dropping of His body. But, she said, looking back, they found that Baba had prepared them, had given them many hints that "now stand out glaringly in the light of the Event." She added that what He had disclosed with one hand, He had covered with the other.

Soon afterwards, Mani remembered a dream that became very meaningful to Mehera after Baba dropped His body:

> When we women would sit around Baba in His room, in His endearingly human way He would often ask after our health, or about any little household matter, or even something specific. One day in January 1969, Baba turned to

me and asked, "Did you dream last night, did you see a dream?"

And I said, "No, Baba, I didn't see a dream. But would You like to hear a dream I had a long time ago?"

"OK. Relate it."

So I told Him a dream—I don't remember which. But looking back, I felt as if Baba was preparing me for something He had in store for later, for a message that would come through a dream I would have later on.

Because what happened was, on 29th January 1969, I had another dream that I related to Mehera at teatime the next morning. Baba was not at all well at the time; He would seem better one day and then worse the next, and we were waiting for Him to get well. So Mehera said, "Well, we won't tell it to Him today. Maybe tomorrow He'll be stronger. Tomorrow we'll tell Him."

We thought His illness was just a temporary thing. It affected us tremendously, but we were looking forward to the time when Baba would get over it.

So, the dream I had that night of 29th January was this. Mehera and I are alone together with Baba in His room. Baba is reclining on the bed and Mehera is standing by Him. I am standing nearer His feet, opposite Him. And the top half of Baba, up to and below the waist, is covered with a towel. His head is covered, His face is covered, His arms are covered, and up till here [Mani gestures]. He's covered with a big white Turkish towel. To this day I can see the tassels at the edges of that towel.

Then Baba puts out His hands from under the towel, only His hands. And He tells me inwardly, very clearly, "Now, you interpret, and tell aloud to Mehera, My gestures.

Interpret My gestures, and tell it to Mehera." So I said, "Yes, Baba." I used to read the alphabet board and, later, His gestures pretty often, more often than the other women.

So Baba puts out His beautiful hands and although now I don't remember what gestures He made, in the dream it's very clear to me what Baba is saying. And what Baba said is, "You know, you see Me covered, you see Me like this, but what you see is not for real. It's not real. It's only make-believe." Meaning, "I'm really here. This is only make-believe. You see Me lying down and covered up, but this is not the Real. This is only mock, a make-believe."

And just that one sentence was so filling. It seemed to fill the whole room. And I woke up with it. I couldn't contain it. So in the early morning after we snatched a cup of tea and before we were called to be with Baba, I told Mehera. We didn't know what it meant, not until afterwards. But still it was a delightful dream.

So, because of the earlier incident when Baba asked me for a dream and I hadn't had one, this time I said to myself, "Oh, I must tell this dream to Baba." Now I had a dream to tell Him.

But this dream could be Reality!

Mani never did get the chance to tell Baba that dream. But it helped console Mehera afterwards.

Mani recalled:

Another instance of His giving us messages concerned three couplets of Hafiz in Persian, that were here in Meherazad, written on a backing of cardboard. I think Aloba had written them out, or had had someone do it. It wasn't framed.

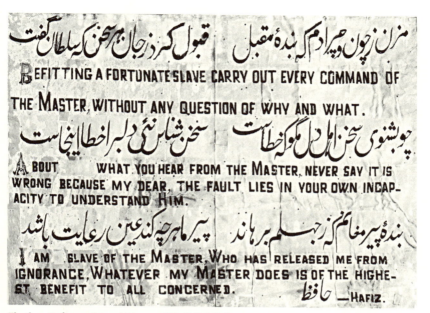

The three Hafiz couplets, which are still in Baba's bedroom.

Now and then when others were with Him, Baba would call for this board, point to the couplets and have Aloba read them out. One says, "Befitting a fortunate slave, carry out every command of the Master without any question of why and what." Actually now that I'm learning a bit of Persian, it actually says, ". . . carry out with heart, with all your heart . . ."

The other two Hafiz couplets written on the board are:

ABOUT WHAT YOU HEAR FROM THE MASTER NEVER SAY IT IS WRONG BECAUSE MY DEAR, THE FAULT LIES IN YOUR OWN INCAPACITY TO UNDERSTAND HIM.

I AM [THE] SLAVE OF THE MASTER WHO HAS RELEASED ME FROM IGNORANCE; WHATEVER MY MASTER DOES IS OF THE HIGHEST BENEFIT TO ALL CONCERNED.

                    HAFIZ

On the day before Baba dropped His body, Baba said He wanted this cardboard brought over to His room. They must have told Aloba; I don't know, I wasn't there. The gist of it is, that Baba wanted this written verse of Hafiz in His bedroom on that last morning.

But when it was brought by Aloba on the 31st, the mandali told him, "Keep it aside, Aloba, just put it by. Afterwards, when Baba's feeling better, when He's rested, He can see it." Baba did not see it, but afterwards, when He dropped His body, it was still there in the room. Now we have framed it and kept it in there.

By calling for that, Baba made it clear to us that His attention was on those couplets.

So many little things Baba had provided for us. Baba provides what you want before you even want it. Baba provides answers before you even think of asking, if only you look.

HE LISTENS

Mani would often tell us, "You're looking for our Baba and we're looking for your Baba." It was touching to see and hear how much the mandali, too, had to search to experience Him in a new way after He had dropped His body.

Mani, speaking to visitors in the early 1980s, shared:

> You've just heard a love story from someone who has met Baba physically. Most of you haven't seen Him, but we

who have wouldn't change that for anything. But now it's Act II, as I say. Ever since Baba dropped His body, we are simply witnesses, understanding and feeling with you your experience of Baba—which is that He is ever present, but that you cannot see Him physically.

This reminds me of Dr. Harry Kenmore, a blind chiropractor who was a very close Baba-lover. He could not see Baba physically, but he could feel His presence. One day when he was here with Baba, Baba said to the mandali, as He often would, "I am not this coat; I am not this body." Harry piped up, "Baba, I can't even see what You are not!"

We, too, have experienced His presence, His being, after He has dropped His physical form. One story is about the sheep and the shepherd, which I've told you again and again. Another is from a time when Baba and the first early group [of men mandali] that were with Him in Manzil-e-Meem had all traveled to Quetta.

You know, Baba has always provided the answers before the questions arise, has always provided for a need before we are aware of it. And in this story I'm about to tell, I'm sure that Baba provided for this time now, when He is not present physically.

It took place in 1923, and Baba was still talking at the time. They were all staying in the home of Dr. Goher and Katie's parents. Goher's father had a very successful restaurant and bakery, and a big house with all the latest contrivances. For example, there was something that was not exactly a telephone, but a system for people upstairs and downstairs to talk to one another. So if you were downstairs, you could pick up the phone and it would ring upstairs, and someone upstairs would pick it up and you could talk to each other.

It only worked inside the house, a house phone of sorts, which was rare in those days. But they had it.

Adi Sr.'s mother Gulmai was also along with Baba on that trip, and one day she heard the phone ringing downstairs. She picked it up and she could hear Baba's voice through the phone. He was upstairs.

"Can you hear Me?" Baba said.

"Oh, Baba. Yes, yes, I can hear You."

"But you can't see Me, can you?"

"No, I can't see You."

And then Baba said, "No matter. You don't have to see Me. But as long as this connection is there between Me and you over this phone, you can always talk to Me and hear Me."

He again asked, "You can't see Me, can you?"

And she said, "No."

"And yet you're in touch with Me. I'm talking to you. You're talking to Me."

So, in short, Baba has promised that although we can't see Him, when you talk to Him, He assured us that He listens.

Just a few days before Baba dropped His body, He reinforced that message. As Mani told it:

Now, as I've said before, I used to read books out loud to Baba, detective stories, novels like Baroness Orczy's *Scarlet Pimpernel*, the Saint series, Carter Dickson, Edgar Wallace was [his] first love, Agatha Christie, Wodehouse, *The Hobbit* and others by Tolkien, and—most favourite—Rex Stout's books about Nero Wolfe, the fat detective. Sometimes spiritual books also, *The Song Celestial* [an English version of the *Bhagavad Gita*], and other such things.

Margaret used to supply almost all the books for us to

read to Baba. And I would use a different voice for each character. Sometimes, when Baba had other work for me, Rano would read another book, not Poirot or Nero Wolfe, but some other detective story. So sometimes the reading would be a number of times in the day, at any time when He wished it. It could be three times, four times, two times, one time. It could be fifteen minutes a session, it could be an hour and a half, whatever Baba would like.

As I've said before, Baba's bedroom here in Meherazad was not just a bedroom, but His room where we gathered together, where I would read out books to Him and where, in the very later days, Baba would have His meals.

So, one day in late January 1969, we women were in Baba's room. His health was not at all good at that time. One day He would seem really strong and we would think, "Fine, it'll be just a few days and Baba will be as before." Then the next day Baba would be very weak.

On this day, when I was reading something out to Baba, He walked with the support of Mehera's arm over from His bed to sit on that very comfortable chair you can still see in the corner of His room. Harry Kenmore had brought it over on the plane, paying for that chair like a passenger!

Baba was always beautiful, but as He sat in that chair with only His sadra on, He looked so beautiful that His beauty drew your attention. Yet He looked tired. Well, not in the sense that you or I would be tired, but as if a great work had been done and now He could relax. And as He sat there while I read out loud one of His favourite books—*The Red Box*, a Rex Stout mystery about Baba's favourite detective, Nero Wolfe—His eyes closed, the only words I can use to describe how He looked are "supremely relaxed."

I've thought a lot over this: how could I describe the feeling that we had, seeing Baba seated there in that chair during that period? The nearest I can think of is that it was like seeing a ship that has just begun to sail away from the shore. It's there, but it's moving.

The other women were sitting around Him on stools or chairs—I was on a chair—quietly listening as usual. After a while, Baba began breathing deeply, until it became a light snore. Obviously He was sleeping. But I went on reading. It was a book I had read to Baba before; these Rex Stout books were repeats because there just weren't enough of them. He only wrote one a year. Margaret would send a new one as soon as it would come out, but Rex Stout couldn't keep up with Baba. So I would wait until enough time had elapsed since the last reading of a certain book, and then I would read it again; each book would be read once a year or every two years. When I came to a certain passage that I remembered Baba had enjoyed very much, I thought, "Oh, pity Baba can't hear this now. He is fast asleep and I'm reading this out. Better wait." It had been some time since we had felt He was sleeping, so I stopped. "When Baba wakes up, then I'll read this passage again and continue on."

The moment I stopped, although Baba's eyes were still closed, He snapped His fingers and gestured, "Why did you stop?" Then He opened His eyes.

"Oh Baba, because You were resting and this is a passage You like so much."

Baba gestured, "But I heard, I heard."

Then I was a bit naughty. I said, "What did I read?"

And that whole passage, the whole incident I had just

read out, Baba told me. So I blushed, I was embarrassed, and we all laughed and I said, "Yes, Baba."

Now this gesture [Mani demonstrated by moving a finger in front of her lips] is for reading aloud, talking, asking, singing, anything that is uttered from the lips. We interpret that gesture to fit the context of whatever is being spoken of at the time. So this meant, "Go on. Read."

Very, very humbled, I started reading. I read another chapter or two, and again the same thing happened. Again Baba's eyes were closed, again He was resting deeply and that light snore was there. I was getting a bit hoarse also, and everybody was trying to keep from nodding, and what to do? So after a while I looked around me, at Mehera, Meheru, and all, and they looked at me. And we made a silent sign to each other with our eyebrows, "Isn't it better to stop? He's resting. Let Baba rest."

So I stopped. The moment I stopped, Baba said, "Why did you stop?" Again He opened His eyes.

Mehera said, "Baba, You were resting and . . . "

And I said, "Because I'd have been reading and You wouldn't be listening."

Then Baba said, "I hear. Remember. Remember, even if you think My eyes are closed, I hear everything. Go on reading." So I continued after that.

At the time I took it to mean He heard my reading, but I realized afterwards that this concerned more than that time, those moments—that it was really a message from Baba: "Even if you think My eyes are closed, go on. Talk to Me. Ask. Say whatever you have to say. I always listen."

That comes back to me so often.

And I have found that's true. He does, He really does.

> He always listens. And if we are silent, if our mind is silent, we always hear the answer.

A BIRTHDAY EMBRACE

Mani's last birthday with Baba was in December 1968. She was born on December 15, but modern Zoroastrians have two birthdays—one by the Western calendar, which is always the same date, and one by the Zoroastrian calendar, which falls on a different date every four years. The women didn't usually observe their Zoroastrian birthdays.

But for some reason, in 1968 Mani felt strongly that she wanted to celebrate her Zoroastrian birthday, which fell on December 3 that year. To "celebrate" her birthday meant garlanding Beloved Baba and receiving His embrace on that day. With this in mind, on the morning of the 3rd she had a garland ready, and she mentioned to Baba that it was her Zoroastrian birthday. Baba looked very happy to hear it, so she garlanded Him and He gave her a specially loving embrace.

She later said, "As it turned out, Baba was not at all well on 15th December, so that kind of special attention from Him would not have been possible on my birthday. I'm so glad I got the impulse to observe my Zoroastrian birthday that year; Baba must have put it in my head. For I had no idea at the time that 3rd December was to be my last birthday with Beloved Baba physically present, and that was to be my last birthday embrace from Him."

MARY BENNETT

Something Mani often talked about, as we've seen, was how Baba's work during His Advent set a pattern, and the small situations of His lifetime were models for a larger plan. After Baba dropped His body, many of the young people who came to Him began to write songs to Baba and they would (and still do) sing them in Meherazad in the Hall, in the garden, on Mehera's porch, all over Meherazad. Observing and appreciating this, Mani would tell a very meaningful story to this generation of singers:

> Maybe all of you don't know that this singing of young hearts, this music that Baba placed in the hearts of so many with love, was ushered in during His physical presence.
>
> First of all, we still can't get over this phase, Act II as I call it, when we see the young ones that Baba promised us would come to Him, the ones He had already chosen and told us about, saying, "You will see, you will see My lovers."
>
> And here you are. It's hard for people to imagine Meherazad as it was before Baba dropped His body, when Baba was in seclusion. Because He was in seclusion, we all were too, in a way, really secluded.
>
> Meherazad is the one place Baba has stayed most, because He stayed here in the later years after the accident, which was a phase when He was not actively traveling. We would just go to Guruprasad for three months in the summer and then come back to Meherazad. And in those latter years it would be a sensation, well, at least a commotion, if someone entered Meherazad.
>
> If one of us saw a car coming down that private road you see going from the gate to the bus stop on the road outside of Meherazad, it became a big thing! Baba would hear it, and He would have the mandali with Him ring the bell outside His door to summon someone, "What was it? Go find out!" We'd rush out to ask the others, who were also excited, "Who is it? Who is it? Who's come?"
>
> Even though it's gone on for many years now, we still wonder to see Meherazad filled with people like the garden is filled with flowers, you all moving about in the garden,

or sitting here before Baba in the Hall, or singing. I stop sometimes, pausing in the wonderment of it all.

As I've said before, all through our lives with Baba, we've seen that everything Baba worked on, He used as a model. If we were with Baba, Baba worked not only on us but through us. Because He looks after the whole universe, His work spreads out in rings. However, the model that represents His plans would always be on a small scale. So we have seen how in His physical presence Baba would usher in something that was to come. We may not have been aware of it at the time but, looking back, the pattern seems clear.

I'll give you a tangible example: electricity. We didn't have electricity at Meherabad or Meherazad, but Baba had electric wires and the bulbs and shades installed here years and years before. So now it has come to pass that we have lights.

In the same way, there was one little model ushering in you all who we see today. Eruch and I have since worked out that it was in January 1969, when a girl named Mary Bennett, from Australia, came here. We had not even heard of hippies then; our first real experience of His young lovers was in Guruprasad during the Great Darshan [1969] when people came in waves to honor His invitation.

So here came Mary Bennett in 1969, carrying a message to Baba from a Baba-lover in Australia. She was traveling through Ahmednagar and she thought it her duty to come to Meherazad and deliver the message. It was not just an oral message; it was a drawing or a sketch or something. I forget the name of the Baba-lover who sent it.

Francis Brabazon was here at the time living with us. There to the gate of Meherazad comes this Mary Bennett, a tall, big girl with a beautiful face. She had a big guitar slung

The surprise visitor, Mary Bennett—a sign of the future.

over her shoulder, and her worldly belongings were all in a little cloth bag. She was barefoot. I think she had contacted Villoo and then come here.

She had the strangest clothing on! I mean, we had always understood Western people from the English who were ruling here in India, with their reserved style of clothes. Mary had on something that looked like a Nepali sarong with a blouse of some kind on top. We've seen that kind of outfit again and again since then!

But at the time we had never seen anything like it. When she came, I don't know if Aloba or who from among the men mandali went to meet her—I heard about it from

Eruch later. Anyway, she was asked who she was, and she said she was from Australia and she had a message for Baba.

Well, the word "Australia" was enough for them to palm her off onto Francis, who was Australian. "You go to Francis; Francis is the right one." In the meantime Goher had gone over on her little cycle and she couldn't believe her eyes, seeing Mary Bennett. She came pedaling back hard to our side to tell Mehera, "Mehera, you just won't believe this!" and she described Mary to Mehera, adding, "You must see her!"

So Mehera said, "Bring her over! Bring her! This sounds very exciting!"

Yes, it was in January 1969 because Baba was more retired then. He was in His room reclining on His bed. At that point He wasn't going to the Mandali Hall to be with the men. The men and women mandali would be called into His room in turns. The men would be called and when they would leave by the outside door, they would ring the bell to give the signal that they were leaving, and then Mehera, Goher, and all of us would go in from the inside door and attend to Baba.

So, after a while, Mary Bennett was brought over to our side. Sure enough, we just couldn't believe her either, "What, nothing on her feet? What, this is all she has; she's traveling so much and everything she has is in this little cloth satchel?"

Then Mehera, of course, had Mary sit at the table and began stuffing things onto her plate and making her eat. "You must eat this, you must eat that!" Then Mehera began stuffing a lot of things into Mary's cloth bag, things that she might need along the way.

In the meantime, I ran back to the men's side to tell Eruch about it. The same story: "You wouldn't believe this girl." When he heard, he said, "Go take a picture of her! It must be on record that such a personality has come here!"

After all, a Westerner with her peculiar blend of clothes and bare feet and all was something new, something novel, something that had never happened before in our world.

So I said, "I'll film her! I have the movie camera."

"So much the better," said Eruch.

At the time I didn't know where my movie film was, but I found it and put it in the movie camera. After Mary had eaten and we were sitting around on the verandah, she sat at the bottom of the staircase where now you all sit and sing and play the guitar, and very softly she sang a song for Mehera, accompanying herself on the guitar. It wasn't a Baba-song as such. It was by some well-known person—I've forgotten the name. But it could have been a Baba-song, because the words were just as if they were written for Him, out of love for Him.

Anyway, Mehera thought, "Baba must see her. Such a thing might never happen again." So she knocked at Baba's room door, and Baba sent the men out, Mehera went in, and we followed.

"Baba," Mehera said to Him, "you know, such-and-such a girl has come from Australia."

Baba played at being reluctant. "No, no, I don't want, no…"

And Mehera said, "But Baba, You won't mind her. She's just like a mastani," which means a woman mast. "Only she's like a Western mastani. You won't mind her at all, Baba. Really, she should come."

"All right," Baba said, "let her come."

So we were excited. "Mary, Mary, come in, come to see Baba." So she followed us into Baba's room. You've all been in Baba's room. It was not only a bedroom for Baba but also where

He would relax. He would sit on the bed facing the window while I read out to Him from some storybook, a Wodehouse or Rex Stout or whatever, and sometimes Mehera and the others would put a folding table before Him, and He'd have His meals. He would say about the window He looked out through from His bed, "That's My television." So we still call the hill that faces right across from Baba's bed "Television Hill."

Baba was reclining when Mary came in, and He looked at her and put out His hand like this, which meant, if you went near Him, Baba would caress your chin and cheek. Baba did this first, "Come," but Mary didn't understand, so we said, "Go, Mary, go near to Baba."

She went and stood near Him and Baba gestured. So we said, "Mary, put your head down," and she put her head down and Baba caressed her face. Then He said, "Come in May."

"Come in May" meant "Come to Guruprasad, Poona, in May, where I'm going to give darshan." But all He said was, "Come in May." Then He said, "Now you can go."

At that, Mehera said, "Baba, she sings very nicely. Oh, one song, Baba, one."

"All right, one song."

So Mary took out the stool from behind the dressing table in Baba's room, sat on it, took out her guitar, and played and sang for Baba. See what I mean by ushering in something which grows. That was only a point from which all this has grown. And it's going to go on growing and growing.

As she was leaving, I ran up to the Mandali Hall by this door to take a film of Mary. I had already taken a picture of her, but I didn't know whether it would come out—I have a very silly school-kid kind of camera—but it did come out after all.

So I took a film of her coming down the house steps with Mehera. Then I put the camera by.

Which leads me to another thing. This is an amazing instance of how Baba provides something before the need arises, which is something He still does. Answers before the question is asked, so that when the question comes up, you look back and you find that the answer has already been put in a particular box for you to discover.

After filming Mary Bennett, I pushed the camera with the film still in it into my cupboard. I didn't pick it up to film again later, as Baba's health was such that we didn't want to be away from Him and there was no time for anything else.

A little time went by, and then Baba dropped His body. At that time He lay here in the middle of the Hall before we accompanied Him into the ambulance to go to Meherabad. Many practical things had to be done, but we were so numb we just went through them automatically.

At some point Eruch said to me, "Get your movie camera and take some footage; film this." I thought Eruch had gone mad. A camera at a time like this? And I must have looked at him like I thought he was mad. "Movie camera?" I said, "Taking pictures of Baba? At this time you can think of cameras?"

Then he splashed cold water in my face, as it were; he looked very impassive and stern and said, "Look, now is not the time to start thinking of ourselves. We've got to continue to do what Baba would want." Then he said, "Do you realize how many of His lovers there are who would want to be here at this moment? How their hearts would long to be here?"

That hit me: the word *continue*. That first "slap" brought everything into perspective: I realised it's a continuation. There is no break. This is still for Baba. I cannot give up now. After all, nothing is different. This part, this side of our life is not different. Because this is what we have been doing all along: trying to do what He wants. So this is also a continuity. And at that time I said to myself, "All right, Baba, if this is what You want, we'll accept it. If this is the tune You're playing, this is the dance we'll dance."

But where was the camera? And when I went and opened the cupboard, still in a daze, there it was, with film inside and everything ready to go. I took a few feet of footage of Baba's body in Meherazad; it was very hard, but I did it. And when Don Stevens came, he took over the project of having a film taken when Baba was lying in the crypt during those seven days at Meherabad and arranged it all.

I gave Don the film magazine of what I had taken—it's about the size of a soapbox—and said, "Here, you can add this to what you are doing. Do what you like with it. I don't want it. This is simply given to you. It wasn't for me, it was for the others." I even said he could edit it.

That went out of my mind; I didn't want to even think of that time. Sometime later in 1969, that film was developed and Don sent it to us through some professor. I remember that very well, I think because he was one of the first professors I'd ever met.

Don brought the whole film of the entombment along when he came for the darshan in Poona, and when all the Baba-lovers had gathered in Guruprasad for the darshan, they wanted to see the film. But I didn't want to see it. So I said to myself, "I can't escape this, but never mind, when it's on I can look down, I can keep my eyes closed." The screen was put up, the film started, the lights went out, which was a blessing for us, and then the film began.

And I did look up at that point, because I thought I really should see it, I had to see it. And there was this girl walking along onscreen, with a guitar slung over her shoulder and a little satchel in her hand, and it broke the whole tension. "My God, that's Mary Bennett! What is she doing in this?"

Then I realized that Don had not cut off the first part of the film that I'd given him, and here was Mary, in May, or whatever the month Baba had said, in Guruprasad, even though she didn't know it. She hadn't consciously come to Guruprasad as He had said. But His word never goes out in vain. It's only a matter of timing. And He had given the timing, "Come in May." And Mary Bennett was there in Guruprasad in May.

BEGIN THE BEGUINE

As with the camera, so with the record of "Begin the Beguine." As we've seen, Mani wrote down the story about this song very briefly in her Family Letter to the Baba-world, but see how Baba provided the record before the need arose:

> As I said, Baba had told us to play the record of "Begin the Beguine" when He dropped His body. Now see how He helps again.
>
> That record was not handy, you know; it was in a box of records. At a time like that, you don't have your wits about you; how would you remember where you've put your keys or where you've put your records?
>
> So I would not have been able to lay my hand on the "Begin the Beguine" record as easily as I was able to after Baba dropped His body, had the following incident not happened.
>
> We had a record of "Begin the Beguine" by Chick Henderson, the one we played for Baba again and again

in the old days from the Bangalore time. Over the years something happened to that record; I don't know where it was misplaced, or if it was given away or whether we still have it. This much I know, that I was anxious to have a record of "Begin the Beguine" from somewhere. You see, we had a gramophone that only played 78 rpm records.

So I'd written to my brother, Adi, in England, Baba's youngest brother, and asked, "Could you get a record of 'Begin the Beguine'?" Adi looked in many places and then he entrusted this job to Fred Marks. Fred searched out many things for Baba. So he went to little shops, looking in the corners, and at last he found a record of "Begin the Beguine," sung by A. Hutchinson [Leslie A. "Hutch" Hutchinson]. It was sent in '68 with my brother Adi to India when my niece and the whole family came here from England.

So that record, A. ["Hutch"] Hutchinson's version of "Begin the Beguine," came, and Baba had me play it here in the Hall. Baba was seated in the chair, and the gramophone was right at His feet. I sat there and played it for Him. And He loved it! Because A. Hutchinson has a voice that has, well, the only word we can use, is "pain." Baba would say, "He has *dard* [a Persian word that signifies "pain" or "longing"] in his voice." There's a pain in his voice, the depth and maturity of a pain, and oh, he really sings it. His voice breaks when he sings it. There's some feeling in his rendering of "Begin the Beguine" that Baba liked very much.

So, for the first time, A. Hutchinson's "Begin the Beguine" was played before Baba in '68. And then there was no time after that to put the record away among the rest of the records—what you call albums but we call records. Usually I put records back, but there was no time.

We were so busy with Baba, and so many things were happening. That was the time Mehera's birthday function was to be held here, along with Dara-Amrit's wedding reception, and Baba wasn't too well. Therefore I just put the record in my cupboard along with my clothes, thinking I'd see to it afterwards.

So when Baba dropped His body, Eruch reminded me, "Where is the record? 'Begin the Beguine' has to be played by Baba's side." Again I said to myself, "This guy's gone crazy! First he says, 'Bring out the movie camera,' then he says, 'Bring out the gramophone' "; and for a moment I said to myself, "My God, now it's the gramophone!" Then I realised that it was as he said, Baba had said "Begin the Beguine" has to be played.

But where am I going to find "Begin the Beguine"? Then I remembered: it was so handy! It's just on top of my dress! I didn't even have to look for it.

So I played "Begin the Beguine" with A. Hutchinson singing, in Baba's room on 31st January evening. I played it, I think, at least three times. And then it accompanied us when we went to Meherabad that evening, Baba in the ambulance and all of us with Him. I think I played it in the Cabin while we sat by the stretcher. It was a very intimate moment in the Cabin, while Mehera and we women waited with Baba, when the preparations were being made in the crypt. That was a very intimate moment. It was before the skies had burst, as it were, and all His lovers poured in. We were just a few, and we just sat silently with Baba. I think I played it there.

And I played it every day in the Tomb for the first few days, before Baba's body was covered. Now every time you hear that singing by A. Hutchinson of "Begin the Beguine," it just goes through you.

Mani playing "Begin the Beguine" near Baba's body, in keeping with His orders.

But you see, even before I knew there would be a need for this record, Baba had arranged for it, had seen to it, had already provided the circumstances whereby I would keep the record handy because there was going to be a need for it that I didn't know of.

So it is with everything in our lives; when we have placed our lives in His hands, there is nothing to worry about. Which is why He says, "Don't worry; be happy." He is not giving this as advice; He knows. He is not giving this as a doctor telling you it's good for you to be happy, so don't worry. He is saying it because He knows, because He sees it all, but we don't.

That's where trust comes in, such absolute and perfect trust that you relax. When I'm in the car and Yusef [the Meherazad driver] is driving, I relax. Don't even look, because I trust the driver. I know that when the wheel is in his hands it's all right. But if it's the other driver, I practically sit on the edge of my seat, point out every goat that comes by, every child.

Baba has given us the illustration of a babe in its mother's arms. It doesn't matter what the mother is walking through, whether she's in a bazaar or on a mountain or in the kitchen or whether she's in the garden. The child is in its mother's arms. The child is not concerned where the mother is. But the child is completely relaxed because it is safe in the arms of its mother.

Trust, that complete trust that He will take care of it.

JAI BABA

There is another example of Baba setting a pattern for the future before dropping His body. This occurred in 1968, and involved Mehera. Mehera, of course, had been completely secluded from men for decades. Other than Baba, she never talked with a man or saw one face-to-face unless a very rare exception was made by Baba.

Even in the New Life when they were camping, the men were

absolutely separate; Mani recalls that at night the women could see only the men's lanterns, far away.

Then on January 31, 1968, exactly one year before Baba dropped His body, Baba asked Mehera to come out and stand with Him on the verandah of the house and greet the men mandali. As Mani recalled:

> Baba told Mehera, "Stand by My side, and I will bring the mandali and all the others over, whoever are here. Just look up and say, 'Jai Baba'."
>
> She looked at Him, and Baba said, "It's all right. I'll be right here."
>
> So Mehera dressed in a sari and went out onto the verandah and stood beside Baba. There, standing down in the garden before them, were the [men] mandali of Meherazad (the household mandali), and the mandali from Ahmednagar, Adi and so on, and Meherabad—I'm sure Padri and the others from Meherabad were there.
>
> Baba said, "Look at her," and they looked up at Mehera.
>
> And she said, "Jai Baba," and they all said, "Jai Baba." And that was that.
>
> Therefore, after Baba dropped His body in 1969— exactly one year later to the day—when it came time for the Great Darshan in Poona, Mehera felt that, yes, He wished her to greet and speak with Baba-lovers, even men, about Baba. You see, Baba had physically enacted in His presence what was to happen in the future. So every time before a program began in the 1969 darshan, when all had gathered in Guruprasad, Mehera would come to the mic and say, "Jai Baba," and the whole room would resound, "Jai Baba." And then the program would start.

THE GONG

You can read in the book *Mehera*, and also in *Baba Loved Us Too*, how Baba's dog Mastan mourned for Him after Baba dropped His body. He stopped eating, and Mehera had to feed him every morsel by hand. But although they had carefully arranged for his care when they went away to Poona for the Great Darshan, Mastan, who had been a perfectly healthy dog only months before, passed away, they felt from grief.

Mastan's grave in Meherazad.

It wasn't only animate things that felt the impact of Baba's absence. In Mandali Hall, Mani—often joined by Eruch—would tell the story of two inanimate things affected by it:

> Again and again we have witnessed Baba's love for His people, for His animals, for His mandali, for His creation, for His lovers. And we have seen His lovers' love for Him—men, women, children, young, old. We have seen children's love for Baba, old people's love for Baba, strangers' love for Baba.
>
> And we've seen the same with animals, their love for Baba. You must have seen the picture of Baba with the goat—a divine romance, I call it—Baba looking down and the goat looking up adoringly at Baba.
>
> But we were also witness to inanimate beings dying for Baba. There's only one word I could use when I speak of what happened to the gong on 31st January 1969. The gong died. Died of a broken heart. That's how I like to say it.
>
> Here's the gong I'm talking about. [Mani holds up the gong for people to see.] My youngest brother, Adi, brought this gong to Baba in 1968, when he and his wife and children, Shireen and Dara, had come for Dara's own wedding.

Baba had me ring it for the first time; He was seated here, and the gong was placed there. Baba had me ring it, and it had such a beautiful, resonant sound; it just went on and on—a deep, mellow, resonant and yet sweet sound. It made you think of a water bird floating on waves—*whooommmmm*—on and on and on . . .

Baba said, "Very nice. Do it again." I used the little gavel and rang it again. And again. It just filled the Mandali Hall. It was lovely hearing that voice, that sound, of the gong.

A month afterwards, Baba was persuaded not to go over to the Mandali Hall anymore because He was weak and unwell. So, from about the 14th of January 1969, Baba stopped coming here to the Hall. He stayed in His room, where He eventually dropped His form, or as we say, "took off His coat."

We can say only of Baba that He "dropped His body." We cannot say it of any ordinary person, because we don't drop the body. The body drops us, whether we want it or not. But Baba puts the body on like a garment and takes it off when His work is done.

Anyway, Baba agreed that He would stay in His bedroom from 14th January, and that when He wanted His men mandali, they could be summoned. They could come and go from the side door, which was always used by the men when Baba wanted them at night. One night watchman would go out and another would come in, always from that side door.

Baba asked, "How do you summon [the men]?" Then He said, "Use the gong!" And He told Eruch and some of the others, "The moment that you hear the gong, drop everything and come."

So the gong was hung on a nail on Mehera's porch, on the side of that cupboard where Dr. Goher has her office table and where Meheru writes, too. I would pick it up and hit it when Baba wanted the men.

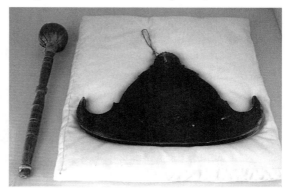

The gong used to summon the men.

The first strike would barely finish sounding and I'd see Eruch running over. Once I saw him come with only one sandal on, his other foot bare, because Baba had said drop everything and come.

Now to give you an idea of the sound of the original gong, this is a baby gong that my brother had sent over the next year with Pete Townshend, who was coming here. Even this little one will give you some idea of the resonance and tone of the original gong. [Mani strikes the little gong.] I timed it one day and the sound continues for over a minute.

The last time I struck the big gong was on 31st January 1969, at about 10:30 in the morning. The men had been sent away for a while so that Mehera could come and be with Baba. I could be with Him at both times, with the women and with the men; for His work I had been given more freedom in seeing the men, for work or under Baba's direction or in His presence.

So Mehera was with Baba that morning for quite some time, we women were with Him also, and then we went back into the house, and I struck the gong so that the men would come back. That was about 10:30 or 11:00. Then the men were with Baba.

And Baba sent a message with me to Mehera, "Tell Mehera, 'Be brave!'" And because Baba said it, she could be brave afterwards. You see, as I've said before, when Baba asks something of you, He's really giving you something. He said, "Be brave!" Therefore she could be brave. He's not asking her to be brave, He's giving it to her to be brave. So when Baba tells us, "Love Me more and more," He's giving it. That is why we can love Him. That is why we will love Him more and more.

So the gong was struck, and the men came over and after that, well, what can we say about all that happened on the 31st of January? Baba's dropping His body was so unexpected! So incredible for us!

You all know what happened.

Months later, when we finally came back to Meherazad from Poona after the Great Darshan, we really could be with ourselves, with Baba. We could drown in our private tears, in our personal memories. Each one was moving about in a world of her memories. I would say to myself, "Ah, this is the gramophone I used to play for Baba, playing these favourite records that He enjoyed. This is the chair He sat on. This is what Baba said when He was at the dining table; here's the radio that I used to play for Baba in the mornings . . ." And so on.

So I was moving about in my world of Baba-memories, and He was everywhere in memory; it was a very deep feeling and presence . . .

And one day I came upon the gong. "Ah," I said to

myself, "this is the gong that I used to strike for the others to come running for Baba." And I picked it up and struck it. And it was as if I'd been slapped. It was the deadest sound imaginable, like the flat of a hand striking a table.

I was shocked. That's the only word I can use, hearing that sound in contrast to the beauty and resonance and sweetness of the tone that had filled Mandali Hall. This was dead. The only word you could apply to it. The gong died, as I like to say, of a broken heart, having done its service to the Lord, having been honoured to do that.

Later, one of the Indian Baba-lovers, a noted physicist, on hearing this story, asked to x-ray the gong. He said that maybe it had been dropped sometime. Maybe there was a fine hairline crack in it. He was trying to find a practical cause for the lack of sound. He had it x-rayed. We still have the x-ray. Clear as anything. There is no crack of any kind.

THE AMBULANCE

Mani continued:

Speaking of the gong, I must tell you of another object that died on 31st January 1969. You have seen the stretcher that's in the Cabin near the Samadhi on Meherabad Hill. That stretcher was used for Baba to rest on when we accompanied Him to Meherabad on 31st January from Meherazad. So that stretcher has great sentimental value for everyone.

It belonged to the ambulance that was given to us by Dr. [Mel] Brieseman of the Evangeline Booth Salvation Army Hospital to transport Beloved Baba's form to Meherabad. He was one of the doctors called by Goher on that day. He was a very fine person, a good friend.

Some time later Dr. Donkin wrote a letter to Dr. Brieseman, explaining why we could not send the ambulance stretcher back to the hospital. But he wrote that, if Dr. Brieseman allowed, he, Don, would get it replaced with a foreign stretcher from England through his father and family there.

A most unexpected reply came from Dr. Brieseman. He said, "You may keep the stretcher. It will be of no use in the ambulance, because the ambulance has stopped working ever since it returned from Meherabad on 31st January."

Despite all efforts, they could not find the cause of the machine suddenly just giving way. And he said, "Unless we replace it with a new machine [engine] or buy a new ambulance, what good is a stretcher to us?"

And that was so touching! It was as if the ambulance was overwhelmed with the honour and privilege of carrying the most precious burden of His form to Meherabad. And when it came back, it just lay down and died. Again, that's the only word you could use.

We heard some three years later that they had to replace the engine inside with an imported one.

So that is the story of the stretcher you see in the Cabin, where we were first with Baba at Meherabad on 31st January. Baba was resting on the stretcher, exactly where it is now. And we few women mandali from Meherazad were seated around Him.

Sometimes Mani would speak of how much they missed Baba:

> After Baba dropped His body, when we came back from Poona, from the Darshan in Guruprasad in 1969, it seemed the first time we had any little time to be conscious of our own feelings, of how much we were missing His physical presence. And a flood of memories came up all at once. Because in Meherazad, there is nothing here that Baba has not either touched or used or is not associated very personally with Baba.
>
> And so there was so much to keep us engrossed in His presence, with so many memories. "This, oh this is the gramophone; remember how Baba sat here and we played those records just a short while before He dropped His form?" "Remember this?" "Remember that?"
>
> We never imagined that we could ever continue to move about, breathe, without Baba's presence. We've had it just about all our lives. And for those who were living with Baba, not a single thing was done without His direction. Big or small or silly or whatever, everything was under Baba's direction. Everything passed through His hand, at His wish. Baba would direct. We only followed Baba's orders. And then suddenly, it was different. But it was also not different in a sense.
>
> When Baba was with us physically, when our life was so involved with Him day to day, He'd tell us, "This is all not real." "I'm not what you see." But when Reality is in illusion, among us, as one of us, so that He's tangible, so that He's approachable, that Reality of His Being gave life even to illusion, to every little thing. We had interest in every little thing. Just like when the sun shines on a bush and you see every leaf sparkle where the sun touches it, so it was with Baba. Because Baba was with us, everything was sparkling.

We were not waiting for the breaking of His silence. We were not waiting for experiences and light. We were not longing for it or even thinking about it. We had only one thing in mind. We were not perfect at it, but that doesn't matter. Our one thing was to do what Baba would want, at least what Baba said that He would want. So, as Eruch said, it was a continuation—what else? Had we wanted something [from Him], we would have felt the tremendous lack of it. And you can drown in that vacuum. So what Eruch said is it: we have to continue to do what Baba would want. From the moment Eruch said that, it was in place for me. Not easy, but it was in place.

THE GREAT DARSHAN

WITNESSES

One of the first questions the mandali faced after Baba dropped His body was—should they go ahead with the darshan He said He would give in April, May, and June of 1969? It was mid-February when they settled back in Meherazad after staying near the Samadhi at Meherabad. If the darshan was to be cancelled, it had to be cancelled soon.

"In the beginning," Mani shared with pilgrims, "the very thought floored us. 'My God! What are we supposed to do? We're supposed to hold a darshan? A darshan is when you see Baba!' What were we going to do?"

Thinking it over and scratching their heads about it, the mandali remembered a hint Baba had given them. When Baba's health was so bad, Eruch had pointed out to Him that it was still possible to cancel the upcoming darshan if He wished to do so. Baba smiled and said, "No, it is not to be cancelled. I will give My Darshan to My lovers. I will give it on My own terms."

So, in March 1969, the mandali sent out an announcement that the 1969 darshan would be held as planned: from April 10 to June 10 in

Guruprasad, strictly for Baba-lovers old and new and not for the general public. People could come for a week at most. No more than five hundred lovers could attend each darshan week, at fixed times of two hours in the morning for Westerners and two hours in the afternoon for Easterners. The week would now include a day visit to Meherabad and Meherazad.

Returning to Guruprasad.

Of those Westerners who attended the Great Darshan, many remembered one moment in particular: on the first morning of each darshan week, when all the Baba-lovers in attendance were sitting in Guruprasad Hall and the clock had struck 9:00 a.m., Eruch would stand at the microphone and say, "You have kept your appointment with God."

Mani described the 1969 darshan to pilgrims in Mandali Hall a few years later:

> We have been witnesses, from the day Baba dropped His body. We were witnesses to the darshan in 1969 at Guruprasad, and that was our first experience of seeing Baba really give darshan without being physically present. And it was an overwhelming feeling. Baba was there. It was like the darshans we had witnessed with Him seated in the chair and visible. At this darshan you did not see Baba in the chair, but everything was exactly as it would be when He was there. It was between each lover and Baba. We had nothing to do with it. And they came because Baba invited them. And they were full when they left. How often we heard those who came say, upon leaving, "I have certainly had Baba's darshan." And

Baba's chair in the main hall of Guruprasad, the heart of the 1969 darshan.

they hadn't even seen Baba physically. Even we, who were apprehensive about it, we felt it; we received it.

That was our first experience of witnessing Baba's presence without seeing His physical form. We were simply witnesses to all He did. And we have been witnesses right from then up until now.

THE DOUBTING MAN

Mani would sometimes go on to tell stories that reflected the atmosphere of that unique darshan:

> When Baba-lovers from all parts of India, Iran, Pakistan, Australia, England, Europe, and America came to

Eruch looking out over the gardens and entry to Guruprasad from the portico. Mani nearby on the left, filming another scene from the balustrade.

Guruprasad for the darshan, we asked them, "What made you all come?" They looked surprised. "We had an appointment with God!" And He did keep His appointment; we saw that. They knew it, and we knew it.

But to start with, we didn't know what to do to get ready for it. So we placed the chair in which Baba used to sit when giving darshan in the Guruprasad Hall. Some Baba-lovers afterwards said that they saw Baba sitting in the chair. Whether during the morning time with the Westerners or afternoon time with the Easterners, Baba was there for them all, all the time.

Eruch would make it very clear: it's between you and Baba. Everybody was free to be with Baba there as each one liked. It was a relationship purely and personally between Baba and each one.

People would come up to the mic and speak; some would tell jokes, like Minoo Kharas, because Baba enjoyed jokes. Minoo used to do it with Baba, so he told jokes. Some sang songs. It was a free atmosphere, a free getting together. Each one expressed their love in whatever way they felt.

One afternoon, an Indian said, "May I say something on the mic, may I say something to all my brothers and sisters here?" "Sure," said Eruch. "That is what you're here for. Whatever you all like." So he came up to the mic and told us what a fool he had been all these years, and what a lot he had missed because he was a fool.

He said he used to follow Baba. And every now and then Meher Baba would say, "I am going to break My silence at such and such a time." "And then," the man said, "He doesn't just say it quietly to a few of His followers. No sir, He declares it. He has it printed, and says, 'Be sure to give it to everybody,' makes a big thing out of it. And then He doesn't do it.

"And not only doesn't He do it, He doesn't even explain why He didn't do it. He doesn't say, 'I'm sorry. I meant to, but . . . '"

And, the man went on, this happened once, this happened twice, this happened a number of times.

"He cannot be who He says He is, because He doesn't know His own mind! How could anyone who doesn't know his own mind be God!"

Then, he said, after some time, after he had missed a number of darshans, missed being with Baba a number of times when His lovers could come, "One day I was sitting and my mind was like a still pool. And a thought dropped in, like a pebble, and that thought was, 'Yes, He does what you say He does. But why don't His followers get less? Why don't they leave Him? Why do they flock more and more around Him? Why don't they mind? And why is it all growing, and getting bigger and bigger, bringing people to Him more and more?'"

Then he said, "Well, He must be God. Because only God can do that and get away with it!"

Mani and Eruch would often tell another story from those sessions:

[MANI:] One day when it was the turn of the Indian side, another Baba-lover said, "Can I—I would like to say something." We said, "Sure."

So he got up and spoke about Baba's love. He said how Baba's love was greater, far greater, than even a mother's love, or a father's love. And he told us an instance.

Often when somebody would tell us a story, we would find that it was the other side of a coin, the other half of something we had witnessed, but because we didn't know this other half, the story would not be complete. This would happen often.

Baba always took great pains to appear natural and to do things through a natural medium, so that we would never suspect that He was doing something. He took great pains to hide what He was really doing, and to show us more of His humanness than His Divinity. Of course He didn't succeed at all this, but He did it.

This man said that a number of years ago, he was transferred for his job to a very far-away place in India, a backward area that was very isolated. The language was different there, the people were different, and communication with the outside world was difficult. Even mail was hard to receive.

This man was very sorry to have to go there, because there would be no Baba-lovers in that place, and his family also couldn't be there with him. He had written to Baba about it, and Baba had said, "Don't worry. You're not going alone. I'm there with you."

So the man went and stayed there for a time. It was as bad as he had expected. After some time his birthday came around and that made him feel more low than ever. He asked himself, "Now do my parents remember me? Does my family remember me? Anyway, even if they did write, how would I get the letter in this place?" He was very sorry for himself.

On the morning of his birthday, when he was about to go for work—he lived alone, of course—he saw the postman coming. He was a bit surprised. And the postman gave him a telegram.

Now in India, the system is that a telegram is delivered through the post office; it takes a long time.

[ERUCH:] Where you don't have the regular postal services, there are postal runners. They have a long staff with a gong on it, that rings—*tong, tong, tong*—and they go running through the forests and deliver the mail.

[MANI:] In a place like that, nobody would be sending a telegram to somebody unless it was very good news or very bad news. It still is like that in India: you don't just send telegrams to say, "How are you?" or "I love you." It's mostly to say somebody's dead or somebody's born, or something's happened.

And the postman waits, looking at the face of the man whom he delivers the telelgram to. If it lights up and the man's happy, the postman waits longer because he knows he'll get a tip, some baksheesh. If the face is sad, then the postman bows and walks out quietly without the man's knowing it.

Mehera, Mani, Meheru, Khorshed, and Rano posing for a photo among Baba-lovers.

Now this time the postman was very puzzled, because after reading the telegram, the man was beaming, glowing, laughing, but also crying at the same time. Tears were rolling down his face, so the postman didn't know which it was, good news or bad!

At last the postman said to the man, "Bad news, sir?" And suddenly the man became aware of him. "No," he said, "the best news in the world!" And he went and embraced the postman, and of course gave him something in his joy.

The telegram was from Baba, saying:

I SEND MY LOVE AND BLESSINGS TO YOU
ON YOUR BIRTHDAY AND ALWAYS.

That man told us, "See, even a mother and father would not do that. His love is unsurpassable." He gave other instances, but this one meant so much to him because his need for love at that time was excruciating and it came in perfect time. Baba does not neglect the least, or the furthest, no matter where one is.

For us, this side of the story fit with the other half of the story, which we already knew. As I told you in the beginning, Baba would take great pains to make something appear as if it were coincidental, or natural, or just happened. Whereas actually He would be giving it very special attention.

What happened was: just two days before the birthday of the lover we are talking about, Eruch as usual was reading out correspondence to Baba. Baba was listening but at the same time He was having somebody ring the bell for Goher to bring a glass of water or do this or that.

In the midst of Eruch reading, suddenly Baba said, "This letter that you're reading, Eruch, isn't it from—isn't this man that you are reading about, wasn't he transferred somewhere?" Eruch was reading about another man who had been in the same place for twenty years. So he told Baba, "He's in a solid position. Certainly not—no, Baba, he's not been transferred."

"Yes," Baba said, "Yes, my mistake, you know. Probably it wasn't [him]. Yes, go on. Go on. Read it."

After a while, something entered Eruch's head and he said, "Oh, I know, Baba, the one you mistook is so-and-so, and he was transferred to so-and-so."

"Aha," said Baba. "That's it. Yes, I mistook them, mixed them up. I mixed them up. That's right. Yeah, yeah." Very casually. So Eruch went on reading. Suddenly Eruch said, "Oh, by the way, Baba, his birthday is the day after tomorrow." (Eruch would keep a list of birthdays of Baba's close lovers.)

So Baba looked up, surprised, and said, "Is that so? Well, why not send him a telegram? Why not send him a telegram? My love and blessing, you know." So Eruch said, "All right."

So you see, for us it seemed that this just happened. But when we heard the man's story, we knew it all was aimed at him. In such perfect time, it was a fulfillment of that need of his.

GREETING HIS CHILDREN

Mani remembered:

> By having Mehera greet the men mandali in His presence on 31st January 1968, Baba provided for the part Mehera would be playing after He dropped His body. So at the beginning of the darshan gathering each morning, which Eruch would conduct, Mehera would come to the mic, look up, see that hall full of Baba-lovers, and say, "Jai Baba."

In the beginning with you all, it was very difficult for her to look at any of the male Baba-lovers because of that life-long habit of never seeing men. It was something very different from what she had ever done. So she would look at one of the women, but talk to one of the men. She would look at the girls, but talk to the boys. But Baba helped her.

Mehera at ease with girls.

In earlier times, we other women also had those restrictions of not touching [men] in any way, and had never met the men or gone over to the men's side. Later that restriction was withdrawn for some of us, although we still didn't touch men. Goher, of course, was the link between the men and the women, so it was Goher who took the messages from Baba to the women's side, or brought a glass of water or whatever Baba needed that Mehera would send, from the women's side to the men's side. Goher was always the bridge.

But at the Great Darshan, we were touched, we were moved to open not only our hearts but our arms. We [except Mehera, who never touched men] embraced all the promised children who came in 1969—men, women, and children.

And we still do. You are all, for us, Baba's children. It has touched us so deeply that you all—who haven't seen Baba physically—can love Him, adore Him, the way you do.

> We didn't know how to express that love for you all, so we opened our arms. Because you all love Him, His children.
>
> Remember His love for you all. It is because of His love for you that He has left us behind for a while, so that we can tell you of God's life on earth—so we can tell you about the Beloved's love for His lovers.

In *The Empty Chair,* a book about the experiences of several Western Baba-lovers at the 1969 darshan, Barbara Bamberger Scott recalled:

> Mani played a significant part in the darshan experience of many Baba lovers, especially on that first day. The stories are many of her appearing out of nowhere at just the right moment to give a hug, to remind one, by her gracious presence, of Meher Baba's love. She was there when people were feeling left out or wavering. She was there when they needed a friend. But how could she have been in so many places in such a sort span of time, and also have been, as most of us believe we remember, right there inside Guruprasad, sitting with the women Mandali?[1]

After Mani passed away, a Baba-lover who had been to the 1969 darshan wrote to the mandali about her:

> The first hug Mani gave me was on Guruprasad's porch, right after I had taken Baba's darshan (in front of His chair with picture) in 1969 (April). I said to her, "Oh Mani, this is like coming home," and she rightly corrected me by saying, "No, this is not *like* coming home, this *is* coming home!" And her embrace was a joy for me! As I missed the embrace of the Avatar in form.

SONG OF THE GREAT DARSHAN

Mani sent out her very last Family Letter on August 26, 1969, from Meherazad.[2] It was a song of the Great Darshan and the tremendous give and take of Baba's Love that the mandali witnessed and experienced themselves. She began:

> JAI BABA to you from all your brothers and sisters at Meherazad. We returned from Poona on July 1, as we have done each year with Baba. And I am writing to you dear ones as I have been doing each time on our return, but I find it is not the same. To write an account of what has most occupied our days and hearts, means to make a word picture of the indescribable Darshan—and what word colours can paint that Master-piece, what can I recount that you yourselves have not experienced or shared from personal accounts? At best I can make it a chat, a thinking aloud, a reminiscing on behalf of dear Mehera, all men and women Mandali, lovers, workers, volunteers—each of us who was privileged to share with many of you the Beloved's darshan given on His terms, at the time and place appointed by Him: Guruprasad, Poona, from 10th April to 10th June 1969. . . .

She went on:

> You who came, honouring God-Man's invitation, accepting His terms without knowing what they were, not expecting anything or not knowing what to expect, you received more than you could contain. That which you received, we saw it flow over from your eyes reflecting His beloved image. We heard it flow over from your lips making His Name resound wherever you went.

She described the darshan as His family in miniature, a model that

He created for the building of the world Baba-family, formed of all shades of religion and color. She spoke of the obstacles that darshanees overcame to get there, the songs and performances, plays and poems and skits and puppet shows they gave to Him there. She wrote:

> ... In you younger ones, His "Boys and Girls" who formed the main body of this gathering, in you we heard the first strains of His "New Life" song. From His Ocean you brought to us a breath of the New Humanity which will awaken a dead world to His Life. ...
>
> ...We thank our Beloved for His gift of the Family.
> We bow down to His Love for you.
> We bow down to your love for Him. ...

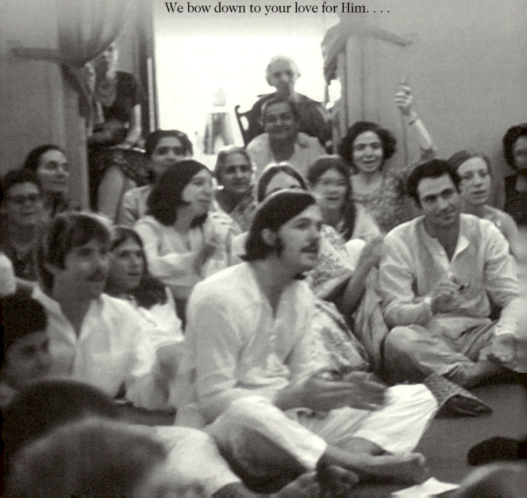

...You had the Beloved's darshan. And you had His sahavas, seated for hours before Him in Guruprasad, communing with Him in silence and in speech. Often you crowded the Hall, yet you were never a crowd to us. It was not a sea of faces we saw, but so many shining drops in His Ocean. . . .

Mani also quoted several of the darshanees:

"I am striving to write the unwriteable, because it is not possible to say what Love I was the receiver of."

"Baba has dipped us in such divine colours, we will never be the same again!"

The women mandali and Baba-lovers singing together before Baba's chair.

Mani playing her sitar for Baba-friends.

"At Darshan I began to feel the Beloved's personal special humanness, through all of you. Before He was overpoweringly God and Christ; now He is infinitely more, being our beautiful Baba, the man, our friend. Every day He is more God, more a 'mighty Beloved'. . . . and every day more Man, more specially Meher Baba. I remember on the third day of Darshan, Baba was so close and full of love that every time I heard His Name or saw His Picture I just cried, it was so incredible—for He is the only One, the Only one in my life, and He has come and let us know of Him. . . . "

"Thank You, Thank You, Thank You Beloved Baba, for fulfilling Your great promise: 'sometime, somewhere, somehow'. . . ."

In this Family Letter, too, she gave glimpses of what the 1969 darshan meant for the mandali:

> ... on March 30 we marched to Poona, our minds bare of expectation, our hearts a desert. Three months later when we left Poona, the desert had changed to a dazzling expanse of flowers which had sprung up in the merciful downpour of His Darshan—it had been a time of Spring for His many lovers, and we had shared in the miracle.
>
> So hungry were our hearts for Baba's nearness, that the Darshan fare we feasted on for a solid two months did not tire us.
>
> On the pink sheets [of the book they kept at the Darshan for comments] and in your letters that followed, you also express such dear praise for all that you received from us at this Darshan. And it makes us wonder if you will ever know what we received from you! What it meant to us to be with you in the Beloved's overwhelming presence—to see Him in your eyes, to embrace Him in your arms, to mingle our love's tears and laughter with yours, to welcome Him in you! You brought Baba with you and He was already here to receive you, you took Him with you and He is as ever with us—such is the profound God-humour that makes life's joke bearable. . . .
>
> Now, back at Meherazad, I speak only for the Meherazad family. And first of all we want to say to you: All that has come to us in your letters, letters so filled with Love of Baba, so full of dear concern for our well-being, has gone deep into our hearts that hold you very close.

Back at Meherazad, Mani wrote, they were kept as busy as ever with household duties and work related directly to Baba. But in one of the most touching and beautiful passages in all the Family Letters, Mani spoke of how much they missed Him:

His holding the reins as tightly as ever, is one of the things which most reveals His presence. He reveals it in so many ways. And the more the Beloved's presence is revealed, the more we miss Him!

Beloved Baba's presence fills each part and particle of Meherazad. Every room where He sat or slept in, every piece of furniture that He used, every article of clothing that He wore, the paths and ground that He walked on, the trees and flowers that He admired, the birds that He inquired after in dear concern, the Hill where He sat in seclusion, the books that He enjoyed having read out, the records of songs which He liked to listen to on the old gramaphone—each object unveils His beloved presence. So it is not that we grieve for His absence from us, but for our separation from His form—the exquisite garment which wrapped our hearts so fully that we desired nothing else. God-realization was not our concern. Striving to realize God's Love expressed through the garment worn and suffered for His creation was enough to occupy lifetimes. Since He has put aside His garment, we realize it more and more. His every act of grace and compassion that is recalled, every form of His suffering that is remembered, adds a little to our realizing it. Our growing realization of His Love is a large part of our pain of separation.

Toward the end of this Letter, Mani included Baba's "favourite saying of Hafiz," the three couplets printed in Persian and English on a board that Baba had Aloba bring into His bedroom on the last day.

Then she reminded the lovers of Baba's warning to them, which He gave more often as the Time drew nearer: "Hold on to My daaman—do not let it slip away under any circumstance." Mani elaborated on what that means:

Now, when the daaman appears invisible, is the time to hold on as never before. Now the "umbrella" has begun to revolve, and time will spin it faster and faster. Drops that are settled on its surface, clinging to the glossy material of promises, are bound to shake off. Drops that surrender their selfness get soaked into the heart of the substance and become part of the fabric. This is what is really meant by holding on to Baba's daaman; to get so absorbed in it that there is nothing of one's self left to hold on with; to live so completely as He wills that one lives as His Will. And what else is there worthy of being lived, when one lives for Baba, for God?

Mani closed this final Family Letter with an account taken from a letter from an Indian Baba-lover:

My youngest daughter aged 2 years and 3 months, suddenly got up from sleep at about 1:15 in the night of March 10, and five times uttered clearly:

"Meher Baba is God."

And so ended what Mani would call "Act One" of her incredible life. As she put it so simply:

To have what one wants, is to have everything.
To us, being with Baba was everything—and we had it.

PART III

Continuing On

Continuing On

CONTINUING ON

Now began what Mani called "Act Two" of Baba's Advent: the time when His mandali and those who had known Him in physical form lived on, sharing their memories with those who had not been so fortunate.

Mani spent twenty-seven years—a little over a third of her life—in Act Two, twenty of them with Mehera. The support and companionship she gave to Baba's bereaved beloved, the inspiration and example she gave to Baba's followers—both those who had met Him and especially those who hadn't—her brilliant chairmanship of His fledgling Trust over all those years make another whole story, as Mani—who turned to "face the Ocean" in 1969—went on growing and changing in her lifelong effort to efface herself.

Before the resident mandali returned to Meherazad following the Great Darshan in Poona, Mani remembered that they met to talk about simplifying life at Meherazad, cutting back, making everything smaller. The Trust that Baba had set up in 1959 to provide for them was just becoming active. There was very little money and no idea of what was to come.

As Mani and Goher recalled, Baba had told them that after the Great Darshan, He would give darshan every day, that the "gates would be open," that He would be available to everyone. Of course, the mandali couldn't understand: How would this be possible with Baba in such poor health? He had been so secluded. What did He mean?

Later, of course, they understood as, little by little, it started to happen: people, many of them having never met Baba or having heard of Him only recently, started coming to Meherabad and Meherazad for darshan, and to meet the mandali and hear their stories of life with Baba. And so, as Mani recalled, the mandali had to do just the opposite of what they had planned in Poona— they had to expand, not cut back! A verandah went up at Meherazad, a portico in front of the Samadhi, and what started as a trickle of pilgrims became a stream, then a river, and sometimes (at Amartithi, an annual gathering in commemoration of Baba dropping His body) a flood.

Eruch and Mani getting to know new Baba-lovers.

Mehera, too, came out to sit with the visiting Baba-lovers. She was mostly with the women pilgrims, telling them stories on the porch of Baba's House, having them for tea at Baba's dining table, being most relaxed and natural in their company. But although Mehera never touched men—nor were men permitted to touch her—she talked with them about Baba. It is hard for us to imagine what an act of courage this was for someone who, for so many years, had never been allowed to hear a man's name or voice, who had been secluded from even the sight of men!

On the first anniversary of Baba's dropping His body, January 31,

Heartbroken Mehera addressing Baba-lovers at the first Amartithi.

1970, someone made a film of the gathering at Meherabad. There you see Mehera giving a message on the stage over the microphone. Her fragile vulnerability and the poignancy of her grief are startling. Mani is standing by her side, holding her arm and directing her steps. It is an apt illustration of the support Mani and all the close women gave Mehera in those first years.

Meeting Mehera in the early 1970s, as I did, you could sense every moment how terribly she missed Him. She could hardly say Baba's Name without crying. And yet she was so gracious and so brave, sitting with pilgrims for hours whenever they came, telling her Baba stories.

Somewhere in those years, Mani wrote a song about Mehera's longing to be with her Beloved. It is written in Mehera's voice, and begins:

*In the dark hour of separation
of endless days and years,
I see you by the light of my burning heart,
I see you in the pool of my tears . . .
Meher Baba, You are with me, it's true,
But hold me by the hand, Lord, keep me with You.*

THE TRUST

Although Mani was a trustee of the Avatar Meher Baba Trust, at first she didn't go regularly to the Trust Office that had been set up in the compound of Adi K. Irani's family in Ahmednagar. She stayed at Meherazad, continuing her active but secluded life, corresponding with Baba-lovers, helping Goher in a new medical clinic for villagers (she and Eruch used to roll bandages!), visiting with the occasional pilgrims, and mostly being with Mehera.

Meanwhile, an earthquake was rumbling beneath their feet, which in 1970 changed the outer direction of Mani's life. All was not well with Baba's Trust and its first chairman, whose ways of doing things, now that Baba had dropped His body, stepped outside the parameters of the Trust Deed. When this was challenged by the other trustees (all mandali members), the case went to court; there was a huge and very tense legal fight, during which Mani took the chair. The role of chairman was one she was to play from 1971 through the rest of her life; it was a responsibility that pulled her out of her cloistered activities and placed her in the world.

Years later, she said to us that she felt Baba created this crisis with the ex-chairman to "wake up" the mandali to their responsibility to the Trust; that before this, they had been asleep. She recalled how, at a trustees' meeting in Baba's time, when Sarosh was casual about attending (I think he had gone off to take a nap!), Baba became very stern and warned him: Keep your eyes open or this Trust will come around your neck!

This is just what happened. Once awake, with Mani in the chair, the lions Nariman, Sarosh, Adi, Padri, Pendu, Meherjee and other trustees steered the beleaguered Trust through a very rough patch. They made numerous court appearances, Mani with her friend and fellow trustee Rano keeping each other company in the totally alien world of a courtroom. Eruch, too, got involved and began coming with Mani to the office from Meherazad every day she went.

I first met Mani in 1971. She was known among our generation of young, new Baba-lovers for being lively and funny, full of wit and sparkle. We were on pilgrimage to Meherabad and Meherazad (most of us hadn't met Baba physically) and we didn't, couldn't, know the tremendous difficulties in Mani's life at that time, her worry for Mehera, the lack of money for the mandali to live on, the crisis with the Trust. She hid all this superbly. In retrospect, it was amazing that she could.

About this time, Mani had a dream. "In the dream," Mani wrote in her book *Dreaming of The Beloved*, "I was walking along a country road in Ahmednagar, and came across Adi K. Irani squatting by the edge of a field, frantically trying to put together

Mani in the early 1970s, full of wit and sparkle.

two ends of a burst pipeline which was flooding the whole area. Water was gushing out at a tremendous rate, no matter how hard Adi tried to fix the pipes." Seeing that the situation was out of control, Mani started to run for help, calling out for Eruch. The dream continued with Mani finally coming upon Eruch writing in the central room of a beautiful crystal castle on a hill. She called out, "Eruch, Eruch, you have to help Adi! He can't control the water which is gushing out from the broken pipes. It won't stop! It will cause a flood and everything will be drowned!"

Eruch calmly looked up from his writing and said, "It will stop when Baba turns it off at the mains."

"I woke up," Mani wrote, "and said to myself, 'Yes, Baba is at the mains, and in control of every situation.' And so it was with the court case. It ended suddenly when the person who had initiated it [the ex-chairman] passed away at his home town shortly after the dream."[1]

As with everything she did for Baba, Mani turned the full force of her creative energy to her new job. Although she missed her "open-air office" on the small verandah at Meherazad, ruefully joking that she had wound up working in a real office in the end, she brought to the Trust Office tremendous charm and liveliness. And her keen intelligence was more than a match for the many problems of the job. She used to laugh and say, "I may not know how to do it, but I can point you to somebody who does!" It was true. She brilliantly utilized the help of the other trustees and the volunteers drawn to work with her over the years.

From 1974 until she passed away in 1996, I had the great privilege of working with Mani at the Trust Office. In the later years, I also joined her at Meherazad on one or two days of the week, to help her out with this and that in any way she wished. There were a number of us on her "team," and we used to wonder how she managed to have so many of us simultaneously scrambling to keep up with her!

One day after Mani passed away, Bal Natu, who as a trustee worked in the office alongside Mani, said to me, "You should write about all the fun we had with Mani in the Trust Office." When I told him I was trying to write a biography of her life, he smiled and just repeated, "You should write about the fun we had in the Trust Office."

On the night Balaji died, I suddenly understood the value of what he'd suggested. The following reminiscences give some flavor of the fun (and sometimes not-so-fun) we had with Mani during those years at the Trust Office, and also at Meherazad and Meherabad.

Fun with Mani at the Trust Office

THE CHAIRMAN

Mani as Chairman of the Trust.

The Avatar Meher Baba Trust Office is located in Meher Nazar—what used to be Adi K. Irani's family compound—in the town of Ahmednagar, midway between Meherazad and Meherabad. For years Mani worked there Monday through Thursday. Friday was for catching up on personal things at home in Meherazad, and Saturday and Sunday were reserved for the pilgrims to Meherazad.

At about 9:50 a.m. on her Trust Office days, all Trust helpers and employees would line up outside the office door under the jasmine arbor, waiting for the car to arrive from Meherazad. After a few minutes, in it would sweep—a grey Ambassador—Eruch in the front, Mani, Rano, and Bal Natu in the back. We'd open the door for the ladies, and Mani would hop out, smile, and quip, "What's for lunch?"

Hugs all around, a special greeting for Adi and later for Bhau (who moved to the compound from Meherazad for Trust work soon after he became a trustee), nods to the staff, and then everyone would squeeze in through the door to stand in a semi-circle as Mani balanced on a stool and garlanded Baba's picture: "AVATAR MEHER BABA ki JAI!"

After a while, Mani would sit at her desk ("I've been waiting to sit down since I got up!"). Behind her was Baba's picture, with a map of the world right under it. "The Boss is on top of the world," she'd say, gesturing to His photo and the map, which was studded with colored stickpins marking places around the world where Baba-lovers lived.

And the day would begin.

. . .

It's worth taking a moment to set the scene: Mani at her desk, Eruch at his small table on the verandah out back, Rano across the room from Mani, Bal Natu out on the verandah in front (and later at Rano's desk). Adi—and later Bhauji—coming in to see them from down the verandah. Helpers floated from place to place.

According to the two purposes Baba dictated in the original Trust Deed, in 1975 the Trust was divided into Avatar Meher Baba Trust (Firstly), and Avatar Meher Baba Trust (Secondly), now the Avatar Meher Baba Perpetual Public Charitable Trust. Mani presided over the entire compound, filled with people and activity connected to the work of the Trust. There was the "Firstly" office on the side of the compound near the gate, where the board meetings were held and the accountant and his staff did their daily work. There was a room next to Mani's office where the head clerk and a number of office workers did a variety of tasks and errands. Down the verandah on the opposite side of the gate was Adi's office, which, after Adi passed away, became Bhauji's office. Reservations for visiting pilgrims were handled in a room next to that, and across the compound from Mani's office were rooms and work areas for various helpers. Typewriters could be heard clacking away from all corners of Meher Nazar. In this compound, all were working for Baba's cause, and all were devoted to Mani. She in turn always took a very personal interest in each one and his or her area of work, the mark of a true leader.

In many ways Eruch was Mani's right-hand man, conferring with her on all important Trust affairs and supporting and helping her with them. His small table on the verandah behind her office was very understated and out of the way, but when you saw him sitting there, dealing with receipts, correspondence, employees, accountants, clerks, trustees, residents, pilgrims . . . his essential role became obvious.

Bhauji, who became a trustee in 1973, was a wonder in the legal, governmental, and banking side of the world that the mandali had entered so abruptly. It turned out that he had studied law before joining Baba. And he had great vision; he could sense what had to be done now to prepare for the future—when Meherabad would become, as Baba foretold, a world center of pilgrimage. Mani relied on him for his expertise in many areas of the Trust's work.

Rano, also a trustee, was her buddy, secretary, and support. Bal Natu, another trustee, was one of Mani's great fans. We loved his respect and admiration for her. He delighted in her humor and her stories, her wisdom and her style. "Mani's letters are alive," he once said. And reflecting on our times at the lunch table, he remembered, "Even the way she ate was graceful." She was very special in his eyes, and she returned his regard.

THE DESK

On Mani's desk sat a huge collection of things that Eruch found troublesome (they always got in the way): a tortoise, a pair of brass swans, stand-up cards she liked (some stayed for years), a toy gavel that went "squeek!" when you pounded it (which she would take to the board meetings and bonk whenever the discussions got too heated), two or three Baba-pictures, extra stationery, and so on. Luckily, the desk was large.

Under the desktop glass were a slew of photographs: Baba, of

course, and pals (Mani posing with black-leather-clad friends beside a motorcycle, "Mani" the dog and her owner in America, Elizabeth and Kitty, and others). And a peacock feather, a leaf, and other mementos of nature. And quotes she liked, and . . .

As with the desk, Mani filled the innards of the office with personality. There was a cupboard just for the photographs and addresses of Baba-lovers who had visited, so that Mani could look up the pictures of those who had written to her or who were planning to visit again, to picture them clearly before seeing or writing to them.

There were drawers full of eccentric postcards and different kinds of stationery (Mani almost always wrote on something attractive: heart-bordered, or studded with animals or stars or sparkly things.) Each postcard or piece of stationery was carefully matched to the recipient.

She had a pad of chairman's letterhead for formal Trust business, and her own letterhead for personal letters of a certain significance. Her letterhead was white with her name and address in blue at the top, and a quote from Baba. The quote was her favorite:

"If you have that love for Me that St. Francis had for
Jesus, not only will you realize Me, but you will please Me."

She rated His pleasure higher than Realization.

She made the Trust Office days fun. And they were fun—for her much of the time, and certainly for everyone else.

Yet, as you've read, she would often say, "Life with Baba is fun, but it's no joke."

Once in the late 1970s, Dr. Alu Khambatta, an old-time Baba-lover who lived at Meherabad, quietly murmured while looking at Mani, "She bears a crushing burden."

I was so surprised. Mani never seemed to be bearing a burden. But thinking it over, I realized that she did. She was the chairman of a trust, a job she came to straight from a life of seclusion. She had been entrusted by Baba with care for His Mehera, who was bravely struggling to adjust to a world without Baba's physical presence. She was—along with Goher, Arnavaz, and Eruch—responsible for or consulted about everything regarding Meherazad. And she was the head of Baba's own family.

I suppose it hadn't occurred to me because Mani never seemed crushed. Tired, yes; overwhelmed, yes; perplexed, yes. But never crushed. Why not?

Once, near the end of her life, she quietly said to me, "I want you to remember that Baba does His own work."

"Yes, Mani," I said.

"No!" she said. "I mean it. This is not just theory. I didn't know it at first, but it is my *experience*."

In style, the chairmanship followed Mani, and not vice versa. She gave it her own lively touch. She once told someone that she thought she didn't make a great chairman because, "I like small things; I don't like big things."

But it was just this that gave her chairmanship such beauty: she tried to see the big problems that came to her from "the Baba angle," and gave a lot of attention to the "small things"—people's feelings, little courtesies, informal, *personal* touches.

She didn't ignore the big. But just because it was big didn't automatically mean that it was more important. I was often impressed by her priorities. One morning, she was intensely busy with "big" things, when suddenly she asked me to go out with her. We took off for the canteen next door, where

Mani at Sarosh Canteen near the Trust Office.

Mani bought a bottle of jam. She chatted a little with her friend the proprietor, and then we strolled back to the office. On the way, she mentioned that the jam was for Elizabeth Patterson, who was staying with them at Meherazad. Elizabeth liked jam with her breakfast.

She had two things going for her in the big things department: One was her absorption in Baba, which seemed to give her a distance from worldly results. The other was her great intelligence that could indeed grasp and solve problems with far-reaching consequences. (As we've seen, Baba said of her, "Mani is very intellectual. You all say so, but even Eruch, who is himself very clever, says so. . . . The Americans, too, say Mani is really very bright.")

She set the Trust's fundamental direction and tone, kept abreast of each and every thing going on, oversaw huge projects (including the initial development of Meherabad), and initiated undertakings no one else could have, such as the restoration of Baba's tomb. She not only chaired the Trust board meetings: for twenty-one years she wrote out every word of the minutes by hand. She was in touch with every detail.

Her other gifts as an executive were a genius for delegating, and an ability to form and sustain a team. She had many supports in the first years (Sarosh, Nariman, Adi, Eruch, Pendu, Padri, among others) and two great pillars in the later years, Eruch and Bhau, who shouldered whole areas of the tasks she faced. She knew what to ask them to do.

And she had a slew of untried helpers to whom she gave both responsibility and the freedom to exercise it (and to learn from their mistakes). She was a true leader, leading not by coercion but by example. No one in that office worked harder or longer or with more focus than Mani. We spring chickens were always running to keep up. And each of us was dying to stay on her team.

. . .

Occasionally, in an introspective mood, Mani would speculate on how she came to be the chairman of Baba's Trust. She was a person who loved the natural world, informality, and homey atmospheres like her "open-air office" on the verandah overlooking the garden at Meherazad. Now she was surrounded by steel desks, fluorescent overhead lights, and a view onto cars, motorcycles, and bikes (although she got involved in the Trust compound garden, too.)

In a serious mood, she once told us about two Baba-incidents that she speculated *might* have been connected with her later role as chairman. One was that He wrapped a turban around her head as they prepared for the New Life, demonstrating to the women how to do it. The other was that when her neck went out (from the whiplash of the 1952 accident), He told Goher to give Mani His own neck-brace to wear.

There were two stories she loved to share in Meherazad Mandali Hall with pilgrims, as a way of "telling on" herself as she acted out the role of chairman:

Once, a group of officials from one of the local banks came to meet the Chairman. As a matter of course, they were offered tea and biscuits. Mani would mime how she sat listening to everything they were saying. At one point, in the midst of seemingly rapt attention, she dipped her biscuit into her tea. And then kept listening—as the soggy half of the biscuit plopped right into the cup, splashing tea everywhere. She didn't blink. Madame Chairman maintained her poise to the end: "Oh, yes, I understand perfectly. Yes, of course. Well, we will get back to you on that." How she laughed when they finally left!

The other story was about when Eruch first showed her the statement of the Trust accounts. She looked carefully at the credit side and then at the debit side—and then looked at Eruch in amazement: "Isn't that something! They match down to the last *pie* [penny]! How do they ever do that?"

. . .

One of Mani's favorite quotations was one that Kitty sent her. She would sometimes remind herself of it: "As thy day, so shall thy strength be."

Her office days were usually very long and relentlessly busy. At day's end, when everything was packed and ready to go into the car, she would linger in the office after everyone else had left, and silently bow to Baba's picture. She was alone with Him. It was a beautiful sight I glimpsed through the doorway. Then she'd head out to the verandah, where she'd hug us all. Once in a while, when she had gotten through an unusually large stack of work, she'd clap her hands and say with gusto, "We did it!"

As the car drove out of the compound, headed for Meherazad, she never once failed to turn and wave her hands at us from the rear window.

ERUCH

Mani called Eruch "Chechoo-mummy." "Chechoo" was a pet name for Eruch coined by Mani, and "mummy" was her affectionate way of referring to his motherly clucking. He nagged her, she teased him, they squabbled with each other and joked together and worked at many tasks in tandem, as when Baba would send Mani to Eruch to get information for the Family Letters, from the late 1950s until Mani passed away in 1996.

As mentioned, Mani and Eruch had never exchanged a word until 1958, when Mani sang "Begin the Beguine" to him. (For those in the ashram, of course, this was perfectly understandable. As we've seen, from the time

Eruch and Mani, dear partners in service.

she joined Baba, Mani—and certainly Mehera—never spoke to men, or looked directly at them, unless Baba ordered her to. The separation between the very secluded women and the men was that absolute.)

Some time after Baba dropped His body, Eruch told Mani and others how Baba had once asked him for a favor. A favor, Eruch said, not an order. The favor Baba requested was that Eruch take care of Mehera and Mani if and when anything should happen to Him. Eruch agreed.

Perhaps that is why Eruch was so particular about accompanying Mani to the Trust Office. Or perhaps it was because Eruch had asked Baba not to put him on the Trust board, and now the burden of the chairmanship had fallen on Mani and not on him. Who knows? At any rate, he faithfully attended the office and the board meetings (as a "special invitee"), and helped Mani immeasurably, his great shoulders sharing many of her burdens.

He was also very funny with her. As mentioned before, he had a fond accusation that he leveled at Mani from time to time—"You're just a Loni girl!"—Loni being the small village in the ghats beyond Poona where Mani had occasionally stayed with her aunt Dowla and uncle Faredoon as a child. In Loni she had great fun: she played with the goats, drank from the stream, went to the weekly village bazaar (where all the wares were laid out on the street) holding her aunt's hand, and came back with spinach and rice and dal and perhaps a little trinket to play with. The "Loni girl" was the one who squatted down on the Trust Office floor to play with wind-up toys with the children. She was straight from the village.

Mani's and Eruch's office styles were opposite. Mani made the office into an extension of her personality: colorful, lively, homey. When she was working, her desk was a sea of papers, letters, pens, stickers, checkbooks, all mixed together. Eruch's table at the back was shipshape at all times. There was nothing extraneous anywhere; God forbid! As usual, he left no trace of himself.

Eruch at work on the back verandah of the Trust Office.

This contrast in desk appearances drew forth at least one remark a day from Eruch. "This is Office here" was a frequent refrain, especially after peals of laughter or busy chatter could be heard around Mani's desk.

In the office, a decidedly "Pappa Jessawala" streak emerged in Pappa's son Eruch. (As we've seen, Pappa was the martinet who had driven Gustadji and three other seasoned mandali, living on a mountain under Pappa's orders, to write to Baba, "We will keep silence for eternity and fast to death—only if Pistol [Pappa] is not here!") But to the many residents, trustees, pilgrims, family members, and others who dropped in to see him, Eruch remained the avuncular friend of the Meherazad verandah, and the wise, compassionate, adroit, engaging raconteur of Mandali Hall.

Of course, Mani was a match for Eruch's "office mood." When he would start in about some work he wanted her to finish, she would give him a warning look over her glasses—"Chechoo-mummy . . ." —and the dialogue would begin:

"Mani, have you signed that bank letter yet?"

"Chechoo-mummy, I'm going to. See, it's right here."

"Come along now, Mani, it's three-thirty; you have a lot of work left to do!"

"All right, there, I've signed it. Take it."

That he waited until three-thirty to nag her was a miracle, but he had a soft spot for her, and he knew how hard she worked. Long before then, he would come out to the front verandah and start in on us. We were the ones distracting Mani with other, less important, tasks. It wasn't her fault, it was *our* fault. And look at our desks! How could we work in such a mess?

I still remember Eruch coming into the office with a booklet of checks for Mani to sign and standing stock-still in amazement. She was sitting by herself at her desk, folding an origami form out of scratch paper. It was either a crane (with a movable neck and head; she was very proud of that one) or a nun—one of the two. This was too much for him. "Your Brother," he fumed accusingly, "had this same habit of suddenly dropping everything and starting to play!"

How Mani beamed at that!

They were partners in Baba's work in the office and at Meherazad. In Meherazad, Mani would go over to Eruch's room for a little "check-in" every morning. Each would have notes of things to tell the other or discuss together. Sometimes Goher would join them, if the topic centered on the household or the bazaar or the dispensary.

They were a wonderful team, an inspiring team.

When Mani became sick with cancer in 1996, Eruch would come

to the house at Meherazad to visit her occasionally, and Goher would call him inside, alone or along with some of the other men mandali. Before her, he was the same old Eruch, even bringing her papers to sign (!). But he was deeply gentle and loving. Away from her, we could see his pain at her pain. He had his own illness to contend with, and the stress of Mani's ordeal noticeably exacerbated his own.

One day, when she was almost completely bedridden, Eruch, after ascertaining that it was a good time to visit, came over alone. He brought no work. She could not walk or stand unassisted by then, but when he came in with Goher, and Mani saw him, she smiled. As he came around to greet her, she struggled out of bed, stood by herself, and hugged him. Somehow those of us there knew—and surely they knew—that it was their goodbye.

After Mani passed away, Eruch changed. Both Mehera and Mani were gone; he had fulfilled his promise to Baba. Looking at him, I felt like this great crock full of honey had cracked down the sides, yet it still held its shape; and through the cracks, honey was streaming out.

GIVING IT TO THE RESIDENTS

Along with pilgrims, trustees and residents were always dropping in to the office to talk with Mani about things, sometimes Trust work and sometimes personal. Mani would often greet them with some humorous remark (I remember a tall, particularly drooly resident coming up to kiss her on the head and Mani saying, "It's OK, I already had a shampoo today").

She was available to help however she could. She really cared. Mani was interested in everything about us, our families, our concerns, how we were doing, how we were surviving. She never said no to a request for a personal talk. She gave us very practical advice on how to live in India and manage our lives here. When I first came to stay, I was very enthusiastic, all fired up to work seven days a week. Mani insisted that I take a day off, "to wash your hair," as she said. She always talked about the importance of keeping balance in our lives. (Actually, the Meherazad mandali's own day for tending to personal things, Friday, was forced upon them by Sarosh in the very early '70s. He didn't think they would take a day for their personal work, which they wouldn't, so he told all of us pilgrims there at the time that if we went out to Meherazad on Fridays, we'd have to answer to him!)

When we got too "ascetic" in our personal habits, Mani would quote Margaret: "A little of what you fancy does you good." And she confided a secret about her own austere life, "I extract happiness from tiny corners with pincers!"

And she was so loving. She could warm you right up with just a twinkle from her eyes, a smile, a hug, a little joke, a nickname.

Mani stressed communication among people, among those working together. She herself made sure she let people know what was going on, and she wanted us to do the same: "You've got to communicate." (Eruch put it another way: "What's the matter with you people? Don't you ever *talk* to each other?")

There was another side to Chairman Mani S. Irani that some people came to know: the strong, tough, strict, straight-talking Mani who called you on your laziness, your sloppiness, your dropping the ball. Meheru once told me that this was a side that Mani had to develop after becoming chairman.

Mani was very clear about what she felt was acceptable and

unacceptable behavior at Meherabad and Meherazad. For the unacceptable, her expressive face had a great range of looks: "What could you possibly have been thinking?"; "I just don't get it; how could you *do* that?"; or, the worst—"Spare me the explanation."

She was an Irani, after all; she could clearly express what she felt.

Yet Mani never expected others to have the degree of focus on Baba, discipline, dedication, clarity of purpose, or lack of self-interest that the mandali had. She just expected people to try their best. And she expected their best from them. She lovingly understood when you couldn't do something. But she couldn't understand it when you didn't try. And she hated to be told, "I'm sorry." When, out of casualness or inattention, you failed to do something that you should have done and then said, "I'm sorry" to get yourself off the hook, she would reply, "What good does 'sorry' do me?" And if you offered the explanation, "Well, I thought . . ."—*boom*—you would be cut off with, "Don't think!"

One day in the early 1990s, Mani and I were looking through a portfolio of photographs of the mandali. They were taken by a Baba-lover in the early years just after Baba had dropped His body. I forget whose photo she was looking for, perhaps Mehera's, but before she found it, we came across a picture of Mani herself. I had seen it once; it was really "her"—lively, laughing, reaching out in a gesture of giving. I said, "Oh, that's a good one!" and she smiled and we went on looking.

Mani, lively and outgoing . . .

. . . and Mani in a more serious mood.

As we neared the end of the pictures, we came upon another one of her, one I had never seen before. It was the direct opposite of the one we had just looked at. In it, Mani is standing, her hands at her sides, gazing directly at the camera. We looked at it in silence for a moment, and then Mani said, "That's how I was with Baba."

At first I was surprised. Then I could see it, the reflection of her inner experience: her resolution, her implacable determination to be His, to stick with Him whatever the cost, to make the very most of her unbelievable good fortune.

So it's not surprising that she expected just a mite of that from us, not for her own sake but for ours.

Once in a while, we'd get a talk.

Before the opening of the Pilgrim Centre in 1980, Mani came out to Meherabad and spoke about working for Baba to those of us who were going to volunteer there. I'm including some relevant excerpts:

> **[On working for Baba:]**
> Never lose sight of the purpose of your being here. You are here because of Meher Baba . . . and while you are working here for Baba, never forget the real work that Baba does through whatever work you do: Each of you is Baba's special work. While He gives you an opportunity to work for Him, He is working on you. He uses the work you do, to do

His work within you. He is quite tricky, you see! Another thing, don't lose perspective; even though He wants you to wholeheartedly do the work entrusted to you, don't be so attached to the work itself that you find yourself failing to give what He really wants from you.

Keep an eye on yourself. It's the little things that you trip over, things too small to make a show of, with no reward of glory attached, only service and the effort to please Him. Like the jeweler who tests the metal to see if it is gold, test your acts and words with the touchstone of His pleasure, to see whether they are pleasing to Him. Remember, Baba does not need us. Baba only loves us, with that incredible love that He alone has to give. It is we who need Him.

Baba is not like anybody else. He has taken all of you, as you are. You have to take all of Baba, not just the parts that suit you, not just His compassion and love, but His fire and tests as well. He gives all these, and when He gives, He gives in large doses.

[On working together:]

Of course there will be problems . . . but when you have a problem you have to look at it from Baba's angle, think of what would please Baba in that situation. The problem looks real because you are looking at it from your angle, you are putting yourself in the way. You have to get yourself out of the way and see the situation from Baba's angle. If you do that, you will find that no problem exists.

In your work for Him there should be harmony and communication among you as a team. There should be no islands, islands are what separate the ocean . . . You are all spokes in the one wheel which revolves round the Hub—

MEHER BABA. And all the spokes have to move rhythmically together for the wheel to keep rolling . . . Your hearts are His, that is certain, but it is the mind; the mind goes on its own sweet way. Remember that the work you do and the problems and conflicts you face are all His way of working on the mind.

It is to deal with the mind that He creates these situations. That is His business. What we have to do is to remember Him, to try to please Him. As I said, Baba is tricky. He plays you along, and when you are too pleased with yourself He pulls the rug out from under all the things you are so proud of in yourself. He will pull the rug right out from under you, but He will sustain you in His hands.

[On preparing to work for Baba:]

When you are about to go on a journey, you prepare for it and equip yourself with the things you need to have with you . . . well, on our journey to Him, too, we have to be equipped. To work for Him you have to equip yourself with humility, tolerance, acceptance, and the will to serve Him with joy . . . and of course keep your sense of humour, an essential ingredient in life with Baba. You cannot take God, Baba, without a pinch of humour!

[On being with Him:]

The important thing is to be with Him. Whatever you do, wherever you are, don't be absent from Him. I am reminded of a line from a ghazal which Baba would quote: *"Masti me bhi sir apna saki key qadam per ho,"* which means "Even in intoxication, keep your head on the Wine Giver's feet." So remember, in the intoxication of work, achievement, service, love, always keep your head at His feet.

. . .

Right across the compound from Mani's office is the Ahmednagar Baba Centre. Baba went there a number of times. Anyway, in 1984, when Mani felt the residents needed to hear a few things "straight from the shoulder," we were called to the centre on a certain day. Mani and Bhauji and Eruch and Bal Natu and Rano came over from the office, everyone sat in front of Baba's picture, and Mani started in.

I jotted down a few points from the talk she gave us. They could have been from any time during her term, they are so central to her point of view about community life:

> Don't forget the little courtesies with each other. Baba always gave a lot of importance to that.
>
> While He allows you to work for Him, He is working on you. As I always say, His work is each one of us, all His lovers. We are His real work.
>
> Don't be too critical. What's behind the other person's posturing and big noise? Think of that, of what they may be feeling. They're new at this too.
>
> Don't be so quick to pull back. Have more trust.
>
> See that His breath comes through. That's the most important thing.
>
> Things to come in future are seeds now; it takes time for them to grow.

At the end of another particularly stern talk, as if in answer to our unspoken thought that the mandali had had Baba with them and we didn't, she said, "If you don't have Baba with you, what the hell are you doing here?"

Then in 1993, she gave us another talk in the Ahmednagar Centre, one that was taped. The beautiful thoughts on working for Baba she shared that day are typical of the advice she would give on many occasions. Here are a number of excerpts:

The last talk I gave was quite some time ago, and I think it's lying somewhere in the attics of your minds—the ones who have heard it—collecting dust and perhaps some cobwebs, and it is necessary once in a while to clean up the attics. To weed things out, to see whether the items still serve the purpose for which they were gotten. Open the windows, let the light in, so that we feel once again the pure and powerful breath of Baba, of His Love. To refresh again, to revive and to throw away some of the junk that is no longer necessary, to renew our vows to ourselves, the resolutions that we make in all sincerity and honesty, and then see to it that all this dust that has collected doesn't obscure our view of His beautiful face, which must be before us at all times. That is the main thing . . .

Back to the things in the attic which we must dispose of: think about them, make a decision and throw away some things.

I don't mean wants; desires are not that easy to just dismiss. You can't throw them away; you can't fast them away; but you can diet them. Let's learn to diet our wants. We are so keen and eager to diet for our physical appearance. But before Him, we are beyond physical. His love is a see-through love, and yet He accepts us. So doesn't it behoove us to give Him more than what we give to the physical? It is for us; it is for you all to decide how and what to give.

Baba's work is to crush the ego. One of the lines Baba liked very much in one of the ghazals was about henna leaves, the juice of which gives a red colour on whatever you put it—it's used for decorating women's hands at marriage time, for instance . . . To get the red colour, you have to grind up the leaves. You cannot get the colour without the

Mani talking earnestly from the Chairman's desk, with a map of the world behind her.

grinding. So for Him to use the henna [within us], He has to grind [us].

. . . So, having made your resolve, re-avowed your vows to yourselves to get rid of some of this junk in the attics—such as the arrogance that comes up when something goes against what you have decided and made up your mind about, and obstinacy and all those things—then you have to replace the junk with something else, because then there will be more room in the attic.

So then we have to nurture and cultivate humility. That's a very important item in your spiritual equipment, in your love equipment for the Beloved. A humility that I would like to see a little more of. Baba was humility personified. Just like His Love is unfathomable, so was His humility. That I would like to see you give to yourselves, because it's a gift.

It's a gift from Him. All these things that I've mentioned are gifts from Him. You can give it to yourselves. He has put it there for you. You have to help yourselves to it. It is much better to help yourself to that than to these other things.

One thing there is no excuse for—there's no excuse for impoliteness; there's no excuse for discourtesy. We have to be courteous. Remember how totally Baba has accepted us . . . The point is that what is important is how one does what one does. How you carry out the duty, not what you do. You serve? OK; they do that out in the world. There are missions, missionaries who serve; we are not them. You are different . . . When [a visitor] said "We come here for a little love," I realized: that is the difference. You all are working with love; that's what gives your work meaning; otherwise without love—you know that *ghanna*, the sugar cane stalks that you see the Indian children eat, and then the fiber that's left over when they take out the juice? Love is the sap. Love for Baba—that love is the sap. The rest is just like that fiber; nobody will even pick it up. You don't even give it to the cat.

What I'm trying to say is: keep yourself aware of what He has given and keeps giving. What can you do for Him? Nothing that you can do obliges Him. Nothing, nothing that we can do, nothing anybody can do. He is so compassionate that although He does not need us, He accepts us. He gives; He gives with a giving that nobody can understand. He forgives with a forgiveness that is beyond everything, that is incredible. And here we have all that.

 . . . One has to become aware of anger. I read the other day, when I just opened a Baba book, a message where Baba says, anger is like a whirlwind that blows out the flame which He has lighted for us. And that whirlwind has to be kept away. We have to work on that. There are things that we have to do ourselves.

The only thing we like to see is you all growing inwardly. Remember the inner life is a very important thing. The outer, yes, you can write it down, you can list it, you can talk about it, you can tick it off. What about the inner? The inner is very important. And the inner reflects in the outer.

And another thing, if you are doing anything for Baba—OK, you all work for Baba, I appreciate that, I admit that. But you have to do it happily. If you're doing your work happily, then you're not overtired and therefore not getting snappy at other people or angry. That happens, I know. I know also that it's very hard. I'm not saying it's easy, I know that it's hard. Sometimes it's so hard that you tell yourself, "Oh, it's impossible. I can't do it. I can't take anymore." Now here I'm talking about myself. "This is the limit. It couldn't possibly cross this line. It's impossible."

So why does our Baba ask us to do the impossible? He asks you to do the impossible because He knows it is possible, because He will make it possible if you want to do it. That is the one thing which Baba keeps stressing: try. What does "try" mean? He hasn't made it anywhere near as hard as it is for people who want to win in the Olympics. My God, we see in those little serials and videos what they do in order to win a medal! What should we do then for the personification of God, the personification of Love? Is that too much? Is anything we are doing too much? No, He is too much.

We were totally full and happy to have Baba, so we never thought, "Oh, how lucky we are." And Baba had to remind us. He said, "You folks have no idea, no idea, how lucky you all are. Angels envy you because they can see Me, but they cannot touch Me." And what were we doing? Bringing the basin for Baba to wash His hands, handing Him a soap. And all these little things—bringing the food, Mehera combing His hair—they cannot do even if they're angels. And He would say that yogis up in the mountains, in the Himalayas, in the snows, they sit there—and Baba, of course, who has to be the most wonderful actor in the whole world, otherwise He wouldn't act so beautifully as Man being God—He would act it out, saying, "You know those yogis sit up in the top of the Himalayas till their eyebrows grow like this, their nails grow like that, and till their beards almost seem like a river growing, to get what you already have." But could we get it in our heads? We didn't care. We had Baba. As I said, we were with the Tavern Keeper. Our business was with the Tavern Keeper, not with the tavern, not with the wine. We were ready to sweep the tavern floor, to wash the glasses in which He served wine to the others who came. We were content, totally full. We didn't want the wine. We wanted the company of our Saki, and towards that you are now going.

So remember, you have not only received a big thing, but you're going towards such a fulfilling and stupendous thing . . .

Baba is making it very easy for you all, believe me, even compared to us. What you're having is very easy, very smooth. No other, not even a Perfect Master, would do that, Baba Himself has said. So kind and compassionate is the Avatar. And we are blessed to have Him. And what do we do? Do we kneel in our hearts every moment in acceptance of that, in appreciation of that? Oh, no; we are angry and we are hungry . . . And these dusts that accumulate on the mirror of our hearts fog His image, and nothing is worth that. No one is worth that and nothing is worth that. Even if it comes for a while, wipe it out. Prove, if not to anybody else, prove to yourself that you are different.

You have Meher Baba. You represent His name. You have a banner in your heart which says "Meher Baba" . . .

Ask for His help to please Him. Working for Him is fine; pleasing Him is better—best. Ask Him; ask Him to help. He never refuses a request.

You see, in the songs that Baba has loved most, there is repetitively this one line that comes in and I noticed that, having wondered why these ghazals were Baba's favorites. The line is: "Your pleasure is my pleasure." When His wish becomes your wish, when you make His wish your wish. If He wants you to stand on one leg, and you do it, then that means that your wish has merged in His . . .

So as I said, please Him, and by pleasing Him, we're not giving Him anything. I'm not talking about that. I'm talking about your receiving, because to receive the gift of pleasing Him is no small thing. And how blessed you all are. We can all have it. It is not earmarked for Indians or Westerners or princes or beggars or blacks or whites. It is for all.

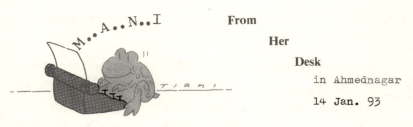

From Her Desk in Ahmednagar
14 Jan. 93

LETTERS

In the middle of the morning, Mani would call for, or we would suggest, a "bump." This was a good jolt of strong coffee (or her favorite Café Français) to "bump" us up for the rest of the morning till lunch. (Mani had a penchant for the cartoon show "The Simpsons." Homer, the father in the show, used to call out to his wife, Marge, "Beer me, Marge," and Marge would run for a beer. We used to joke that all you had to do in the office was call out, "Bump me," and you'd get a cup of coffee.) At Mani's invitation, we all bumped up on coffee along with her.

She'd often drink her bump while working on letters. Baba had involved her in correspondence for ages, and she was used to it and wonderful at it. But the sheer volume of mail after He dropped His body just kept growing as more people came to Baba. Unlike Eruch, who wrote to his correspondents, "Friend is he, friend is she, who keeps the mandali correspondence-free," Mani couldn't help responding to the hearts who wrote to her; she felt how much it meant to people to receive a word or a line from Baba's Meherazad family. When she wrote, whatever she wrote, her aim was always to reach the person, to affirm the personal heart-to-heart contact of Baba's Love.

Extracts from her own letters best tell what she could convey through words.

Mani had great beginnings to her letters.

(to an oldtime Baba-lover, on a bird card):
"Reading your letter, a flock of memories flew up onto this card—Oh yes, dear pen-pal, what olden golden times we shared with The King!"

(to a child who just moved to a new house):

"My heart-lens took this picture: it's you, cute [K.], enjoying your new home. . . . I liked your sunny card, and I love you in Baba's beautiful Love. Beloved Baba is going to New Mexico with you, so I'm sure you'll like it. Maybe He'll also bring you to India before long—we'd sure like that!"

(to someone who'd been out of touch):

"Getting your letter is like seeing a dear familiar face after a long time—and what joy the last lines of your letter brought to my heart: 'I have not forgotten Baba.'"

(to someone who used to work at the Trust Office):

"Jai Baba dear [A.],—here I am at the Trust Office and feel like declaring a holiday because the office lights are ON (yesterday no lights all day and my brain was on the blink) [smiley doodle here]."

(to someone seeking guidance from Baba):

"Your letter of . . . just reached me, but all that you expressed in it has reached Beloved Baba before you wrote, and what you strongly feel inside of you (as to what you want to do) is His answer I'm sure. 'Talking to Baba' is the best prayer of a heart privileged to house His Love—as you would to a true friend, and Baba is the truest Friend ever! Rest always assured of His Love for you and know that He will guide you in His silent way, through the course of circumstances and the voice of your heart."

(to a newcomer):

"Dear [M.], greetings to you in Meher Baba's Love from Mehera and all your Meherazad family. It was a joy to meet you through your most heart-warming letter and we too are 'so glad you finally made it'—wondrous are His ways! It is Beloved Baba's Love for you that has brought you to Him, and your touching experience made our old hearts glow with His Smile."

(to a Baba-lover who could not come to India):
"Your letter was like an embrace in Baba's Love—you touched my heart so gently and deeply. Some day, in His perfect time, Baba will bring you here in person—all things are possible in our Beloved's Love. And remember, when others are here with Baba, Baba is there with you.

"Now Mehera and I come over (in a picture) to meet you my dear—till we meet in person in His perfect plan."

(written in August):
"I received your letter in July—but it seems my pen thought it was still Silence Day till now!"

The endings of Mani's letters were pretty good, too.

(to an old friend):
"Well, the lunch whistle just went off (translation: [P.] Is shouting for us)—it happily synchronizes with my tummy's alarm clock (also ringing loudly). Will sign off with my favourite exit-line: AVATAR MEHER BABA ki JAI from your Meherazad family, to you with cabooses of love."

(to Margaret Craske):
"I always seem to end my letters with saying Mehera and we all Girls remember you a lot—and as it is a fact I will repeat it again, and add 'you are so close to our hearts always.'"

(written at a busy time):
"A short letter on paper is better than a long one in the head, and at the speed Beloved Baba is spinning His merry-go-round

I'll never get the time to write a long one—So get out your lorgnettes to pick up all the love that's packed between these lines for a special delivery to you and your lovely family."

(in the midst of a long letter:)

"Dr. Freny (Foreman) has just come in, and seeing me writing this long letter in December she's ready to take my temperature!"

(to dear old-timers who had just visited India)

"A Jai Baba hug to you dears from me. Your short but love-full visit remains fresh and fragrant in my heart in Beloved Baba's Love."

(and this family favorite:)

". . . with lots and lots of love and a united AVATAR MEHER BABA ki JAI from all your Meherazad family."

Good beginnings and good endings. But what Mani did best was the middle. I loved how personal her letters were, how much warmth she could pack into a sentence:

"The Baba-joy in your visit was mutual."

"You are so often in my thoughts and always in my heart."

She gave such support and encouragement to Baba-lovers going through hard times:

"Your total faith in Beloved's Love and your simple acceptance of His Will are the true offerings that please Him—how blessed and fortunate you are."

―

"I placed your letter and all you poured out in it onto Beloved Baba's lap—on His chair in His room at Meherazad. And I will also deliver a prayer on your behalf, in the shape of a rose from Mehera's garden, at Baba's Samadhi when next we

> Heather Angel, I know all about it — but I won't tell anyone! I'll keep Baba & Erico's secret plan to have you quietly at Meherabad on this Thursday when all the world is at Meherazad — and the Trust Office is in a whirl of its own 🌀 Jai Baba — ENJOY 😊 + get perfectly well & strong soon — you hear me? ♡ We all miss you — See you Monday — Mani T.O. 27-9-90

From Mani: an amusing, clever note and a typical example of her kindness to residents, ill or well.

go to Meherabad. Try and keep happy; remember that He loves you and is with you. Though you may feel in low moments that He has turned His face from you, that is never so. Keep your gaze on Baba with the full assurance of what He has told His lovers 'I am always with you.'"

"As an old-timer you know our Beloved's habit to see to each and everything where His lovers are concerned—So indeed He is with you and holding you in His precious care. Keep on dancing to His tune, [S.] dear—keep reflecting your Beloved's smile in your constant remembrance of Him."

(to someone who had been through a difficult experience:)
"We are happy you have taken it as you have, that this lesson (experience) has not lessened you, but has added to your depth and growth in Baba's unfathomable ways and Love—This is His Compassion and grace."

(sent to a sick woman, along with a picture of Baba holding a lamb:)
"This is how Beloved Meher Baba holds you, in His lovely arms, close to His Heart. I've no doubt Baba kept this picture specially for you—I've just found it in a most unexpected place in my cupboard! It has rested on Baba's bed (in Meherazad) all morning, and goes to you by hand of dear [N.] who will also carry lots of love to you from each of your Meherazad family. JAI-BABA, in His Ocean."

"Don't ever think that our Mighty Beloved would ever ever reject for a moment someone He has given His Love to!! Such an unworthy thought or fear belittles His Love!"

> "Your remorse and regret were a real prayer from your heart to Beloved Baba . . . know that Beloved Baba is forgiveness itself: and when your repentance is so deep, it means that He has already forgiven you and dissolved your past failings in His Ocean of Mercy. . . . Just keep remembering Baba—His help and comfort will never fail you."

The following excerpt is from a letter Mani wrote in the early 1980s to a Baba-lover in great physical pain. I quote so much of it because it shows Mani's deep understanding of the sometimes terrible trials of ordinary life:

> "Your letter of . . . has been very lovingly received. In reply I must tell you first of all that it has been placed at Beloved Baba's feet in His Samadhi where you and all your concerns rest in the Ocean of His Love. Dear [A.], your love for Baba shines out from your letter and touches our hearts, reflecting His own greater Love for you. Rest assured that your Divine Physician has your care monitored in the 'intensive care' of His Heart—so don't for a moment think that you are 'far' from Him. You would be absolutely wrong, [A.], to think that Baba can be 'indifferent' to your situation when He Himself has picked you for His own! Why, even this pain you are given, proves that He has His special attention on you. Baba will not ever let go of you, He has promised His lovers 'You can never get rid of Me'! Keep holding onto your Beloved Baba through everything, and remember it is a tiny portion of the suffering He went through for us.
>
> "He also tells us that suffering is never in vain; that is why in His Ocean of Mercy Baba allows His lovers to suffer. But at the same time, He <u>shares</u> our suffering. . . .
>
> "You write that you hesitate to ask Baba for help. Dear

[A.], while we should not dictate to Baba about our problems, feel free to tell Him your troubles. He is <u>The</u> Friend, and as the Perfect Friend He is there to share all our hearts' tribulations. If we don't tell Him, who have we to tell—and I can assure you from my experience that He always listens.

"I have been through pain, and know that it is totally distracting, and well understand how wearied and helpless you (and your dear wife) must feel while this pain doesn't leave you. Your letter was shared with the Meherazad mandali and we feel much concerned about your condition—especially our Doctor Goher. She feels first of all [here follows some medical aspects and advice]. . . .

"We were all very touched to read of your wife's love and support, which is the beautiful silver lining Baba has provided to the cloud of these present circumstances. The cloud will pass away, nothing is lasting except Baba's Love."

And to end these excerpts, here's a "NOT"-letter, written to an old-timer leaving India after a pilgrimage:

> Dear [L.]
> As you can see
> this is NOT a letter,
> but something better:
> a Jai Baba hug at parting time
> in Baba's Love which needs no rhyme
> but is the very Reason
> for the Pilgrim Season
> by His grace sublime!

As Meheru said, "Mani was never shy to use words." As Bal Natu remembered, "Mani's letters had life."

. . .

"Mani. Mani. MANI!" Rano would shout, standing in front of Mani's desk. She once timed it: it had taken her ten minutes to break through Mani's concentration. There at her desk, glasses perched on the end of her nose, hand writing a letter with a small Flair pen, Mani was oblivious to it all: the outside chatting of the crowd waiting for the bus to Meherabad, the steady stream of visitors to Eruch that passed right in front of her, Rano and others typing two desks away. Yet there on the paper before her would be emerging line after line of advice, comfort, care.

Rano and Mani.

But it took time and terrific energy. She would sometimes write to friends, "Baba doesn't retire us; He re-tyres us" (re-tires, as with a car), or "we keep on rolling 'cause He keeps on pushing," or she would describe the mandali as "dizzily busy." And when she was very busy, or ill, she used to laugh, "Sometimes I say to Baba, 'You never were good at arithmetic, were You? Look at all this and look how old I am!'"

Or with a twinkle, as they rush, rush, rushed through day after day of activity, effort, problems, and work: "We used to have nothing and enjoy everything; now we have everything and enjoy nothing!"—no time!

THE FAX

The Trust Office was not what you'd call technologically state of the art in those days. There were no phones in the office, and no computers (these were just beginning to loom on the Indian horizon). There were lots of typewriters. And lots of communiqués by written message.

The messages would usually come in envelopes that had been reused about five times. There would be the original "To So-and-so" and "From So-and-so" on the envelope, which would be scratched out—except for the "To" and "From"—and new names put in, and then those would be scratched out, and other names put in, and so on and so forth until there was no more space to write. Then the envelope *might* be thrown away, but more likely passed on to another incarnation as a pill carrier for patients at the dispensary. This was the mandali's style of office economy. I once received a manila envelope from Mani in the mid-1980s that had originally been sent by Rano to Ivy Duce in America in 1962 (the stamps were there, postmarked). Then it had somehow returned to Mani in India (must have been hand-carried, obviously with something in it). I think there was a back and forth between Mani and Eruch also there, before Mani sent something in it to me. That envelope had been circulating for twenty years! By the time I got it, the thing was an archival object.

Of course, the messages themselves were written on the back side of scrap paper that had been previously used for something else (typed address lists were a favorite.) God help you if you used *new* paper for a *local message*. They were usually carried from Meherabad to the Trust Office to Meherazad and vice versa, either in the office car or by the bazaar rickshaw or by an office worker on a bicycle. It sounds impossible, but it worked.

Although the office itself had no phone, there was a phone down the verandah. If Mani wasn't at her desk, you were sure to find her either in conference with Bhauji (and sometimes Eruch) down in Bhauji's office, where they had privacy (and God forbid you interrupted those sessions!), or she might be visiting Khorshed, swapping old stories and songs or guessing who was who in an ancient photo. (From the 1970s, Khorshed lived down the verandah from the office of her cousin Adi Sr., which was later Bhauji's office.) Or Mani might be at the reservations office, checking out the new frames for Baba photos or the latest Baba-trinkets, and in the meantime finding out what was for lunch. Or she might be using the phone.

Mani had an executive relationship with the phone—i.e., it was kept a little at a distance. Her phonewalli (almost always the same person) would dial the number and get the desired party. Then Mani would take the phone, holding her list of points to be conveyed. She had rarely talked on the phone in her life before the office (they didn't have a phone back then at Meherazad, only in Guruprasad), but she quickly became adept at its use. It was a perfect vehicle for communication with her family in Poona (Baba had asked her to look after them for His sake) and close Baba-friends in Bombay. The conversations were usually short, a little bit of chat, a lot of communication.

Mani on the office phone.

There was no e-mail at that time, but one day the phonewalli told Mani about a new invention over at the Post Office: the fax. Mani was already very fond of the xerox (her handwritten letters were often sent out to be copied), so she grasped the idea immediately. Like a xerox, only long distance. It was an interesting news item.

About two weeks later, we had a problem. Mani had heard rather late about something new about to happen at the Meher Spiritual Center in Myrtle Beach. She was really excited about it: they were going to have a sahavas for young people. With her strong belief in nurturing young people's love for Baba, Mani jumped at the chance to support it. She hand-wrote an inspiring poem for the kids about loving Baba. The problem was: how to get it to the Center in time for the sahavas?

Who was leaving India for America who could hand-carry the message? Out came the pilgrim departure list. No one. Could it go by regular mail? Everyone counted the days before the sahavas all over again. No use. The fact remained: there wasn't enough time.

Suddenly Mani said, "Fax!" We all said, "Huh?" and she said, "We'll send it by fax!" And down the message went to the Post Office and off to America over the phone line, just like that.

BABA'S PHOTOS

The day a box of Baba photographs arrived from a photowalla in America was always a big day at the office. Mani, on receiving the big flat box, would push aside the papers on her desk and sit with the photo box in her lap. Then, one by one, she would take out the printed pictures.

She used to say, "Mehera never handled Baba's pictures casually," and as far as we could see, Mani never did either. Slowly, carefully, she looked through the photos. Almost every picture won some comment or murmur from her. Looking at one, she might mention His eyebrows or some facial feature emphasized by the fall of light, or what His glance conveyed. She could quickly interpret not only His hand gestures but His expressions: "He's very tired here"; "Look at the fire in His eyes!"; or she'd construct a whole context—"He's not at all happy with what's happening."

Baba photos.

Coming upon a picture she had taken herself—and there were many of those—more description would follow. The beautiful, luminous picture [page 163] of young Baba standing on Meherabad Hill against a bamboo matting wall—gazing upward, looking like an angel—she had taken with her good old box camera.

The pictures would be laid out on her desk in piles. These here were too good to let go of so soon—she wanted to look at them some more; she'd take them home. These here were to be offered for sale in the Reservations office down the verandah.

Pictures of Mehera got almost as much attention. We came to know, as Mani murmured and sighed her way through these boxes, that almost all the early pictures of Mehera (and the women) were taken by her or under her direction. And so many classics of Baba and Mehera together! Like her artistic brother Beheram, Mani had an eye for composition, and could capture Baba and Mehera at their ease.

A photo of Mehera and Baba from the 1940s near Meherazad.

One day I said to her, "It's so wonderful for our generation to see pictures of Baba." She replied, "Baba's pictures are very important." And we saw Mani's work to preserve and share them: supporting many people to collect and protect the negatives, and making sure Baba's photos were available.

After Mani passed away, the women mandali were shown a rare movie of Baba. It was taken in Meherazad garden—and Mehera was behind the camera! A little later, Mehera appeared in the movie, and Goher was now behind the camera. And then the funny part came: into the movie stepped Mani holding a still camera, so then Goher was taking a movie of Mani taking photographs of Baba!

But more often it was Mani behind the movie camera that Elizabeth gave her, filming Baba, or directing her brother Beheram or nephew-in-law Jangu as they filmed Him.

In this way, Mani gained a lot of experience making movies. And consequently one had to be very careful about showing her any home video footage: "Why didn't you pan the scene to show us where you are?"; "Take your time; we couldn't even see that"; "Zoom in SLOWLY!"; and so on. I learned a lot just watching her watch videos. Because, of course, she was the movie-making queen—maker of the "family films" of Baba in Meherazad, and at Guruprasad, which she would then send to Baba-lovers in the West.

So it was only natural that she became very involved in promoting the collection and preservation of Baba-films, too—and Baba-videos, when they came onto the scene. (As she said, "I can never do things half-way.")

An enthusiastic photographer.

What I found touching about Mani's lifelong work with photographs and films of Baba was that it was all oriented toward sharing Him with other people. It was not "art for art's sake," although both endeavors called forth her creative talents. It was art for His lovers' sake. Many of the photos and films that carried Him across the long miles to distant disciples in earlier times, and across the years to us now, are a legacy of that selflessness.

RACHEL

In front of the Trust Office—in fact, on three-and-a-half sides of the Trust compound—is a verandah facing the common courtyard. To get from one place to another—to Bhauji's office, the lunchroom, the Reservations office, Khorshed's, wherever—you went down that verandah.

One day, when Mani was walking down the verandah in a fun mood, she spotted a new pilgrim, obviously an American, coming toward her. "Hi!" drawled Mani in her put-on American accent, "Jai Baba!"

"Jai Baba," replied the young woman. "What's your name?"

"Oh, I'm Rachel." (Rachel?) "Who are you?"

The woman introduced herself.

"Rachel" then revealed that she, too, was from the United States. They hugged and, after exchanging a few more details, went their own ways. "See you later!" called out "Rachel," as her new acquaintance moved toward the bus.

Of course, they did see each other later at Meherazad, when the new pilgrim was formally introduced to . . . well, let's just say it wasn't "Rachel"!

You wouldn't call her playfulness a characteristic. It was more of a life force, an elemental aspect of her nature.

Once, when she was in her early seventies, I told her something that Eruch had said to me. He had been very serious. He was trying to impress upon me the importance of people ridding themselves of bad habits when they were still young. "All your traits," he insisted, "become much more exaggerated as you get older. And when you're older, you can't change or stop yourself. If you go on talking to yourself and waving your arms around, you'll end up like those muttering mad women in the street."

Mani listened very carefully to all this, nodding her head. "I know what he means. That's happening to me."

"To you?" I asked, surprised. "How?"

"I'm becoming too funny."

"Too funny?"

"Yes." She was perfectly serious. "More and more, I see the funny side of everything. I never know what I'm going to say next. It's a problem!"

INTO THE BAZAAR

Eruch always viewed Mani's excursions into the bazaar with suspicion. She and Rano would bundle into a rickshaw and off they would go shopping. Mani called Rano her *dosi,* sort of the equivalent of "dear old gal." Not only did Rano support and help her in the office, but she was up for any adventure Mani had in mind.

In later years, after Rano passed away, others of us would be her companion on these outings. Eruch couldn't lecture Rano much (she would give it right back), but he could lecture us, and did: about all the things we weren't supposed to let Mani do, and how soon we were supposed to be back (usually in about five minutes) because were we aware of how much work she *still had to do?*

Once out of the compound gates, we were free. Mani would drink in everything: the goats lounging in the doorways (she would always point these out), little bare-bottomed children, the old woman sitting on the pavement selling spinach, the old man with a white beard entering a mosque. Like her Brother, she had a special fondness for old people, especially "characters," and for the charm and chaos of India—in fact, for all of life. She was eager to see it all and chat about it all. And she was a great shopper, could make a selection in about three minutes and still be happy with it later on, which is a miracle.

One day in early December we went to the Christian bookstore. Mani had a few people she sent Christmas cards to (among them, Mrs. Burleson, the wife of the doctor who had taken care of Baba and Mehera after the 1952 accident. They had become dear friends at the accident time, and always exchanged affectionate greetings at Christmas).

The Christmas card selection was spread out on tables around the bookstore. We went in and started looking around. Having gone to a convent school with nuns, Mani had a good eye for a Christmas card.

I was taken back to my Catholic childhood—all those scenes of baby Jesus with Our Lady and Joseph in a manger. And all of a sudden, it struck me. I turned to Mani and said, "It's so funny! Here I am, shopping for Christmas cards with Jesus' sister!"

Mani looked at me, chuckled, and, without missing a beat, turned back to the cards.

LUNCH

It's summer and boiling hot. Standing outside the Trust Office with Rama Kalchuri (Bhauji's wife), Mani is inspecting the sugarcane juice extractor. A little man has hauled it into the compound. It is a work of folk art: the crusher—a beautifully carved wooden spindle with spiral edges for squeezing out the juice from the sugarcane stalks—is turned by a wooden handle, the cart is on huge bicycle wheels, and the whole contraption is painted with flowers and other designs, just like Indian trucks of the time.

Rama has had it thoroughly cleaned, and Mani is conferring with her about the recipe. Will they mix the juice with ginger this time, or with lemon? They fix on lemon, which Rama gets ready, and we are all called out. Glasses are filled, juice gulped, seconds served out, the old man turns and turns the rough handle, Rama mixes in the lemon, Mani makes sure no one is forgotten. A hot office morning is transformed into an "occasion."

Mani was wonderful at bringing herself into the present. I used to wonder how it was possible for a person with such a spectacular past to go on living as if the humdrum present was something special. But she did. We particularly noticed this at the office lunch table.

It began with her arrival. As we've seen, as soon as she got down from the car, she'd quip, "What's for lunch?" Then the office whirlwind would snatch her up in a thousand things happening all at once: correspondence, visitors, trustees and residents with work issues, pilgrims in for a "private talk" in the Parlour (more on this special room later), phone calls, cables with news both happy and sad, checks to sign, Bhauji to confer with . . . Whew! And finally, at about 1:30, it was lunchtime.

Now you'd think she'd be so preoccupied with work that she'd just gobble down the food and plunge back into the fray—so much to do, so little time! But Mani never did that. From the first, lunchtime was not a pause on the way to something else. It was not a fueling stop. It was its own occasion. Wherever we'd been before that, we were in the present at lunch.

Lunchtime fun at the office!

There were lunch-table "rules":

(1) no business at the table (just as with Nero Wolfe!), and
(2) we were there not just to eat but to share each other's company.

"With Baba," Mani said, "we had feasts and we had fasts." The lunchroom offered moderate, simple fare, though there was the occasional feast. That is, when Mani and the rest of us weren't on the latest diet (a different version of a "fast"!) For a number of years, lunch was hard-boiled eggs, plain dal (cold), chappatis, and uncut salad vegetables sent from Meherazad. Later on, when Mani was older and needed to eat more at midday (her only real meal), everyone got into the act and provided lunch in turns. We started calling it "The Lunch Club."

Mani took a keen interest in the menu. Sometimes she arranged it herself. At her request, Asha (who, with her husband, Sudam, took care of Khorshed), would make an eggplant-potato dish and bhakri characteristic of Maharashtrian villages, or her special *dahi-wada* (a yogurt-based dish); Rhoda Dubash, who also worked in the office some days, would make Parsi spiced dal and rice and accoutrements; Rama and her daughter-in-law Raj would bring to the lunchroom some special Indian snacks. Sometimes Mani ordered out for her favorite bhajia—the kind Baba, too, loved. And then, every once in a while, Mani would be inspired: "Let's order from that lady. She'll send a good mutton biryani." That lady was a Parsi connected with the Zorastrian fire-temple in town, and she really could cook. Actually we all cooked, struggling to bring our contributions up to the mark. If Mani asked for seconds, we'd made it!

But even in eating, Mani had wonderful discipline. Once I remember her relishing a piece of cake. When we offered her another, bigger, piece, she said, "No, thanks. Cake tastes good. Greed doesn't taste good."

The best part of lunch at the office was the company. Sometimes Mani would have a guest, but whoever was there, Mani's mere presence set the tone. Newsy stories, or funny stories, or stories of how people came to Baba were popular. Jokes were always appreciated. There was a phase of about three weeks when everyone struggled to come up with conundrums:

Q: What's the difference between a football and Prince Charles?
A: One is thrown in the air and the other is heir to the throne.

A recurring theme was epitaphs. I remember one Mani particularly liked:

> "Here lie I
> Martin Elginbrod
> Have mercy on my soul,
> Lord God
> As I would do
> Were I Lord God
> And Thou
> Were Martin Elginbrod."

And my personal favorite:
> "Here lies Lester Moore
> Shot to death by a 44
> No Les, no More."

And she had a favorite little poem that she often recited in a Scottish accent:
> "My soul is like a rusty lock.
> Oil it with Thy grace,
> And rub it, rub it, rub it, Lord
> Until I see Thy Face."

Mani loved conversations between Rhoda Dubash (who was quite hard of hearing) and anyone like Rano, who was going a bit deaf herself. If important word cues were missed and the two misunderstood each other, Mani would blithely (and intentionally) insert comments to mislead them further. Some crazy conversations went round that table!

On birthdays, the birthday person brought the food (agreed on by all beforehand), and Mani supplied the flowers (carried in a little vase on Rano's or her lap from Meherazad) and The Card. This was always the same birthday card, recycled: an accordion-style card that was stretched out in front of the birthday plate. On it, Mani would tack a post-it note on which she had written the person's name. After the lunch, the card (with the post-it still attached) would go back to Meherazad, to be stored in Mani's cupboard for the next birthday.

Then there were the rare and unforgettable times when Mani, stirred to memory by some remark or story, would talk very softly about Baba. Not in her engaging "story-telling way," which she did often, but almost to herself: she'd talk about His beauty, or His hands (which she particularly loved), or a quality of His presence. Or perhaps it would be an instance of His compassion or Love. How her descriptions evoked

Him! At those times, we would fall silent, entranced, for some moments after she was done, basking with her in the glorious past.

At lunch's end, when everyone was getting up and the magical lunchroom world was beginning to evaporate, Mani would unobtrusively turn and bow to Baba's picture hanging on the wall. She never failed to bow to Him when she came in for lunch or bow to Him when she went out.

THE PARLOUR

The "Parlour" was a small room behind the office where Mani received "guests"—i.e., people who wanted to have a private talk with her. Heaven knows how she came up with that name: I think she liked the Victorian associations. It was simply furnished with a bed and a sofa and a little coffee table.

Coffee played a big part in the Parlour sessions. When Mani took off down the small back verandah to the Parlour with her guest, she would call out to one of us: "Two coffees, please, and don't make them decapitated." Which meant decaffeinated—oh, no. Good, strong fully "leaded" coffee was all you saw in that office.

Mani was a wonderful confidante. She would show her guest into the Parlour with a little bow. She would gesture to the sofa, and when the guest sat, she would sit next to him or her. She would turn toward the person with a gentle gravity—all empathy, all ears—because often people came to the Parlour in trouble, or anguish, or confusion, or facing a problem they just couldn't handle.

So, what did she say?

Well, the Parlour's secrets rest in the hearts of those who exchanged them, and her advice would be very personal, but here's some advice I heard her give others away from the Parlour (or received myself) at various times:

> "I always say, you have to look at things from Baba's angle. Any problem, see it from His angle."

"The simplest thing we have to do—all we have to do—is just hold on."

"Love is sacrifice."

"It is not this or that that matters. He can use any means, any excuse, any medium. And that is what it means to hold on to Baba's daaman. It means being with Him. And anything that helps you get closer to Baba, that is the thing. Never forget, the purpose is to get closer to Him. That's what you are here for."

When problems overwhelmed you, and you lost perspective, she'd say, "When you face the shadows, they can seem very long, but if you face the Sun, Baba, all the shadows will be behind you."

When you were disappointed because things didn't go as you wanted, she'd advise, "Accept, don't expect."

She could be so encouraging when one felt weak or unworthy or far from Baba. She had a favorite prayer called "Paradoxes of Prayer," written by an unknown author, that she xeroxed to give to friends:

> I asked God for strength that I might achieve;
> I was made weak that I might learn humbly to obey.
> I asked for health that I might do greater things;
> I was given infirmity that I might do better things.
> I asked for riches that I might be happy;
> I was given poverty that I might be wise.
> I asked for power that I might have the praise of men;
> I was given weakness that I might feel the need of God.
> I asked for all things that I might enjoy life;
> I was given life that I might enjoy all things.
> I got nothing that I asked for but everything I hoped for.
> Almost despite myself, my unspoken prayers were answered.

Her advice was always to trust Baba:

> Sometimes one feels, "Oh no, how can I let Baba, God in human form, see this weakness of mine, see this side of me." And so the intimacy of give and take in love is lost. The natural way is to approach Baba the way we would a beloved friend or member of our family who has grown up with us and who therefore knows all of our faults and weaknesses. One time when someone hesitated to approach Baba because of a sense of unworthiness, Baba reassured the person, saying in effect, "I am the Ocean. Do not wait to purify yourself before coming to Me. Come and dump all your filth into My Ocean, so that you may become the Ocean that you really are." None is worthy of Baba's Love, but the great miracle of His Love is that none is excluded from it!

And she'd talk of how He helps:

> Baba has said through circulars and told us on several occasions, "I am with My lovers." Now, His words one must not take to be ordinary. If He says, "I am with My lovers," remember, He is. It is you who cannot see. It is I who cannot see. But if He says, "I am", He is.

She would speak of His enduring presence:

> Baba has said that He comes to give the greatest treasure which can ever be given, but it is up to us to receive it. And the way to receive it is through sahavas, through simply allowing ourselves to sit in His presence. And it seems to me that the opportunity to simply sit and spend time in Baba's company is still very much here for all of us. All we have to do is stop trying to figure out how to "find" Baba, stop worrying about our problems and simply relax in His company, allowing ourselves to open up to His love.

To those enduring a "dry spell" in their inner relationship with Baba, she offered reassurance: "He loves you always and in all ways."

To those struggling with problems, she'd give her version of the 12-step saying, "Let go and let God," which was, of course, "Let go and let Baba!"

We noticed that Mani put a lot of emphasis on Baba's timing: things happen only "in Baba's time," not our time. You'd finally get to India, or recover from an illness, or meet the long-awaited mate, or get the job you were working toward "in Baba's perfect time."

And if someone was suffering greatly, she would pass on what in similar circumstances she told herself, "This too will pass."

She often spent an hour, or even two, in the Parlour with her guests, no matter who they were, new or old. With her desk piled high with correspondence, policy proposals, checks to sign, she would take whatever time was needed to talk to a troubled person about Baba. You saw that people truly mattered to her; the chairman set that example: Baba-lovers in need deserved attention and care.

And about her own advice, served up so lovingly with that strong coffee, she once said, "If anything we say brings you closer to Baba, it is His grace. If anything takes you further from Baba, crumble it up and toss it away."

TEATIME

Teatime was a rough time of the day for Eruch. First of all, a lot of people would come to hang out with him. For Eruch, the office was for office work, and that was that. But he could adroitly manage any situation. Worse for him was that a lot of people would come to visit Mani, and she liked it. Office discipline went right out the window.

If Mani's visitors were children, she would reach into her top desk drawer and pull out a little box of chocolate M&M'S. "These are vitamins," she'd say. "Now which color would you like?" The kid would look seriously into the box and choose a color, and Mani would give a couple of red or green or yellow "vitamins" to him or her with a hug. Then, if the kid lingered, down came the toys (she kept a box of them on the top shelf of a stand next to her desk). She was known to have squatted down on the floor with small children right there in the office! Egads! The duck, the car, the bug—all the wind-up cast—would perform, racing, sidling, hopping across the Trust Office, with the chairman running and fetching errant toys . . .

A child visitor in the office delighting Mani.

The most famous toy was the "magic pig" (pronounced "peeeeg" because it had been given by two French children). The magic pig permanently occupied one of the office tables, and when pulled by a string, walked across it, came up to the edge and—watch for the magic!—mysteriously stopped. This never failed to warm up even the shyest child.

Adults would all sit around Mani's desk with their tea and biscuits. By teatime Mani had had it with paper and was ready for people. Stories, jokes, banter, dreams flowed back and forth across the desk. She was in her element: a lively crowd, a give-and-take atmosphere, good hot strong tea (two cups), and a morning and half-an-afternoon of work behind her.

She would also use teatime to visit with her friends, often inviting someone to the office for tea. Mani had a gift for friendship. She was a very loyal friend, and a very considerate one. Over the years she made a great effort to remain in touch with her old friends. At the same time, she was constantly reaching out to new people.

For years I thought that her extreme friendliness was a part of her "role" in Baba's work, a way of giving. But Goher and Meheru told us that Mani had always made friends (with women, of course—they had no contact with men) wherever they traveled. For example, she had befriended the two elderly English sisters in Dehra Dun who gave them Peter the dog, and the doctor's wife and children in Oklahoma when Baba had His first car accident, and so on.

We came to see that Mani was very curious about people. This was strikingly demonstrated when she was in the hospital in Poona recovering from her brain surgery in 1995. She made friends with all the nurses, knew their names, how many children they had, what their problems were, etc. This might be expected. But her interest went beyond that.

She was supposed to exercise every day by taking a walk in the hall with one of us, her caregivers, helping her. So here is Mani in her pajamas, her head wrapped up in a bandage and scarf, walking with support down the open-air hospital corridor, when she sees a woman, obviously a patient, looking down at the view below. The woman seems a little low. Mani walks right over to her and begins chatting. What is she in the hospital for? How many days to go? Is she from Poona? How is she feeling? Then comes the comforting advice: don't worry, trust in God, all will be well, you'll feel better in a couple of days, it's always hard at first . . .

A few hours later, the woman plus her whole family come by Mani's room to visit. They become a regular feature in the room. This happens with another patient chatted up in the hall. A nurse appears with her friend. Finally Meheru—there to support Mani through the hospital ordeal—draws the line: Mani can't make any more friends. She isn't getting enough rest! The room is becoming a train station!

It was in the hospital that I truly understood that friendliness was a part of her *nature,* just like the women mandali had always said.

I loved to watch Mani talking to people. For one thing, she was an avid giver of nicknames, and her affectionate nicknames reflected something very individual about each person. (One Baba-lover came to Baba in a cave, and learning this, Mani lovingly called him "Caveman" ever after. She would actually write him letters addressed to "Caveman." His sweet wife she nicknamed "Open Secret.") She had the gift of remembering the small details about people; in their talks together, she would ask about particular family members, remember the name of a beloved pet, request a picture of the kids for her "children's album" at Meherazad.

A frequent pilgrim remembered: "Mani greeted me with her warm embrace, saying with a lively twinkle in her eyes, 'It can't be, it just can't be a whole year!'" (that is, since they'd seen each other).

I loved to watch her making friends. A new person would shyly look into the office, perhaps wanting to make a donation. They would pass by Mani's desk. She would be looking down, working on a letter. But if she happened to look up: that was all it took. No matter how occupied she was, or how exhausted, or how much she still had to do, she would beam, and stand, and smile, and hug, and make the person feel like a million dollars. Why, you felt Mani had been waiting years just to meet you. And before you knew it, you were sitting across from her—God's sister!—having a cup of tea.

When the teatime hour had gone by and the friends, new and old, were just settling in for some heavy-duty chatting, Eruch would start muttering in the back. Then he would send one of us to "scold" Mani for playing and not working, at which point the friends would obligingly rise and depart, and Mani, with a mock-scowl at Eruch over her glasses, would take up her pen again.

Fun with Mani at Meherazad

BABA'S ROOM

Early one morning, a few of us went to Baba's Room at Meherazad with a video camera. We had a date with Mani. She was going to give us a tour of Baba's Room for a home-video we were making about the Trust.

When we walked in, we were charmed to see that Mani was still wearing her "home clothes"—comfy clothes that she wore around the house when no visitors were there—with a scarf wrapped around her head to keep out the early morning chill. It was such an intimate touch.

The tour she gave us was as "at home" as her clothes, as "at home" as she herself was in Baba's Room, which she referred to as "this most precious Room on earth."

Mani told us how Mehera brought the garden of Baba's remembrance, which bloomed in her heart, into Baba's Room. Until late each night, after the others had gone to bed, Mehera would stand for a long time in Baba's Room, thinking of Him, remembering the past with Him, and sometimes making notes in pencil on little cards of things to tell someone or memories to share with pilgrims the next day.

Mehera arranging roses on Baba's photo on His bed.

One tangible expression of her love for Baba was the flowers from the garden that she would place on His bed and chairs and by His pictures in the room. She was very particular about it, as with everything for Him, and she told Mani, "You do the flowers when I'm gone," and taught her how.

Baba's bedroom in Meherazad.

So, after Mehera passed away, one of Mani's "meditations" was to arrange the flowers in Baba's Room. She added her own touches, of course, like playing a tape of Baba-songs or ghazals when she did it, and when the garlands brought by the flower-man were not up to snuff, substituting a sparkly garland for the Baba-picture on His bed. Those flowers were an expression of love, offered as much from Mehera as from herself.

In Baba's bedroom, there is a bronze bust of Baba on a pedestal in the corner across from His bed. It was brought from Australia in 1996 by Bernard Bruford and given by the Bruford family for Baba's home. The sculptor was John Bruford, Bernard's father, a master sculptor and one of the Australian old-time Baba-lovers; the original plaster-of-Paris head study had been carried to India in 1967 for Baba to approve. It was a work "in progress" according to John, and Baba was very pleased with it, remarking that it was perfect and that Bruford had truly captured Him.

The day the bust was brought to Meherazad, Mani was not very well, but it was carefully unwrapped for her to see. Sitting on the sofa chair inside the house, she was silent as she looked at it. After a long while, she began to touch the sculpture with her fingertips, gently caressing Baba's cheeks. She looked at it from every angle, marveling at the perfection of the resemblance. You could tell she was deeply moved, lost in remembrance. As she looked at Baba's ear, she murmured, "I loved His ear. Look how beautiful His ear is . . ." And stroked His face with utter tenderness again and again.

"Aussie Baba."

Mani promptly named the bust "Aussie Baba," and had it placed in Baba's Room. When Bernard came to Meherazad the next day, although she wasn't seeing people, Mani had him come into Baba's Room with her, so she could show it to him. Every morning from that time, she offered a flower to Aussie Baba, and that is continued to this day.

One day Mani paused at the doorway to Baba's Room (on the inside of the house) to recall an incident for those of us who were with her. In the later years, when Baba was not well, He would lean on Mehera's arm as He walked into His room from the sitting room or the dining room. Mehera went first, supporting Him as He walked through the door, and Mani walked behind Him. Mani would put her hand between Baba's shoulder and the doorframe as she followed Him in, just in case His shoulder should hit the frame.

One day Baba swayed a little while walking in, and bumped into the doorway. But Mani's hand was there in between, cushioning His shoulder.

Afterwards she felt He had done it on purpose, in response to her gesture of care.

Mehera-Mani.

MEHERA–MANI

When Baba's beloved, Mehera, went to Him in 1989, Mani had been her closest companion for fifty-seven years. They had shared a room since Mani had joined the ashram in 1932 and, until 1970, when Mani began to go to the Trust Office just before she became chairman, they were constantly together. And it was not just in this life, for Baba had gestured to Mani that she and Mehera had been connected for ages "from way, way back."

One might say that Mani had two beloveds: her Beloved Baba, who was her "all in all," as she put it; and her beloved Mehera, for whom she would do anything.

The group of women who lived with Mehera in the early years after Baba dropped His body were absorbed in caring for her. Their attention

Mehera and Mani in a photo of them together on Meherabad Hill, taken at Mehera's request.

on her was subtle but pervasive. It was a current running through all of their days: How is Mehera? Is she sad today? Is she eating? Did she sleep at all? (As we've seen, Mehera would stay up in Baba's room until the early hours of the morning, thinking of Him, praying to Him, talking to Him. When the women would plead with her to come away to bed, she used to say, "But when do I have time to be with Baba?" because she spent the daytime talking to pilgrims about Him!)

Mani's focus on Mehera underlay everything she did. I saw this one day in the Trust Office. An Indian Baba-lover came in during the morning rush, sat with Mani for a few minutes, and when leaving, gave her a dozen pretty bangles as a gift. Mani thanked her and then immediately counted out six, which she carefully wrapped up and put aside "for Mehera." Then she put on the other six. When the woman had gone, I said, "How sweet that you thought of Mehera!" "Of course," Mani said. "It's automatic. I always first take out some for Mehera."

. . .

Mani shielding Mehera from the sun on the Hill.

Always sharing a room, they naturally had "friendly squabbles," as Mani called them. One morning they had a disagreement. Mehera said something to the effect that she hoped this was their last incarnation together, and Mani replied, "Suits me!" Then Mani went off to work at the office. When she came home, she found, neatly placed in her little wash-up area, a new bar of oatmeal soap. Mehera knew that Mani had delicate skin, and oatmeal soap was supposed to be good for that. It was, Mani said, a little peace offering. Immediately she rushed to tell Mehera how much she liked oatmeal soap.

Once, when the women came to Meherabad to visit Baba's Samadhi, I saw Mani reach out and adjust a barrette in Mehera's hair. I'd rarely seen her do anything with such tenderness.

Some years after Mani went to Baba, I was watching a video of her that Sheriar Foundation put out. It was *so* her: expressive, vivacious, wise, funny, full of warmth and focus. After it was over, I wondered when it had been taped. Then I read on the cover that it was made in September 1989, which was only four months after Mehera passed away. *Four months*!

How could Mani be so composed, so poised, after only four months? Knowing her tremendous love for her beloved friend, and a little about the grief she had felt at her passing, I found it hard to believe.

"It is not easy," she said in the video, "but it's simple. Because either you want it your way, or you accept His way. It's as simple as that. And once you continue to do what you've always been doing, accept His way, His Will, it's simple. And He helps very much. Baba's Love through you all helps a lot. And in fact we're adjusting well. After all, it has got to be as He wants. I still remember once we were all together and something happened and Baba said, eyes flashing, 'Either you want what you want or you want what I want! You can't want both.'"

What He wanted, of course, was for Mehera to come to Him and for Mani to stay behind.

Mani sometimes shared how Baba had helped her. When Mehera was so sick and it was clear that she was going to Baba, Mani wondered how she could bear the emptiness in their room at night. They had shared a room for nearly sixty years; naturally, Mani could not imagine being there without Mehera.

But when Mehera went to Baba, Mani was amazed to find that the room never felt empty. On the contrary, it felt just as though Mehera was still there. Mani said that when she woke in the night, she would look over to make sure Mehera was all right, that her mosquito net was still tucked in!

"That fullness of Mehera is very much here. I have to remind myself that she's not with us at times. And yet at times I feel lonely in my heart for her. But it's beautiful, it's fine. It's as He wants it and we are happy to accept what He wants."

On Mani's cupboard by the door is taped a piece of paper with a dream written on it. A Baba-lover in America had dreamt about Mehera. As she wrote to Mani, in the dream "Mehera was talking about you as though she was still with you daily, 'Mani and I were talking about this or that!' I said to her, 'You see Mani?' and she said, 'Oh yes, Mani and I are always together. I'm with Mani all the time.'" Mani was deeply touched by this and had it written out and posted it, where she could see it every day.

Mani at Mehera's shrine.

MEHERA–MANI'S ROOM

Some time after Mani passed away, just for fun a Meherazad resident and I counted all the representations of animals, birds, bugs—in short, the animate natural world—in Mehera-Mani's room. The room is not that big and quite tidy, but we came up with twenty-two items. These included, on Mehera's side, a white horse music box and a jeweled peacock (from Margaret), and on Mani's side, her moth collection (she collected dead moths with interesting wing decorations and kept them in a plastic-lidded box), various stuffed animals, a statuette of two cocker spaniels (mementos of Peter?), and some fluorescent-shelled beetles.

Mani with Agoos, their beloved pet tortoise.

These beetles were very beautiful, blue-black with an opalescent gleam. Mani loved them. She had spotted a beetle in the garden, say. If it were already dead (that is, "had received promotion"), she would scoop it up. If it was still crawling, she would follow it for a while—or mark the place and keep returning there to check on its progress toward its next life. Eventually the little thing would give up the ghost, and its shell would be a new treasure.

A lot of Mani's rocks, moths, feathers, leaves, moss, and bugs were collected in the morning when she would go walking with the dogs on the paths and in the fields around Meherazad. All through their life with Baba the women were intimately linked to the natural world: through pets (dogs, cats, horses, deer, donkeys, pigs, cows, rabbits, monkeys, birds—even a snake!), through the walks Baba went on with

CONTINUING ON 947

Mani working at a table in her room in the concentrated stillness of Meherazad.

them and encouraged them to take without Him, through Mehera's love for nature, and through living many years in the countryside (at Meherabad, Meherazad, Satara, Mahabaleshwar, and so on).

When they first moved to Meherazad, it was the most pastoral place imaginable. And today the natural world—its energy of breezes, sun, starlight, creatures, cycles of planting and reaping, green things—still sweeps in and through Meherazad's open-air dwellings and Mehera–Mani's big-windowed, garden-facing room like a balm.

On the way out of the room, Mani's dressing table by the door reaches out and snags your attention. Here in microcosm is Mani: the playful, the spiritual, the deep, and the light. A colorful picture of Baba, a tiny one of Mehera, an origami nun, a Virgin of Guadalupe card and pictures of angels, and Ganesh, the elephant god; a small bell, that she would gently ring in the

The top of her dressing table.

evening before she prayed at the dresser; and all around the mirror, tiny stick-on earrings that they sell in malls in America for teenage girls.

On the dresser top sits the framed postcard-sized photo of Baba where "I am the Highest of the High" is written out in Mani's handwriting, followed by Baba's own signature.

SOFA CHAIR

The "sofa chair," a big armchair just inside the door of the house at Meherazad, was where Mani relaxed before and after lunch. Picking up a book, munching on potato chips or bhajia, she would drop into another world. She could completely shut out everyone and everything, except for Nero Wolfe or Rumpole or St. Teresa or a Georgette Heyer heroine or whoever lived in her book of the moment.

The sofa chair was a mini-office too: there she'd go over her to-do lists—small notecards with words or initials or phrases indicating things to remember, scribbled down in a mixture of English, Gujerati, and shorthand. She'd have conferences around the sofa chair, give dictation, talk with Goher and the others (Goher's bed was right nearby), read the mail. She dictated her last book, *Dreaming of The Beloved*, from there. It was the venue for all kinds of communiqués.

Oddly enough, one of my favorite memories of Mani is of a scolding she gave me and one of her Meherazad helpers from the sofa chair. Maybe it

Mani having a good exchange from the cozy sofa chair.

was because she was so creative even when acerbic. I had forgotten something, an important detail of work, I can't remember what, and she had called the two of us. After listening to my lame explanation, Mani narrowed her eyes at both of us and said, "If I had fifty years, I might be able to train you two. But I don't have fifty years. So you tell me what I should do!"

One morning, a few months before she knew she was terminally ill, Mani sat in the sofa chair and gave some of us instructions on things she wanted us to do "after." They were very carefully listed and delegated. She had not received any diagnosis for her continual pain, but this was one of the indications she gave us that she knew her end was close. I think she had long been prepared, because she once mused, "No one in the family has lived to be 80"; she was 77 at the time.

PERFECT SLAVE

One morning, during the time she was ill, Mani was sitting in the sofa chair listening to a draft of a book about the women mandali written by a Baba-lover. I was reading it to Mani at the author's request, in case she had any corrections to pass on.

The writer recounted a time in the Hall when Mani shared how Baba had said she would have one more life, as a man. Someone in the Hall had asked if Baba had indicated that Mani would be a Perfect Master, and she had said yes.

As I was reading this out, I looked up at Mani to make sure the version was correct. She nodded, yes, that was so. I had a flabbergasted moment (yikes! I was sitting on a stool in front of a soon-to-be Perfect Master!), and then read on. The writer then quoted Mani as saying, "But all I want is to be His perfect slave!"

Again I paused and looked up. "That's right!" said Mani very emphatically. And as I was digesting this, she gestured impatiently, "Get on with it."

I could see being a Perfect Master meant nothing to her. It didn't matter in the least. She wanted to be a perfect slave, and the perfect slave just wanted to get on with the work.

THE PASSAGEWAY

The sofa chair sits in a large room that the women called the "passageway." Baba used to stride through this room to the dining room's far wall, and then back to the far wall of Mehera-Mani's room, back and forth, back and forth, for exercise.

Here are a couple of vignettes of amusing times with Mani in the passageway:

Mani was very funny about her appearance. Her liveliness extended to occasional, rather startling, reinventions of her image. I remember when she took scissors and cut off her hair, which she had worn in a small bun at the back of her neck for years. She wasn't planning on telling anyone why she did it, but she was so guileless in matters like this that she couldn't help letting it slip to about fifty people: she had gotten lice (from embracing people at Amartithi), and the hair just had to go.

Her hair was a lovely white by that time, but as her face was so fair, she would use a little shampoo rinse that would make her hair slightly more gray. Someone gave her a bluish rinse to try out. Once, she got a little carried away with the amount of the rinse, and her hair came out quite blue. I remember her emerging into the passageway with this blue hair. And I mean *blue!* She was trying it out on everyone around the house, including Goher and Meheru. We teased her that she looked like Marge in "The Simpsons" (Marge has a tower of bright blue hair in the cartoon show). Everyone, including Mani, had a good laugh.

But all day long she kept inspecting herself in the mirror, and it gradually dawned on the women mandali that she was thinking about keeping it that way. (She was very creative with color.) When she saw the looks from Goher and Meheru, she said, "What's so wrong with it? I kind of like it." Wrong with it? Well, for a start, it was blue . . . It took their combined nagging to finally convince her to wash it out.

At the end of the passageway stood a little dressing table, right by the foot of Goher's bed. Mani kept her mail on it. There was a laminated photo of her there, sitting down, all dressed up in a magenta sari, with her white hair and a formal smile. She looked a little matronly; in fact, as she herself admitted, she looked like the Queen Mother. The funny thing was: she *liked* that photo. It was the opposite of her usual girlish image, but she liked it; maybe because it showed a certain inherent dignity that you didn't often see in her pictures. She kept it around forever; just when you thought it was finally gone, it would pop up somewhere in her room. Everyone gradually got used to it, and the Queen Mother won out: she had a long reign over that little end of the passageway.

On one wall of the passageway, the one by the dining room door, there is a photograph of Baba standing in Meherazad garden, holding an umbrella. Mani once pointed it out: "That's a photo of Baba and me!" "Me?" Where was Mani?

Then I looked carefully, and there on the ground was Mani's shadow, a silhouette of her distinctive haircut just by Baba's feet. She was taking the picture!

Photo of Baba (and Mani somewhere in the picture).

AT THE DINING TABLE

After Mehera went to Baba, some of us who worked with Mani at the office also worked with her at Meherazad one or two days a week. On those days we usually joined her for tea in the dining room. Seated by Baba's chair (on His left; Mehera's seat was on His right), Mani was in a different mood than at the office—more casual, "at home."

Sometimes she'd reminisce about playing the radio for Baba at the table. I remember something she shared with us once: they were listening to the news broadcast with Baba when the rape of a young girl was reported. Hearing this, Baba became very solemn; He then held out the index finger of His left hand and made chopping motions along it with the index finger of His right. Imitating the gesture, Mani interpreted, "mincemeat—he'll be made into mincemeat," a prophecy of divine retribution for the rapist, that sent chills down our spines.

Each of the women mandali had her own place at the table. Once, looking around at their empty chairs, Mani said, "We were together but we were not attached to each other. We were like the spokes of a wheel, each one separately joined to the hub—Baba—each one focused on Him alone. We were linked to each other only by the outer rim." The round outer rim of a wheel holds the spokes together, but with plenty of space between each one.

Mehera praying to Baba's photo in the dining room.

As she once remarked, "The path to God is single file."

In Mehera's time, Mehera would invite women pilgrims into the dining room for tea at Baba's table. After teatime, she would pray to Baba's picture so sweetly and devotedly, it could move you to tears. She had several prayers that she would whisper aloud to Him, and sometimes her prayer would be, "Baba, may the whole world come to know You and love You." If Mani was there and you stood close to her—she who was reeling from dealing with the people already coming to Him—you might hear her as she whispered, "Easy, Mehera, easy. Say 'may the whole world come to know You and love You *after* we're gone!'"

VERANDAH DESK

The cottage just in front of Baba's house in Meherazad has a small verandah on which sits Mani's desk. You can tell it's hers: who else of the women would have hung on the wall behind her desk a photo of Baba kissing Mehera's horse Sheba, and a large picture of a black cocker spaniel with chipmunks crawling up and down his legs? (That was Peter with his charges.) A later addition was a garish green clay-fired parrot. It must have reminded Mani of their parrot Mittu. There was also at one time a china figurine of an elderly Chinese man with a green plant growing out of his arms that Mani called Gandalf (a wizard in J.R.R. Tolkien's *The Lord of the Rings*). Now a painting of Baba with young Mani holding onto His arm hangs there, gifted to Mani by the artist and her friend, Jane Haynes.

Mani working at her desk in Meherazad.

The eighty-two Family Letters that went out to the Western Baba-family from 1956 until 1969 were mostly written in this homey venue.

Kitty once wrote her, "Mani dear, how can I ever convey to you what your letters mean to Baba lovers here. On all sides they are deeply appreciated—their whole atmosphere of Baba that goes with them. Never think you are just writing a letter—you are doing something far beyond the scope of a letter."

So, that little desk has a big history. As we know, Mani, who had always been so happy that she got to work on a verandah in a garden and not in an office, ended up sitting in the Trust Office in town. Yet she never stopped using her verandah desk. It was for more intimate letters, the often handwritten ones full of personal details to her ashram pals Elizabeth, Kitty, Margaret, and Delia (who she called "England's National Treasure"), or to her friend and "sister" Jane (because of the difference in the time zones of India and the United States, they shared the same birthday), or to her own family members in England or America.

As new waves of Baba-lovers flowed onto the scene, Mehera, Mani, and all the women continued to deeply appreciate and empathize with the old-timers. When Baba was planning the Great Darshan, He would describe all the new lovers coming with great enthusiasm. "Yes, Baba," Mani would put in, "and Your old lovers want to see You too." She was remembering a line in a letter from Elizabeth, written after Baba had postponed calling the Westerners for a sahavas: "Baba dear, don't let it be too long."

So she was very particular about keeping in touch—and more than that. She wrote a song for Kitty's 100th birthday at that desk and taught it to a Baba-lover from Myrtle Beach so the woman could sing it to Kitty in person on her great day. A Scottish tune, no less! The chorus went:

"Hoorah hoorah, hurray, hurray,
It's Kitty's 100th Birthday!
Hoorah, hoorah, hurray, hurray,
Avatar Meher Baba ki Jai, Avatar Meher Baba ki Jai!"

Mani, Goher, Kitty: dear, dear friends.

When Kitty was very ill, one day Mani had a deep prompting to write to her. She was sitting at her desk, on the same verandah where Elizabeth and Kitty would have their breakfast when they came to stay at Meherazad, and she spotted a red hibiscus flower growing on a bush nearby. She plucked and dried it. When flat and dry, it formed the shape of a fan, and Mani signed her loving message, "from your fan." As it turned out, that flower with its message reached Kitty just before she passed away.

Such were the letters written on the quiet Fridays (the "no visitors" day), or on Silence Day, or early in the morning after remembering someone in Baba's Room. Her attention to the personal especially shone at the verandah desk. I once saw her spend an entire morning creating a birthday card for one of her newer friends. Made out of one of her "minis" (very small, folded, thick paper notes), it was a real Mani creation—3½ x 3 inches of stickers, stars, drawings, poetry (lines in different colored ink), and her signature doodles—a little gift of time and care that carried so much.

. . .

A funny moment with Mani, Rano, and someone silly.

The verandah desk had other uses, too: one year, as the great Hindu festival of lights, Divali, approached, I saw Mani assembling her gifts for the female servants working in Meherazad. She arranged to get a number of new little cloth *pishwis* (tiny satchels that traditionally serve as "purses" for village women), and she tucked a holiday bonus inside one of the multiple pockets of each pishwi. Then she carefully selected which pishwi went to which person, knowing the individual servants and their tastes very well.

That was fun. But when she would handwrite the Trust board meeting minutes at that desk, I got a glimpse of the inner discipline that had enabled her to walk her very narrow path. The minutes were very formal and very long, and it could take a couple of days to complete them. She would get out the right pen (there were special, thick black ones for this job), and a ruler, and a pencil for drawing straight lines with the ruler, and an eraser for erasing them afterwards. She would set herself times, and adhere to them to the minute. She was almost relentless in her focus.

The beauty was that her neat, regular handwriting would look exactly the same in the first line as it did—countless pages later—in the last!

I have another memory associated with that verandah desk. It is of a day in May 1989, when Mehera was lying in their room in a semi-coma. Mani sent a message for me to come and see her at her desk. She was sitting with a piece of paper in her hand. She said to me very simply, in a neutral tone, "We have to be practical; I want you to type this out."

I looked at it and saw with a shock that it was a draft for a cable announcing Mehera's going to Baba. Of course it had to be written in advance. Baba-lovers should know as soon as possible, and how could Mani write something worthy of Mehera in the emotion of such a moment? But still it was a shock.

I held it for a minute and then said, "Yes, Mani." Then, turning to go, I saw tears streaming down her beautiful cheeks as she sat at her desk, completely still.

A last memory of the desk: Twenty-three years after Baba had dropped His body and two years after Mehera went to Him, Mani wrote down the stories of her childhood that she had been telling in Mandali Hall for years. She started in the summer (which in India is in March, April, and May) and wrote every morning and every afternoon on a pad in pencil, sitting at the verandah desk. Summer in Meherazad used to be a very still, quiet time, a rare time, without interruptions.

Looking back, I felt that in that summer Mani began to heal from her great grief over Mehera's passing. After Mehera went to Baba, Mani had risen to every occasion; she had gracefully and courageously accepted her tremendous loss; her cheerfulness and surrender were an inspiration. But for the first two years after Mehera's reunion, if you were around Mani enough, you could feel a deep sadness in her; she missed her beloved, incomparable companion very much.

When she was writing *God-Brother,* she became totally immersed in her childhood world. There was nothing to distract her from it, and gradually we saw her becoming more and more her old self. She would sing in the morning, and get up excited about what she was going to write that day. She started remembering incidents and small details that she had forgotten for years. Naturally, it was a very happy time for everyone.

Mani sharing stories from God-Brother, *her book of childhood stories with Baba.*

Seeing how much joy Mani got from reliving her childhood showed me how truly happy it had been—a time apart, and full of her God-Brother.

ST. FRANCIS AND ST. TERESA

As we've seen, Mani would read out to Baba passages from St. Francis of Assisi and St. Teresa of Avila and other saints and Perfect Ones. A Baba-quote mentioning St. Francis was on her letterhead, and St. Teresa (along with others) was on her bookshelf. Other little books in her cupboard that she'd read occasionally included a small copy of the New

Testament (in English), the "101 Names of God" (in Gujerati), *Meher Chalisa* (in Hindi), poems by Hafiz, a book of funny poems/prayers, and the songs of Tukaram.

Jane Haynes used to send her books by and about St. Teresa because Jane enjoyed them herself and knew Mani did, and also because she found so many similarities between Teresa and Mani. Once Jane sent a description of St. Teresa to Mani that Jane had read in a book:

> She [St. Teresa] was a mystic: that is one who knows God by experience. She made mysticism into music, poetry and an ecstatic dance with the Beloved. But not without walking the path of suffering like every genius.
>
> She was stunning to look at, outgoing, cheerful and charming. Everyone adored her. She was a scintillating conversationalist. People of all walks of life listened to her—men, women, bishops, mule drivers and the King himself. She enjoyed both talking and silence. She enjoyed being alone, *and* having a good time! She loved to laugh and laughed often. When she did everyone around her laughed! She liked perfume, jewelry, chivalry and the color orange.
>
> Hear the musical sounds of her voice . . . imagine sitting down with her for a good visit, basking in her sweet embrace, her gaiety and the depth of her wisdom; for she was a woman of substance as well as charm. Imagine her at a party or at prayer; laughing over a lizard that crawled up her arm and landed in the face of her friend. Or weeping over the death of her brother. Composing verses to sing at celebrations for her Beloved; or falling and breaking her arm so badly it was useless for the last five years of her life.
>
> She was a poet and a brilliant administrator; a shrewd politician, and a *faithful friend;* walking a dangerous

> tightrope; holding the delicate balance between realism and idealism, common and uncommon sense.
>
> She knew fear and human weakness, loneliness, illness and exhaustion; the joy of love and pain of misunderstanding.
>
> Throughout her suffering she was humbly and heroically aware of destiny and God's designs and she clung to these tenaciously. She grew into a giant, a conquistador of the spiritual life . . . a saint for all seasons.
>
> If she prayed well she first lived well. The best secret we learn from her example is to live life as she did—to the hilt![2]

What struck me was how, like Teresa, Mani's closeness to the Avatar poured out to nourish others; that she combined a private, rich, inner life with unceasing creative outer activity; that living exclusively for Him, she lived so much for other people.

Like St. Francis and St. Teresa (and like the other Baba-mandali), Mani helped shape the Baba-world's idea of how to love Him and serve Him. How? Of course by her advice, personal, and in letters. And by her example, which taught the obvious lessons: self-giving, inner discipline, sacrifice.

But there was another, subtler lesson, too, that seemed to come through her in particular: the beauty and freedom of the light touch. She would tell jokes for hours in Mandali Hall. She would draw a doodle at the end of a letter full of empathy and advice. As Baba wished, she was one who "took God seriously and life lightly."

And it was as if, while taking God absolutely seriously and playing her part as His sister one hundred percent, she herself didn't matter all that much. Really, only He mattered; all the rest was nothing.

As if to illustrate this, she told me once, "Don't lose *Him* in your service to Him; many have fallen by that way."

A glance that was hard to forget.

THE INNER VOICE

"A seed germinates in soft soil. I plant the seed of My Love in weaknesses, not in strengths."

(7-1-92 Mzd) (between 1 + 2 p.m. when I woke up during nap)

This mysterious notation appears in one of the little notebooks that Mani kept around by her bed, by the sofa chair, and at her verandah desk. In them she would record thoughts and things she wanted to remember. This particular saying was among those she heard in her mind from time to time, spoken by a clear "voice."

These sayings came to her at unexpected moments right out of the blue. Mani would be excited whenever she heard the voice, as the messages were quite meaningful to her. She used to tell us about them, sometimes with a little explanation of what they meant.

Here are some of the sayings she heard, as she wrote them down [italics are added]:

> "*I am the bird, not the cage.*"
> (1987–88)
>
> "*Let the world wait.*"
> (1987–88)
>
> "*God is not a plus.*"
> (1987–88)
>
> "*Liquid light.*"
>
> "*I order [the drink], you drink [it].*"
> (3 Jan 94 – morning)
>
> "*You cannot wish against My Will.*"
> (21-3-94) (21st March morning '94 heard clearly in mind Voice)
>
> "*Edifice of faith*"
> for Him to occupy, and when He does you leave.
> (3-7-94)

> *"It is God's Hand that pours it in the bowl."*
> '94

And the following are two "clear thoughts," as she described them:

> *"What is the purest thing in Creation?"*
> (answer) *"Stone."*
>
> *"There is no shadow without light."*
> (31-10-95)

Her explanations would make them meaningful to us, too. She told one of us that she had been struggling to understand the weaknesses of the resident helpers, who couldn't seem to serve Him in the way she expected, when she heard the voice say, "A seed germinates in soft soil. I plant the seed of My Love in weaknesses, not in strengths."

"God is not a plus," she explained, meant that He was not something you added onto your life. He wasn't an addition. He was primary; everything else was additional.

"Let the world wait" is one of my favorites. Mani thought of it as a message for those times when you are absorbed with Baba and something external is nagging at you or calling you away. "Let the world wait"—yeah!

The words "I am the bird, not the cage." came to her in the late 1980s, but they assumed a very poignant meaning years later, when she was very ill.

And she loved the authority in, "I order, you drink"—the "I", of course, being God/Baba. As she would explain, whatever He puts before us is what we get and what we take! And the companion saying to that—"It is God's Hand that pours it in the bowl"—emphasized that it is *He* who gives whatever comes.

In the little notebooks (there are several) are also some creative musings Mani would jot down:

> "the Victory of losing
> the fullness of poverty
> the power of purity
> are incredible."

> "By the Light of His Love
> falling on my darkness
> I shall see, I shall see His lovely Face."

> "Alone I stand within
> this crowd of desires –
> only your Onlyness
> can banish my loneliness –
>
> let me drop,
> without a stop,
> into Your ocean of oneness
> so that only You are,
> and I'm no more."

In one notebook, she wrote down "for 1995 . . . Story-points to remember
BABA STORIES for PILGRIMS IN MANDLI- HALL & PORCH."
First among the points:

> "Baba: sternly, to us around Him: -
> 'Either you please yourself, or you please Me, you can't do both!'"

A few pages later she writes:

> "Walk in the garden but don't pluck the flowers (i.e. be in the world but not of it.)"

And in another notebook:
> "Why called Perfect MASKERS –
>> because they have mastered themselves – have gained mastery over their lower self – they are <u>masters</u>, not slaves (of lust, greed, anger etc) as humans are."
>
> "When we say God is deaf to our prayers, it means we are deaf to His answer."
>
> "If you can't stop, pause
> If you can't fast (your desires), diet."
>
> "STOP we can't, so PAUSE as habit and think of Him."
>
> "Baba's forgiveness is always there, natural to Him – but to save us from suffering He gives orders."
>
> "Mind always running, because chasing shadows. You don't have to chase Truth because it is there, real – you become still."

Among the notebooks is a card with a New Year's quotation that she would often repeat:

> "I said to the Man Who stood at the gate of the Year,
> 'Give me a light that I may tread safely into the unknown.'
> And he replied, 'Go out into the darkness and put your hand into the hand of God. That shall be to you better than light and safer than a known way!'"[3]

SPEED-BREAKERS

Mani used to say that in life with Baba, you need speed-breakers: built-in pauses that slow you down and slow the mind down long enough to remember Him. She talked a lot about the importance of putting such speed-breakers in your daily life: setting aside times to think of Baba, remember His Name, look at His photos.

Mani practiced what she preached. She seemed to think about Baba or be doing something for Him all day long. So her speed-breakers seemed very natural, subtle outpourings of her inner feeling or remembrance.

Impressed by the idea of speed-breakers, I once drew up a list of Mani's (only the ones I knew about, that is). Just see:

Upon waking, Mani would sit up and repeat Baba's Name before getting ready for the day. After breakfast at His table, of course remembering Him, at about 8:15 a.m. in the morning she would go to her steel cupboard on the verandah of the small cottage and spend fifteen minutes or so in silent prayer and in company with Baba.

The women would say Baba's prayers in His bedroom morning and evening (the Master's Prayer and the Beloved God prayer in the morning, the Bujave Arti and the Repentance Prayer at night—because, as Mehera would say, the time to repent is after the day is done). Mehera would put the flowers on the bed, chair, and photos in His bedroom before the women's morning arti. She gave Mani careful instructions on just what to do, which pictures should have flowers, how to arrange them, and so on.

Mani used to laugh as she remembered standing first on one foot and then the other in Baba's bedroom with Mehera on the days when Mani had to go to the Trust Office. Eruch was on the other side of Meherazad, Mr. Punctual, ticking off the minutes as he waited for her to get in the car. And Mehera would be doing the flowers with all her usual love and care. Mehera was not bound by time when offering flowers to Baba. Nothing else existed when she was doing it. Each offering had to be perfect, each flower placed with pure love. She would search for two identical flowers (or as near as possible) to place on either side of a picture, hesitating between these two or those two, as Mani would stand looking at the clock as the time for her departure for the office neared and then passed.

"Mani," Mehera would say, "which rose do you think is better?"

"They're both beautiful, Mehera," Mani would say as the seconds ticked by.

"But isn't this one a little larger?"

"Oh, no," Mani would say, "not a bit!" and then sigh as Mehera would become absorbed again, murmuring lovingly to Baba as she placed first this flower and then that one, caught up in His remembrance, beyond time. And she would talk to the flowers, too, Mani said, gently opening them out with her fingers to make them prettier, or scolding one that wouldn't stay put on the top of a picture.

In the years after Mehera went to Baba, Mani savored the memory of those times together in Baba's room, and all Mehera's absorption and wonderful tricks with flowers Mani now took up herself.

Walking through the garden to go to Mandali Hall, Mani would bow to a green bench near Baba's House, because of a very special memory of Baba seated there. And she'd bow to a spot at the back of the Hall, where she would offer flowers as well because of another precious memory of Him there.

On office days, Mani would leave in the car with Eruch, Rano, Bal Natu or whoever else and head to town. On the road out of Meherazad, Mani would turn her mind to the day ahead. Once they arrived at the office, Mani would clean Baba's photo over her desk and then garland it with all present. And start to work.

When the call "lunchtime!" resounded at the Trust Office, Mani would finish whatever sentence she was writing, put away her glasses, and walk quickly down the verandah to the lunchroom. It had been a long time since breakfast at 7:00 a.m.! Yet, as I mentioned before, with all the commotion inside the lunchroom, she never once failed, upon stepping in, to put her hands together over her heart and unobtrusively bow to Baba's picture.

After lunch, she would bow again to Baba's photo in the lunchroom and, at departure time, again to His photo in the office. At home in Meherazad in the evening, Mani had another personal time for remembering Baba, this one at her dressing table in the room she shared with Mehera. She would ring a little handbell before she started, and would face the dressing table, a miniature cupboard itself. And of course there would be evening arti with all the women in Baba's Room, and His name before sleeping.

All these speed-breakers for a person who was totally involved in serving Him all the rest of the time, all the rest of the day. Her *life* was a speed-breaker!

MANI'S CUPBOARD

When I came to know that Mani visited her steel cupboard on the small verandah every morning, I wondered what was inside of it. For most people, a steel cupboard is for storing things, but not for Mani: she created a little three-dimensional altar-world inside hers.

The first time I saw the inside of Mani's steel cupboard, my mind boggled. On the top shelf was the Trust file I was looking for, stacked neatly among other official-looking files. So far, so good. But on the second shelf (at eye-level) was a "Lilliput" for Baba—an arrangement of the most incongruous collection of little items you could imagine. At the back was a large color photo of Beloved Baba, beaming. To the side was one of Mehera and then there was a stained-glass Our Lady, a blue fluorescent beetle (deceased), several rocks and shells, an angel statuette, a tuft of shiny ribbon from a package, a hoopoe feather, a crystal, and so on. The other shelves mixed stationery, the hole-punch, papers, etc., with similar items. On the inside of the doors were pictures of Mehera and each of Mani's siblings.

The most arresting thing about the cupboard was its atmosphere:

Inside Mani's personal cupboard.

you opened the door and out poured the richest, headiest, most intimate perfume. You almost wanted to quickly close it up again, so it wouldn't all seep away.

If you were looking for Mani between 8:30 and 8:45 a.m. at Meherazad, you would probably be told, "She's at the cupboard." We all knew what that meant: she was not to be disturbed. Both of the cupboard doors would be open and she would be standing in between them, silently looking in and praying, perhaps swaying a little to silent music. She often had on her Walkman, listening to, say, circus music (a cupboard favorite), or Baba-music, or a bhajan/qawwali tape or something like that.

She would be completely absorbed in another world. This was her private time with Baba and Mehera. You could walk right behind her and she wouldn't even register. The cupboard was a repository of love and remembrance, and her time there was deliberately set apart for Baba. It must have deeply refreshed her because she rarely ever missed it, and even when she was sick, you could tell how bad it was if Mani hadn't been able to "go to the cupboard."

THE TOY CUPBOARD

Halfway down the verandah from Mani's cupboard and very near Mani's desk was the toy cupboard. On a Meherazad pilgrim day, Mani and one of her helpers would round up the children and, like Pied Pipers, lead them to the small verandah. They might stop on the way and float origami boats on the small duck pond in the garden, or Mani might form shadow puppets (a swan, duck, bird, or rabbit, for example) against the wall near Mandali Hall. But the toy cupboard was a great destination.

Opened, it revealed row upon row of toys: wind-up toys and stuffed

Children playing with wind-ups, stuffed animals and Mani at Meherazad.

animals that walked (and sometimes talked). Mani and the kids would get right down to playing. I think generations of Baba-lovers must have memories of first feeling at home in Meherazad on that verandah, amid the chaos of toys.

Whenever I caught a glimpse of the toy scene, there was always some small person clutching a stuffed animal to his or her heart, engaged in earnest conversation with Mani, as toys and kids hopped, crawled, fought, laughed, shouted, *oom-pahhed* all around the verandah. You see, word would get around, and often kids would bring their own toys to show to Mani. She took these introductions as they were given—very seriously, talking with both toy and child at length.

It was always touching how Mani carved out a place at Meherazad for children. She had a swing put up in the garden, and a see-saw. She carried chocolates around in her pockets for them. She gave them lots of her time, and right down at their eye level. I took this for granted: it seemed an expression of her personality. Everyone knew Mani had a huge streak of kid in her, and she really did love the company of children.

A happy conversation.

But I came to see it in another light one day. It was a Sunday and there was a program at Meherazad. On Sunday, pilgrims would turn the tables and entertain the mandali, with songs or poems or skits or dances, and it all would end with a movie of Baba. On this Sunday, a thirteen-year-old boy read out a poem he had written himself. It was a brilliant poem, an astonishing poem, really, on the theme of Infinite Consciousness. I was amazed by it.

As I walked with Mani back toward the house after the program, I mentioned the poem. "How could a thirteen-year-old write a poem like that?" I wondered out loud.

Instantly she came back with, "What's so surprising about it? Where do you think all the old souls have gone?"

Then I realized that Mani didn't just play with children because she liked them. She was also honoring Baba's lovers on pilgrimage on their own level, and she was striving to make sure that in Meherazad, the young-bodied old souls had a place and a welcome to remember.

So how did children see *her*? I caught a glimpse of that one day at the Trust Office. A family had come from the West and one of their children was seven. He was a slightly wary, reserved boy, who Mani took care to talk to in adult tones. She didn't baby him or patronize him, which he seemed to appreciate—a little.

The day came for their departure, and the family stopped by the office in a jeep on their way to Bombay. The parents got out to say goodbye to the mandali, but the boy stayed in the back of the jeep. So, Mani went around to say goodbye to him. She leaned into the open door, and he tolerated her hug. The door was closed, and she continued to stand by the back as the jeep started up. Just as they were about to pull away, he totally dropped his guard, popped his head out of the window and, in a slightly desperate voice, called out loudly, "Mani! Can I ask you a question?"

Mani stepped right up to him. "Of course!" Obviously it was something he just *had* to know.

"Are you young or are you old?"

"I'm old, but I feel young."

Her answer completely satisfied him. He nodded, turned around to face the front, and they drove off, Mani waving with both hands until they were out of sight.

UPSTAIRS

It's hard to imagine just how much music was woven into Baba's life. Mehera remembers Him always singing or humming (or talking!) before His silence, and from the early days He had music, both live and recorded, played for Him often.

Mani was one of His primary musicwallis. She sang songs to Him, played instruments (sitar and harmonium), wrote songs for the other women to sing in plays and concerts for Him, assembled records to play for Him, searched the radio for music He'd enjoy.

Mani was big on music after Baba dropped His body, too. She suggested that everyone be welcome to sing following the women mandali's arti at Meherabad, and that music be played and sung in the Hall at Meherazad on Sundays or on the porch with Mehera on any visiting day; Mani even wrote songs, and sometimes just lyrics, for both individuals and groups. And like her Brother before His silence, she was always singing or humming to herself. I was amazed when, in her seventies, she taught herself the *forty* Hindi couplets of a famous praise-song, "Meher Chalisa," practicing every few days in the bath!

One day she led me upstairs in Baba's house to a room next to His former bedroom that stored precious and household things. There she squatted down and opened up a cabinet; inside were crates of vinyl records—some 78 rpms, some 33⅓ rpms—carefully stored in their original paper jackets or LP covers. They were the Indian and Western records that she had collected and played to Baba; she wanted to look through them to check names of songs and singers.

Just the sight of the records themselves (78 rpms!) was a blast into the past, but I was particularly touched by the way Mani handled them. They were obviously old friends; she picked them up so deftly, surely, lovingly, and with the familiarity of long practice. She must have pulled them out and played them for Baba many times.

As she went through them, I was given a small window into the sound-landscape of Baba's time: the tones, words, tunes, and histories of ghazals sung by master qawwali singers, of bhajans by saints and Perfect Ones sung by singers still revered in India, and even of vintage Western hits.

The Master Singer loved our earthly music, the seventh shadow of His own Eternal Song.

MANDALI HALL

Sitting next to Baba's chair, Mani told stories to pilgrims in Mandali Hall on pilgrim visiting days, on weekends, tag-teaming with Eruch, and later, after Mehera went to Baba, also on Tuesdays by herself.

She was a vivacious storyteller and an expert at sketching a scene and bringing its characters to life. You had to keep an eye on her not to miss anything, she was so lively. Her mother, Shireenmai, was a great raconteur too, so maybe it was in the blood. (Of course, when you think of what her Brother could convey with just a raised eyebrow . . . !)

Of these Hall sessions, she would often say, "Baba made the stories; we only tell them." And she'd joke:

It reminds me of a professor of music who had retired. Years later, he goes back to the university where he'd taught; he's a fine old man, the students give him an ovation. Then they call out, "Professor, professor, play for us! Play for us!" On his horn or trombone or whatever musical instrument he played, he plays a few songs, and then the students clamor for their favorite: "Professor, professor! Play 'The Poet and the Peasant'!"

"But," says the Professor, "I just played 'The Poet and the Peasant'!"

"You did? You played 'The Poet and the Peasant'?"

"Well, he replies, "I put in 'The Poet and the Peasant.' What came out, I don't know!"

Here Mani would laugh: "Sometimes we feel like that about the talks we give!"

But if you've ever heard a tape of hers, or seen a video, or heard her personally, you know just how her love for Baba, her wisdom, humor, experience, and perspective, came out in magical stories. She never told the same story the same way. And she could make you tear up as often as she'd make you laugh.

She once said:

> We're natural talkers, but we're not speakers. So when we try to express, convey, the essence of Baba's presence and ways of working as Man and God on earth, we find ourselves fumbling for the right words.
>
> You see, there's so much to say and so much to share of so many years of living with Baba. So our problem is not what to say. Our problem is which to say. And when to stop. We're like the little girl who was asked by her teacher, " Do you know how to spell *banana*?" "Oh, yes, I know

how to spell *banana*. I just don't know when to stop. Bana-na-na-na-na . . ."

People loved her company and her stories. Speaking of the pilgrims who would come to visit the mandali, Mani recollected:

> One morning I said to myself, "Why do they all say, 'Oh, we receive so much from you?'" How is Baba doing this? Because we feel so emptied out, scrubbed out, hollowed out. So where is it coming from?
>
> And then it came to me. But of course. That is how a flute is: it's hollow. Over the years with Baba we have been hollowed out, and now we're also holey—that is, h-o-l-e-y. Like bamboo flutes. And it is His breath that makes the music that you hear from us, the music of God's glory on earth. Not only God's glory on earth, but God's Love, which is unfathomable and the only thing worth having.
>
> And therefore, when Baba says, "I do My own Work," it is true—for it is His breath that keeps all this alive. There is a song that says [and here Mani sang a line from an Urdu ghazal], "Oh Saki, it is Your breath which keeps the tavern prosperous." It lives because of Him.

But her story-telling skill was only the icing on the cake—or at least this is how I saw it. The real beauty was how much Mani and Eruch and Aloba and Bal and Katie and the others gave of themselves and shared their memories to convey Baba's human side and ways. "You are looking in us for His humanity and we are looking in you for His Divinity," she would say, or, putting it more simply, "You're looking for our Baba and we're looking for your Baba."

They would sometimes repeat what Baba had told them about the new generation who would come to Him in the future. One day He gestured, "You will see My children, My lovers"—and then, tapping His ring finger— "they are gems."

Perhaps that is why even if there were only, say, five pilgrims who came out to Meherazad on a given day in the 1970s, the mandali would still devote their whole day to sharing "their Baba." This sharing went on for years (and still goes on). At first it was seven long days a week—until, as we've seen, Sarosh put his foot down and forced them to take Fridays off ("so we could wash our hair!" Mani explained). Later, as the mandali aged, pilgrim visits were limited to half-days on Tuesday, Thursday, Saturday, and Sunday.

Mani's respect for Baba's pilgrims was deep. I've heard her refer to His lovers as "our royal family." Once in the later years when someone grumbled about the problems of dealing with so many visitors, she responded instantly, "But they come with so much love!"

"We're empty reeds," Mani would say of the mandali, "and all we have to give are Baba-stories, stories of life with Him. And believe me, that's all there is."

She explained, "You see, we were there for the Saki, not for the wine. We would sweep the tavern and put out the glasses and even help pour the wine for the guests, but we were only interested in the Saki."

Funny stories, serious stories, talks on topics related to Baba (following Him, pilgrimage, arti, and so on), the Hall saw them all. Mani had a little scratchpad on her cupboard on which she would jot down topics for Hall talks that might come to her in odd moments.

Most often she was funny, but sometimes she was quite stern. She once gave a very serious talk on Baba and Mehera's relationship of Divine

Love and purity (one that can be seen and heard in the video, "Mehera, Meher Baba's Beloved"), saying, "This role, of being the chosen counterpart to the God-Man, amounts to the highest, purest, most spiritual relationship, consisting of a divine love which the world cannot imagine."

Most pilgrims and residents came to Meherazad in the pilgrims' bus arranged by the Trust. One day in the Hall, in another mood, Mani asked people to raise their hands if they thought the horn on the pilgrims' bus, that beeped often along the road, was too loud for those inside. (There had been a lot of complaints about the loudness of the horn.) A host of hands shot up. Oh boy, what a talk followed that! Had we any idea of what it was like to travel on the Blue Bus, day after day, squished together, jolting over horrible dirt roads, the bus full of dust, everyone short on sleep and food and many not at all young? Well, all she could say was that we were "delicate darlings" if the horn of a comfortable bus traveling over good roads was too much for people with full stomachs and a good night's sleep behind them!

She thought of the mandali's lives of sacrifice and hardship as a blessing worth sharing: "We can't give you the experience, but you should have at least a fragrance of what we had!"

On some days, she'd tell only jokes, which is a good excuse to follow with two of Mani's favorites:

> One day, Little Johnny was on the bus with his mother.
> After a little while, he tugged on mother's coat.
> "Mother?"
> "Yes, Johnny?"
> "Is it true that we are here to help others?"
> "Why yes, Johnny! What a good boy you are!"
> A minute or two later, he tugged her coat again.
> "Yes, Johnny?"
> "What are the others here for?"

At an exclusive private school, the boys were told to write on the subject of "poverty."

One wrote:

"There was a very poor family.
The father was poor.
The mother was poor.
The children were poor.
Even the butler was poor."

On other days in the Hall, Mani would show around a box of Baba-treasures that included a brooch Mani made for Mehera in the mid-1930s at Meherabad from Baba's nails and hair, and a tiny crown and pair of sandals Mani had made for Baba as a child. Occasionally she would bring out her sitar, and play and sing. These were special times; she loved to do this.

When a Hall session had flowed along in a lively fashion, Mani would come back to the house after the pilgrims' bus had departed and beam: "It went with a swing!" She'd be so happy.

Sometimes, when hearing news of someone who had missed an opportunity with Baba or had drifted away, Mani would shake her head, "What could she do? It wasn't in her suitcase."

Suitcase?

"She didn't pack it in her last life. So when she opened her suitcase this life, it wasn't there."

That's why she would exhort people to make the most of the

opportunity to love and serve Baba: "Pack as much as you can in your suitcase for next time!"

Many of her talks consisted of that kind of advice, from the heart:

> It is for us to yearn for Him, yearn to be with Him when He comes again. How blessed we are in that we have been given the authority to love Him. Yearning is a grace from Him. Grace is earned by your longing—your longing to serve Him, to please Him. To yearn for Baba is to earn your place with Him next time He comes.

Over and over Mani would emphasize the importance of maintaining

our connection to Baba, the Powerhouse of Love and Truth, by seeing that the "wires" of our connection to Him "are not gnawed by the mice of anger, greed, lust and jealousy." And that our hearts are kept clean and not "coated with the dust of ignorance."

In short: "Stop running away with your desires and anchor yourself in Him."

And she would point out how He helps us:

> He tells us, "Love Me more and more," and yet He says He's the one who gives the love to us. But because He Himself says, "Love Me"— coming from the Truth Itself, this is substantial; it has to be. So even the very fact of His saying, "Love Me more and more" makes it possible for us to love Him more and more. He has said, "Let there be Light," and there was light; "Love Me," and so we are loving Him. Even that is His giving—by giving these words, "Love Me," He is giving us this love.

. . .

On one occasion, Mani summed up the heart of what the mandali so often tried to convey:

> We have tried to put the essence of life with Baba, of His Love, His Compassion, His Attributes, wrapped up in these words. If you find that the mandali do not agree on certain versions [of the same story]—say, the date or the place—that is not important. You have received the wheat with the chaff. It is for your love now to blow away the chaff and just take the wheat, which is Baba.
>
> And I'd like to say a few words from my heart for all who see us on the screen or hear us, but who receive us in their hearts with Baba. Remember, Baba is with you. He has promised, He has given that assurance to each and all of you: "I am with My lovers." Remember that He is with you. And my wish for you is, may He bless you to be with Him always. May He bless you to love Him more and more and more. May He bless you to please Him more.
>
> During this silence of thirty seconds that they've asked for, for the video [most likely for starting another tape, which would need a short silence at the beginning], you can hear the clock so clearly—*tick tick tick*. But actually it's ticking all the time. It was ticking while I was talking. It was ticking while you were laughing or sharing. It was ticking all the time. But when I'm still, when there's no sound, you can hear it.
>
> That is how remembrance of Baba must be. It must be there all the time, even though you're only conscious of it when your mind is still or when you have a break in your preoccupations. So I also wish you more and more "speed-breakers" as I said before. More and more speed-breakers in your very busy and occupied world, in

life, till there is only one road, till the speed-breakers become the road itself, and there is no break in between.

Because, as I've always said, in that fast pace of life, especially out in the West, it is not easy to check yourself and to remember Baba consciously. So you must create speed-breakers in your life. Even if it's an artificial creation, even if it's crutches, it doesn't matter. Say to yourself, "At this time, I will do this, so that I stop whatever else I'm doing in my mind and consciously be with Baba, even for a few seconds."

That is the speed-breaker. Then you start fast again, do what you like—but then again, there is a speed-breaker. And each time, if you can bring the speed-breakers closer and closer to each other, by creating more and more speed-breakers in your life, in your days, then eventually there will be just ONE speed-breaker! Just be with Baba, consciously and still.

Here's a final excerpt from a Mani talk to Baba-lovers in Mandali Hall. Having lived a life with no "freedom" as the world knows it, in the later years Mani spoke a lot about the modern concept of freedom:

If our life, so full of restrictions and confinements, was really a binding, then how was it that we felt so full in our hearts? How was it that we felt the joy of His being so deeply?

In the world's dictionary, freedom means doing as you please, doing whatever you feel like. And it is something you want to attain. Drugs, permissiveness, the rebellion against discipline: there is an epidemic of craving for such freedom these days.

Why then, we ask ourselves, is it that this pursuit of

freedom is not making people happy? From where comes the misery, the frustration, the sad rise in young suicides we see all around us? If there is so much freedom, why all this?

It's what happens when you are chasing a shadow. And running after false freedom is nothing but that. Running away with your desires is chasing a shadow. And you can't stop running. All this wanting to be high, high, and higher by whatever means, drugs or physical self-indulgence, is like building a skyscraper without a foundation. In time, it's going to collapse like a castle of sand.

To gain real freedom, you have to bind yourself to the Real. You have to bind yourself to God, to Baba.

After all, how many lives have we had the freedom to do these things? We've done them again and again, but all we've done is go round in circles. We've gone very "fast forward," but we've come back again.

This lifetime with Him is where it breaks up, where He takes you out of that circle, straight to Him. How can we expect it to be easy? But at last we are on a route that really goes forward.

We don't know what we have been through just to get to this point when we can do what we should be doing: loving God, surrendering to Him, being His.

He doesn't want many lives. He wants just one life. But to get to that one life, we have to keep on repeating, repeating, repeating, until we can come to this point and say, "This one is completely Yours."

IN THE GARDEN

Standing in the middle of the garden, between Mehera's porch and Mandali Hall, a story comes to mind with nearly every view. Baba called this the "Garden of Allah," created by Mehera to refresh Him with beauty.

There's a bougainvillea arbor by the Hall's back door, site of many home-movie shots of Baba with Mehera and the women. In a late '60s film vignette: Baba walks haltingly under the arbor, smiling for the camera, as Mehera holds His hand and beams at Him—Baba's walking!—and Mani is on the other side, supporting His arm, her expression startlingly concentrated and concerned.

A shadow puppet.

Turn again, and there's the duck pond. Here is Mani's vision of the Garden of Allah as a playground for children: the duck pond for floating paper boats, the white wall by the Hall for making hand shadow puppets, the swing and see-saw for burning off all that zip.

. . .

Right near the duck pond is a spot that held a special memory for Mani. During the last weeks of Mehera's life, she often sat out on her porch so that she could enjoy looking at the garden. Mani was often with Mehera, but sometimes she would walk through the garden to her desk on the small verandah to work. One morning, as Mani was coming out of the small verandah into the garden, Mehera spotted her. Mehera then joined her hands together and bowed slightly in the ancient Indian gesture of namaste. Seeing this from her spot near the duck pond, Mani was a bit confused. This was not a gesture Mehera ever used with Mani; it is quite formal, a greeting of regard and respect. Mani thought to herself, "Well, Mehera must not be able to see me so well. She thinks I'm someone else!" But as Mani stood there, Mehera did it again, and so Mani gestured namaste back to her. Then Mehera did it a third time, very intently. Mani returned the gesture, not quite knowing what to make of it, and then, as Mehera seemed finished, Mani walked on.

Mehera happily in the garden.

That turned out to be the last day Mehera ever sat on her porch. Soon after she went in to rest that afternoon, she slipped into a light coma. Four days later, she went to her Beloved. Mani realized that the greeting in the garden was Mehera's goodbye.

Mani once mentioned to me that if she had the time to write another book after *Dreaming of The Beloved,* she would write one about the memorable trees of Baba's Advent. The *trees?* She was perfectly serious. The trees . . . Thinking it over, I could see what she meant.

I mean, really, what a part the umar tree with Baba's image on it played in Baba's story: it brought His beloved Mehera back to life! Consider how Mehera (and later Mani) would honor that tree, Mehera praying to it by the hour, putting little marigolds around Baba's face in the bark, or sometimes a long flower garland around the trunk.

If you think about it, other trees served Him, too: the big neem that sheltered Baba and the mandali when they first arrived on foot at Meherabad; the neem and karunja and banyan trees that Valubai planted to shade Him when He walked up Meherabad Hill; the banyan near the Samadhi that shaded Him and the women in the early years; the mango tree at Meherazad that gave mangoes in the off-season, little sweet ones for sucking when all the other mangoes had gone—it grew from a seed given to Baba by a mast. Then there was the coconut palm in the garden behind Baba's house that gave coconut water for Him to drink on fasts and when He wasn't eating much; a pipal tree in Madras under which He gave darshan; and on and on.

Mani amid the trees.

Sometimes down the approach road, sometimes back by Seclusion Hill, Mani would walk in the early mornings with the dogs loping along (so excited!). As we've seen, she often picked up an odd-shaped leaf, a shiny stone, a hoopoe or crow feather, a dead beetle or moth to bring back to her cupboard collection. The women's intimate world extended beyond the garden into the fields and hills nearby and to all the trees around their home.

After Mehera went to Baba, on special occasions Mani garlanded another tree—the ancient mango on the approach road to Meherazad. She had dreamt of this tree years before. In her dream, she was hurrying down the road toward Meherazad when she saw a blue light emanating from the tree. Turning toward it, she saw Mary, the mother of Jesus,

The tree on the approach road.

sitting on a throne in a niche in the tree, looking glorious, with a little jeweled crown on her head. Mani was instantly drawn to her, and, kneeling, put her head in Mary's lap. As she rested there, deeply at peace, she looked up and saw—to her astonishment—Mary's face turning into Mehera's and then back into Mary's, again and again. It was a very beautiful dream-vision, full of feeling and light and meaning for Mani. (When she told it to Mehera, Mani said, Mehera giggled!)

There's one Meherazad tree, the gulmohr by the gate, that holds not a memory but a feeling for me. Gulmohrs are tall, gracious trees, red-flowering in summer, with bright green fronds of tiny leaves that turn yellow in the hot season. This stately gulmohr had stood sentinel at the Meherazad gates from Baba's time.

In June 1996, Mani was driven to town to have a sonogram to determine what might be causing her incessant abdominal pain. (The scan showed a mass that turned out to be cancer.) As she was driven out between the Meherazad gates to go for the scan, some of us stood in the garden to wave her off. The car went down the road, and Mani's waving hand drew back inside the window. Just as we were turning to go, suddenly a breeze came up and from the gulmohr tree fell thousands of tiny yellow leaves, twirling down and down—a shower of gold veiling the receding car from sight, as if in salute, beautiful and sad.

Soon after, in August, when Mani was in her final week of life, I noticed something from inside her room that I had never marked before. It seemed as though the tree with Baba's image, the umar, was leaning in toward Mehera-Mani's room—toward Mehera in her yearning in 1969, and now toward Mani in her suffering. A fancy, of course, but the feeling was so strong that I went outside to look at the tree. Sure enough, it did lean toward their window, and then straighten and climb upwards from there.

The umar tree is sacred to the Hindus as the seat of the god Dattatreya. Dattatreya, a symbol of the Avatar, is depicted with three heads representing God's triune nature of Creator, Sustainer, and Dissolver.

Going closer to the tree that day, my gaze was drawn down the trunk, and I saw something else for the first time: a small niche formed in the trunk at the bottom. Wait a minute—was there something in the niche? I got down on my hands and knees to see. There was something: a tiny bronze statue of Dattatreya, standing in the naturally carved little "throne room" of His tree.

As I guessed (and another helper later confirmed), Mani had tucked it in there.

For many years Goher had a motorized wheelchair (a "scoota") nicknamed "Ducky" to ferry her around Meherazad when her legs could no longer push her famous little bicycle easily. When Mani's health began to fail, Baba-lovers brought over another scoota—for Mani— piece by piece in their luggage. Mani christened it "Begum," after the little horse they had in earlier years. The very back of Mandali Hall became the two duckies' garage, where their batteries could be plugged into the wall socket for recharging.

Goher and Mani on their duckies.

So, for a few years, both Goher and Mani would ride through the garden on their duckies. Of course, with her sense of humor, it wasn't long before Mani got into the idea of ducky races with Goher, and she would tease Goher about it on pilgrim days. Although I never saw it, I believe a race may have happened after all. It would have been a sure bet if Mani was calling the shots, and a non-starter if left up to Goher!

Fun with Mani at Meherabad

AT BABA'S SAMADHI

Mehera, Mani, and Katie inside the Samadhi.

Although Mani came countless times by herself, it is always with Mehera that I picture her at Baba's Samadhi. They would come from Meherazad to Meherabad (about a forty-five minute drive) with the other women mandali every fifteen days, and after placing garlands, saying the prayers, and singing arti, they would all sit down inside the Samadhi. Mehera and Mani sat together on mats on the floor to Baba's right, Mehera slightly forward, leaning on the upper flagstone level (or later, sitting on it), and Mani sitting next to her and a little back. Baba-lovers were welcome to come, too, and lucky women would help the ladies offer garlands and, if there was room after the prayers, sit inside with them.

These visits, known as the "Women's Arti," became much-anticipated occasions for both pilgrims and residents. It was a true privilege to be with the women at Baba's Samadhi, and all seemed touchingly aware of this.

It is impossible to imagine all that

the women mandali had gone through since first seeing their Beloved's precious body placed in the crypt in 1969. Even years later, these twice-monthly visits had a poignant beauty. Mehera seemed especially absorbed in that timeless, devotional, unique inner world she shared with Baba, and when she stepped out of the Samadhi and smiled at those outside, she would bring its atmosphere with her and send it—*zing*—right to your heart.

As usual when in public, Mani was on her toes, balancing her private communion with the needs of the occasion: follow Mehera's lead so that everyone said the prayers and sang the arti together (in tune and in time!), request a lively group song when there were too many dirges in a row—or a song that Mehera particularly liked, or a song from a singer too shy to come forward. After Mehera passed away, when Mani and the others sat on benches on the Samadhi portico during the singing, Mani often translated lines from an Indian bhajan or ghazal that had been sung, or shared a comment Baba had made about a song, or tossed in a pun to put a nervous performer at ease.

One time, a few days after the women had visited the Samadhi for darshan, Mani mentioned that Baba had answered a question in her heart while at Meherabad. At that time, the mandali were deluged with the Trust's teething problems and concerns. Of course, Mani would "tell" Baba all this, but she sometimes wondered, was He listening? That day at Meherabad, a Baba-lover sang a song with the chorus, "There's a singing in your heart, are you listening?"

Listening carefully.

To Mani, it was her answer: Baba saying, "I'm here—are *you* listening?"

. . .

Baba had the present Samadhi dome and structure built in 1938, and as we've seen, Mani remembered Him taking Mehera and the secluded women over from their Hill quarters in the evening to see "what Helen was doing." Helen was Helen Dahm, a fellow ashramite and famous Swiss painter, and what she was doing was painting murals on the four Samadhi walls and inner dome at His order. "Eyes, eyes, eyes" was what Mani remembered about Helen's painting, eyes on the figures everywhere.

Fifty-two years later, she stood inside the Samadhi, speaking of those eyes to the team she had assembled to restore the murals to their original beauty. This effort, the restoration of Baba's Samadhi (1990–1992) was one of Mani's greatest gifts to Meherabad. She thought it up and she put her whole heart into pulling it off, knowing that only she, Baba's sister and chairman, could set in motion such a major project involving His tomb.

In 1971, the Helen Dahm murals in the Samadhi were repainted under Adi's direction by Bhaiya Panday, an Ahmednagar artist and photographer. Mani felt that when the time came to refresh the murals again, they should be done in a restorative way to more correctly resemble the original paintings. So she assembled a team of Baba-lovers with special skills to undertake this project. There were fine artists, restoration experts, plasterers and painting helpers, researchers, logistical supporters . . . it was quite a well-orchestrated effort.

In that blazing hot summer of 1990, Mani often took the long car ride from Meherazad via the Trust Office to Meherabad Hill to check on the restoration work, give suggestions and encouragement to the team, and share tea, snacks, and old stories with Mansari and with Kaikobad's daughters Guloo and Jaloo. She was involved with every aspect of the project, including the artistry itself in the restoration of the paintings, suggesting subtle changes in color, hue, shape, and offering her

Restored section of the murals (in the dome of the Tomb), on the left. How Helen Dahm's original painting looked in the same section in 1971 (before being repainted by Panday), on the right.

remembrances of the feeling of the original paintings. She, who with her pale skin was so sensitive to sun and heat, spared no effort to make sure everything was going well, to smooth out any hitches, and to ensure that the project was harmoniously received.

Maybe she also knew—I used to think this at the time—that there wasn't much time left for her to do it.

After the painting was done, she decided that no one should sit inside the Samadhi for a year to give the plaster and paint time to thoroughly dry out. Take darshan, yes, but not sit inside. And during Amartithi that year, the thousands of visiting pilgrims took darshan only at the threshold.

I was astonished by this. Mani would go to enormous lengths to make one pilgrim feel welcome. How could she not consider the feelings of thousands? But from this I soon came to see how much she valued and upheld the Samadhi, and the primary importance and tremendous responsibility she placed on taking care of it. As she explained, it was not just for us now, for the individuals who would be affected for a year. It was His gift to the future, and as she and Eruch said, it was a privilege for His lovers to sacrifice something precious to themselves to preserve it for the world.

Besides, Baba Himself had indicated that eventually the Samadhi threshold was where His lovers would bow down to Him.

MEHERA'S SHRINE

After Mehera passed away in 1989, the women mandali continued to visit the Samadhi on a regular basis. After darshan and arti inside Baba's Samadhi, they would gather by Mehera's shrine, and Mani would pray aloud: "Mehera, help us to love Him as He should be loved. Help us to please Him as He should be pleased." And sometimes she would talk about Mehera's matchless, unfathomable love for her Beloved.

The women would offer flowers, and sometimes showers of rose petals that Mani said were for all the "hearts" around the world that wished to be there at Meherabad that day. No one is allowed to photograph pilgrims inside the Samadhi or outside on the portico, but it was revealing that Mani always requested no photographs be taken when the women were at Mehera's shrine. She didn't mind people taking pictures of them anywhere else on the Hill, but in the Samadhi, on the portico, and in this place, too, she wished to keep some measure of privacy.

Then they would bow at Mehera's feet. Soon after Mehera went to Baba, a Baba-lover wrote to Mani, wondering—was it all right to bow down to Mehera's shrine? Mehera and all the mandali emphasized one-pointed devotion to only Baba. Mani's reply showed Mehera's place in their hearts:

> . . . this is a private matter concerning the heart. There is no rule which says you shall do so, and none that says you shall not. When your heart prompts you, it is right to do it. Otherwise, it is right not to do it. When you talk to Mehera, garland her shrine or bow to her, you are simply acknowledging and honouring Mehera's supreme love for Beloved Baba and Baba's highest love for beloved Mehera—Love is reason enough. After all, why would one feel like remembering and honouring Mehera in such a profound way? Because of her love for Baba and Baba's love for her which alone prompts that response

of love from you. Honouring Mehera is honouring pure, one-pointed, whole-hearted love for the One Beloved, to whom she directed all honour, veneration or adoration expressed towards her at any time . . .

In conclusion, Mani said, "Follow your heart, which will take you only one place: up the high road to your Beloved Baba."

BABA'S CABIN

After Mehera's passing, Mani had two stories she almost always told those who crammed into Baba's Cabin with them on the women's visit to Meherabad. You've heard them before: one was of the dog Chum, chasing a calf round and round the Cabin after Baba gave the calf some millet bread. This was a big hit with the kids, as Mani would act out the chase.

(Speaking of Chum, I noticed that Mani never placed a flower on the Cabin picture of Baba standing there with Chum at His side. You might remember that Chum had once bitten her—on the chin—when she had come too near to him as he sat by Baba. Although Mani grudgingly admired how Chum took the beating Baba gave him for it—"that dog just sat there and took it"—he didn't get a flower!)

The other story was about the stretcher. As we've seen, the stretcher in the Cabin was very precious to the women, being the stretcher on which Baba's body lay both in the ambulance coming from Meherazad and in the Cabin while the men were preparing the crypt in Baba's

At the threshold of Baba's Cabin.

Tomb. It was the place where Mehera, Mani, and the intimate women mandali sat with Him, in grief and farewell, just before they had to give Him up to the world. (Visiting the Cabin, Mani would not talk of that night, but rather about the ambulance that broke down after carrying Baba's body from Meherazad to Meherabad.)

After Mehera passed away, Mani would put flowers in the Cabin in just the same places as Mehera, even following Mehera's choice of colors.

We saw Mehera's wonderful intimacy with flowers when she offered them to His photos in the Cabin. She would take a marigold and mime tucking it behind Baba's ear in a photo, murmur lovingly to Him, and then kiss the flower and patiently stand it up against the frame. Mani once said that Mehera didn't just look at Baba's photo; it was a meeting.

In another Cabin photo, Baba's hand is seen very clearly, slim and graceful, and Mehera would hold a flower by its stem and stroke Baba's hand with the blossom. She would kneel on the floor to kiss the stretcher pillow and place a fresh garland where His body had lain, every gesture redolent with love.

Mani told us that when they were placing Baba's body on the stretcher in Meherazad just after He passed away, she had run and brought her pillow to place under His head. Afterwards she realized that the pillow had been His mother Shireenmai's. Mani was so touched that Baba's Memo, with such a huge part to play in His beginning, had a part to play, too, at the end.

The last year of her life, before she was sick, Mani struck me as extraordinarily radiant on her visits to the Cabin. As she told her stories to pilgrims there, she was so animated, so funny, so intensely alive. Chum had never chased the calf so hard. It scared me. She was like a candle blazing up. I was somehow afraid that she was about to go out. And that did come to pass.

DRESSING DOWN

I once asked some of the mandali what they thought was Baba's most characteristic personality trait. I only remember a few of the responses. Adi K. Irani said it was Baba's mastery of psychology, that He was a Master psychologist. Eruch said: His compassion (in fact, he said, "Baba was too compassionate!"). I forget what Mani said; perhaps it was His humor. But Mehera said, "He was so sporting." When asked for clarification, she said, "He always entered into the spirit of everything we did."

I saw that wholeheartedness in all of the women mandali, too. It manifested in many ways: one was how particular they were about their clothes. Not what Mani would call their "home clothes," to be worn when no one was around; those had to be comfortable, soft, preferably patched. But when the pilgrims came to Meherazad, the women dressed to receive their "royal family," each in her own distinct way.

Mani's outfit for many years was a variation on a little waisted dress over loose white pants gathered at the ankle (the Indian *lengha*). And there was the ubiquitous scarf, carefully coordinated. (She had a patterned top that she thought was a little dull until a Baba-friend who was a clown gave her a set of different colored buttons. Onto the dress they went, every button a separate color, and it became a favorite, her "clown dress.")

Mani all dressed up.

Visits to Baba's Samadhi at Meherabad, when they were going to honor His precious form, called for a special effort. Mehera almost always wore a sari, lovely earrings, and a carefully chosen Baba-pin or locket. Mani and the others wore saris or

Punjabi outfits and matching jewelry, all varying with personal taste. They took care not to wear the same color or anything close to the color that Mehera had chosen. But they dressed up. There's a picture of Mani taken at Meherabad after Mehera had passed away that was a favorite among her friends; she's in a bright, spangly ensemble holding a bamboo parasol and posing.

This spirit permeated the atmosphere; most of the women attending, young and old, visitors and residents, entered into it and dressed up for "Women's Arti." I had a number of outfits for these occasions. But one day, after years of dressing up, I had a fit of laziness and decided to dress down. I wore an old, comfortable, respectable but somewhat faded number that I decided I would wear every time they came from then on.

Mehera and the women arrived. After arti and darshan at Baba's tomb, they went into the Cabin, and some other women and I went in, too. As Mehera was talking to a few of the others over by the stretcher, Mani gave me a quick look up and down and commented wryly, in Hindi, "Have you come in from the kitchen or from the garden?"

Translation: If you've decided not to make an effort for our occasion, be good enough not to flaunt it! (Needless to say, that was the end of that outfit of mine!)

BABA'S GAADI

Baba's wooden couch on the Hill, the gaadi, was kid-sized in the sense that it was very low and long, so a lot of small people could stand around it at a time. Taking advantage of this when they visited Meherabad, Mehera and Mani would always call the pilgrim children to help them offer a garland to Baba on His gaadi.

The gaadi was where, in the early days on Meherabad Hill, Baba would sit out with the women in the evenings. Standing by the gaadi, Mani would sometimes recall being with Baba there many years ago. At that time, He had gestured a circle that seemed to cover the whole Hill and all the way to the horizon, describing how many pilgrims from the East and West would come in the future.

At Amartithi, Mani would point out, His words came true in a very literal sense: the whole Hill was covered with people from all over the world. Watching Mehera, Mani, and all the women interact with this immense crowd of lovers was a lesson in graciousness and giving. It was also exhausting, for they would embrace hundreds of women who were just dying to touch them, and, from a short distance, greet hundreds of men. Old-timers seemed to understand that they were flesh and blood, but the newcomers, for whom Mehera and Mani were practically mythical figures, sometimes hugged them as tightly as they might a metal statue! Yet by the end of Amartithi, Mehera always looked radiant, filled to the brim and overflowing with love. How was it possible? The women got almost no sleep for three days (they stayed in the East Room and another room right at the top of the Hill in the midst of a heightened twenty-four-hour-a-day atmosphere of noise, dust, and a particular sort of chaos). But Mehera in particular and the women in general seemed

to thrive on the love at Amartithi: the love of all those lovers for their Beloved and the unique atmosphere of His Love that, like the dust and light, permeates the very air at Amartithi time.

It was the small things the women did for individuals that touched me then. In that mass of people they remained so *personal*. I remember Mani coming back to the East Room to catch a little rest, exhausted by the fever pitch of activity (they had been up since 3:00 a.m.). She would lie down in the room, where the din of the loudspeakers, announcements, broadcasted singing, chatting, and crowd hubbub was only slightly diminished, and after about an hour (of no sleep), she would get up and go outside for her "Hindi talk." The Hindi talk was for a couple from North India who brought their big black tape recorder along to Amartithi. This was an annual event. The couple would be waiting by the gaadi's place (on Amartithi the gaadi itself was placed on the Sabha Mandap, the large platform near the Samadhi). Mani would greet them and then sit down, holding her little card of notes. They would click on the recorder, and off she would go in Hindi, not just telling stories, but acting them out, facial expressions, imitations, gestures, and all. After a while, a crowd of Hindi-speaking lovers would gather, from Delhi, Hamirpur District, Dehra Dun, and so on, and stand or sit on the flattened cow-dung "floor," absolutely tickled to hear Manibahen ("Sister Mani") talking about their Baba in their language.

What pleasure she gave that couple and those people at Amartithi! And how gladly she did it, overriding her exhaustion, giving her all. Mani used to say, "Love is sacrifice," and at Amartithi particularly, we saw this in the mandali.

But Mani herself would often say after such occasions as the Hindi talk: "I thought I was giving, but I received." She used to illustrate this with an Amartithi story. During the early Amartithis, the women would stay in the East Room (and some in another room) from noon on January 30 through noon on February 2. One year, February 1, while standing by the gaadi, Mehera and Mani were approached by a couple from Andhra Pradesh holding a baby and a package. In the package were two saris, which they wanted Mehera and Mani to wear that day in honor of their baby son's first birthday (Mani reproduced their regional accent to a tee as she brought the story alive). Now these saris were very bright, quite vivid actually, not really to Mehera's or Mani's taste. Besides, they had no matching sari blouses to wear with them. And no time to change. Mani assured the couple that they would happily wear the saris on a different occasion. But the parents were crestfallen. As they said, in English, "It's the first birthday! Please wear—today only!"

At last, Mehera and Mani gave in. Somehow, from among the other women, semi-matching blouses were produced, and the saris put on. "Well," recalled Mani, "we got so many compliments on those saris, you wouldn't believe it! We thought we were giving, but in the end it was we who received." In fact, that vivid sari became one of her favorites.

This story has a touching sequel. Many years later, after both Mehera and Mani had gone to Baba, the Meherabad Young Adult Sahavas hosted two discussion sessions, one remembering Mehera and the other Mani. One of the sahavasees at the remembrance of Mani was a young man from Andhra. At the very end of the hour's discussion, he shyly spoke up. He had a memory of Mani. You see, February 1 was his birthday and . . . Yes, it was the first-birthday baby, all grown up! It turned out that his parents took him to meet Mehera and Mani on his birthday every year at Amartithi from then on. "As a child, I didn't really understand about going to meet Baba at Amartithi; Baba was in our house already," he said. "But all year long I wanted to go to Meherabad to meet Mehera-aunty and Mani-aunty on my birthday." And both Mehera and Mani always remembered to keep a little present ready for him.

The story went on. The last year of Mani's life, she was too ill to stay at Meherabad for all of Amartithi. So, it was arranged that she would visit only on the morning of January 30, take darshan at the Samadhi, and return to Meherazad. The young man from Andhra knew he would not be able to meet her at all that year. But on the first of February, at Meherabad, Mansari sought him out. She had something for him. As she put it in his hand, she said, "Mani gave this to me to give you on your birthday." When he told us this, he began to cry. (So did we.) He never saw Mani again.

THE PILGRIM CENTRE

"Let them have a whiff, just a whiff, of what we had!" Mani would say, meaning what she had expressed in Mandali Hall: let the pilgrims experience some hardship, discomfort, deprivation, so that they could have a scent of the life of sacrifice the mandali had with Baba. She wanted to give us the chance to give up something for Him.

So when, under the watchful eye of Padri, that prince of austerity, Mani and Goher set up the first pilgrim accommodations at Meherabad in the old ashram buildings in 1970 or 1971, they kept it simple. Even then pilgrims had all kinds of things the mandali often went without in their years with Baba: beds, mosquito nets, three meals a day, a full bucket of water for a bath—for a start! And, like them, we had kerosene lanterns for light, extremely simple food, and no media whatever to distract us.

Mani was the reservationwalli: she would take the pilgrim list and fill up the twelve spots available at Meherabad. Each pilgrim could stay for four days at a time, from Monday to Friday.

When the Meher Pilgrim Centre opened in 1980, Padri, with Mani's input, drew up the rules and policies. They bear his stamp. The written introduction to the rules says (in part):

> You have come to stay in this building—the Meher Pilgrim Centre—situated in Meherabad where Avatar Meher Baba did a major portion of His Universal Work, and to which people journey from all over the world to pay homage

at His Tomb on Meherabad Hill . . . [therefore] this building is
not to be treated as a hotel but a pilgrim accommodation.

You have come to pay homage to the Avatar, so please
observe the discipline outlined by the rules given below.

. . . [At the end of the list of the six Pilgrim Centre rules:]
All pilgrims are asked to abide by the rules, thereby
upholding the spirit of true pilgrimage.

Mani used to become impatient when people complained about the six rules of the Pilgrim Centre. "I just don't get it," she'd say. "You obey the rules of your country, you obey traffic rules, you obey the rules at school, you obey rules on the airplane, you even obey rules in the grocery store! Can't you obey the rules of God's place?"

A few years later (in 1994) Eruch wrote to a pilgrim who had complained about the food:

We His lovers, must not forget why we come to
Meherabad in the first place. Meherabad is a place of Holy
Pilgrimage. It is not a vacation spot, resort or retreat. It
behooves each pilgrim blessed to cross His Threshold, to
accept all conditions of their pilgrimage as the prasad given
to them by their Beloved Lord. To have one's pilgrimage
accepted by the Lord is no easy task, for it means more than
to merely bow down at His Samadhi. We must accept wholeheartedly any and all trials and tribulations that may beset
us during our pilgrimage, knowing full well, that these very
difficulties when happily accepted without reservation or
expectation mark His acceptance of our pilgrimage. Doubly
blessed is the pilgrim who, in spite of all hardships, remains
cheerfully resigned to the conditions of his pilgrimage.

And yet, Beloved Avatar Meher Baba, in His Infinite
Compassion and Benevolence, has made our pilgrimage so

comfortable and easy that we have forgotten all that He Himself, as Man amongst men, suffered throughout His Ministry to awaken His Love in our hearts.

Dear brothers and sisters, we have been blessed to receive His gift of love, now it is time for us to return that love by dissolving all expectations, reservations and desires in total gratitude and resignation to His Will.

With warm regards in Love and Service of our Beloved Lord Avatar Meher Baba.

Yours lovingly,
(signed) ERUCH

The Meher Pilgrim Centre, conceived as a place where Baba-lovers could all stay together at Meherabad (instead of scattered around Ahmednagar in various accommodations) opened on June 17, 1980. Mehera, Mani, and the women came there for lunch a few days before the opening. As they garlanded a photo of Baba [page 163] in the foyer, Mani smiled, "I took that picture with my box camera!"

Mehera arriving at the Pilgrim Centre.

Just beyond the photo, on the foyer wall, was a plaque that Mani had requested be made and installed. It was a quote from Baba to His Sahavasees in 1958:

> I may give you more, much more than you expect
> or maybe nothing, and that nothing may prove to be

everything. So I say, come with open hearts to receive much or nothing from your Divine Beloved. Come to receive not so much of My words but of My Silence.

Also on the other foyer wall was Padri's contribution: a plaque of the same three couplets of the Perfect Master Hafiz that Baba had brought to His room the day He dropped His body.

After the garlanding, the women went on an informal tour of the building, although Mani didn't need one, having been consulted by the architect at each stage of the planning and design. Then everyone had lunch.

On another day, about a week or two before the opening, Mani set the tone for the staff by talking to us about the importance of working together harmoniously for Baba. (Excerpts are given in an earlier section [page 900] as "On Working for Baba".)

Two years after the Pilgrim Centre opened, Padri passed away, and we began going to Mani with problems. "Tell me now; it's going to come to me in the end," she would say, because somehow word always got back to her when things weren't going right. Sometimes she would counsel the pilgrim who had come to her with a difficulty or she would take the time to explain the history or reason behind a policy or rule. Often she would use an incident to point out how someone might grow with Baba through it. But many times the staff were the ones needing the perspective. She would give us a chance to explain ourselves (God help you if the explanation was wimpy), but over and over she would remind us: "It's not only what you do for Baba; it's how you do it."

And she had an expansive view. Once, when I told Mani that a pilgrim's way of following Baba seemed very "off-course" to me, she replied severely, "Don't limit Baba!" I then saw that this was exactly what I had been doing. The mandali's perspective on Baba's ways of bringing people to Him was so much broader. As Eruch used to say, "There are as many paths to Baba as there are Baba-lovers."

Mani beaming at Baba's 100th Birthday celebration.

On the walls in the Pilgrim Centre dining hall were a number of Baba-paintings, but also two photographs, one of Baba eating and one of Him drinking tea. Mani had given them to the cook to place right near where the food and chai were dished out. She introduced Baba's pictures wherever she could (in the Museum on Meherabad Hill, for example, she had Baba-pictures put in every cupboard, to "tell the story" about the article on display). There in the Pilgrim Centre dining hall, the photographs did just what she intended: very simply, they brought Baba among the pilgrims as they ate and drank in His place.

Having been raised a Catholic ("all roads lead to Rome"), I had always had a vague question in my mind about the place of the Trust in the Baba-world. Of course Baba had said that Meherabad (the Trust Estate) would be a world center of pilgrimage, and the deed He gave outlined many charitable directions for it. But aside from that, did it have a role among the wider Baba community?

One day something happened that helped shape my thoughts on this. The Pilgrim Centre occasionally would receive notices of other

Baba center activities, either by mail or from individuals, to be posted on its notice board. One day one of these came to the Trust Office and I mentioned to Mani that I would take it to the Pilgrim Centre to post on the board there. Surprised, she asked, "What for?" I replied that we posted these notices so that Baba-lovers would know of other centers' activities. Immediately Mani shook her head, no, and went on to say that we should post only notices about our own activities, the activities at Meherabad and Meherazad.

Her decentralized view answered my unspoken question. The Trust was not to be a central clearinghouse for the Baba-world; it should do only what it was given to do by Baba in the deed.

One of my favorite pictures of Mani was taken in the Pilgrim Centre. It's Mani, beaming, tired, and a little flushed, in a cream, gold-trimmed, spangly sari with sparkling confetti in her hair. The occasion was Baba's 100th Birthday party. Because Baba always encouraged His lovers to celebrate His Birthday at their own centers, as the centennial of His Birth approached, Eruch suggested (and the trustees agreed) that Meherabad's pilgrim accommodations be closed starting on February 15 that year. This would encourage Baba-lovers to observe this unique Birthday at their centers, often through public programs.

Soon after this was decided, Mani said, "But what about our own celebration? We have to celebrate His 100th Birthday too!" She thought about it for a while and came up with a plan. We'd have a play (as usual) but this time it wouldn't be in the theater, it would be in the Pilgrim Centre, because there would not be a big audience, just the mandali and a few local folks. From the late 1970s on, a play was put on for Baba's Birthday, first at Meherazad and later in the theater at Meherabad. What would the play for His 100th Birthday be about? She thought about this, and one day said, "We've done everything on earth, so why not do heaven?"

Heaven? Turns out what she had in mind was not a play with lots of dialogue, but more like a spectacle, with music and movement. And the theme? The rejoicing in heaven at the birth of the Avatar as baby Merwan.

Of course "heaven" did not mean just angels. Oh, no, we had to have it all: angels, sure, and archangels absolutely, but also Hindu gods, goddesses, and *apsaras* (heavenly beings), Muslim *houris* (fairies/angels), and the five Perfect Masters to boot. You see, it could start with Mother Earth beseeching the Beloved to return and save Earth from the crushing, destructive ignorance of humanity, and then the five Perfect Masters could come out, holding candles, and then . . .

Under Mani's guidance, the spectacle took shape. Other work at Meherabad except the most essential was suspended for the ten days leading up to the Birthday, and all of the residents worked with excitement, each in his or her own capacity.

Midday on Baba's 100th Birthday, about eighty curious audience members assembled in the Pilgrim Centre dining hall to see this mysterious production: all the mandali, all Meherabad's older residents, and most of Ahmednagar's very close lovers.

The spectacle took just fifteen minutes. But what a fifteen minutes! The grand finale was baby Merwan descending from the rafters (on invisible guy wires) in a cradle as the celestial cast sang the "Hallelujah" chorus from Handel's "Messiah" and showered rose petals on the baby (a very cute Ahmednagar doll in Zoroastrian baby clothes). Even the skeptics got goose bumps. He certainly came down from heaven into our hearts that day.

Mani could not have been more pleased.

The Birthday entertainment had another memorable moment. Midway through the post-spectacle variety show, Sushila, a close disciple who lived at Meherabad from Baba's time, had a heart attack at her seat in the second row. I was the MC and had my glasses off, but suddenly I dimly made out a lot of commotion right behind the women mandali. Someone was being put on a stretcher and carried out. Hazarding a guess that someone had died or was dying, I looked at Mani for guidance. What the heck do I do now? Mani looked back at me and gestured, "Well, get on with it!" (Had someone I dearly loved just conked out? No idea.) I stuttered a bit, introduced the next number, the performers dutifully got ready for a song, and the show went on.

(As it turned out, Sushila went on, too, for another five years. Her heart had actually stopped, but she received CPR right there in the dining hall, which revived her, and after a long hospital stay, she came home quite tickled at being reborn on His 100th.)

At the end of the show, glittery confetti was loosed from the rafters, and it so happened that most of it showered onto Mani. We asked her up for the curtain call, and in the photo I mentioned, she is standing on stage thrilled, surrounded by gods, goddesses, and angels, and sparkling from head to toe. (She didn't comb the confetti out of her hair for days!)

Fun with Mani in Baba-House, Poona

BABA-HOUSE

As you enter the main hall of Baba-House, Baba's family home in Poona, you see a big picture of Beloved Baba, a big picture (to His right) of Mehera, and a big picture (to His left) of Mani. On a couch under these three is a photo of Perinmai, Baba's sister-in-law, wife of His brother Beheram, right where she used to sit. You could certainly find the above three pictures inscribed on Perinmai's heart: she loved—just as Baba told her to—"First Me, then Mehera, then Mani, then Beheram, then your children."

Mani coming out of Baba's Room in Baba-House.

Mani felt at home in Baba-House, not only because she grew up there, but because the family were all completely Baba's and loved her deeply—and vice versa. After separating her completely from the family for years, in the 1960s Baba asked her "to look after the family . . . for My sake." Her heart carried out His request one hundred percent. And among the family, their focus was first Baba, then Mehera, then Mani, then one another.

Mani herself writes about her parents, Sheriarji and Shireenmai, in her book *God-Brother*. And they're all over Baba-House: in the main hall, brought alive in paintings by a Baba-artist of Father and Mother on either side of young Merwan; in the courtyard, where a chikoo tree planted by Sheriarji still gives fruit; in the well, from which, in Shireenmai's dream, goddesses came out to take baby Merwan away from her; in Baba's Room, where there is a formal photograph of Sheriarji and Shireenmai posing together.

As mentioned early on, in the corner of Baba's Room, a note handwritten by Mani tells us what Baba Himself said about His Room in Baba-House. Baba's brothers—Jal, Beheram, Adi Jr.—are hanging around in photos here and there. Then there's the TV and the kitchen and the cupboards and the dining room and bedrooms off to the side. In short, it's a family home—with a divine difference: it just happens that one of the children is God, and one of the bedrooms is a site of world pilgrimage!

After Baba dropped His body, His injunction to Mani to "look after the family" came into effect more than ever. So, among all of her other worlds—Mehera, Meherazad, Baba-lovers, the Trust—orbited the world of "the family."

She kept in close touch with everyone: her niece Gulnar and the Poona family by frequent phone calls; her brother Adi's family in England by frequent letters; and Adi's son, Dara, and Dara's wife, Amrit, and their children by personal contact. And they all visited Meherabad, Meherazad, and the Trust Office often, too.

I was often moved by the extra touches Mani put into looking after the family. I remember on several occasions she composed original songs for her twin nephews, Rustom and Sohrab, to sing on their Baba-tours in the West. She helped her brother Adi's family design and build a house in Ahmednagar. She helped her Poona family build one near Meherabad. She was consulted about everything and responded to everything, going not "the extra mile" but about 150 extra miles to give support and advice to any of them whenever wanted or needed. (Mani told Gulnar and Gulnar's husband, Jangu, that the day she went to Baba, the family should have ice cream, knowing how Gulnar loved it!) And her love and care was deeply appreciated and reciprocated.

But what I found most revealing of her heart's loyalty to the family was the way she defended Shireenmai and Shireenmai's natural, maternal love for Baba and the great price she paid in suffering to play the role of His mother.

After Baba dropped His body, Mehera, Mani, Goher, and Meheru continued to visit Poona in the Indian summer for three weeks. He set this up in 1969, when He told them "in March we march to Poona" (for the Great Darshan at Guruprasad). All year long the women looked forward to their holiday (for many years they also visited a nearby hill station, usually Panchgani, on the same trip). In Poona, they stayed in Bindra House with the Jessawala family for some years, and later on they stayed in Poona Club.

The holiday took a lot of planning. As the time approached, endless phone calls would fly back and forth between Mani in Ahmednagar and Gulnar in Poona, and Mani would laugh, "It's hard work getting ready to relax!" One of their Poona treats was an evening at Baba-House with the Irani neighborhood gang. A fond family memory is that Mehera particularly would want Baba's nephew Sheroo to sing a song to her. He was so shy about it, but Mehera kept on persuading him until he finally gave in. It was always a film song, and Mehera would giggle like a girl, very pleased. After he was finished she would comment, "He's childlike; he has a pure heart." The whole gang would then start up, and their joyous singing for Mehera raised that much-blessed roof.

In Mani's account of Mehera's reunion with Baba in May 1989, Mani gives a touching view of their Poona holiday in April, which turned out to be Mehera's last and the precursor to her going to Baba.

~ *Finale* ~

MEHERA'S PASSING

Next to Baba, Mani loved and served Mehera with all her heart. In the Indian summer of 1989, when Mehera began to weaken mysteriously, first having trouble with her speech and then with her balance and walking, Mani and the women were heartbroken. Mehera's reunion with Baba followed swiftly.

Mani wrote the account of Mehera's last weeks to share with the Baba-world at her little verandah desk in the days right after Mehera passed away. It was something that, despite her great grief, she knew she had to do. She had been struggling with the question of how to begin it when, among Mehera's things, she came across a little china box in the form of a panda, which contained a strip of paper on which was written a lovely and meaningful "fortune" for Mehera. The words in that "fortune" (described by Mani in her account) turned the key for Mani, and out poured the deeply moving account that follows.

MEHERA'S REUNION

Meherazad
25th May 1989

Dear Family,
A cable from Meherazad family dated 20th May 1989 carried the following news to Baba lovers round the world:

> BELOVED AVATAR MEHER BABA HAS TAKEN MEHERA HIS BELOVED UNTO HIMSELF ON 20 MAY 1989 MORNING STOP WHILE MEHERAS BODY IS BEING BURIED NEXT TO SAMADHI ON MEHERABAD HILL AS SPECIFIED BY BABA THE LIGHT OF

> MEHERAS PURE SUPREME LOVE FOR HER ONLY
> BELOVED WILL FOREVER ILLUMINE THE EARTH
> AND THE HEARTS OF HIS LOVERS EVERYWHERE
>
> — MANI AND ALL MEHERAZAD FAMILY —

The report on Mehera's health sent to Kitty-Margaret-Jane on 9th May 1989 served as a prelude to the following account of Mehera's final days:

Years ago, a Baba lover from the States sent us a batch of Fortune cookies which had a Baba-saying enclosed in each one. The little pink slip in the cookie which Mehera picked said: "The more you think of Me, the more you will realize My love for you."

This message from the Beloved, preserved by Mehera in a decorative little china box all these years, serves as a fitting opening to this account of the last weeks of Mehera's most precious life on earth in the highest role of God's Avataric Advent as Meher Baba. For the more we think of the period of Mehera's illness, the more we realize Baba's love for her, Baba's tender compassion in veiling her suffering when most needed, His saving her from a prolonged illness as He carried her swiftly through the last crucial week when each day brought on a new and humiliating binding to her freedom of movement and self-expression. Except for the great sharing in Baba's car accident in America in 1952, Mehera had rarely undergone a physical suffering, and even a mild pain or upset was difficult for her to bear. And so it was hard for us, her Companions, to watch her go through this ordeal at such a pace, and we couldn't help questioning as to why He should allow it to happen this way! But we fully realized later that Beloved Baba had planned and timed this momentous event perfectly, in His perfect Love for His Mehera.

His speed in the final days was such that Dr. Goher and Baba lover doctors and nurses helping her, as well as all of us from Meherazad and Meherabad surrounding her, were unable to catch up with it or think over it calmly. But His speed was compassion in disguise, the more swiftly to gather to Himself His beloved Mehera who had waited for Him for twenty years in bitter-sweet resignation to His Will.

Looking back we still cannot believe that so much happened so quickly at the last. In fact from the moment that a serious investigation was indicated, to the moment Mehera passed away from us, it was less than a week. On Sunday 14th [May] we took Mehera to Poona for a C.T. Scan at the up-to-date Medinova Diagnostic Centre, where it was discovered that Mehera had a large growth in the brain, resembling a tubercular tumour. What astounded the doctors was the absence of any of the symptoms that go with such a growth pressing on the brain—they shook their heads in disbelief when told she hadn't even had a headache! The next Sunday, we were saying goodbye to Mehera on Meherabad Hill, laying garlands and nets of fragrant flowers on a mound of earth by the side of the Beloved's Samadhi, which covered the beautiful form of Baba's Beloved Mehera.

A song I only remember the title of, "In how many ways does my Beloved love me," sings in my heart as I recall the days and nights that Mehera lay in her bedroom surrounded by the group of women destined to serve her night and day at this time. Every moment was a witness that Baba was with her. We could all but see Baba's hand pass tenderly over her face to ease the moments of pain and acute discomfort during the final days when her physical condition required medicated saline drips, and nasal feeding, etc. Each time, after a moment of resistance or painful look on her face, she would ease off into the slumber of a child, her expression calm and sweet, far away with Baba. As Arnavaz remarked, Baba had put a veil over Mehera's consciousness, so that she was not wholly aware of what was happening. She knew that she was ill, and that to begin with she could not be understood when she spoke and needed support to walk or stand —yet she seemed unaware of the enormity of all that was happening. Even when taken to Poona for the C.T. Scan, she accepted it calmly, knowing she had to go to the hospital for some purpose. She did not ask about it; she seemed a bit far away from all the events surrounding her, as if she was more and more with Baba and less and less with us. Mehera was never told that she had a tumour, but it broke our hearts. Later, it helped to soothe our bewilderment when we saw Baba's clear touch visible in one of the x-rays where the tumour appeared in the shape of a heart.

Just see how Baba had planned it all! The Medinova Diagnostic Centre in Poona where Mehera would have to be taken from Meherazad for the C.T. Scan was one that Goher and I had just visited while on our Poona holiday, at the invitation of Dr. Arvind Chopra, who wanted us to see the up-to-date place where he serves as consultant and to talk to some of the doctors and staff interested in hearing about Baba. We even saw a C.T. Scan being taken! So Goher knew exactly what it would involve when agreeing to take Mehera to Poona for the Scan. As I have said, the Scan showed a large growth in the brain, closely resembling tuberculosis. Full treatment for it was begun immediately, along with medication for a possible abscess. Mehera was dearly cooperative in taking the incessant medicines and tonics and pills, and without complaint submitted to the doctors' various tests and to all our nursing, but to make her take in enough nourishment became more and more difficult with time.

Mehera had never been a hearty eater, and all these years we would be constantly reminding her to please come to the table because if she wasn't hungry we were! So feeding her was one of our biggest problems during her illness, requiring much coaxing to make her accept some of the nutritious and delicious concoctions that Meheru made for her throughout the day. Later, before she was put on nasal feed, she was refusing even coconut water or buttermilk. Her gesture of refusal touched and delighted all who saw it: slightly turning her head away and raising her hand to hide her eyes, as though she could make the drink disappear by not looking at it!

But before all this happened, Baba had prepared for us a package of three happy weeks in Poona, the holiday that Mehera, Goher, Meheru, and myself took each year in April. It was only when we got there that we realized how tired we were after the long period of the Pilgrim Season, and how much we needed this change from our unbroken routine of nine months at Meherazad. And what a gem of a holiday He prepared for us! It was choreographed and conducted by Jangu and Gulnar (Baba's niece) along with others of the family, seeing to our every comfort and entertainment from dawn to night, sending us meals cooked by Perin for her Mehera-Radha and us, taking us for treats to the Sizzler and Ashok, and the Sagar Plaza with the glass elevator (lift) which Mehera much enjoyed riding in with us, arranging for a Victoria (horse-carriage) ride to Empress Gardens, *faluda* (a sweet drink) at the Badshah, and so on and on.

For our holiday, our favourite cottage in Poona Club was reserved for three weeks, and apart from our most popular relaxation of watching films on Video, we went for quiet walks in the old gardens where we used to go with Baba, visiting beloved Babajan's, and Guruprasad, and Meherjee's, and sharing old-time Baba memories at Eruch's home with his gracious mother and family; and the inevitable visit to BABA HOUSE where all the neighbouring Baba lovers came to honour Mehera and receive Baba's prasad from her. The Meher Kawwals, comprising of the Twins and the rest of the Alley gang, including children clapping to the music to their hearts' content, gave a resounding singing program. And all said they felt it to be the best of visits from Mehera, with Baba's presence pouring silently from her on all who had assembled in His Love.

An unexpectedly interesting visit we made during this holiday was (for the sake of a walk on its spacious verandah) to the Synagogue known to Indians as "Lal Deval" (Red Temple). We thought it remained as neglected as we had heard it to be in recent years since the exodus of Jews from India to Israel, and were surprised at the approach of a Jewish gentleman who opened the doors of the Synagogue for us, welcomed us inside and showed us round the lovely hall with its distinctive atmosphere and Presence. The Synagogue's redstone structure with the clock tower had served as a prominent landmark for Poona from before Baba's childhood days, and as a young boy Baba used to practice cycling in its grounds. During our summers in

Poona Baba always pointed out the Red Temple to us whenever we drove past it.

Yet another unexpected outing was to the Poona School & Home for the Blind, where free education and housing is provided to poor blind boys. Goher needed to get information about their sister school for blind girls, where she was keen to admit her little blind patient from Pimpalgaon, a 5-year-old girl who comes regularly to the Meher Free dispensary at Meherazad and wins Goher's heart each time by her cute smile and bright JAI BABA with folded hands!

Mehera walked over with Meheru and me to some of the boys seen in the grounds, to praise the roses in the little garden they tended and to ask about themselves. As more boys joined them, it was obvious that now was their turn to ask questions. Mehera made it clear that we were Meher Baba people from Ahmednagar, and that as Meher Baba is God He will help them and that they must always remember Him during their exams and at all times. When Goher came out of the superintendent's office, her hands were loaded with items made by the blind boys and available for sale at the school: sheets, dusters, and candles, some of which were later used for Mehera. How blessed are these children, and how significant that their candles were among those whose bright flames served to keep a continual vigil on Mehera's bed and in Baba's Room for 4 days after she left us.

And then there was that morning of shopping: our little visit to Kashmir House, and then to Bombay Dyeing to get material for curtains and cushion covers and Baba's gaadi cover. With her subtle sense of colour harmony, Mehera was always very particular about matching shades, and on this occasion once again we marveled at her perfect choice.

I relate these different facets of our holiday so you can see how normal was the range of Mehera's activities a few weeks before the serious condition of her health became evident.

Watching video films amused and interested Mehera a lot. Whenever we wished to awaken her from an extended nap, I would just turn on the TV and the start up noise which was like a steam engine would make Mehera sit up and walk over to watch what was coming on! Of course the most delightful video we saw was the "Frivolous Three"— our dear old-time companions Margaret, Kitty and Delia! And we couldn't get over the minor miracle of phone calls from Myrtle Beach to Poona Club! Kitty and Margaret talking from Myrtle Beach with Mehera, Meheru, Goher, and myself in our bedroom in Poona Club! Mehera spoke clearly on both calls, and happily Margaret's call was recorded—what turned out to be the last recording of Mehera's voice. Once again, Baba's timing was perfect —Margaret and Kitty, both so dear to Mehera, were able to converse with her not long before she passed away.

Mehera always looked forward to the evening "ice cream" visits from Gulnar and Mehernaz, sometimes accompanied by Eruch's sister Manu, on the private little lawn in front of our cottage. From here Mehera would watch at a distance the stream of people dressed in a variety of fashions and colours going in and out of the nearby library, or the large bullock cart rolling by with the regular load of ice for parties held at the Club. To the end of our stay, our ice cream sessions were followed by a regular little walk up and down the lawn before Arti. This was remembered by us with deep nostalgia on our return to Meherazad when we watched Mehera's physical movements becoming speedily restricted day by day—from walking by herself to being supported by others more and more, from being helped down the steps to being practically lifted down, to using Beloved Baba's little wheelchair for moving about indoors and for outdoors using the big one which we wheeled right into the TV room for a video session. She was ever happily ready to attend these film shows at any time—but by now we were not sure how much she took in.

Several times over the years I've heard Mehera relate how she told Baba she was getting forgetful, that she couldn't remember where she had put this or that, or the things she had to do. Baba said to her, "Don't worry. Remembering Me is what matters. It doesn't matter what else you forget, as long as you remember Me."

Remembering Baba was of course so natural for Mehera. But during this sickness, which we were first made aware of by the sudden and unnatural degree of her forgetfulness when she couldn't remember our names and failed to name simple objects most familiar to her, her remembrance of Him was strong and clear as a Church bell, surfacing from her heart to reach all who were with her. Not only was her Beloved's Name on her lips at every excuse, but she remembered every word of the Parvardigar Prayer and Bujave Nar Arti which we sang together in Baba's Room for as long as she was able to be moved about in her little wheelchair.*

The mention of Baba's Name or the sight of His pictures were reminders of Baba stories she had told others, and which were now being fed back to her by the ones tending to her.

---

* Elizabeth had also used this Baba-chair when she was last at Meherazad, always referring to it as her "throne."

It was as food for her heart, which in turn refreshed and nourished her body as could be seen by the glowing expression of interest and pleasure on her face. Nothing else won such response from her. Every day Mehera would look through the book of Baba's beautiful photos: LOVE PERSONIFIED, kissing each picture, and caressing it with her gentle hand. She was only His and only for Him, to the end.

Before her health took the serious and dramatic turn which confined her to bed totally, there was a happy spell of quiet days with Mehera, when her intimate companionship was enjoyed by the dear group of Residents from Meherabad and Meher Nazar tending to her every need, while she sat for long periods in her usual armchair on the verandah. Her sense of humour and flashes of teasing often caught her companions off guard and dissolved them into laughter, while her gentle sweetness seemed to radiate from every pore of her being.

As therapy for her aphasia, speech lessons were instituted, and Mehera's one-pointed attention in trying to relearn simple words was very touching. As Heather describes it: "She would concentrate so fixedly on trying to say 'cup' and come out with 'How extraordinary! I just can't get it!'" In each attempt invariably the word she would get first would be 'Baba'! With tenacity, Mehera did manage to relearn a few simple words, which pleased her very much and she would look forward to her lessons. Many Baba-lovers entertained Mehera at this time with their singing on tape. We played tapes of her favourite Baba songs, and also Indian favourites like Mirabai, Begum Akhtar, and others. Simple games like 'ludo' won giggles and smiles from her; and we would play animatedly, with Mehera taking her turn and watching the others' progress with much interest. In the evening, the trip across the garden to the TV room for TV sessions was a favourite event of the day—most favourite being the Arti sung together on the porch. Which is why at feeding time when we wished to arouse her from deep sleep we would resort to calling out "time for arti"—she always responded to it!

Later the picture kept changing quickly as though Baba was snapping His fingers to say "Hurry, hurry." A couple of instances will give you an idea of these startling changes in Mehera's condition:

Dr. Goher, sick with anxiety and responsibility, was so relieved by Dr. Arvind Chopra's daily directions by phone and his personal visits from Poona. The morning of 16th May, Tuesday, was a surprisingly good one when Arvind arrived and Mehera greeted him with a charming smile and said, "I am happy to see you." That same evening, Mehera closed her eyes to all external objects for all time and did not open them again till the final moment when her Lord and Beloved came to receive her.

Two days later, on Thursday 18th morning, when our Poona team drove over, Mehera clearly responded to Gulnar's greeting with a sweet smile and slight raising of eyebrows, which showed us she was aware of what was going on around her. Whereas the same evening, when the welcome medical team from Bombay and Ahmednagar arrived to help care for Mehera—doctors and nurses who had been with Baba as children and closely associated with Him from the early years—Mehera was entering a light coma.

We strove to hold her back from slipping into a deep coma. I kept talking to her, pleading that she see us—

"Mehera, open your eyes, Mehera darling please, open your eyes, see I am holding this beautiful picture of Baba before you." I would speak in Gujerati, and in Irani (Dari) which her much loved grandmother used to speak. But although a couple of times Mehera acknowledged my plea with the slightest movement of lips and brow, she did not open her eyes. As she would not or could not open them of her own volition, I tried to help her by lifting an eyelid, raising it with my little finger. Doing it to both the lids revealed eyes that were seeing but not looking at anything. When I let go of her delicate eyelids, they came down clumsily and haltingly over eyes now reserved for seeing only her Beloved, eyes which had thirsted too long for a sight of Him.

The night of Friday 19th gave some very anxious moments to the ones keeping vigil with her, but this fleeting experience did not in any way prepare us for what was to happen the following morning.

It began as a morning of "normal" activities. We heard no ringing of bells, felt no brushing of angel wings, to announce her dawning reunion with her Beloved that morning; but simply for a moment "Welcome to My World" bubbled over in my heart as I watched Mehera being given an alcohol rub and mild massage. Could I but see, He was surely standing beside her with open arms.

But we were not aware of the Moment's arrival until it was upon us. We were around Mehera, together singing the Beloved's Name as we often did. I was sitting by her side holding her hand, with the others of the women mandali close by. Through the waves of His Name-Song I could see the anguished face of Dr. Goher, and heard Dr. Meher Desai softly declare, "Her pulse is rapid and blood pressure is dropping." The Signal was clear—I pressed to Mehera's forehead her favourite picture of Baba, as well as His Sandals, while with one voice we all kept loudly singing Meher Baba, Meher Baba. And with one heart we decided that when the Moment arrived we would resonantly call out seven times "AVATAR MEHER BABA KI JAI."

With the great sense of urgency now upon us, we sent for our Meherazad men mandali to come over. They streamed in and stood with folded hands, joining the old faithful servants who were quietly gathered by the door, and Dr. Arvind whom Jangu had driven over from Poona in perfect time to be by Mehera during her last moments.

We who had shared in the miracle of Baba's love through Mehera, did not anticipate any unusual revelation to happen at the last. When it happened, it was as a brilliant flash of lightning that we were totally unprepared for!

Mehera was lying on her side, and my face was near to hers at the time. Suddenly, as though the shutters she had kept locked all these days were flung open, Mehera opened her eyes in a swift strong movement, completely and totally open, the circles of the irises fully in view. It was as if the heavens had opened to welcome Him. Her bright shining eyes had an unfathomable look in them, with a drop of moisture on the outer corners of both eyes, teardrops of joy. Each of us witnessing this powerful moment knew she was gazing on the beauty and glory of her Lord and Beloved.

Then she let the lids down with amazing ease, took in a sharp breath, and nodded her head in two graceful movements like a queen making a regal adieu to the assembly.

Mehera had gone to Baba.

It was 9:45 in the morning of 20th May 1989.

"AVATAR MEHER BABA ki JAI" called out loudly seven times by us all, was a song to Mehera's Joy of Reunion, and a testimony to our tears of parting. In that fleeting moment, all her pain and stress, all her waiting and yearning, was wiped away by Him. From then on, a gently happy smile adorned her face and joy streamed out from her slightly parted eyelids. This expression of her happiness was witnessed by all 'til our very last glimpse of her.

In the bedroom's privacy, Goher and I washed Mehera's body with rose water and dressed her in a dusky pink skirt and flowered blouse, framing her face with a soft mauve pink chiffon scarf. Mehera's smile reflected her ecstasy. Her face and hands took on the eternal youth of the Madonna as depicted in the holy images. She looked so young and sweet that I was reminded of the Mehera I knew at Nasik in 1932—the year which began Mehera-Mani's continual companionship in a link unbroken for fifty-seven years.

In Heather's words:

"Throughout the day, Mehera's body lay on her bed in her room, as Baba lovers from Ahmednagar, Poona, and nearby places came to pay their last homage. A most beautiful smile was on Mehera's face, an air of purity and deep serenity around her. The women mandali, whose grief can scarcely be imagined, received each one graciously—handling the situation with courage as they had when Baba passed away.

"It was Mehera's very strongly expressed wish that she not be photographed after she passed away. She wanted to be remembered as she was in life. I doubt if even a camera could have captured the radiance of her face in her last repose, the sublime peace and triumph of a supremely loved being!

"Ice coolers and fans kept the room cool throughout the day, despite the intense summer heat outside. Near sundown Mehera's body was transferred onto a stretcher and carried by a group of women to Baba's bedroom for a final darshan. Then she was carried across her garden to Mandali Hall, arriving there just at sundown, as the full moon was rising over the trees and bushes and flowers of her beloved Meherazad."

Mehera's stretcher was placed before Beloved Baba's chair, and there her body rested until morning, surrounded by large blocks of ice which gave an ascetic touch, a feeling of the Himalayas reflecting her supreme purity.

A Baba lover recollects, "A number of Baba people had gathered and were sitting quietly around Mehera. My heart skipped a beat because to me she looked alive and present; not like someone sleeping, but like someone resting fully awake with their eyes closed. Mani, Meheru, Goher, Arnavaz, Katie, were sitting by her side. Although in deep grief, they were generous to share with others an account of Mehera's last weeks. It was all so intimate, yet so informal, often there were tears but also there was laughter. Mehera seemed to be participating in all that happened. The vigil lasted all night, full and deep, like Amartithi at night. It will ever remain vivid in my memory."

The all-night vigil in Mandali Hall was like a darshan, filled with Baba's Presence, vibrating with His beloved Name sung together in varied tunes, as well as other songs loved by Mehera. And there were the still silences, when the sound of the whirring fans seemed to say: this is goodbye, goodbye, goodbye. But above all, it was a reminder of words given by God, Meher Baba: "It is all a going forward, forward, always a going forward."

I had taken some rose petals from the Beloved's Body as He lay in the crypt of His Samadhi at Meherabad in 1969. I had taken them for Mehera, and kept them with me all these years for just this moment in the galaxy of time. At one point during the vigil in Mandali Hall, I stepped forward and gently placed the rose petals near to Mehera's heart.

One of the close ones gazing at Mehera's face at the time, was overwhelmed with amazement to see it flush with happiness at the touch of these precious petals from her Beloved.

As 21st May dawned, so did our awareness that the time had come to prepare for Mehera's final journey to Meherabad. The men mandali were seeing to the many practical details involved in arranging for the funeral, and we continued to see to our various duties by Beloved Baba's help and grace. But when I try to review the consecutive events of that Morning, the screen of my memory is hazy. I'm therefore very thankful for the following report from Heather:

"It was 6:00 a.m. by the clock in Mandali Hall. The atmosphere was very solemn, the women mandali approaching Mehera one by one for a final caress, covering her hands and feet with kisses, and apparently asking her to convey their private messages to Baba. Mehera was suddenly Queen, and the occasion was of universal significance. Artis were sung to Baba. Mehera's body was transferred to her coffin, and covered with a lovely pink sari. Mani and Goher garlanded her with a garland of roses from Meherazad's rose garden—which had been specially created for Mehera's pleasure of offering them to her Beloved at Prayer time in His Room each morning and evening.

"At 6:45 a.m. our caravan of seven cars left Meherazad for Meherabad Hill. On the Hill were gathered about one hundred lovers from distant places who were able to make it in time. The coffin was placed on the Sabha Mandap for the convenience of Baba lovers awaiting their turn to bow to Mehera. Wonderment showed on their faces as they gazed at Mehera. Still smiling with her lips and eyes, Mehera looked unbelievably beautiful, and we heard someone remark, 'No artist or sculptor could ever capture such beauty.'

"From there Mehera was carried into the Beloved's Tomb and placed at the Feet of her Lord, to the exact place where she has bowed down a thousand times, while we recited Prayers and Arti. All around Mehera's form, Mani scattered some of the earth that had covered Beloved Baba's body in 1969, and was saved by her for the unknown day and moment which had now arrived.

"After this last obeisance, Mehera's coffin was carried outside to the colorful mandap (tent) shading the pit that was so lovingly dug and prepared to receive its most precious burden. Mehera's coffin, now a mound of fresh fragrant flowers from loved ones present and absent, was lowered in the grave next to the Beloved's Samadhi as specified by Him long ago, at His righthand as she had the privilege to be all her life. Shouts of AVATAR MEHER BABA ki JAI went out in waves and circled Meherabad Hill in a garland of obeisance from hearts round the world.

"The women mandali came forward to glimpse the coffin for the last time—no words can describe their love and grief. Some more of the earth that had been around Baba's dear body in 1969 was gently tossed upon it. It was the first earth to cover Mehera's coffin. Mani also found herself distributing pinches of it into eager hands so that most of them shared in showering this precious earth on her coffin in the grave, along with a shower of flowers in tribute to Mehera's great love for her Beloved, which God lovers will strive for and minstrels will sing of for timeless centuries.

"Not long afterward the men, women, and children were filling bucketfuls of earth from nearby mounds to pour into the grave. As the iron pans went from hand to hand, Baba's Twin nephews and His 'Irani gang' from Poona and Bombay led the crowd in lively ghazals and songs. Everyone began singing as the many hearts and hands joined together in joyful, deepest remembrance of Baba's most loved Mehera. When the grave was finally filled and smoothed over with soft earth, the women mandali placed a sparkling fresh net of flowers over it. When their AVATAR MEHER BABA ki JAI rose to the skies, someone drew our attention to the time—9:45 a.m.—exactly 24 hours to the minute from the time Mehera went to her Beloved the day before, on 20th May."

20th May 1989. A date made immortal in the lives of Baba lovers, to receive a permanent place in their hearts and calendars, and to be observed by Baba families, groups, and countries everywhere. On Indian calendars, 20th May was a red-letter day declaring a national holiday in honour of Buddha Purnima ["full moon"], the day of Lord Buddha's birth, also said to be the day of His enlightenment and of His passing away. 20th May also happens to be the date of our Sister-companion Naja going to Baba seven years ago.

From past experience we find ourselves expecting special Baba-events to be marked by a shower of rain, or at least a sprinkle. There was no such outpouring from the skies on the momentous occasion of Mehera's funeral. The showers were of silent tears from the hearts of His World family, tears of love raining on us in a torrent of cables expressing joy for Mehera, sorrow for us. Many wished to rush over and be by our side at this time, but refrained at our request, respecting our need to be by ourselves for a while—till Meherazad welcomes His lovers from 1st July.

Our beginning this new phase of life without Mehera's physical companionship requires much adjustment and time, but we bow to His Will and we know that He will continue to conduct every act of His daily drama in our lives and to prompt us from behind the stage whenever we fumble. Truly, as He has repeatedly assured us, HE does His own work!

We also feel deeply for all Baba lovers who will miss seeing her, and the ones who did not see Baba in His physical form but received so much of Him through Mehera's companionship and love. One of them expresses it so well in a little picture card depicting Spring.

"Jai Baba! Our hearts are with you all during this time which now marks an end to a very precious period for those of us who never met Baba physically. We feel so grateful to Baba to have met His beloved Mehera and witness through her example how He ought to be loved. Thank-you Baba!"

In her message for you all, of last July, Mehera says:

"When each of you tries 100 percent to do as Baba wants He is surely near you helping you. To do so is often not easy, but with Baba's help it is not impossible. Beloved

Avatar Meher Baba's Advent on earth as man is to help us on our spiritual journey. Know that He does help and guide us on the path to the Goal, which is to Himself. And by offering us His Daaman to hold, Beloved Baba is making the journey so much easier for us. So hold fast to Meher's Daaman with both hands and love Him more and more."

And here's what Mehera says to her Beloved. During the 20 long years of absence from Him, Mehera sometimes expressed her love and longing for Him in lines scribbled on odd scraps of paper. They are variations of the same sweet refrain from her heart:

> "Oh Baba my darling come to me—Come back to me sweet love. O how I miss you—When will I see you and hold you. I love you and I know you love me. My heart's love is all for you. I will be true to your love for me. Come, we'll be together for ever and ever."

The wish of a pure heart is fulfilled.

And just as the song of the Indian koyal (bird) heard on a summer's day heralds the coming of rain, Mehera's eternal reunion with her Beloved was proclaimed by several dreams a few days previously. These dreams were dreamt by Baba-folk in different parts of the world, but were fashioned from the same material, depicting the JOY of Mehera's sublime reunion with her Divine Beloved: Mehera radiant in a bridal gown, Mehera beside a flower-bedecked bridal car, Mehera seated among soft swirls of pink lace in some ethereal place, a voice announcing it is Mehera's wedding day, a big gathering of people celebrating the happy event, and so on.

We can imagine the celestial Celebration, the music and singing and dancing, unseen and unheard by us, but amazingly revealed by Hafiz, Baba's most favourite Persian poet. When two Baba-lovers in the States had opened at random the book of Hafiz' ghazals on 13th May for a message about Mehera, they both independently arrived at the same answer. The ghazal they opened to is entitled "Dance of Life," and signifies an outburst of Mehera's ecstasy, as would be expressed by clashes of joyous cymbals, singing of angel's choirs, and rapturous dancing in Nataraja's Court:

"DANCE OF LIFE"

"Waiting. Straining to hear—your voice
       that I may rise
I am heaven's dove that from the earthly cage will rise.
If I am bid but to be your slave
       I gladly shall foreswear
Dominion over worldly things as now I rise.
Let the rain fall from your cloud of grace,
       oh Lord;
Before, to dust I would be changed—I rise.
Bring a minstrel to my grave and a bottle of good wine.
       Your fragrant presence
Shall lift me dancing full of joy as I rise.
Hold high your lordly stature that I may see
       You draw me nigh.
With clapping hands I leave this life, and I rise.
Though I am old yet in a night—
       from your embrace

> In Dawn's new light a youth will rise.
> On the day that I die, a glimpse of you may I behold
> and, as Hafiz,
> From Life's desire leap into eternity, and I will rise!"[4]

AVATAR MEHER BABA ki JAI!
AVATAR MEHER BABA ki JAI!
AVATAR MEHER BABA ki JAI!

Mani

Mani and others offering garlands with love at Mehera's shrine.

A GOING FORWARD

We all felt that for Mani, Goher, Meheru, and her other close ones, losing Mehera was in some way like losing Baba all over again. I got a little insight into Mani's grief when she quoted the poet Keats in a letter to a friend soon afterwards:

> To know the change and feel it
> when there's none to heal it,
> nor numbed sense to steel it . . .

After Mehera passed away, Mani received a beautiful card, full of empathy for Mani's sadness. She asked me to write the sender, a mutual friend, the following thoughts in reply:

> "We must think of Mehera's passing as a fulfillment and not an end—as [her nephew] Sheroo said, sitting in the Trust Office with Mani, 'Manifui, everything will be fine! Baba's completed a great work!' But most of all, as Mani and Goher and they all remind themselves, how long Mehera waited for this reunion, how much she longed for it, and how dearly she earned it. The last 20 years were so hard for her, but she went ahead, doing her best for Baba. Mani says, 'Now we cannot begrudge her her happiness.' Thinking of her happiness keeps them going. Mani says, 'We have to draw on her happiness. That's what I do when I am low. Yes, sometimes it overwhelms, but we must think of her.' And lastly, Mani so beautifully reminds us that from Baba's perspective it's all just a going forward, and in the play of creation from the timeless beginning, how many eons and ages have passed, lifetimes and lifetimes, and life goes on (here Mani used Baba's graceful gestures) like a wave rolling on and on. Now we have to do what life and creation and consciousness are all doing—going forward towards the Goal."

Mani herself designed Mehera's shrine (and the shrines of all the women mandali next to Baba's Samadhi) along with the resident architect. Its special place on Baba's right-hand side, right next to His Samadhi, was chosen by Baba Himself.

CONTINUING ON TOWARDS REUNION

Mani lived seven years after Mehera. One day, four years after Mehera passed away, I mentioned something to Mani about my stepmother's ongoing grief at the loss of my father. Mani said, yes, she understood, she felt that way about Mehera. It didn't get easier over time; it seemed to get harder. Then she added, "You don't get over it; but you get through it."

Soon after Mehera went to Baba, Mani developed heart trouble, and I always felt that Mehera's going had broken her heart.

With her parasol at Meherabad.

To me, she seemed to grow more radiant as the years went by, more loving and caring. It was as if all the love she had kept for Mehera now poured out onto His lovers. As if she felt she did not have much more time, and she wanted to give all she could. We knew she did not expect to live to be 80.

During these years she continued on as the Trust's chairman, attending the office now three days a week (and two in the last years), and spending three days a week with pilgrims in Meherazad. In the early 1990s, as mentioned before, she wrote the book of her childhood stories, *God-Brother*.

. . .

And she continued to write songs, most memorably "The Glory of Love," a song for Mehera on Mehera's birthday the year she passed away. It has a number of versions; Mani sent the lyrics out to Baba-singers around the world, who brought their own melodies to the song. The words show a little of what Mehera was to the women mandali:

> *Gentle breath of His mercy,*
> *Song of His silence pure,*
> *Beat of His Universal Heart . . .*

And what they felt without her:

> *Now we are out in the open*
> *In the strong unshaded Sun,*
> *The wings of good fortune protect us*
> *For the Love of our Beloved One.*

Life went on—and then suddenly everything changed. On November 27, 1995, Dr. Goher sent out a circular to Baba-lovers that began:

> As many Baba-lovers know, Beloved Baba's sister Mani has not been in good health for some months. As she herself cheerfully puts it, "The bird is singing away, but the cage is in need of repairs."
>
> Her recent health problems began about eight months ago, when Mani suddenly developed a "foggy" sensation in her head accompanied by difficulties with her balance and walking.

They thought at first that it was due to her cardiac medication, but finally determined that Mani had normal pressure hydrocephalus, or NPH, in which there is an increase in the cerebrospinal fluid in the ventricles of the brain, causing pressure on the brain.

It was a great shock to everyone, especially in Meherazad and

Meherabad. How could Mani be ill? She was so strong, so full of life! It was unimaginable. Because of the fuzziness she felt in her head and general weakness, she had to withdraw from her many activities for some time, and everyone keenly felt the absence of her wisdom and care.

As Goher's circular went on to say, on November 21, 1995, Mani had an operation in Poona in which a shunt was successfully inserted from the ventricle in the brain to the abdomen. After two and a half weeks in the Poona hospital, Mani was able to return to Meherazad. All the messages, gifts, and cards sent from Baba-lovers touched her very much. In response, she wrote a little poem:

Mani recuperating at Meherazad.

> *Like a shower of rose petals,*
> *your thoughts and prayers for me*
> *have carried the fragrance of His Love*
> *to heal me tenderly.*

Mani wrote Jane Haynes a little story about how Baba helped her get through her ordeal in the hospital:

Meherazad
12-12-95

Very dear Jane,

During the 2½ weeks I was in hospital in Poona, Baba showed in many little ways that He was with me all the time. One incident I write here for you my sister, knowing it will hold most special interest for you. It concerned a personal vanity—mine of course.

When the shunt was to be inserted in the scalp,

I believed that only a limited area around the spot would be shaved for the purpose. The usual procedure for the surgeon was to shave the entire head, but when he heard from our Dr. Arvind that I was apt to be sensitive to becoming totally 'bald' he agreed to the partial shave.

Just a short while later I felt a strong conviction that I was holding out on Baba by doing this, that you don't deal with The Beloved in halves, when you give yourself to Him you give wholly.

I sent word to the surgeon requesting a full shave, as I was opting for a totally bald head for him to work on. The hospital barber was immediately sent up to my room, with his big pair of scissors and long unsheathed blade and set to work shearing me. My thoughts were of Beloved Baba and Mehera.

Meheru and Shelley were with me and I heard Meheru say "look at the barber's watch". I thought "how crazy, here I am going through this moment with Baba, and here she is asking me to look at the man's watch!" while his hands fluttered all over and around my head as he wielded his blade. When Meheru repeated her request, the barber helped by stopping his work for a moment and holding up his wrist for me to see – his watch revealed what became for me a message from Baba.

The face of the watch bore no figures but was fully covered by a beautiful coloured picture of Jesus Christ, a school favourite of mine called "the Sacred Heart of Jesus"! You can imagine what this meant to me!

I had no doubt that while the barber's hands moved over my head, it was Beloved Baba as Jesus blessing me – Yes, Baba was keeping watch over me.

(signed) Mani

. . .

But even after the operation, poor Mani was not freed from her suffering. Incredibly and against all odds, the first shunt failed, which amazed her surgeons. She had to have a second operation to replace it. On February 8, 1996, Mani again entered the hospital in Poona.

Around that time, Mani wrote a little piece, "On the Topic of Suffering," a reflection on her recent ordeal. She wanted it printed in a Baba-magazine. I feel that she gave this out to Baba-lovers to help them digest and deal with the questions and doubts that naturally come up when one faces great suffering, to help them stay close to Baba through their own ordeals and see His compassion and support within their pain.

On the Topic of Suffering

From the time I was little I knew that suffering, like everything else in creation, comes from God. I noticed how much suffering my loved ones had to go through in one way or another, especially my close family.

Later I would wonder why the good people I knew received more suffering while the not-good people I knew got away with whatever they did. The answer came from within me that suffering must surely be a very good thing, such a good thing that God would want to share it with His special ones. I asked Father about it, and he said, "Never question God's Love and Wisdom my child, suffering is a passing thing given to you for your lasting benefit."

When you belong to the Lord, He takes over all that is yours—your failures, your victories, your joys and your sorrows, to work with as He wishes. With all the Baba lovers that we know of going through all the suffering that we hear of, it is not easy to see all the compassion that we are assured of. His unseen compassion is spoken of by His great lovers in the past, and illustrated by a Perfect Master in a simple analogy of [the] village potter.

You may have been among one of the groups accompanying Eruch on a tour of Pimpalgaon Village in the old days when he took Baba-lovers around the village. One of the favourite sights was the village potter at work making a pot on a primitive wheel turned by hand. While the clay is whirling around on the wheel, the potter is shaping the pot by whacking it with a wooden mallet. As his right hand is visibly raining these blows on the outside of the pot, his left hand is inside the pot, unseen, silently supporting and upholding it so that it does not break.

Thus a Perfect Master illustrates God's unseen compassion.

Avatar Meher Baba ki Jai !!!

–Mani

Before her first brain surgery in November 1995, Mani had asked Aloba to consult the Divan of Hafiz to see what Hafiz had to say about her operation. As mentioned earlier, there is an Irani custom of consulting the Divan, known as "taking a fal," that Baba Himself practiced on occasion. Aloba was the one who would consult the Divan for Him.

So, when Mani asked, Aloba prayed to Baba and opened his Persian edition of the Divan to ghazal number 224. Aloba translated it and showed it to Mani, and later to Goher and Bal Natu. He told them all that it was not a hopeful ghazal; it was a farewell ghazal. And he privately mentioned to Balaji that it portended a final farewell.

Although Mani survived the ordeal of the two brain surgeries, Hafiz's prediction came true. Despite the fact that her second shunt seemed to be working, her health continued to decline over the Indian summer of 1996. She had a lot of mysterious abdominal pain, and despite numerous treatments urged on her by Goher, she seemed to only get worse.

THE DREAM BOOK

Mani returned to Meherazad from her second brain operation in time for Baba's Birthday. Her visits to the Trust Office had stopped after her surgeries, and when the pilgrim season ended, she made her usual hot-season visit to Poona with Goher and Meheru "for a change." But it was not a restful visit, because Mani's pain continued.

Back in Meherazad after Poona, she carried on with her usual home routine, and also began spending some time each day reviewing chapters of a book written by a Baba-lover. It was May, it was really hot, and Mani was really uncomfortable.

One day, in the middle of this rather difficult review project, Mani suddenly blurted out to me, "Here I am doing someone else's book. What about the book I want to do?"

"Your dream book, Mani?"

"Yes!"

"Well, let's do it!"

Snap-closed goes the folder on "someone else's book" (which she eventually did finish reviewing), open goes the notebook for dictation, and away goes Mani into her world of dreams.

It always struck me as funny that when she finished *God-Brother,* her book of childhood stories, and people wrote asking her for stories of her later life, Mani always said, "No, I won't write about that. There's no end to it. If I ever write another book, it will be about my Baba-dreams."

As we've seen, Mani loved dreams; loved to tell her dreams to people, loved to hear other people's dreams. If someone had a dream of Baba, Mani always wanted to know all about it. She had started dreaming of God when she was seven, so her dream life had an early start. Most of her significant dreams she told to Baba. And sometimes in the morning He would ask her if she had had a dream the night before.

So now in Meherazad, in May, out poured the dreams, the early dreams, the dreams she told to Baba, the Baba-dreams and Mehera-dreams, the Babajan-dreams and God-dreams, and a few odd dreams that had deep feelings attached.

After she dictated a dream, I would type it up and read it back to her. (She had written *God-Brother* by hand in pencil, but now she was too uncomfortable to write herself.)

We could see that despite her pain, the shaping up of the dream book interested her. But we didn't know how much until one day, deep in the hot heart of May. The morning dreams were typed and placed by the sofa chair so she could hear them after tea. It was naptime. As Mani was still so unwell, Goher had stressed to her and everyone else that it was essential for Mani to rest. (There were plenty of side comments and askance glances at the activity evoked by the dream-book project!)

One of Mani's dreams, "Baba, Please Don't Wake Me Up!," told and illustrated in Dreaming of The Beloved.

So, it was naptime and Mani was resting. Goher was resting, too, on her bed nearby the sofa chair. Suddenly, out of the corner of my eye, I saw Mani clandestinely tiptoeing past Goher to the sofa chair. She sat down and quietly picked up the dream papers and started going through them. I went over to her, horrified. "But, Mani," I whispered, "you should rest! We can do this later!"

She looked at me very seriously and whispered back, "You can help me or not, Heather, but I have to do this. I feel a push."

From that day, she worked on it as much as she could (and so did I!). In the end, she had twenty-three dreams done. A few people commented that it should be twenty-four dreams—twenty-four was a round number, two times twelve. They were ignored. She had twenty-three, and twenty-three it would be.

The morning before the book drafts were to be sent to the publisher, Mani greeted everyone with a huge grin. "I had it! I just had the twenty-fourth dream!" And it was a beauty: a dream of Baba and Mehera sitting together on Mehera's bed in Mehera-Mani's room, handing Mani an exquisite box tied up with a ribbon. She didn't know what was inside, but she knew it was something wonderful.

The dream ended with Mani kneeling before Baba and Mehera, gazing at her two beloveds, cradling her precious, mysterious gift.

I typed up the dream, Mani reviewed it, and we sent it off in the packet to the publisher.

The very next day, Mani went to the doctor in Ahmednagar for a sonogram in an attempt to diagnose her pain. The sonogram showed a large mass in her abdomen that sent her off to Poona for further tests and the fatal diagnosis of cancer. There would never have been another time for the dream book.

LAST DARSHAN

On May 20 of that year, Mani had made a great effort to go to Meherabad with the other women mandali in the sweltering summer heat for Mehera's Day, the seventh anniversary of Mehera's reunion with Baba. During the women's visit to Poona a month earlier they had gone for darshan at Babajan's shrine. Quite unexpectedly the caretaker there had presented Mani with a brilliant green and red cloth that had been on Babajan's tomb. It was shiny, satiny green with red borders and silver braid, very beautiful. Mani had brought it home with her and sent it to Meherabad to be placed on Baba's Samadhi on Mehera's Day.

There was a small gathering of people at the Samadhi when Mani and the women arrived. She had to be helped to stand and to walk, but she turned a loving smile on those waiting outside the Samadhi as she went in. After the prayers and arti, as Mani stepped out toward Mehera's shrine, she paused, murmuring, "*This* is restoration; *this* is rejuvenation," and then— gazing out on the banyan tree and the wide fields and hills beyond—"I don't feel like leaving." Very slowly and with difficulty she bowed and kissed Mehera's shrine with great tenderness.

After the women had gone and I was walking down the Hill, I looked back. The seven-colored flag was flying from the tower, and in the intense heat the atmosphere was very bright, solemn and yet strangely charged, full of feeling. I, too, didn't feel like leaving. No one knew it then, but this was Mani's last darshan at Baba's Samadhi, on her darling Mehera's seventh anniversary, with Babajan's cloth on His tomb.

Mani had a dream in early June of that year right before she went to the hospital. In the dream she was laughing, singing, and dancing, and she felt as if she were soaring upwards. The next morning, Mani went over to the men's side of the Meherazad compound, as usual. As Bal Natu remembered that morning: "She seemed in an especially buoyant mood and her manner was as it had been in years past. She sang a Marathi line from an *abhanga* [Marathi devotional song] she had heard that morning on the radio, three or four times by the window of Pendu's room while sitting in Begum [her electric cart], which she had been using for the past year. In a very cheerful mood she also swayed gracefully from side to side and moved her arms as if dancing while she sang. The transliteration of the line is '*Nirgunache bhetisathi Ahlow Saguna Sange*', which means, 'To meet the Attributeless (Formless) One, I have come with all my attributes (Form).'"

MANI'S REUNION

On June 12, 1996, Mani went to the hospital in Poona for the third time in eight months, for tests and possible treatment for the mass shown in the Ahmednagar sonogram.

On June 26, Dr. Goher wrote to Baba-lovers:

> As I wrote earlier, the initial test results revealed a tumor in Mani's abdominal cavity and further investigations of this tumor show that it is malignant. After careful review by Mani's physicians both in Pune and Bombay, it has been determined that the type and extent of cancer she has will not be responsive to conventional medical treatment. Therefore surgery and chemotherapy are not indicated....
>
> In view of this I have started Mani on a program of alternative medicine which has been highly recommended by Baba-family members and practitioners....

> Mani remains ever resigned to her 'Divine Doctor's' Will, as Beloved Baba goes on showing in so many ways each day His infinite love and care for her. . . .

In the hospital in Poona, Mani had yet another dream of Baba. In this one, He appeared resplendent before her, and she garlanded His beautiful form from head to foot. As soon as Goher came for a visit, Mani asked that on Goher's return to Meherazad, she purchase a Rs. 100 garland and garland Baba's chair in Mandali Hall from head to foot. This Goher did, along with all the men and women mandali.

Recently, as I looked through notes I jotted down from those weeks in the hospital, I found the following recollection. Every morning at the hospital, Mani, with Meheru and others attending on Mani, would say the Parvardigar and Beloved God prayers, and in the evening would say the Repentance Prayer and sing the Gujerati Arti, following the practice of the Meherazad ladies. One evening, when Meheru was out attending to some work for Mani, Mani began the evening prayers. Sitting on her bed, her back to us, Mani started to sing the Gujerati Arti. That day, or the day before, she had received the diagnosis of inoperable, terminal cancer.

As I stood behind her, I could not see Baba's picture on the bedside table that she was facing. I saw only her back, as she sat on the edge of the bed, rounded at the shoulders like Baba. She had her hands folded together, and when she started to sing, somehow the rest of us knew that we should remain silent.

I had heard Mani sing the Gujerati Arti many times, parts of it for people, all of it with the other women mandali in the Samadhi or at Meherazad. But I had never heard her sing it like this. As she sang, her voice was the voice of an angel. That's what I thought as I listened: this is the voice of an angel. Not high, not a soprano, but pure, so pure, full of love and adoration, one-pointedly absorbed, the most beautiful singing I had ever heard. She had hardly spoken all day, but had remained absorbed within herself since getting the news. From her place of silence came pouring out this pure adoration.

Since an allopathic treatment was no longer indicated and alternative therapies could be continued at home, Mani returned to Meherazad in the beginning of July, as she deeply wished to do.

Another little memory, from the day we left the hospital: I was to sit in the front seat of the car that was bringing Mani home from Poona. Naturally, I was heartbroken, as we all were, to be bringing Mani back in this condition and with this prognosis. She was sitting behind me in the car, and just as the car pulled out of the hospital driveway, she reached forward and patted me encouragingly on the shoulder. In her state, in her situation, she was encouraging me.

> *Nothing in me is mine,*
> *Everything belongs to You*
> *Having given You what is Yours,*
> *What concern is it of mine.*

In her last illness, Mani often quoted these lines, translated from a Hindi poem by Kabir, the Perfect Master poet. As Meheru recalled, Mani completely accepted Baba's charge of her and never questioned what she was going through.

Back at Meherazad, Mani remained in the house under the care of Dr. Goher, the other women mandali, and helpers. This period of her illness lasted about two months, and on August 19, 1996, in her room in Meherazad, Mani went to Baba.

The following message from Eruch and the mandali was sent out to Baba-lovers:

> Mani Sheriar Irani, dearest sister of Avatar Meher Baba, soared triumphantly into her God-Brother's open arms on

19 August, 1996, at 7:01 a.m. to be reunited with Him whom she adored with all her heart and served with joyous dedication.

The time had come for her darling God-Brother and Lord to free His beautiful nightingale sister to be with Him evermore. As Mani wrote to the Baba-family recently, the bird was singing sweetly, but the cage was in need of repair. Now the Eternal Beloved has released His little sister from the cage of illusion to fly freely in His eternal domain and presence.

The Ancient One, whom Mani served faithfully and tirelessly till the end, called Mani His true sister in service. Whatever the duty Baba entrusted to her, whether it be as close companion to His beloved Mehera, scribe to the West, or Chairman of the Avatar Meher Baba Trust, Mani ceaselessly endeavoured to please her Beloved Lord. Her exemplary life shall be a guiding star to all Baba's lovers.

Mani not only leaves behind generations of Baba-lovers whose hearts have been deeply touched by Baba's Love through personal contact with her, but an invaluable legacy to the generations to come of a life lived in His company, shared through stories, songs and wisdom, which will continue to light the way for all His lovers until He comes again.

We shall miss our dearest Mani whose lively presence and loving company, sparkling vivacity, warmth, unique wit and humour shall ever remain alive in our memories. We, Mani's lifelong companions, join our worldwide Baba family in saluting her unparalleled life of supreme love and total dedication as sister to the Lord of the Universe, Beloved Avatar Meher Baba.

AVATAR MEHER BABA KI JAI!!!

=Eruch, Goher and all Meherazad
men and women mandali

This evening, August 19th, at 6:00 p.m., Mani's body will be cremated at Meherabad and after some time her ashes will be interred on Meherabad Hill on the left side of Beloved Baba's Samadhi (Baba's left, towards the East) according to Baba's express wish.

At a remembrance gathering in Meherazad a few days later, Meheru spoke very movingly about Mani's weeks in the hospital and at Meherazad just before she passed away. The following are her remarks from that gathering:

Baba's dear ones gathered here today, we greet you with Jai Meher Baba!

Our Beloved One, the Highest of the High, the Omnipotent and Omnipresent is the One who brought us all here, He is the One who will ever be our friend and our guide all the way on our journey Home to Him.

For His beloved sister Mani as it was for His beloved Mehera, the journey has been completed and they are in blissful reunion with their Beloved Lord. For the moment in all our hearts there is a bottomless grief for our loss that only His Love sustains and helps us to bear.

I have known them both all my life, and was fortunate that all my adult life with Baba I was permitted to be so close to Mehera and Mani. It was a privilege and honour for me to be with Mani and help care for her in her time of need. They were not always painful times for us in the hospital. Baba's and Mehera's love was around us, and those precious times when we talked of them and remembered them or sang to them—especially since Mani initiated the singing—are for me truly beautiful memories imprinted on my heart for always.

And we have felt all the love and good wishes and prayers of our Baba family the world over pouring in on her behalf in oceanic waves. He holds the key and it was so easy for Him to turn it on her behalf. But Baba's ways are unfathomable, and He who is all Merciful and Eternally Benevolent sees so much beyond our limited vision into far infinity. No matter how much we pleaded and prayed for His Mani's recovery, His is always the last say—the only say, as it has always been. And this Mani wholly accepted.

Mani was so courageous and cheerful, yet at one point in the hospital when her spirits were very low, she said in a small voice while sitting on her bed, "If this is what He wants of me, I must have Baba on one side of me and Mehera on the other," pointing to either side.

I immediately came to her and looking into her eyes said in Gujerati, "Of course they will be. They are both here with you now, encircling you in their loving care." And I know she felt comforted.

In the last week at Inlak's Hospital, there was an urgency in Mani—a yearning to return to Meherazad to Baba's Home, so filled with precious memories of her times with Baba and Mehera. How could we know the time was to be so short?

Beloved Baba in His tender caring of her had gathered around His dear Mani really wonderful dedicated helpers to care for her every need under Goher's supervision—especially Shelley [Marrich] who was with her night and day. This great responsibility of caring for His sister was a privilege, an honour that touched each heart to its very core.

Such an atmosphere of His presence and love coming through Mani permeated all around. It was a gift of His

Sahavas, which even in her frailest state she was giving to us each and all.

At night time [in Meherazad] we would all gather around her in her room whether she was conscious of us or not, and we would sing together Baba songs or talk of our times in Baba together—it was with reluctance that we left her presence.

Every morning as long as she was able to walk, Mani would come to Baba's room for Darshan. One day after bowing down to the cast of Baba's lotus feet, she mentioned Mehera's name. Not wishing to interrupt her Darshan, I did not remember till the next day to ask her about it. Quite matter-of-factly she replied, "Yes I see Mehera continually —she is here all the time." And I knew that Baba was there too. She once tried to point Him out to us and describe His radiant beauty. We felt their presence around very tangibly.

Even when we were not with her, we felt Mani with us all the time. Every night I always fell asleep remembering her, and often woke up several times in the dark thinking of Mani and how she was doing. In the early hours of August 2nd, around 3:00 a.m., I was lying awake thinking of her, when around 3:30 a.m. I heard these words:

I do not know when or how I go,
But this I know to where I go:
It is to a place of indescribable beauty,
Where God's love enfolds completely.

And I know it was from Mani. Knowing if I fell asleep I would forget the message, I got out of bed and scribbled it down on an old envelope I found.

Well, you all know that in spite of all our heartfelt prayers Mani went to Baba, but in the gentlest way.

Seeing her face and form relax beyond the bonds of pain is what sustained us all. She was now completely in her Beloved's loving care where her heart had yearned to be these many years, especially after Mehera's passing from our midst. Our pain and grief for her suffering, and our loss, are beyond words. The two roses of Baba's garden are now hidden from our eyes, entirely in His care in blissful reunion with their Beloved.

. . .

The last journey with Mani to Meherabad was spent by all who accompanied her just gazing at her beautiful face and delicate form, savouring those last moments of the time she was to be with us. And for me, in remembering her lifetime of service for her Beloved Lord. What work she had done, what responsibility she had shouldered with love and grace and cheerfulness and what joy and caring she had given to all around. This was reflected in the loving homage given to her by all who came to bow down to this perfect life lived in and for her God Brother.

During the cremation, as with dazed and saddened heart I looked on not really seeing, I suddenly realized that the flames were dancing with a joyful gladness, and I realized how happy Mani would have been watching them trying to spring higher and ever higher in the wind. And I asked Janet [Judson] that Ted [Judson] sing "The Lord of the Dance."

Observing the fire with more attentive eyes I saw a host of forms bowing towards Mani in humble adoration. And in the center I kept seeing Baba's face one moment and Zoroaster's face the next. It was deeply comforting.

Naturally our tears also flowed freely for the loss of our sister. In Meherazad [afterwards], quite wiped out with emotion, I heard Goher softly giving way to grief in her bed as I was entering Baba's room. I tried to console her as best I could and repeated Mani's words spoken to Heather in a dream:

"You have no idea how much He loves me.
You have no idea how much I love Him.
You have no idea how happy I am."

Then going into Baba's room, I heard Baba say in Gujerati, "She is mad to weep because Mani has come to Me." And He repeated it again, "Because Mani has come to Me, she's weeping. She's crazy."

That night we all felt a lightness in our hearts, for we all felt that Mani had been freed from pain and was in indescribable bliss.

May these two whom Baba loved the best ever be watching over us and guiding us, with Beloved Baba, to help us to always please and obey Him as He should be pleased and obeyed.

One of Mani's frequent requests to Ted when we visited Baba's Samadhi was for him to sing "Have Thine Own Way, Lord," but she would always say, "Have It Your Way." And that was the way it was for her with Baba all her life—that it should be His Way.

Jai Baba!

= Meheru

. . .

As Mani had so many people who loved her out in the Baba-world, on the afternoon of that remembrance gathering, I wrote something about her final weeks to be sent out to Baba-lovers who were not here. I find that I now cannot describe the feeling of that time any better than I did then. So here is that account:

MANI'S REUNION

As Beloved Baba's family around the world now knows, His darling sister Mani rejoined Him on 19th August 1996, in Meherazad after a prolonged illness. This account is to share with you some of the events of her final days of love and service to Him.

A few years ago, Mani related that she had heard a voice, clear and distinct, saying within her:

"I am the bird, I am not the cage."

Perhaps that is why, when her health first began to fail in March 1995, she often would remark, "The bird is singing away, but the cage is in need of repair!" Despite her ensuing struggle against "NPH" (Normal Pressure Hydrocephalus) that involved two surgeries (in November '95 and February '96) Mani remained a radiant singing "bird"—meeting Baba-lovers in Meherazad whenever she could, scooting around Mehera's garden in her "Begum" (motorized scooter) as her walking became more and more difficult, and finally greeting people for a few moments from the confines of her chair inside the house in Meherazad. At the end of February 1996, having returned to Meherazad from her second surgery, she appeared on Mehera's porch just before Meherazad closed for the season. She was eager to spend time with her Baba family, and she loved the hour that followed as she "held forth" to a porch full of people and they performed for her, a wonderful giving and receiving of His love. Afterwards many remarked that Mani was more joyous and radiant than they had ever seen her.

That memorable day in February turned out to be her last "love-feast" with pilgrims at Meherazad. When pilgrim season opened again in July 1996, Mani was in the hospital in Poona, having been diagnosed with an inoperable malignant tumor.

How touching in retrospect was the vision of Mehera that Mani had just before leaving Meherazad to go to Poona for what we thought at the time would be a simple investigation! In the middle of the night, Mani sat up for a moment, and gazing over towards Mehera's bed, was amazed to see her darling Mehera lying there. "Oh!" she thought happily, "Mehera's come back to her old place!" and then she saw that Mehera was looking at her with an expression of great compassion and sadness. Mani was deeply touched, and soon afterwards in the hospital, when her diagnosis became known, she was heartened by this evidence of Mehera's loving presence and care.

After three weeks in the hospital, how happy and grateful Mani was to return home to Meherazad in early July! There she was often joyful in spite of her growing pain, and more than anything else in her last weeks, except gazing at pictures and slides of her beloveds, Baba and Mehera, Mani would love to sing. The bird indeed was singing, despite the condition of the cage, and Mani often entertained us with wonderful renditions of all kinds of songs, Baba's artis, her own songs, Baba-songs by others, hymns, traditional Indian songs, Mirabai songs, bhajans, village songs, lines from ghazals. She'd sing alone, or with Khorshed, Katie, Manu or Roda [Mistry], or with a chorus of us, always very happily.

One day, as Mani was being helped to the dining room, she said, "So this is what Baba wants me to do now." And she turned to this new, most difficult task, with the wholehearted concentration and discipline that always characterized her work for Him. She participated in her care with 100% focus, carefully taking the pills and alternative medicines prescribed for her with such great love and concern by Dr. Goher and Shelley, resting when she was tired (something it had always been hard to get her to do), and in spite of the pain, almost never complaining. In fact, her sweetness and at times genuine cheerfulness often cheered up her caregivers! And we felt she was doing all this for Baba, not for herself. As always, she was striving to live as He wished, moment to moment, wholeheartedly accepting whatever He ordained.

As the weeks went by, Mani seemed to become less and less attached to the world and more and more immersed in thoughts of Baba and Mehera. She would recall old days and reminisce with the women about their happy times with Baba. Or sometimes she'd tell jokes, complete of course with fantastic facial expressions, perfect mimicry, and a myriad of funny voices that would leave everyone in stitches. On Silence Day, she gestured as eloquently as she used to speak—and of all of us, she was the one who managed to maintain total silence! At tea when we inquired through signs as to whether she had finished her nutritional drink, she scribbled on the chalkboard, "Fait accompli"!

"Thank God for a sense of humour," she had remarked during her earlier illness, and her humour lightened many moments as she became weaker and weaker and more and more confined to bed. In the beginning she was able to sit up in her chair in the sitting room or on the porch for short periods, and enjoyed hearing Get-Well cards and heart-messages from Baba-lovers, and especially attending to last-minute details about her new manuscript *Dreaming of The Beloved* that she had dictated in May with such interest and meticulous attention. Something else she really enjoyed was hearing stories read aloud from her book *God-Brother*. She would become so childlike and excited reliving her childhood times with Baba, and amused and impressed with her own remarkable story-telling!

Gradually, the sessions at the dining table and in her chair became shorter and more infrequent as she became too weak to sit for long. Eventually she could no longer walk to Baba's Room for her morning darshan which had meant so much.

It was so hard to see her weak and in pain, but true to what she had written in her article "On the Topic of Suffering," Baba was upholding her from within as He dealt her blows of pain and weakness from without. This we knew from things she would say. Once we remarked to her how strongly we felt Baba's and Mehera's presence in her room, and Mani said that she felt as if Baba was there with her always, and even more so Mehera whom she often felt was moving around in their room "doing this and that." One day after hearing from Arnavaz of a beautiful Baba dream had by one of the men mandali, she said so happily, "Baba keeps sending me messages!"

On one of the last days she was able to sit up, Mani sat for a little while on her bed, facing Mehera's bed. All the windows of her room were open and from outside the room, Baba's image tree seemed to lean in to lend her support and strength. As she sat there, our tapewalli played a tape of Mani's song written for Mehera, "To the Glory of Love," and Mani swayed back and forth in time to the music, singing along with closed eyes and a gentle smile, lost in the beauty of the song. Baba and Mehera seemed specially present then, in the atmosphere of the pink room and in the joy of her glowing face.

It was to be our last such session. Despite an IV drip and all possible treatment, a few days later Mani slipped into a semi-conscious state. This was hardest to bear for Goher and the other women, her close companions of so many years. In their distress and concern for Mani, they would often wake at night, and one night around this time, waking from sleep and thinking of Mani, these comforting words came to Meheru as if from her:

*"I do not know when or how I go,
But this I know to where I go:
It is to a place of indescribable beauty,
Where God's love enfolds completely."*

Yet despite Mani's condition and our sorrow, there remained an atmosphere of overflowing love, sweetness, purity and innocence radiating from her that seemed to grow as the days went by.

Mohammed Mast had said on 9th August, Friday, that "Baba's sister will go tomorrow. Her pain will be over." Mani lived on past that Saturday. But looking back later, we all felt that her state changed that day and as Mohammed had "predicted," she did indeed "go," turning further and further away from this world and closer than ever to Baba. Soon after she was in a coma, and her niece Gulnar, visiting a few days later, upon entering the room perceived the difference immediately, remarking, "She's with Baba now." It was at this time that I dreamt of Mani saying to me, "You have no idea how much He loves me. You have no idea how much I love Him. You have no idea how happy I am."

Many dreams about this time heralded her reunion with Baba: dreams of Mani lying weak and sick then suddenly turning into Baba, of Mani skipping and dancing full of joy, of a great celebration soon to take place, of Mani walking down the front steps of her childhood home Baba-House on the arms of her brothers Beheram and Adi and touching each step with reverence as they stepped down and walked away, of Mani entering Baba's Room and inviting everyone outside to come in and meet her. Earlier Mani had been touched by a letter from a Baba-lover who wrote that while watching the video of Mani gesturing to "Welcome to My World," she saw Mani's face turn into Baba's face. And my husband Erico, who was close to the family, saw Baba's brothers Beheram, Jal and Adi, plus Pendu and Padri, standing on Meherabad Hill awaiting Mani, proud of all she had done for her Brother.

Mani had always told her family, "I will go at the moment Baba has chosen for me—not one second before or one second after." His chosen moment for their Reunion was early morning, 7:01 a.m., Monday, the 19th of August, when Mani opened her eyes with a look full of love and wonder, and after a few quiet breaths, slipped softly and gently into her Beloved's welcoming arms. It was as she had wished, in her room in Meherazad, facing her beloved Mehera's bed with the women mandali and a few others around her holding Baba's picture and saying His Name.

From the moment she went, her face assumed an expression of joy and triumph, and as the moments went by her luminous smile seemed to deepen until you could not look at her without feeling her happiness. Once years ago, seeing a picture of herself in which she appeared composed, self-contained, almost regal, Mani had said, "That is me as I was with Baba" and it was that same Mani that I saw now in her.

How could we not rejoice to see the end of all her suffering written so clearly on her beautiful face? We said the prayers around her, and then Eruch—her dear partner in His service these past 27 years—and the rest of the men mandali filed in for their own farewells.

They departed, and after being dressed by the women in one of her favorite "dress up" outfits of pink, mauve and beige, with a chiffon pink scarf framing her lovely face and a tiny "diamond" tilak on her forehead, Mani was gently placed on the same stretcher used for Mehera and taken by Mehera's bed where Arti was sung. Then she was carried into Beloved Baba's Room and as she rested at His feet, the prayers were recited, the Seven Names of God sung, and rose petals and flowers that had been offered to Baba were showered over her form. From there, across Mehera's garden past her favorite flowering china-box bush, she was carried into Mandali Hall.

As she lay in her last repose before Baba's chair in the Hall, her face shining, her form covered with flowers, surrounded by singing, Baba-lovers from Meherabad, Ahmednagar, Poona and Bombay streamed in to pay homage. Bhau was first to come, and DaraAmrit, followed soon by Khorshed. What a tribute to her loving personality to see the variety of people who came to honor her: the trustees of His Trust, all of the devoted Trust Office staff from the head clerk and chief accountant to the peons, government officials, Pimpalgaon villagers young and old, the tailor and many other local people who had been touched by her kindness. Late morning, her family from Poona arrived, and despite their grief, RustomSohrab and the "Irani gang" from Baba-House entertained Mani with zest as they had so often before, singing ghazals, songs she had written for them, and comic songs that used to make her laugh.

At 3:15 p.m. it was time for a final Arti, and the Meherazad women mandali, with great love and grief, tenderly kissed their precious sister for the last time in Meherazad, the home she loved so dearly. It was moving to hear even the Meherazad pet dogs calling out a farewell. Then Mani's form was carried on the stretcher into the Swanee [a small van], and with Goher, Meheru, Katie, Gulnar and a few other women, she began her last journey to Meherabad. Reaching there, as they turned into the road going up the Hill, some of the women saw her face flush, as if she was exulting in the approach of her final goal.

On the Hill, a group of Baba-lovers carried the stretcher into Baba's Samadhi, where Mani was placed on Baba's right hand side as the prayers were said. From there, she was taken to Mehera's shrine, and lying in the space between her beloveds, she seemed to grow pinker with happiness.

Mani's form was then placed on the Sabha Mandap. It is hard to describe the amazing atmosphere of this gathering,

the heightened sense of Baba's presence, of Mani's joy, of
the immensity of the event of her Reunion with Him, all
against a background of flowers garlanding her form, songs
in English, Marathi and Hindi, an outpouring of reverence
and respect from the villagers, the intimate moments of
farewell from her dear old friends Mansari and Gulu,
and others who had just arrived from Bombay, and the
combined focus of the huge crowd on her glowing form.

At about 5:30 p.m. once again Mani was carried into
the Swanee, and a caravan of cars, motorcycles and people
on foot wound down the Hill to the Meherabad cremation
ground at the southernmost end of the property.

Mani had always loved the atmosphere of freedom and
renunciation surrounding cremations, and especially those
that took place at evening time. As her form rested on the
pyre, she looked sublime and serene, like the Princess she
truly is. Poignant farewells from her dearest ones, heartbroken
with grief. And then all stepped back for the final covering
of her form with sandalwood, and the finishing of the pyre.*
Sometime after 6:00 p.m., at twilight, a time of day she loved,
the men of her devoted family, Jangu, RustomSohrab, Dara,
Arvind, Meherdil and Jamshed lit her pyre to resounding calls
of "Avatar Meher Baba ki Jai!"

If legends are to grow from this farewell to Mani, surely
there will be one about her pyre. For those who have
seen many cremations it was extraordinary in many ways.
Extraordinarily beautiful, as the flames whipped by a west
wind leapt up, dancing, intense, and bright against the deep

---

* Under Mani's head, Eruch put a block of sandalwood he had saved for years for this moment, saying quietly that his work was complete.

blue evening sky. Extraordinarily meaningful, as Meheru, dazed by sadness, suddenly saw forms among the flames dancing and bowing to Mani, and then Baba's face and Zoroaster's face alternating in the center. Extraordinarily rare, for as Eruch was standing silently nearby, two sadhus approached him, asking whose pyre was this? They had been passing by, and observed the smoke—but it was not the black smoke of the pyre of an ordinary person, it was the gray-blue smoke of the pyre of a saint. And so they had come to ask about this great soul and to pay their respects. The sister of Meher Baba? Ah, that explained it.

And the pyre was extraordinarily long-lasting, for when all was done and the mandali had returned to Meherazad and others to their homes and resting places, it went on burning and burning and burning. Normally a pyre will burn for twenty-four hours. A very large one, for thirty-six. The fire of Mani's love must have ignited the very air around her, for her pyre burned for three days. Even thereafter the place where she had lain was warm. Those three days were another kind of darshan for the Baba-lovers who kept round-the-clock vigil at the site, passing the time with songs and stories, energized by the atmosphere of great peace and sweetness that came from the fire. How delighted Mani would have been to see among them young people from the Youth Sahavas recently held at Baba's Center in Myrtle Beach (USA). One of them remarked that Mani's song to Baba, "Open Up the Door," which had been sung so often at the Youth Sahavas, for the first time really meant something to him because of this experience.

Even the flora paid her tribute that night. Years ago, Mehera had given a cutting from a "Christ's Cradle" plant at

Meherazad to grow in the Pilgrim Centre. The Christ's Cradle flower, which Mehera had shown to Baba, is a beautiful white fragrant flower that blooms only at night, and then rarely. On the night of Mani's reunion, all the Christ Cradles in the Pilgrim Centre bloomed. Only the next morning did anyone notice there was one more plant outside, stuck away in the corner of the nursery, that had given seven blooms in the night —in direct view of the distant pyre.

Mani's ashes were interred on Meherabad Hill on September 8th, 1996. As per Meher Baba's wish, she was interred at the side of the Samadhi on His left, just as His beloved Mehera was on His right.

Such touching tributes to Mani have come from Baba-lovers around the world that it is fitting I share some words from them:

"For a while she shone for all of us and lightened our burden with her joy of living, her singing, her laughter, her words of wisdom, her childlike manner—all of her a unique reflection of Baba's diamond that we will always cherish in our hearts. . . . For truly she was teaching us how to love Him. Now when we remember Mani, we will be truly remembering Him, because she was 100% Baba's."

"It is difficult to imagine that our dearest Mani will no longer be at Meherazad to greet us and cheer us with her incomparable personality. For me, she was the one person, besides Kitty Davy, who never seemed to grow old—who always projected such a magnificent, childlike zest for life and fun, and whose unquestioned faith and surrender to

Baba was such that it permeated everything she did. She was, indeed, Beloved Baba's sister, but she was also, in a very real sense, everybody's sister. She was, and is, a beacon of Baba's Light, reflecting not only His Love and Compassion, but also drawing us all closer to Him by her shining example."

"Mani, we always think of you as the one person who helped us the most through our most difficult time. Your compassion and understanding lifted our hearts. We miss your effervescent presence and heartwarming stories."

"So thanks! For the jokes, the toys, the scoldings, the hints, the pictures in words and mime, advice, your own good example, and the precious encouragement you gave us to try to love and please Him."

"The world has lost a luminous star of love and dedication."

"How we will miss your most special presence uniquely energized with such a keen focus upon your divinely human Brother, enlivened with the very intensity and humor and spirit of the Beloved Himself! . . . How much difference you have made—and your memory will continue to make—in the lives of all who have known you! How beautiful and uplifting have been your words and your actions in a life lived solely for your Beloved Meher Baba!"

Mani had a dream towards the very end of her life that she related to us. She woke up from sleep and looking around asked, weren't we going? When we said, no, we weren't going anywhere, she said, "Oh, it must have been a dream. I dreamt we were all dressed up and going to a great celebration."

So now we can imagine that celebration in His highest Court, with Beloved Baba at the head of the table, Mehera on

His right and Mani on His left, as in the celestial company of Perfect Ones, saints and angels, He welcomes her to His World! As one of Mani's close ones wrote: "Surely the heavens and the heavens beyond the heavens are reverberating with Beloved Baba's divine satisfaction at His glorious handiwork in the form of His little sister Mani!"

To end this account, I turn to Mani. Some years ago, while writing her book *God-Brother*, Mani laughingly said, "This is what I want for my epitaph!" She was pointing to a line written by Shireenmai, her mother, in a letter to Baba, describing Mani who was then seven years old. What Shireenmai had written to her Son about His little sister was simply:

"Night and day, Mani remembers You."

There can be no higher tribute than that.

AVATAR MEHER BABA ki JAI!

AT HER SHRINE

As we walk up Meherabad Hill now, we see a row of small shrines at the side of Beloved Baba's Samadhi. The one closest to Baba as we approach is Mani's. It is about 4 by 2½ feet, a bit smaller than Mehera's, which has the place of honor on the other side, at Baba's right-hand.

As designed by Mani, Mehera's shrine is covered by a canopy to protect it from the sun and rain, and after some years, knowing how affected Mani herself was by strong sun and the cold and damp, the architect once asked Mani if she, too, would want a canopy over her own shrine when the time came.

She said no, and she gave two reasons. One was that it was Mehera's privilege to have a canopy, and she did not want to take away from that. The other was that when Baba-lovers walked up the Hill for darshan, as they came to the top of the rise they eagerly looked out for their first glimpse of their Beloved's Tomb. A canopy over her shrine would block the view; it would distract from their first sight of the Tomb. She did not want to come between the lovers and that moment with their Beloved.

At Mani's behest, on Mehera's shrine on the Hill is carved:

MEHERA
BABA'S BELOVED

On Mani's is:

MANI
BABA'S SISTER

. . .

"*Mahara bhai jaan, chhere tun Bhagvaan,*" Mani sang from time to time, in a little Gujerati song that she had written: "My beloved Brother, You are God." And in her native tongue, she would sing on:

My beloved Brother,
You are God.
For the sake of the world,
For the sake of love,
You took human form.

My beloved Brother,
You are God.

Endnotes

VOLUME ONE

PART I: GOD'S SISTER

GOD'S SISTER

1. Mani S. Irani, *God-Brother: Stories from My Childhood with Meher Baba* (North Myrtle Beach, SC: Sheriar Foundation, 1993).
2. From among Mani's personal papers.
3. Mehera J. Irani, *Mehera* (East Windsor, NJ: Beloved Books, 1989), 81.
4. Mani S. Irani, *Dreaming of The Beloved* (North Myrtle Beach, SC: Sheriar Foundation, 1999), 45.
5. "The Editor's Diary or The News about The Master, Shri Sadguru Meher Baba (15th March to 14th April 1929)," *Meher Message* 1, no. 5 (May 1929): 25.

PART II: TO BE WITH YOU ALWAYS

INTO THE FIRE

1. David Fenster, *Mehera-Meher: A Divine Romance* (Ahmednagar: Meher Nazar Publications, 2003), vol. I, 252–54.
2. Mehera J. Irani, *Mehera* (East Windsor, NJ: Beloved Books, 1989), 102.
3. *Mehera*, 104.

4. Mehera J. Irani, *Baba Loved Us Too: Stories of Meher Baba and His Pets* (Myrtle Beach, SC: Sheriar Press, 1989), 39.
5. All quotes attributed to Mehera in the "Pets" section are from *Baba Loved Us Too,* 13, 14–15, 41–42, 9–10.

EAST-WEST

1. Unless otherwise noted, all quotes attributed to Rano in this chapter are from Rano Gayley, *Because of Love: My Life and Art with Meher Baba* (North Myrtle Beach, SC: Sheriar Press, 1983), 16, 19, 20.
2. Margaret Craske, *The Dance of Love: My Life with Meher Baba* (North Myrtle Beach, SC: Sheriar Press, 1980), 56–57.
3. Quotes attributed to Delia in this chapter are from Delia DeLeon, *The Ocean of Love* (Myrtle Beach, SC: Sheriar Press, 1991), 91, 103.
4. Quotes attributed to Kitty in this chapter are from Kitty Davy, *Love Alone Prevails: A Story of Life with Meher Baba* (North Myrtle Beach, SC: Sheriar Foundation, 1981), 204, 207, 214, 229.

THE BLUE BUS

1. Kitty Davy, *Love Alone Prevails: A Story of Life with Meher Baba* (North Myrtle Beach, SC: Sheriar Foundation, 1981), 251.
2. Rano Gayley, *Because of Love: My Life and Art with Meher Baba* (North Myrtle Beach, SC: Sheriar Press, 1983), 29, 41.
3. Mehera J. Irani, *Mehera* (East Windsor, NJ: Beloved Books, 1989), 130.
4. *Because of Love,* 33.
5. *Mehera,* 131.
6. *Love Alone Prevails,* 255.
7. Margaret Craske, *The Dance of Love: My Life with Meher Baba* (North Myrtle Beach, SC: Sheriar Press, 1980), 136–37.
8. *Because of Love,* 31.
9. *Mehera,* 146.
10. *Dance of Love,* 106–7.

11. Bhau Kalchuri, *Lord Meher: The Biography of the Avatar of the Age Meher Baba* (Myrtle Beach, SC: MANifestation, 1996), vol. VIII, 2854.
12. *Lord Meher*, vol. VIII, 2853.

TRAVELING

1. This quote and the next, from a letter written by Margaret Craske, are from Kitty Davy, *Love Alone Prevails: A Story of Life with Meher Baba* (North Myrtle Beach, SC: Sheriar Foundation, 1981), 308.
2. Mehera J. Irani, *Mehera* (East Windsor, NJ: Beloved Books, 1989), 162.
3. *Love Alone Prevails*, 313.
4. *Mehera*, 170.
5. *Love Alone Prevails*, 309–10.
6. *Love Alone Prevails*, 310–11.
7. *Love Alone Prevails*, 315.
8. The quotes from Kitty in this section are from *Love Alone Prevails*, 333.

A NEW LIFE

1. *Tales from the New Life with Meher Baba*, Narrated by Eruch, Mehera, Mani and Meheru, eds. D. E. Stevens, Rick M. Chapman, James M. Hastings, Gary Freeman, and Patty Freeman (Berkeley, CA: The Beguine Library, 1976), 173–74. The other quotes from *Tales from the New Life* in this section are from pages 189 and 176.
2. Judith Garbett, "Mani Part 2," *Lives of Love: The Women Mandali of Avatar Meher Baba* (Woombye, Queensland: Meher Baba Foundation Australia, 1998), 4–5.
3. *Tales from the New Life*, 186–87.
4. *Tales from the New Life*, 177.
5. *Tales from the New Life*, 156.
6. *Tales from the New Life*, 179.
7. "Mani Part 2," *Lives of Love*, 2–3.

8. *Tales from the New Life*, 85.
9. The stories attributed to *Tales from the New Life* in this section are from pages 161 and 179–80.
10. "Mani Part 2," *Lives of Love*, 3–4.
11. *Tales from the New Life*, 79.
12. *Tales from the New Life*, 182–84.
13. This, and the next quote from Mehera, are from *Tales from the New Life*, 184, 166.
14. This and other quotes attributed to Kitty in this chapter are from Kitty Davy, *Love Alone Prevails: A Story of Life with Meher Baba* (North Myrtle Beach, SC: Sheriar Foundation, 1981), 346–47, 349–50, 349, 350.
15. David Fenster, *Mehera-Meher: A Divine Romance* (Ahmednagar: Meher Nazar Publications, 2003), vol. II, 535.
16. Bhau Kalchuri, *Lord Meher: The Biography of the Avatar of the Age Meher Baba* (Myrtle Beach, SC: MANifestation, 1996), vol. X, 3686.
17. C. B. Purdom, *The God-Man: The Life, Journeys and Work of Meher Baba with an Interpretation of his Silence and Spiritual Teaching* (North Myrtle Beach: Sheriar Foundation, 1971), 187–88.
18. *Mehera-Meher*, vol. II, 542–43.
19. *Tales from the New Life*, 167.
20. *Tales from the New Life*, 171.

VOLUME TWO

PART II: TO BE WITH YOU ALWAYS (CONTINUED)

IN THE WEST

1. This and other quotes attributed to Kitty in this chapter are from Kitty Davy, *Love Alone Prevails: A Story of Life with Meher Baba* (North Myrtle Beach, SC: Sheriar Foundation, 1981), 386, 397
2. *Love Alone Prevails*, 398.

3. David Fenster, *Mehera-Meher: A Divine Romance* (Ahmednagar: Meher Nazar Publications, 2003), vol. III, 40.
4. Bhau Kalchuri, *Lord Meher: The Biography of the Avatar of the Age Meher Baba* (Asheville, NC: MANifestation, 1996), vol. XI, 3848.
5. *Love Street Lamp Post* July (2002): 28, 35.
6. *Mehera-Meher*, vol. III, 92–93.

FIERY AND FREE

1. Kitty Davy, *Love Alone Prevails: A Story of Life with Meher Baba* (North Myrtle Beach, SC: Sheriar Foundation, 1981), 435.
2. Mehera J. Irani, *Mehera* (East Windsor, NJ: Beloved Books, 1989), 215–17.
3. Ivy O. Duce, *How a Master Works* (Walnut Creek, CA: Sufism Reoriented, Inc., 1975), 219–20.
4. Bili Eaton, *A Love So Amazing: Memories of Meher Baba* (North Myrtle Beach, SC: Sheriar Press, 1984), 80.
5. This, and Kitty's reply, are from *Love Alone Prevails*, 441, 484.
6. This and the other quotes from letters in this section are from *Love Alone Prevails*, 436–37, 437, 443, 456–57, 475, 460, 474, 455, 444, 443, 459, 455.
7. This and the next quote, from a letter to Kitty, are from *Love Alone Prevails*, 431, 434.
8. This and the next quote are from *How a Master Works*, 219, 203.
9. Don E. Stevens, *Meher Baba's Word and His Three Bridges*, eds. Norah Moore and Laurent Weichberger (London: Companion Books, 2003), 228.
10. *How a Master Works*, 239–40.
11. *Love Alone Prevails*, 476.
12. This and the next quote are from Bhau Kalchuri, *Lord Meher: The Biography of the Avatar of the Age Meher Baba* (Asheville, NC: MANifestation, 1996), vol. XVI, 5511, 5560.
13. Mani S. Irani, *82 Family Letters To the Western Family of Lovers and Followers of Meher Baba* (North Myrtle Beach, SC: Sheriar Press, 1976), 1.

14. David Fenster, *Mehera-Meher: A Divine Romance* (Ahmednagar: Meher Nazar Publications, 2003), vol. III, 164.
15. *82 Family Letters*, 2.
16. *Love Alone Prevails*, 478–79.
17. *82 Family Letters*, 5.
18. Bhau Kalchuri, *Lord Meher: The Biography of the Avatar of the Age Meher Baba* (Asheville, NC: MANifestation, 1996), vol. XV, 5144.
19. *82 Family Letters*, 5.

THE LAST TWELVE YEARS

1. The excerpts from the Family Letters in this chapter are from Mani S. Irani, *82 Family Letters To the Western Family of Lovers and Followers of Meher Baba* (North Myrtle Beach, SC: Sheriar Press, 1976), 11, 15, 20, 47, 52, 137, 200, 173, 151, 22, 151, 81, 168, 24, 54, 53, 33, 42, 45, 277, 300, 304, 274, 308, 314, 315, 310, 314, 313–14, 312, 319, 321–27, 328–33, 334–41.
2. Kitty Davy, *Love Alone Prevails: A Story of Life with Meher Baba* (North Myrtle Beach, SC: Sheriar Foundation, 1981), 559.
3. *82 Family Letters*, from the introduction. The next quote is, as explained in the text, from the back cover.
4. Bhau Kalchuri, *Lord Meher: The Biography of the Avatar of the Age Meher Baba* (Asheville, NC: MANifestation, 1996), vol. XV, 5425.
5. *Lord Meher*, vol. XV, 5465.

ETERNAL BELOVED

1. This and the next quote from Mani are taken from David Fenster, *Mehera-Meher: A Divine Romance* (Ahmednagar: Meher Nazar Publications, 2003), vol. III, 486, 488.
2. Excerpts from Mani's last Family Letters are from Mani S. Irani, *82 Family Letters To the Western Family of Lovers and Followers of Meher Baba* (North Myrtle Beach, SC: Sheriar Press, 1976), 342, 346, 344.
3. Mehera J. Irani, *Mehera* (East Windsor, NJ: Beloved Books, 1989), 238–40.

THE GREAT DARSHAN

1. Barbara Bamberger Scott, *The Empty Chair* (Berkeley, CA: The White Horse Publishing Company, 2010), 187.
2. Excerpts from Mani's last Family Letter are from Mani S. Irani, *82 Family Letters To the Western Family of Lovers and Followers of Meher Baba* (North Myrtle Beach, SC: Sheriar Press, 1976), 353–63.

PART III: CONTINUING ON

CONTINUING ON

1. Mani S. Irani, *Dreaming of The Beloved* (North Myrtle Beach, SC: Sheriar Foundation, 1999), 35–36.
2. Tessa Bielecki, *Holy Daring: An Outrageous Gift to Modern Spirituality from Saint Teresa, the Grand Wild Woman of Avila* (Rockport, MA: Element Books Ltd., 1994).
3. Minnie Louise Haskins, "God Knows." The Rotarian, Oct 1940, vol. 57, no. 4. Rotary International.
4. "Dance of Life," in *Hafez, Dance of Life*, trans. Michael Boylan and Wilberforce Clarke (Washington, DC: Mage Publishers, Inc., 1987).

GLOSSARY

These terms in the Glossary may be spelled differently in British and American English. Throughout the book, when the author is Mani Irani, British spelling is used; when the author is Heather Nadel, American spelling is used.

agyari. The Gujerati term for "fire temple," used by Parsis in India to refer to the main Zoroastrian place of worship, where a sacred fire is kept continuously burning.

Ahuramazda. The Zoroastrian name for Almighty God in the ancient Avestan language.

Amartithi. Literally, "immortal date." The anniversary of the dropping of Meher Baba's body on January 31, 1969.

arti. Devotional song or prayer. In the Hindu tradition, the practice of arti involves waving a tray with lighted camphor (or lamps of oil or ghee) before the master or an image of a deity. Among Baba-lovers, *arti* refers either to a song in praise of Meher Baba or to the performance of the prayers dictated by Baba, as well as songs dedicated to Him.

ashram. The abode of a spiritual master, where he lives with his disciples. Meher Baba established His main ashram at Meherabad, in Maharashtra state, India. He convened several other ashrams at various times, including for the masts and the mad.

Avatar. Literally, "descent." God in human form. In Hinduism, the word *avatar* refers to an incarnation of a deity on earth; most sects of Hinduism specify this deity as Vishnu, or the sustainer of creation. Meher Baba revealed that the Avatar is that same Ancient One—known by such names as the Avatar, Rasul, Christ, Messiah, or Buddha—who descends into human form repeatedly throughout history. His advents in the present cycle of time have been Zoroaster, Rama, Krishna, Buddha, Muhammad, Jesus, and Meher Baba.

Avatar Meher Baba ki Jai. An exclamation or salute meaning "Hail to Avatar Meher Baba!"

Baba-lover. An English version of the Hindi phrase *Baba premi* that has none of the usual connotations of "lover" in English. *Prem* is a Sanskrit word denoting love for God. The term *Baba-lover* is used to refer to people who hold a special place for Meher Baba in their hearts but who did not necessarily meet Him.

Babajan. *See* Perfect Master.

bhajan. A Hindu devotional song in praise of God.

bhajia. A fried savory snack, often made of ground chickpeas.

bhakri. A flatbread made from millet. Traditionally popular in the villages of Maharashtra state, where millet is typically cheaper than wheat.

bhiksha. Alms, usually food. In Hinduism, feeding sadhus and other spiritual mendicants is considered an act of devotion to God.

Bujave Arti. Also known as the Bujave Nar or the Gujarati Arti. A song of praise to Avatar Meher Baba, composed by Baba Himself in the 1920s.

Cabin, the. A small structure in Upper Meherabad, located near the Samadhi, where Baba often stayed in seclusion.

chappati (also chapati). A flatbread made from wheat.

chargeman. A saint or *mast* assigned by a Perfect Master to carry out specific spiritual work in a specific place.

chit. A note written on a small piece of paper, often scrap.

daaman. "The hem of a garment." Just as a child holds on to the hem of its mother's skirt as they make their way through a crowded marketplace, Meher Baba asked His lovers to figuratively hold on to His daaman by remembering Him and depending only on His guidance.

dak bungalow. A government rest house offering basic accommodations, originally established in colonial times for the convenience of touring officers.

dal. A dish prepared from split lentils.

Dari. A Persian dialect traditionally spoken by Zoroastrians.

darshan. "Sight." In India, *darshan* refers to the act of seeing a holy person or an image of a deity, and the blessing derived from this sight. During His lifetime, Meher Baba granted His darshan to large masses of people. Typically, those taking His darshan would fold their hands in adoration and, on special occasions, bow at His feet. Today, people take darshan by bowing down at Meher Baba's Samadhi or other places intimately associated with Him, such as His bedroom in Meherazad or Myrtle Beach.

dastoor. A Zoroastrian priest.

dhansak. A Parsi dish of cooked dal with spices and vegetables, eaten with a rice pilaf.

dharmshala (also dharamshala). A free rest house for travelers.

dhuni. Saints and masters in India often keep a fire burning, usually in a small pit, that symbolizes the purifying inner fire of Divine Love. Meher Baba lit a dhuni at a particular spot at Lower Meherabad on a number of occasions, and invited His lovers to throw into it sandalwood sticks dipped in ghee, symbolizing attachments that they wished to give up. He instructed that the dhuni at Lower Meherabad should continue to be lit on the twelfth day of each month at sunset.

Divali (also Diwali). The Hindu "festival of lights," celebrated across India in autumn.

East Room, the. Originally a water tank with two tank rooms, one on the eastern end and another on the western end of the Meher Retreat on Meherabad Hill. Baba converted these into inhabitable rooms by adding a separate door for each. Mehera and Mani lived in the East Room at one time.

fakir. A wandering Muslim ascetic who subsists on alms and renounces all comforts in devotion to God. The fakir represents the ideal of true poverty in the spiritual sense.

falooda. A sweet drink made with milk and rosewater. Traditionally served by Parsis on Navroz.

gaadi. Literally, "throne." A long reclining seat, or divan.

Ghalib. The pen name of Mirza Asadullah Baig Khan, perhaps the most famous nineteenth-century poet of India. Ghalib is one of the great masters of the poetic form known as the ghazal, and is known for his innovation in the regional vernacular, Urdu. He also wrote in Persian, the traditional literary language of the time.

ghazal. A poetic form with a strict meter and rhyme scheme that involves complicated wordplay and metaphor, sometimes set to music and used to describe the devotion between lover and beloved. In India the ghazal is most often written in Urdu or Persian, although Meher Baba composed ghazals in Hindi and English as well.

ghee. Clarified butter.

God-Realization. The soul's realization of its true Self as God; the "I am God" experience whose achievement fulfills the aim of life and brings release from the cycle of birth and death. In God-Realization one experiences God's triad nature as Knowledge, Power, and Bliss, whereas in *Mukti* one experiences Bliss only.

gopis. "Milkmaids." The female devotees of Lord Krishna, who was a cowherd in His youth.

Gujerati (also Gujarati). The language of Gujarat State, India, adopted by Parsis as a common tongue.

Guruprasad. "Grace of the guru." The name of a palace in Poona (now Pune) belonging to Maharani Shantadevi of Baroda, given to Meher Baba exclusively for His use during summer months in the 1950s and 1960s. The palace has since been torn down, but one small room, made from materials saved from the bedroom used by Baba, and a part of the verandah were preserved on the site as a memorial to Meher Baba.

Hafiz, Shamsuddin Muhammad (c. 1320–1389). Persia's greatest mystic poet, a master of the ghazal, who was Meher Baba's favorite poet. Baba identified Hafiz as a Perfect Master.

Hari. One of the many names for Vishnu or Krishna; Lord.

hill station. A town in the mountains favored by the British for long holidays during India's hot summer months.

Hindi. A vernacular language of North India, instated as the official language of India after the nation gained independence from British rule in 1947. Written in the same script as Sanskrit, Hindi's spoken form is almost identical to Urdu, albeit with many more words derived from Sanskrit. *See* Urdu.

Hu. "He," used by Sufis to refer to God.

Jai Baba. A common greeting or salute among Baba-lovers that literally means "Victory to Baba." *See also* Avatar Meher Baba ki Jai.

jelebi. A pretzel-shaped sweet made of deep-fried wheat flour soaked in sugar syrup.

Jigar. The pen name of Ali Sikander Muradabadi (1890–1961), an Indian poet known for his Urdu ghazals and Meher Baba's favorite contemporary poet. According to an endnote in *Lord Meher* by Bhau Kalchuri, "when Jigar was on his deathbed in 1961, Baba sent a devotee named Baghel (from Hamirpur) to him with a copy of *God Speaks,* as a gift from Baba. Baghel presented the book to him, and Jigar touched his forehead with the book."

Kabir (1440–1518). A mystic poet and saint from North India who is revered by Hindus, Muslims, and Sikhs alike. Meher Baba identified Kabir as a Perfect Master.

kafni. An ankle-length men's garment like a long shirt, made of lightweight cotton, usually white. Meher Baba and His companions wore kafnis during the New Life.

kamli. A rough, hand woven shepherd's blanket.

Krishna, Lord. One of the major advents of the Avatar, worshiped by Hindus as an incarnation of Vishnu. Hindu literature tells of Krishna's life as a village cowherd whose divine personality attracted the devotion of the gopis, or milkmaids. In the *Bhagavad Gita,* Krishna presents His teachings to His disciple Arjuna.

kusti. A handwoven, flat woolen string worn around the waist by orthodox Zoroastrians. A child receives a kusti to wear over the sadra at his or her Navjote ceremony.

Majzoob. In Sufi terms, "divinely absorbed." A Majzoob is a God-merged soul of the seventh plane. Masts may be "majzoob-like" on the lower planes of involving consciousness.

mandali. Literally "a circle, a ring; a group or party." Used by Meher Baba to denote the intimate circle of disciples around the Avatar or a Perfect Master. In the early days, the term was used only for Meher Baba's men mandali; later it came to include the women mandali as well.

Mandali Hall. A hall where Baba met with His disciples and devotees. There is a Mandali Hall in both

Meherazad and Meherabad. Unless otherwise specified, the Mandali Hall referred to in this book is that in Meherazad.

Manonash. "Annihilation of the mind," or passing out of the separative ego-mind to abide in God.

Manonash cabin. A small cabin constructed on Seclusion Hill, near Meherazad, where Baba spent time in seclusion doing His special manonash work in 1951. It was later moved to Meherazad.

Manzil-e-Meem. Baba's first ashram. The Manzil is a large bungalow in Bombay (now Mumbai) where Baba stayed with a number of His men mandali from June 1922 until April 1923.

mast. "Drunk." A Persian word that gains another meaning in the context of Sufi mystical poetry, where wine signifies love for a beloved, master, or God. Meher Baba used the word to indicate a God-intoxicated person on the spiritual path.

mastani. A female mast.

Maya. Illusion; the divine power that causes the illusory world of duality to appear real.

Meher Nazar compound. Originally the home of Adi K. Irani's family and known as Khushru Quarters, it now contains the offices of the Avatar Meher Baba Perpetual Public Charitable Trust and houses Bhau Kalchuri's family and several Trust volunteers and staff.

Meher Retreat. Originally a stone water tank used by the British in World War I, this building in Upper Meherabad has been used in several ways, among them as living quarters for many of the Eastern and Western women disciples who lived in Meher Baba's ashram. Today the building holds a museum, study hall, and library.

Meherabad. The site of Avatar Meher Baba's Tomb-Shrine (Samadhi) and center of world pilgrimage. First visited by Baba in 1923, Meherabad soon became Baba's primary residence, ashram, and headquarters of His activities until 1944. Upper Meherabad ("Meherabad Hill") and Lower Meherabad, divided by a railway track, housed separate mandali quarters, schools, dispensaries, temporary buildings and other external "scaffoldings" Baba created for His spiritual Work. On January 31, 1969, Meher Baba dropped His body at Meherazad; His form was brought to Meherabad Hill and interred in His Tomb-Shrine, constructed at Baba's orders many years before.

Meherazad. Meher Baba's personal residence for the second part of His advent. He stayed at Meherazad on and off from 1944 through 1956, and after His second accident He lived there permanently until He dropped His body in 1969. Alongside Baba's Samadhi at Meherabad, Meherazad is now a primary site of pilgrimage to Avatar Meher Baba in India.

Mirabai. A sixteenth-century princess of North India who renounced her wealth and husband to lead a simple life of devotion to Lord Krishna. The devotional songs composed by Mirabai are still sung today throughout India.

moholla (also muhalla). An urban "neighborhood," which, in traditional Indian cities, often consists of a network of narrow lanes.

Mukti. Emancipation, liberation, release from worldly existence and rebirth (*see* God-Realization).

murshid/murshida. Arabic for guide or teacher. The head of a Sufi order.

naan. An oven-baked wheat flatbread common in the north of India.

'Nagar. Short for Ahmednagar.

Namaste (also namaskar). A greeting or salutation, usually accompanied by a bow of respect with folded hands.

Narayan Maharaj. *See* Perfect Master.

Navjote. Initiation into the Zoroastrian faith (similar to confirmation for Christians), performed when a child is between seven and nine years of age. During this ceremony, the child is invested with a sadra and kusti.

Navroz (also Nowruz). The Persian New Year, celebrated on the first day of spring.

New Life. A special phase of Meher Baba's work (1949–1952), during which He traveled on foot with a number of His close disciples for much of the time. During these travels, He went incognito as one of their companions, sleeping wherever they found shelter, and eating *bhiksha,* or whatever people offered them with love. Throughout the New Life, Baba did not allow His disciples to identify Him as the Avatar.

nullah. A dry ravine or gully.

oodi. Ashes from a dhuni.

pandal. A colorful tent erected temporarily, for a special occasion such as a darshan.

Paramatma. A compound of *param* (highest, first, best) and *atma* (soul). The Supreme Self, or Oversoul. One of the Hindu names of God.

Parsi. A descendent of Zoroastrians who emigrated from Persia to India around the eighth century to avoid religious persecution by Muslim invaders of their homeland. The first Parsis settled in Gujarat State, which is why Gujerati became a common Parsi language.

Parvardigar Prayer, the. A prayer composed by Meher Baba, also known as the Master's Prayer. It is recited at morning and evening Arti at His Samadhi, along with the Prayer of Repentance and the Beloved God prayer, also given by Him.

Perfect Master. A God-Realized man or woman, also called a Sadguru, who retains God-consciousness and creation-consciousness simultaneously and who works in creation to help other souls toward God-Realization. The five Perfect Masters who unveiled Meher Baba as the Avatar were Sai Baba of Shirdi, Upasni Maharaj, Hazrat Babajan, Tajuddin Baba, and Narayan Maharaj.

prasad. "Divine grace or favor." A gift from the master to a seeker. In Hinduism, the term *prasad* refers to offerings to a deity at a temple, which are shared with devotees as a blessing. Among Baba-lovers, *prasad* refers to gifts distributed by Meher Baba, whether at mass darshan programs or more intimate meetings, often in the form of something edible. Prasad bestows the gift of inner contact with the Master and conveys His love blessing.

pulao. A rice dish cooked with spices and meat or vegetables.

qawwali. A genre of ecstatic devotional music popularized by Indian Sufis as a form of worship. The lyrics may be based on a verse from the Qu'ran or a mystical poem, and sung in Persian or Urdu to improvised music.

Radha. The beloved of Lord Krishna. Radha was one of the gopis, or cowherding girls.

Ram, Lord. One of the major advents of the Avatar, Lord Ram (or Rama) was a princely ruler in ancient India and the celebrated hero of the epic *Ramayana.* Hindus worship Him as an incarnation of Vishnu.

rava. A sweet dish made of cream-of-wheat with nuts and raisins, traditionally prepared on birthdays, weddings, and other special occasions in some regional Indian communities.

Sabha Mandap. A platform covered with a tin roof, situated across from the Samadhi.

Sadguru. *See* Perfect Master.

sadhu. A Hindu ascetic or holy man who has renounced the world. A sadhu typically wanders from place to place and begs for his food.

sadra. A thin muslin shirt traditionally worn by Zoroastrians. Meher Baba adapted the sadra into an ankle-length garment that He regularly wore.

sahavas. The company of the master. Also, a gathering held by a master so that his devotees may enjoy and benefit from intimate companionship.

Sai Baba of Shirdi. *See* Perfect Master.

Samadhi, the. Meher Baba's Tomb-Shrine on Meherabad Hill, initially called the Dome. In India, the site of the burial of a holy person is often referred to as a *samadhi,* the Sanskrit word for the highest state of meditation.

sanskaras. In Hindu philosophy, mental impressions, or accumulated imprints of past experiences that determine one's present desires and actions. Meher Baba identified the binding of sanskaras as the primary obstacle to spiritual freedom.

sev. Sweet vermicelli with nuts and raisins.

Shahnameh. A long epic poem by the Persian poet Ferdowsi. It tells the story of the Persian Empire from the beginning of Creation up to its Islamic conquest in the 7th century.

Simab. An acclaimed Urdu poet of India. He is best known for his ghazals.

Sufis. [from *God Speaks*] The mystics whose origins lie in the Middle East. Their beginnings are lost in antiquity. They existed at the time of Zoroaster and were revitalized by Muhammed. They exist today in all parts of the world.

Tajuddin Baba. *See* Perfect Master.

tatta. Bamboo matting.

toddy. The fresh or fermented sap of various Asian palms. Often a hot drink consisting of liquor (such as rum), water, sugar, and spices.

tonga. A two-wheeled, one-horse carriage driven by a tongawalla.

Tower of Silence. A circular tower used by Zoroastrians for disposal of the dead.

umar. A type of tree that in the Hindu tradition is believed to be the seat of Dattatreya, a deity whose three heads express the three aspects of God: Creator, Sustainer, and Dissolver.

Upasni Maharaj. *See* Perfect Master.

Urdu. A language spoken in Pakistan, across much of northern India, and by Muslims throughout India. Written in a script similar to that of Persian, the language's spoken form is almost identical to Hindi, albeit with more loan words from Arabic and Persian. In popular Indian culture, Urdu is portrayed as the "language of love," reflecting the work of celebrated poets and qawwali singers from the subcontinent. See Hindi.

Work, Baba's. The Universal Work accomplished by Meher Baba during His advent as the Avatar. Although He said that ordinary people could not understand His Work, Baba indicated that it included giving a spiritual push to all of creation as well as specific help to individuals.

Yezdan (or Yazdan). The Persian name for Almighty God.

yogi. One who has renounced worldly life to follow the spiritual path; one who practices physical or mental discipline (yoga) for spiritual reasons.

Zend–Avesta. The holy book of the Zoroastrian religion.

Zoroaster. Considered the founder of the ancient Zoroastrian religion and identified by Meher Baba as the earliest known Avatar in the present cycle of time. Also called Zarathustra.

LIST OF ILLUSTRATIVE MATERIALS

The following materials used in The Joyous Path, *are in three parts: Photographs, Historical Materials, and Archival Objects. They are listed by chapter and page number. Where possible, the list identifies the people, places, dates, photographers, and copyrightholders, but this information was not available for all of the materials. Photographs were taken in India, unless otherwise noted, and are used with permission.*

Many images in this book have been identified through the extensive Baba photo database at the Avatar Meher Baba Trust's Archives, and in some cases the image itself has been given digitally for use in this book. Content information has also been provided from the database.

PHOTOGRAPHS

PAGE   DESCRIPTION

Covers

Front cover, Volume I: Mani in Mandali Hall. Photographed by Win Coates. Copyright Susan White.

Front cover, Volume II: Mani in Mandali Hall. Photographed by Win Coates. Copyright Susan White.

Back cover: Mani, Meherazad, 1970s. Photographer unknown. Courtesy of Meher Nazar Publications.

Inside front flap of covers: Mani and Baba, Upper Meherabad, 1934. Photographed by Small Khorshed. Courtesy of MSI Photographic Collection.

1088 LIST OF ILUSTRATIVE MATERIALS

PAGE DESCRIPTION

Frontispiece

iv Mani and Baba, Upper Meherabad, 1934. Photographed by Small Khorshed. Courtesy of MSI Photographic Collection.

VOLUME ONE
PART I: God's Sister

Prologue

2   Baba, Mani, and Shireenmai. Courtesy of Meher Nazar Publications.
4   Baba, Poona, about 1917–18. Courtesy of Meher Nazar Publications.

God's Sister

11 Merwan as a child with Freny and Jamshed Irani, Poona, about 1899. Courtesy of Meher Nazar Publications.
12 Merwan, a paternal cousin Shayr, Adi Jr., Shireenmai, and Jamshed (seated); Beheram and Jal (standing). Probably taken in Poona, 1915–1916. Courtesy of Martin Cook.
14 Baba's parents Sheriarji and Shireenmai, 1920s. Courtesy of Avatar Meher Baba Trust Archives image collection.
15 Hazrat Babajan. Courtesy of Meher Nazar Publications.
20 Upasni Maharaj. Courtesy of Meher Nazar Publications.
23 Baba and Shireenmai, Nasik, about 1929–1931. Courtesy of Meher Nazar Publications.
25 Shireenmai at Pumpkin House, Poona, late 1930s. Courtesy of MSI Photographic Collection.
35 Mani age 4 with her brother Jamshed and his wife Khorshed, Poona, December 1922. Courtesy of Mani Family Collection.
39 Shireenmai. Courtesy of Mani Family Collection.
42 Mehera J. Irani near the East Room doorway, Upper Meherabad, about 1937. Photographed by Elizabeth Patterson. Courtesy of MSI Photographic Collection.
46 Baba standing behind the Jhopdi, Meherabad, about 1926. Photographer unknown. Courtesy of Meher Nazar Publications.
52 Group gathered for Baba's birthday, Post Office, Lower Meherabad, February 18, 1925. Mani standing behind Baba on the right. Photographed by S. S. Deen. Courtesy of Meher Nazar Publications.
57 Baba under neem tree, Sai Darbar cabin, lower Meherabad, February 18, 1927. Photographer unknown. Courtesy of ECPPA.

LIST OF ILUSTRATIVE MATERIALS

PAGE	DESCRIPTION
59	Baba with a gathering of visitors; Mani standing at the back on the verandah with Padri next to her. Lonavla, December 4, 1926. Courtesy of Meher Nazar Publications.
61	Mani, a servant Chandri, Adi Jr., Shireenmai, Sheriarji, and Jal at Baba-House, Poona, about 1922–23. Courtesy of Avatar Meher Baba Trust Archives image collection.
62	Shireenmai, Mani, Adi Jr, Jal, a servant, and Sheriar at Baba-House, Poona, 1922–1923. Courtesy of MSI Photographic Collection.
63	Sheriarji. Courtesy of Meher Nazar Publications.
79	Babajan. Courtesy of Meher Nazar Publications.
80	Narayan Maharaj. Courtesy of Meher Nazar Publications.
107	Shireenmai bowing to Baba, Nasik, February 18, 1937. Courtesy of Martin Cook.
108	Baba (dressed as Zoroaster) and Shireenmai, Upper Meherabad, September 1938. Courtesy of MSI Photographic Collection.
111	Baba with Shireenmai (behind Baba), Gulmai, Daulatmai, Abdulla Haroon Jaffer (Ramjoo's brother-in-law), Kaka Baria, Adi Sr.; Meherabad, 1926. Courtesy of Avatar Meher Baba Trust Archives image collection.
118	Perinmai. Photographed by Beheram S. Irani. Courtesy of Mani Family Collection.
121	R.M.S. *Ausonia*, the ocean liner that Baba sailed on in 1932. Photographed by Stewart Bale/Library and Archives Canada/PA-164781 (Public domain), via Wikimedia Commons.

PART II: To Be With You Always

Into the Fire

125	Mani, Nasik, 1935. Courtesy of MSI Photographic Collection.
127	Khorshed and Mehera (seated); Masi, Naja, Valu, Gulmai, Freiny, and Mani (standing). Dak Bungalow, Nasik, 1935. Courtesy of MSI Photographic Collection.
131	Mani, Nasik. Courtesy of Avatar Meher Baba Trust Archives image collection.
133	Baba, Nasik, 1935. Photographed by Mani. Courtesy of MSI Photographic Collection.
135	Baba with pet goat, Dak Bungalow, Nasik, 1935. Courtesy of MSI Photographic Collection.
136	Mehera, Mani, and Freiny, Nasik, 1935. Courtesy of Mani's Personal Collection at Meherazad.
137	Baba and Soonamasi (seated); Naja, Valu, and Mani (standing). Nasik, 1935. Courtesy of MSI Photographic Collection.
138	Baba dressed in Krishna crown for His birthday, Upper Meherabad, February 1938. Courtesy of Meher Nazar Publications.
141	Beheram and Perin. Courtesy of Meher Nazar Publications.

LIST OF ILUSTRATIVE MATERIALS

PAGE	DESCRIPTION
143	Baba and Eastern and Western women in Marker's house, Kandivli, near Bombay, April 7, 1933. Photographed possibly by Quentin Tod. Courtesy of Avatar Meher Baba Trust Archives image collection.
144	Baba, Kandivli, near Bombay, April 7, 1933. Courtesy of Avatar Meher Baba Trust Archives image collection.
145	Upper Meherabad, early 1930s. Courtesy of MSI Photographic Collection.
146	Baba with Soonamasi, Gulmai, Mehera, Mani, Valu, and Naja outside the east wall of the Meherabad kitchen. Upper Meherabad, about mid-1930s. Photographed by Small Khorshed. Courtesy of MSI Photographic Collection.
148	Baba, Upper Meherabad inside the west corridor, about 1934. Photographed by Mani. Courtesy of MSI Photographic Collection.
149	Mehera in the East Room, Upper Meherabad, about 1938. Courtesy of MSI Photographic Collection.
157	Mani shooting air rifle, Meherabad, 1930s. Courtesy of MSI Photographic Collection.
163	Baba by bamboo matting, Mysore, 1936. Photographed by Mani. Courtesy of MSI Photographic Collection.
164	Mehera with Baba on Champa, Meherabad. Photographed by Mani. Courtesy of MSI Photographic Collection.
168	Baba with Chum in Baba's cabin door. Courtesy of MSI Photographic Collection.
173	Baba outside Meherabad kitchen. Courtesy of MSI Photographic Collection.
177	Baba, Mysore, 1936. Courtesy of MSI Photographic Collection.
186	Two photos of Mani, Bombay, 1936. Photographed by Beheram. Courtesy of Mani Family Collection.

East-West

188	Baba, Nasik or Meherabad, 1936. Courtesy of MSI Photographic Collection.
189	Baba with women at Nasik ashram. Photographed by Elizabeth Patterson. Courtesy of ECPPA.
191	Mani and Mehera outside east corridor, Upper Meherabad, January 1937. Photographed by Elizabeth Patterson. Courtesy of MSI Photographic Collection.
192	Norina, Ramjoo, and Baba at Rahuri ashram. Courtesy of MSI Photographic Collection.
193	Baba as Krishna with the women, Meherabad. Courtesy of MSI Photographic Collection.
194	Baba and women in Villa Caldana, Cannes, France. Courtesy of Meher Nazar Publications.
200	Baba and Mehera on a picnic in France. Courtesy of Avatar Meher Baba Trust Archives image collection.

LIST OF ILUSTRATIVE MATERIALS 1091

PAGE DESCRIPTION

201   Baba and women on a picnic in France. Courtesy of Meher Nazar Publications.
203   Baba aboard ship, upper bunk, 1934. Courtesy of Avatar Meher Baba Trust Archives image collection.
205   Mehera and Mani with Baba in the East Room, Upper Meherabad; Baba is dressed in a crown and robe made by the women, about 1937–1938. Courtesy of MSI Photographic Collection.
206   Mani on a picnic with Baba. Courtesy of Meher Nazar Publications.
207   Krishna's birthday celebration, P.W.D. Bungalow, Ahmednagar, 1938. Photographed by Hedi Mertens. Courtesy of Meher Nazar Publications.
207   Baba dressed as Krishna during the Rang Panchmi celebration at the P.W.D. Bungalow, Ahmednagar, 1938. Photographed by Hedi Mertens. Courtesy of Meher Nazar Publications.
207   Meher Retreat, 1938. Courtesy of Meher Nazar Publications.
211   Meher Retreat stairway. Courtesy of MSI Photographic Collection.
212   Baba with Kippy. Courtesy of MSI Photographic Collection.
212   Mehera with Kippy. Courtesy of MSI Photographic Collection.
215   Irene Billo with servant in kitchen. Courtesy of Meher Nazar Publications.
218–9 Baba and the women against the wall of the water tank, Upper Meherabad, 1937. From the left: Kitty, Khorshed, Nonny, Jean, Norina, Baba, Mehera, Nadine, Mani, Bhagu, Delia, Naja, and Rano. Photographed by Hedi Mertens. Courtesy of Meher Nazar Publications.
221   Baba speaking with Mehera under the Tin Shed, Meherabad, 1937. Rano (beside Mehera); Manu and Meheru Jessawala (bending over). Courtesy of Meher Nazar Publications.
223   Baba on a walk on Meherabad Hill with Irene Billo and the women, 1938–1939. Courtesy of MSI Photographic Collection.
225   Mani on Meherabad Hill, 1938–1939. Photographed by Hedi Mertens. Courtesy of Meher Nazar Publications.
226   Moti the peacock, who roamed the compound at Upper Meherabad when the women lived there in the 1930s. Photographed by Mani. Courtesy of MSI Photographic Collection.
228   Baba outside the tomb at Meherabad. Kitty is sitting next to Baba. Photo taken on Kitty's birthday and the opening of Meher Retreat, August 28, 1938. Gulmai and Norina on the left, Rano and Nonny on the right of Baba. Photographed by Hedi Mertens. Courtesy of Meher Nazar Publications.
229   Baba and Mehera under the Tin Shed, September-November 1938. Photographed by Hedi Mertens. Courtesy of Meher Nazar Publications.
235   Baba seated between Norina (left) and Nadine, Nasik, 1930s. Photographed by Elizabeth Patterson. Courtesy of ECPPA.

LIST OF ILUSTRATIVE MATERIALS

PAGE	DESCRIPTION
241	Baba playing gilli danda. Courtesy of MSI Photographic Collection.
244	The Dome, 1938. Courtesy of MSI Photographic Collection.
245	Baba's family by Baba's cabin. Courtesy of MSI Photographic Collection.
249	Shireenmai with Mani, February 1938. Courtesy of Meher Nazar Publications.
250	Shireenmai with Nadine. Photographer unknown.

The Blue Bus

258	Baba with white turban in open Meherabad field. Photographed by Hedi Mertens. Courtesy of Meher Nazar Publications.
263	Blue Bus packed with luggage. Photographed by Rano Gayley. Courtesy of MSI Photographic Collection.
269	Baba on steps at Taragarh Fort, Ajmer, February 1939. Photographed by Mani. Courtesy of MSI Photographic Collection.
273	Baba in Pandu Lena Caves, Nasik, January 11, 1937. Photographed by Elizabeth Patterson. Courtesy of ECPPA.
274	From the left: Mansari, Gaimai, Meheru Jessawala, Rano, Mani, Valu, and Naja, Jabalpur, early 1939. Photographed by Hedi Mertens. Courtesy of Meher Nazar Publications.
275	Baba dipping hands in Narmada River, near Jabalpur, Christmas 1938. Photographed by Rano Gayley. Courtesy of MSI Photographic Collection.
276	Baba rafting on the Narmada River at Mandla with (from the left) Khorshed, Mehera, and Mani, December 29, 1938. Courtesy of Meher Nazar Publications.
277	Baba at Pushkar Lake, Ajmer, February 1939. With Baba (from the left) are Kitty, Mehera, Gulmai, Soonamasi, Nadine, Helen Dahm, Pilamai, Katie, and Norina. Photographed by Hedi Mertens. Courtesy of Meher Nazar Publications.
278	Elizabeth in the Blue Bus, Hyderabad. Courtesy of MSI Photographic Collection.
281	Mani snapping a photo with box camera on Blue Bus Tours. Photographed by Hedi Mertens. Courtesy of Meher Nazar Publications.
283	Baba in Ellora Caves, Aurangabad, May 18, 1939. Photographed by Rano Gayley. Courtesy of MSI Photographic Collection.
284	Buddha in the Ellora Caves. Photographed by Anne Giles. Copyright Anne Elizabeth Giles.
286	The Blue Bus halts for a brief stop during the Blue Bus Tours. Courtesy of MSI Photographic Collection.
289	Mani and Rano, Agra, 1939. Courtesy of MSI Photographic Collection.

LIST OF ILUSTRATIVE MATERIALS 1093

PAGE	DESCRIPTION
292	Nonny and Baba, Canute and Kippy, Nasik, late 1930s. Photographed by Elizabeth Patterson. Courtesy of ECPPA.
294	Shireenmai and Baba on tour. Photographed by Elizabeth Patterson. Courtesy of ECPPA.
296	Baba with Phulwala, a mast at the Bangalore mast ashram, early 1940. Photographed by Padri. Courtesy of MSI Photographic Collection.
297	Kaka Baria unloading beddings from the Blue Bus in front of Hotel Republica, Panjim, Goa, April 1940. Courtesy of ECPPA.
298	Baba with Sarwar (in topee far left), Meheru Jessawala, Soonamasi, Valu, Soltoon, Gaimai, Mansari, Nargis Dadachanji, Mehera, Irene, Kitty, Khorshed, Nadine, Norina, and Margaret, Goa, April 1940. Photographed by Elizabeth Patterson. Courtesy of ECPPA.
307	Baba with Lucky the monkey, probably in Bangalore, 1939. Courtesy of MSI Photographic Collection.
314	Most likely taken at Fatehpur Sikri, Agra, January 27, 1939. Nadine, Norina, and Rano (behind, taking a photo); Irene, Mehera, Helen, Khorshed (toting the special briefcase); Baba and Mrs. Brown (a neighbor in Agra, acting as their guide that day); Kitty and Naja. Photographed by Elizabeth Patterson. Courtesy of ECPPA.
322	Baba with Mehera, Mani, and other women, including Najoo Kotwal (far right), Meherabad, 1930s. Courtesy of MSI Photographic Collection.
329	Baba, Ceylon, about 1933. Courtesy of Meher Nazar Publications.
330	Baba, Chanji, and Norina, Jabalpur, 1939. Photographed by Hedi Mertens. Courtesy of Meher Nazar Publications.
332	Baba, southern India, 1930s. Photographed by Elizabeth Patterson. Courtesy of ECPPA.
333	Mani at the Red Fort in Delhi during the Blue Bus Tours. Photographed by Hedi Mertens. Courtesy of Meher Nazar Publications.
339	Irene Billo, Meherabad. Photographed by Hedi Mertens. Courtesy of Meher Nazar Publications.
343	Mani's passport photograph, 1937. Photographer unknown.
348	Karim Baba, the mast, Calcutta, 1940s. Courtesy of Meher Nazar Publications.
351	Chacha in tonga with Kaka Baria, Ajmer, 1939. Photographed by Hedi Mertens. Courtesy of Meher Nazar Publications.
353	Chatti Baba in Bangalore mast ashram. Photographed by Padri. Courtesy of MSI Photographic Collection.
358	Baba embracing Mohammed the mast at the back of the old Dharamshala building at Lower Meherabad, mid-1940s. Photographed by Padri. Courtesy of Meher Nazar Publications.
359	Mohammed picking up stones, Meherabad. Courtesy of MSI Photographic Collection.

LIST OF ILUSTRATIVE MATERIALS

PAGE	DESCRIPTION
360	Baba bowing to poor woman. Photographed by Padri. Courtesy of MSI Photographic Collection.
362	Kitty and Baba, Agra, 1939. Courtesy of Meher Nazar Publications.
368	Baba and Upasni Maharaj, Dahigaon, 1941. Photographer unknown. Courtesy of Meher Nazar Publications.
372	Baba in Himalayas during a mast tour, 1942. Courtesy of MSI Photographic Collection.
374	Mani, Lonavla, 1940s. Courtesy of MSI Photographic Collection.
375	Shireenmai, Bangalore, 1939. Photographed by Padri. Courtesy of MSI Photographic Collection.
381	Baba with Kitty opening the door of the Blue Bus for someone to enter. Mani may have taken this photo. Courtesy of M&C Collection, www.martincook.zenfolio.com.

Traveling

383	Mani and Mittu the parrot, Lonavla, 1942. Courtesy of MSI Photographic Collection.
384	Baba and Mittu, Lahore, 1943. Courtesy of Meher Nazar Publications.
390	Baba, Mehera, and Mani, Meherazad, about 1944. Photographed by Naggu. Courtesy of MSI Photographic Collection.
397	Mani, Meherazad, 1940s. Courtesy of MSI Photographic Collection.
399	Meheru, Nagoo, Mani, and Mehera, 1940s. Courtesy of MSI Photographic Collection.
410	Baba standing by the gate at Meherazad with a dog, 1940s. Courtesy of MSI Photographic Collection.
412	Seclusion (Tembi) Hill, before 1946. Courtesy of Meher Nazar Publications.
413	Photo seems to be of Mani on top of Seclusion (Tembi) Hill, 1940s. Courtesy of Avatar Meher Baba Trust Archives image collection.
418	Baba reading a newspaper, Ajmer, 1939. Photographed by Mani. Courtesy of Meher Nazar Publications.
425	Mani with Cracker, Florence Hall, Mahabaleshwar, 1946. Courtesy of MSI Photographic Collection.
427	Baba with Cracker, Florence Hall, Mahabaleshwar, 1946. Courtesy of MSI Photographic Collection.
433	Meheru, Ivy Duce, Mehera, Baba, and Goher (from the left, standing); Mani (sitting). Meherazad, 1948. Photographed by Charmian Duce. Courtesy of Meher Nazar Publications.
438	Baba and Mehera in the garden at Meherazad on the occasion of the housewarming party, 1948. Photographed by Elizabeth Patterson. Courtesy of ECPPA.

LIST OF ILUSTRATIVE MATERIALS 1095

PAGE   DESCRIPTION

439 Meheru outside the verandah of the main house, Meherazad, 1948. Courtesy of MSI Photographic Collection.
442 Meheru and Mani dressed as a pirate and a circus dwarf, Meherabad, 1948. Courtesy of MSI Photographic Collection.
443 Goher dressed as a chicken for the Christmas play, Meherabad, 1948. Courtesy of MSI Photographic Collection.
446 Kitty dressed as a duck, Meherabad, 1948. Courtesy of MSI Photographic Collection.
447 Kitty and Rano as a Parsi couple, Mr. and Mrs. Dhunjishah, Meherazad, 1948–1949. Photographed by Mani. Courtesy of MSI Photographic Collection.
449 Baba on bench, Mt. Abu, 1949. Courtesy of MSI Photographic Collection.
450 Baba and Mehera, Mt. Abu. Courtesy of Meher Nazar Publications.
451 (Left) Baba at Meherazad before going into His Great Seclusion in the Blue Bus, June 21, 1949. Courtesy of Meher Nazar Publications. (Right) Baba at Meherazad at the same time as the photo on the left. Courtesy of Avatar Meher Baba Trust Archives image collection.
452 Mani's passport photo, Hyderabad. Copyright Avatar Meher Baba Trust Archives image collection.

A New Life

467 Baba, Adi Sr., and Babadas begging at Dr. Nath's, Benares, during the New Life, 1949. Photographed by Krishna Prasad Sharma. Courtesy of Meher Nazar Publications.
491 New Life Caravan, Meherazad, 1950s. Courtesy of MSI Photographic Collection.
513 Baba in Mahabaleshwar, October 16, 1950, one day of stepping out of New Life (full figure). Photographed by Padri. Courtesy of MSI Photographic Collection.
513 (Top Left) Baba in Mahabaleshwar, October 16, 1950, one day of stepping out of New Life (close up). Photographed by Padri. Courtesy of MSI Photographic Collection.
513 (Top Right) Baba in Mahabaleshwar, October 16, 1950, one day of stepping out of New Life (close up). Photographed by Padri. Courtesy of MSI Photographic Collection.
515 Baba on the verandah of Florence Hall, Mahabaleshwar, 1951. Photographed by Padri. Courtesy of MSI Photographic Collection.
517 Baba with Begum, Florence Hall, Mahabaleshwar, February 13, 1951. Photographed by Padri. Courtesy of MSI Photographic Collection.
525 Baba meeting with the mandali, Mahabaleshwar. Photographed by Padri. Courtesy of MSI Photographic Collection.

1096 LIST OF ILUSTRATIVE MATERIALS

PAGE	DESCRIPTION
525	Baba meeting with the mandali, Mahabaleshwar. Photographed by Padri. Courtesy of MSI Photographic Collection.
525	Baba meeting with the mandali, Mahabaleshwar. Photographed by Padri. Courtesy of MSI Photographic Collection.
527	Baba with a group of men, Hyderabad, June 1951. Courtesy of Meher Nazar Publications.
533	Seclusion Hill, Meherazad. Photographed by Padri. Courtesy of MSI Photographic Collection.
535	Baba sitting in front of the Blue Bus, Meherazad, at His birthday celebration, February 12, 1952. Photographed by Padri. Courtesy of MSI Photographic Collection.

VOLUME TWO
PART II: To Be With You Always (continued)

In the West

537	Baba at Meher Spiritual Center, Myrtle Beach, May 1952. Courtesy of Avatar Meher Baba Trust Archives image collection.
546	Baba leaning against a tree outside the Guest House where the women mandali stayed, Meher Spiritual Center, Myrtle Beach, May 1952. Courtesy of Sufism Reoriented, Inc.
547	Charmian Duce and Lud Dimpfl on the lake at Meher Spiritual Center, where they set up a fireworks display during Baba's visit, July 1956. Photographed by Hedi Mertens. Courtesy of Meher Nazar Publications.
548	Long Lake at Meher Spiritual Center, seen through the trees, 1960s. Courtesy of Meher Spiritual Center.
551	Goher, Mani, Mehera, and Meheru, during Baba's visit to Myrtle Beach, 1952. Courtesy of Martin Cook.
554	Mehera and Mani, Meher Spiritual Center, Myrtle Beach, 1952. Courtesy of Sufism Reoriented, Inc.
557	Mehera, Baba, Filis Frederick, and Adele Wolkin at Baba's House, Meher Spiritual Center, Myrtle Beach, May 1952. Courtesy of Sufism Reoriented, Inc.
573	The hospital in Prague, Oklahoma, 1950s. Courtesy of Meher Nazar Publications.
574	Some of the Prague hospital staff who treated Meher Baba. From left to right: Velma Davis (head nurse), Jess Dobbs (lab technician), and Dr. Ned Burleson, 1950s. Courtesy of Meher Nazar Publications.
575	Dr. Ned Burleson and his wife Julia. Courtesy of Meher Nazar Publications.
576	Dr. Ned Burleson. Photographed by David Fenster. Courtesy of Meher Nazar Publications.

LIST OF ILUSTRATIVE MATERIALS   1097

PAGE	DESCRIPTION
582	Baba and Mehera on their way to Locarno, Switzerland, 1952. Courtesy of Meher Nazar Publications.
588	View of Youpon Dunes, Elizabeth Patterson's home, where Baba recuperated after the accident. His room was on the top floor (left corner). Courtesy of Meher Spiritual Center.
593	Baba at The Rubens Hotel, London, late July or early August 1952. Mary Backett is at the top left of the photo. Courtesy of Sufism Reoriented, Inc.
595	Delia DeLeon, 1952. Courtesy of Sufism Reoriented, Inc.
598	Baba at the Mertens' home in Locarno, Switzerland, 1952, after His car accident in America. Courtesy of Meher Nazar Publications.
599	Baba with Meherjee and Adi Sr. in Locarno, Switzerland, 1952. Courtesy of Martin Cook.
602	Lunch at Hotel Schweizerhaus, Maloja, Switzerland. Delia DeLeon (seated at table), Mani (arms crossed), Meheru, Mehera, Goher, and Irene Billo's mother, 1952. Photographed by Irene Billo. Courtesy of Meher Nazar Publications.

Fiery and Free

603	Mani, 1950s. Photographed by her brother Beheram. Courtesy of Mani Family Collection.
605	Mani's dog Peter, Mahabaleshwar, 1950s. Photographed by Mani. Courtesy of MSI Photographic Collection.
605	Mani's dog Peter, Mahabaleshwar, 1950s.
607	Mani's dog Peter, Mahabaleshwar, 1953. Photographed by Mani. Courtesy of MSI Photographic Collection.
609	Mehera with Peter, the dog, and Sheba, the horse, Satara, 1953 or 1954. Photographed by Mani. Courtesy of Meher Nazar Publications.
611	Peter's gravestone, Meherazad. Photographed by Anne Giles. Copyright Anne Elizabeth Giles.
620	Mani's photo, signed by Baba as "Highest of the High," on her bedroom bureau, Meherazad. Photographed by Anne Giles. Copyright Anne Elizabeth Giles.
623	Manu Jessawala, Khorshed Jessawala (Eruch's wife), Mehera, Meheru holding Peter, Gulnar, Rano, and Mani, Florence Hall, Mahabaleshwar, 1954. Courtesy of MSI Photographic Collection.
626	Mehera with Bhooti in front of the verandah steps, Meherazad, about 1954 or 1955. Courtesy of MSI Photographic Collection.
628	Baba at Grafton, Satara, 1956. Photographed by Beheram S. Irani. Courtesy of MSI Photographic Collection.
629	Baba kissing Sheba the horse at Grafton, Satara, 1955. Photographed by Mani. Courtesy of MSI Photographic Collection.

LIST OF ILUSTRATIVE MATERIALS

PAGE	DESCRIPTION
629	Baba relaxing at Grafton, Satara, 1955. Photographed by Nagoo or Beheram S. Irani. Courtesy of MSI Photographic Collection.
632	Baba, Satara, about September 7, 1955. In a letter to Beryl Williams September 16, 1955, Mani writes that she took this picture as this is "how I see them [Baba's feet] when I'm reading out loud—just the souls, as he sits back on the gaadi with his feet up on the side-rest." Photographed by Mani. Courtesy of MSI Photographic Collection.
633	Baba, Satara, 1955. Photographed by Mani Courtesy of MSI Photographic Collection.
640	Baba at Grafton, Satara, December 25, 1955. Photographed by Mani. Courtesy of MSI Photographic Collection.
641	Baba and Mehera on her birthday, Satara, December 25, 1955. Photographed by Mani. Courtesy of MSI Photographic Collection.
644	Baba signing *God Speaks*, Satara, March 18, 1955. Photographed by Mani. Courtesy of Meher Nazar Publications.
646	Baba, Satara, 1955. Courtesy of Meher Nazar Publications.

The Last Twelve Years

656	Baba and Mehera, Meherazad, March 1957. Photographed by Beheram S. Irani. Courtesy of MSI Photographic Collection.
659	Mani near Eruch's cabin, Meherazad, 1960s. Courtesy of MSI Photographic Collection.
661	Baba sitting between Mandali Hall and the main house, Meherazad, 1960s. Courtesy of Martin Cook.
662	The gates at Meherazad, 2015. Photographed by Anne Giles. Copyright Anne Elizabeth Giles.
662	The dining room in Baba's house, Meherazad, 2015. Photographed by Anne Giles. Copyright Anne Elizabeth Giles.
663	Meheru, Goher, Irene Conybeare, Mehera, Rano, and Mani, probably taken at Meherazad, July 1957. Mastan is sitting in front. Courtesy of MSI Photographic Collection.
664	Sitting room with Baba's gaadi in Baba's house, Meherazad. Photographed by Adair Adams. Courtesy of Adair Adams.
665	Baba, Meherazad, 1950s. Photographed by Bhaiya Panday. Courtesy of MSI Photographic Collection.
670	Mani typing in her "open-air office." Photographer unknown.
673	Baba and Elizabeth, Meher Spiritual Center, Myrtle Beach, May 1958. Photographed by Hedi Mertens. Courtesy of Meher Nazar Publications.

LIST OF ILUSTRATIVE MATERIALS

PAGE	DESCRIPTION
681	Baba's bedroom, Meherazad. Photographed by Don Stevens shortly after Baba dropped His body. Courtesy of Martin Cook.
684	Baba with Mehera, Naja, and Mani, Meherazad, 1959. Photographed by Goher. Courtesy of Meher Nazar Publications.
687	Baba at the end of the oval garden, Meherazad, 1960s. To the left are Mandali Hall and Bhau's room. Photographed by Beheram S. Irani. Courtesy of MSI Photographic Collection.
695	Mani and Goher, Meherazad, 1960s. Courtesy of MSI Photographic Collection.
701	Jaipuri Qawwal entertaining Baba in Mandali Hall, Meherazad, October 1963. Photographed by Meelan Studio. Courtesy of Meher Nazar Publications.
709	Baba with Kondyala Rao and his three children in Mandali Hall, Meherazad, 1963. Photographed by Meelan Studio. Courtesy of Meher Nazar Publications.
714	Mehera and Baba in Meherazad garden. Courtesy of Meher Nazar Publications.
718	Mehera and Mani in Meherazad garden. Courtesy of Meher Nazar Publications.
720	Baba sitting at the end of the oval garden with Mastan, Meherazad, about 1963–1967. Photographed by Beheram S. Irani. Courtesy of MSI Photographic Collection.
726	Baba in Mandali Hall, Meherazad, early 1960s. Photographed by Beheram S. Irani. Courtesy of MSI Photographic Collection.
731	Mani in her "open-air office," Meherazad, 1960s. From Mani's Family Film "Meherazad Memories." Copyright Sheriar Foundation.
735	Baba at the East-West Gathering, Guruprasad, Poona, November 1962. Photographed by Meelan Studio. Courtesy of Meher Nazar Publications.
750	Baba with a group in Mandali Hall talking to Adi Sr., Meherazad, December 1962. Photographed by Meelan Studio. Courtesy of Meher Nazar Publications.
757	Mehera with Pegu the cat, Guruprasad, Poona, about 1963. Courtesy of MSI Photographic Collection.
758	Baba in front of Guruprasad, Poona, late 1950s or early 1960s. Photographed by Meelan Studio. Courtesy of Meher Nazar Publications.
760	Baba on the verandah at Guruprasad, Poona, 1950s. Eruch is in the doorway behind Baba; Adi Sr. is on the left. Photographed by Meelan Studio. Courtesy of Meher Nazar Publications.
764–5	Baba at the East-West Gathering, Guruprasad, Poona, November 1962. Photographed by Meelan Studio. Courtesy of Meher Nazar Publications.
766	Baba enjoying ghazals during the East-West Gathering, 1962. Photographed by Meelan Studio. Courtesy of Meher Nazar Publications.

LIST OF ILUSTRATIVE MATERIALS

PAGE	DESCRIPTION
767	Baba at the East-West Gathering, Guruprasad, Poona, 1962. Dr. Moorty and Shuddhan Bharati are on the left, and the Maharani Shantadevi of Baroda is on the right. Photographed by Meelan Studio. Courtesy of Meher Nazar Publications.
770	Children dancing for Baba during a program, Guruprasad, Poona, 1963–1964. Photographed by Meelan Studio. Courtesy of Meher Nazar Publications.
773	Baba, Guruprasad. 1950s. Photographed by Meelan Studio. Courtesy of Meher Nazar Publications.
777	Baba on the verandah, Guruprasad, Poona, May 1957. Photographed by Beheram S. Irani. Courtesy of MSI Photographic Collection.
794	Guruprasad, Poona, early 1970s. Courtesy of MSI Photographic Collection.
798	Last photo of Meher Baba, Meherazad, December 23, 1968. Photographed by Rayomand Dadachanji. Copyright Rayomand Dadachanji.

Eternal Beloved

805	Goher, Rano, Mani, Khorshed, Arnavaz, Nargis, Mehera, and Katie during Baba's entombment, Meherabad, January 31 to February 7, 1969. Photographed by Meelan Studio. Courtesy of Meher Nazar Publications.
807	Mani and Goher by the stretcher in Baba's cabin, 1969. Photographed by Meelan Studio. Courtesy of Meher Nazar Publications.
808	Crowds at Baba's Samadhi, Meherabad, January 31 to February 7, 1969. Photographed by Meelan Studio. Courtesy of Meher Nazar Publications.
809	Eruch, Dr. Ginde, Mani, and Dr. Donkin at the Samadhi during Baba's entombment, Meherabad, 1969. Photographed by Meelan Studio. Courtesy of Meher Nazar Publications.
811	Mehera and Mani in the tomb during Baba's entombment, Meherabad, January 31 to February 7, 1969. Photographed by Meelan Studio. Courtesy of Meher Nazar Publications.
812	Cover being lowered over Baba in the Samadhi with Irwin Luck, Pendu, Beheram Irani, and others inside. Mani, Mehera, Arnavaz, and Katie looking on through the rear window. Meherabad, February 7, 1969. Photographed by Meelan Studio. Courtesy of Meher Nazar Publications.
818	The umar tree with Baba's image outside Mehera's and Mani's bedroom window, Meherazad, early 1970s. Photographed by Mani. Courtesy of MSI Photographic Collection.
820	Mehera and Mani by the umar tree, Meherazad, 1970s. Photographed by Bea Muller. Copyright R. Allan Muller.
824	Mehera and Mani, 1970s. Photographer unknown.
837	Mary Bennett from Australia visiting Meherazad, early January 1969. From a film taken by Mani. Copyright Avatar Meher Baba P.P.C. Trust.

LIST OF ILUSTRATIVE MATERIALS 1101

PAGE	DESCRIPTION

846 Mani in the Samadhi during Baba's entombment, Meherabad, January 31 to February 7, 1969. Photographed by Meelan Studio. Courtesy of Meher Nazar Publications.

849 Mastan's gravestone, Meherazad. Photographed by Anne Giles. Copyright Anne Elizabeth Giles.

The Great Darshan

858 Guruprasad, Poona, early 1970s. Photographed by Martin Cook. Copyright Martin Cook.

859 Baba's chair, garlanded by Mehera, in the main hall of Guruprasad, Poona, during the Great Darshan, April to June 1969. Photographed by Felix Schmidt. Copyright Felix Schmidt.

860 Mani and Eruch on the verandah, Guruprasad, Poona, during the Great Darshan. Photographed by Kendra Crossen. Copyright Kendra Crossen.

864 Westerners and women mandali at Guruprasad, Poona, during the Great Darshan. Photographed by Larry Karrasch. Copyright Larry Karrasch.

867 Mehera in the main hall, Guruprasad, Poona, during the Great Darshan. Photographer unknown.

870–1 Westerners and the women mandali, in front of Baba's chair, Guruprasad, Poona, during the Great Darshan. Photographed by Larry Karrasch. Copyright Larry Karrasch.

872 Mani playing the sitar during the darshan program at Guruprasad, Poona, 1969. Photographed by Meelan Studio. Courtesy of Meher Nazar Publications.

PART III: Continuing On

Continuing On

880 Mani and Eruch meeting with visiting Baba-lovers on the verandah, Meherazad, 1970s. Photographer unknown.

881 Mehera addressing the crowd at the first Amartithi, supported by Mani, Meherabad, January 1970. Photographed by Meelan Studio. Courtesy of Meher Nazar Publications.

883 Mani on the verandah, Meherazad, 1970s. Photographer unknown.

886 Mani. Photographed by Jim Braude. Copyright Dr. James Braude.

888 Mani in the Trust Office, early 1970s. Photographed by Anne Giles. Copyright Anne Elizabeth Giles.

890 Mani at the Sarosh Canteen. Photographed by Win Coates. Copyright Susan White.

893 Mani and Eruch, 1972. Photographed by James May. Copyright James May.

895 Eruch on the back verandah of the Trust Office. Photographer unknown.

LIST OF ILUSTRATIVE MATERIALS

PAGE	DESCRIPTION
899	Mani, 1976. Photographed by Goodwin Harding. Copyright Goodwin Harding.
900	Mani, 1972. Photographed by Goodwin Harding. Copyright Goodwin Harding.
905	Mani in the Trust Office. Photographer unknown.
918	Mani and Rano, 1972. Photographed by James May. Copyright James May.
920	Mani on the office phone, 1975. Photographed by James Oppenheim. Copyright James Oppenheim and Robin Reeves-Oppenheim.
921	Baba, Lower Meherabad, 1927–1928. Photographed by Shah. Courtesy of Meher Nazar Publications.
922	Baba and Mehera on Mehera's birthday, Gheun Deolali (near Meherazad), December 22, 1948. Photographed by Mani. Courtesy of Meher Nazar Publications.
923	Mani with camera in the garden, 1972. Photographed by James May. Copyright James May.
924	Mani walking towards Bhau's office at the Trust Office, 1990s. Photographed by Glenn Magrini. Copyright Glenn Magrini.
928	Lunchtime at the Trust Office. Photographer unknown.
935	Mani with a young visitor at the Trust Office, 1993. Photographed by Robin Reeves-Oppenheim. Copyright James Oppenheim and Robin Reeves-Oppenheim.
938	Mehera garlanding photo on Baba's bed, October 15, 1986. Photographed by Wendell Brustman. Copyright Wendell Brustman.
939	Baba's bedroom, Meherazad. Photographed by Sheila Krynski. Copyright Sheila Krynski.
941	Mehera and Mani, 1970s. Photographed by Jack Small. Copyright Jack Small.
942	Mehera and Mani, Upper Meherabad. Photographed by Win Coates. Copyright Susan White.
943	Mehera and Mani, Meherabad Hill, 1972. Photographed by Tim Owens. Copyright Tim Owens.
945	Mani at Mehera's shrine, 1980s. Photographed by Glenn Magrini. Copyright Glenn Magrini.
946	Mani with Agoos, the turtle, 1980s. Photographer unknown.
947	Mani, Meherazad, 1994. Photographed by Kacy Cook. Copyright Kacy Cook.
947	Top of Mani's dressing table. Photographed by Beth Ganz. Copyright Beth Ganz.
948	Mani, Meherazad, 1990s. Photographed by Kacy Cook. Copyright Kacy Cook.
951	Framed photograph of Baba in Meherazad, about 1948. Photographer unknown.
952	Mehera in the dining room, Meherazad, October 15, 1986. Photographed by Wendell Brustman. Copyright Wendell Brustman.
953	Mani at her desk, Meherazad. Photographer unknown.
955	Mani, Goher, and Kitty, Meherazad, November 1980. Photographer unknown.
956	Mani, Rano, and Heather, Meherazad, 1980s. Photographed by Jim Meyer. Copyright Jim Meyer.

LIST OF ILUSTRATIVE MATERIALS

PAGE	DESCRIPTION
958	Mani in Mandali Hall, Meherazad, 1980s. Photographed by Anne Giles. Copyright Anne Elizabeth Giles.
961	Mani, Meherazad, 1970s. Photographer unknown. Courtesy of Meher Nazar Publications.
969	Mani's cupboard, Meherazad. Photographer Beth Ganz. Copyright Beth Ganz.
970	Mani and visiting children playing with her toys, Meherazad, 1980s. Photographed by Anne Giles. Copyright Anne Elizabeth Giles.
971	Mani with children, Meherazad, 1993. Photographed by Amy Romanczuk. Copyright Amy Romanczuk.
974	Mani in Mandali Hall, 1980s. Photographed by Win Coates. Copyright Susan White.
977	Mani in Mandali Hall, 1980s. Photographed by Win Coates. Copyright Susan White.
979	Mani in Mandali Hall, 1980s. Photographed by Win Coates. Copyright Susan White.
980	Mani in Mandali Hall, 1980s. Photographed by Win Coates. Copyright Susan White.
983	Mani in Mandali Hall, 1980s. Photographed by Win Coates. Copyright Susan White.
985	Mani making a shadow puppet, Meherazad. Photographed by Larry Karrasch. Copyright Larry Karrasch.
985	Mani with Freiny-Etta and friends, Meherazad, 1988. Photographed by Raine Eastman-Gannett and Jack Mormon. Copyright Raine Eastman-Gannett and Jack Mormon.
986	Mehera in the garden, Meherazad, 1970s. Photographed by Bea Muller. Copyright R. Allan Muller.
987	Mani, Meherazad. Photographed by Glenn Magrini. Copyright Glenn Magrini.
988	Tree on the approach road to Meherazad. Photographed by Kacy Cook. Copyright Kacy Cook.
989	Mani and Goher, Meherazad. Photographed by Glenn Magrini. Copyright Glenn Magrini.
990	Mehera, Mani, Goher, and Katie inside the Samadhi, Meherabad. Photographed by Win Coates. Copyright Susan White.
991	Mani, 1980s. Photographed by Ed van Buskirk. Copyright Ed van Buskirk.
993	(Left) Restored section of murals in the dome of the Tomb, Meherabad. Photographed by Rustom Vazifdar. Copyright Rustom Vazifdar.
993	(Right) Image of the same section in the dome of the Tomb before restoration, Meherabad, 1971. Photographed by Bhaiya Panday. Copyright Bhaiya Panday.
995	Mani in the doorway of Baba's Cabin, Meherabad. Photographer unknown.
997	Mani, Meherabad, 1990. Photographed by Georgina Erskine. Copyright Georgina Erskine.
999	Mani at Amartithi, Meherabad. Photographed by Glenn Magrini. Copyright Glenn Magrini.
1004	Mehera arriving at the Pilgrim Centre, Meherabad, 1981. Photographed by Scott Himmelsbach. Copyright Scott Himmelsbach.

LIST OF ILUSTRATIVE MATERIALS

PAGE	DESCRIPTION
1006	Mani at Baba's 100th birthday party, Meherabad, 1994. Photographed by Chris Pearson. Copyright Chris Pearson.
1010	Mani by Baba's Room at Baba-House, Poona. Photographed by Paul Comar. Copyright Paul Comar.
1034	Mani at Mehera's shrine, Meherabad, 1980s. Photographed by Glenn Magrini. Copyright Glenn Magrini.
1036	Mani, Meherabad, 1980s. Photographed by Glenn Magrini. Copyright Glenn Magrini.
1038	Mani, Meherazad, 1996. Photographed by Kacy Cook. Copyright Kacy Cook.
1043	Two-page spread of Mani's book *Dreaming of The Beloved*. Photographed by Sheila Krynski. Copyright Sheriar Foundation.
1069	Baba, Andhra, 1954. Photographer unknown. Courtesy of Meher Nazar Publications.

LIST OF HISTORICAL MATERIALS

VOLUME ONE
PART I: God's Sister

God's Sister

97	Mani's childhood letter to Baba, February 26, 1926. Copyright Avatar Meher Baba Trust Archives document collection.
99	Letter to Baba from Mani written in Gujerati. Copyright Avatar Meher Baba Trust Archives document collection.
120	Excerpts from a letter (and its envelope) from Baba on the R.M.S. *Ausonia* to Mani. Copyright Avatar Meher Baba Trust Archives document collection.

PART II: To Be With You Always

Into the Fire

160	(Left) Drawing by Mani of Mehera. Copyright Avatar Meher Baba Trust Archives collections. (Right) Drawing of Baba by Mani. Copyright Avatar Meher Baba Trust Archives collections.
161	(Left) Drawing of ship, "Bon Voyage" by Mani. Copyright Avatar Meher Baba Trust Archives collections. (Right) Drawing of "Freedom" by Mani. Copyright Avatar Meher Baba Trust Archives collections.

LIST OF ILUSTRATIVE MATERIALS 1105

PAGE   DESCRIPTION

East-West

224   Note to Mani from Baba. Copyright Avatar Meher Baba Trust Archives document collection.
232   Collage by Mani of picnic with Baba. Figures around Baba are (from left to right): Khorshed, Rano, Kaku, Masi, Naja, Norina, Nonny, servants, Kitty; (bottom) Mehera, Mani, Kippy (pet). Copyright Avatar Meher Baba Trust Archives collections.

The Blue Bus

266   Page from Mani's Blue Bus diary. Copyright Avatar Meher Baba Trust Archives document collection.
271   Collection of Mani's diaries. Photographed by Sheila Krynski. Copyright Avatar Meher Baba Trust Archives document collection.
299   Pages 78 and 79 from Mani's diary from 1950. Copyright Avatar Meher Baba Trust Archives document collection.
302   Mani's notebook, June 1940 to March 1941. Copyright Avatar Meher Baba Trust Archives document collection.
328   Map of the Fourth Blue Bus Tour. Copyright Avatar Meher Baba Trust.

Traveling

398   Two pages from Mani's knitting notebook. Copyright Avatar Meher Baba Trust Archives document collection.
415   Two pages from Mani's notebook from the 1940s. Copyright Avatar Meher Baba Trust Archives document collection.

A New Life

501   Page from Mani's diary from the 1950s. Copyright Avatar Meher Baba Trust Archives document collection.
528   Two pages from Mani's New Life diary. Copyright Avatar Meher Baba Trust Archives document collection.

LIST OF ILUSTRATIVE MATERIALS

PAGE   DESCRIPTION

VOLUME TWO
PART II: To Be With You Always (continued)

In the West

553   Two pages from Mani's diary, written at Meher Spiritual Center, Myrtle Beach, April 1952. Copyright Avatar Meher Baba Trust Archives document collection.

Fiery and Free

606   Three pages from Mani's "The Dog Book": (Top to bottom) Cover, inside page, title page, and (bottom right) two pages from the same book. Copyright Avatar Meher Baba Trust Archives document collection.

625   Pages from Mani's diary, 1954. Copyright Avatar Meher Baba Trust Archives document collection.

649   Pages from Mani's diary, 1956. Copyright Avatar Meher Baba Trust Archives document collection.

Eternal Beloved

827   Three Hafiz quotes, framed, hanging in Baba's bedroom, Meherazad. Photographed by Adair Adams. Copyright Avatar Meher Baba Trust Archives document collection.

PART III: Continuing On

Continuing On

910   Masthead of letter from Mani to Anne Giles. Copyright Anne Elizabeth Giles.

914   (Top) Back of postcard from Mani to Heather. (Bottom) Front of postcard from Mani to Heather. Copyright Heather Nadel.

PAGE   DESCRIPTION

LIST OF ARCHIVAL OBJECTS

VOLUME ONE
PART II: To Be With You Always

Into the Fire

152   Two views of a brooch with Baba's hair made by Mehera for Mani. Photographed by Sheila Krynski. Copyright Avatar Meher Baba Trust Archives collections.

A New Life

468   Puppet head made by Mani in the New Life. Photographed by Beth Ganz. Copyright Avatar Meher Baba Trust Archives collections.

469   Three hand puppets made by the women mandali in The New Life. Photographed by Beth Ganz. Copyright Avatar Meher Baba Trust Archives collections.

VOLUME TWO
PART II: To Be With You Always (continued)

Eternal Beloved

851   The gong used to summon the men. Photographed by Anne Elizabeth Giles. Copyright Avatar Meher Baba Trust Archives collections.

PART III: Continuing On

Continuing On

940   "Aussie Baba," bust of Baba sculpted by John Bruford. Photographed by Adair Adams. Copyright Avatar Meher Baba Trust Archives collections.

LIST OF SOURCE MATERIALS

Excerpts from the following works are used by permission.

82 Family Letters: To the Western Family of Lovers and Followers of Meher Baba by Mani S. Irani. (North Myrtle Beach, SC: Sheriar Press, 1976).

Baba Loved Us Too: Stories of Meher Baba and His Pets by Mehera J. Irani. (Myrtle Beach, SC: Sheriar Press, 1989).

Because of Love: My Life and Art with Meher Baba by Rano Gayley. (North Myrtle Beach, SC: Sheriar Press, 1983).

"Dance of Life" in *Hafez, Dance of Life*. Translated by Michael Boylan and Wilberforce Clarke. (Washington, DC: Mage Publishers, Inc., 1987).

The Dance of Love: My Life with Meher Baba by Margaret Craske. (North Myrtle Beach, SC: Sheriar Press, 1980).

Dreaming of The Beloved by Mani S. Irani. (North Myrtle Beach, SC: Sheriar Foundation, 1999).

"The Editor's Diary: The News about The Master, Shri Sadguru Meher Baba (15th March to 14th April 1929)." *Meher Message* 1, no. 51 (May 1929).

The Empty Chair by Barbara Bamberger Scott. (Berkeley, CA: The White Horse Publishing Company, 2010).

God-Brother: Stories from My Childhood with Meher Baba by Mani S. Irani. (North Myrtle Beach, SC: Sheriar Foundation, 1993).

"God Knows" by Minnie Louise Haskins. *The Rotarian* 57, no. 4 (Oct 1940). Rotary International.

LIST OF SOURCE MATERIALS

The God-Man: The Life, Journeys and Work of Meher Baba with an Interpretation of his Silence and Spiritual Teaching by C. B. Purdom. (North Myrtle Beach: Sheriar Foundation, 1971).

Holy Daring: An Outrageous Gift to Modern Spirituality from Saint Teresa, the Grand Wild Woman of Avila by Tessa Bielecki. (Rockport, MA: Element Books Ltd., 1994).

How a Master Works by Ivy O. Duce. (Walnut Creek, CA: Sufism Reoriented, Inc., 1975).

Lord Meher: The Biography of the Avatar of the Age Meher Baba by Bhau Kalchuri. (Myrtle Beach, SC: MANifestation, 1996).

Love Alone Prevails: A Story of Life with Meher Baba by Kitty Davy. (North Myrtle Beach, SC: Sheriar Foundation, 1981).

A Love So Amazing: Memories of Meher Baba by Bili Eaton. (North Myrtle Beach, SC: Sheriar Press, 1984).

"Love Street Lamp Post" (July 2002). Avatar Meher Baba Center of Southern California.

"Mani Part 2" in *Lives of Love: The Women Mandali of Avatar Meher Baba* by Judith Garbett. (Woombye, Queensland: Meher Baba Foundation Australia, 1998).

Meher Baba's Word and His Three Bridges by Don E. Stevens. Edited by Norah Moore and Laurent Weichberger. (London: Companion Books, 2003).

Mehera by Mehera J. Irani. (East Windsor, NJ: Beloved Books, 1989).

Mehera-Meher: A Divine Romance by David Fenster. (Ahmednagar: Meher Nazar Publications, 2003).

The Ocean of Love by Delia DeLeon. (Myrtle Beach, SC: Sheriar Press, 1991).

Tales from the New Life with Meher Baba. Narrated by Eruch, Mehera, Mani, and Meheru. Edited by D. E. Stevens, Rick M. Chapman, James M. Hastings, Gary Freeman, and Patty Freeman. (Berkeley, CA: The Beguine Library, 1976).

INDEX OF MANI'S STORIES

The following collection of Mani's stories includes 1) Mani's words verbatim, shown as indented paragraphs in the text; 2) quoted stories that Mani told in Mandali Hall; 3) text from letters sent describing her experiences; and material from Mani's diaries.

VOLUME ONE

DESCRIPTION • PAGE	DESCRIPTION • PAGE

Preface
Delia's box of quotes • *xi*

Prologue
"I didn't come to Baba; Baba came to me." • *3*

God's Sister

Sheriarji's search for God • *5*
Shireenmai and Sheriarji's engagement • *7*
Shireenmai's dream of a river of people • *9*
Childhood of the "Perfect Boy" • *11*
Baba banging His head in the L-shaped room • *16*
Shireenmai's dream of the goddesses in the well • *17*
Golandoon visits Babajan • *19*
Shireenmai visits Upasni • *20*

Merwan at the toddy shop • *23*
Mani born "by special appointment" • *25*
Opposition of Zoroastrian community • *26*
Cruel rumor of Baba's arrest • *28*
Shireenmai attends Pavlova performance • *30*
Dowlamasi and Ferdoonmasa raise Jamshed • *32*
Jamshed's death • *33*

INDEX OF MANI'S STORIES

DESCRIPTION • PAGE	DESCRIPTION • PAGE
Mani wants a tricycle • 40	Visiting Narayan Maharaj • 80
First meeting with Mehera • 41	Ghostly Victoria (carriage) • 81
"Child mandali member" on visits • 44	Dream of Babajan closing shop • 83
"Lucky ducks" salt and pepper shakers • 47	Baba's voice • 84
Mani punished with cooking pot on her head • 49	Convent of Jesus and Mary • 86
	"How could they do that to Baba?" • 89
Mani is bitten by a scorpion • 51	Coming first in her exams • 89
Shireenmai and Baba argue • 53	Lying at the drop of a hat • 91
Flying a kite with Baba • 56	"My brother is Christ!" • 92
"Not all this and heaven, too." • 56	God-Luck 93
Mani forgets to remove her sandals • 58	"Please turn the key." • 94
Sheriarji and his prayers • 63	How she knew her brother was God • 100
Dream of a red goldfish • 65	"Little" and "big" orders • 101
Sheriarji's gift of languages • 66	Crying on the train home • 102
Loss of the toddy shop • 67	Dream of God's Court • 104
Play at home • 70	Dream of God naked on a cloud • 105
The moholla (neighborhood) • 72	Shireenmai's acceptance of Baba as God • 106
Mani's Navjote • 75	Baba to Shireenmai on His Silence • 112
Birthday at the agyari • 77	"Make a wish." • 113
Closeness to Babajan • 78	How Mani joined Baba • 118

Into the Fire

Skipping rope • 125	Baba cheating at games • 155
"Into the fire" of self-denial • 127	Air rifle practice • 157
Special spinach diet • 129	Learning a classic sitar piece • 158
Doing and not doing • 131	"One anna soul" • 165
Pastimes when Baba was away • 135	Ugly baby parrots • 165
Big Khorshed "dies" at Baba's feet • 138	"Make the most of this time." • 170
Life in the East Room on Meherabad Hill • 144	Thinking of Him constantly • 171
Learning how to serve Baba • 151	Embroidered poem to Lord Meher Shree • 172
Crafts using Baba's hair • 151	"I say, can you tell me the time?" • 175
Playing the sitar when workers around • 153	Making friends at the Mysore Hospital • 177
Covering labels so no words appear • 154	Mani's mastoid operation • 181
	Baba blesses the babies • 183

INDEX OF MANI'S STORIES

DESCRIPTION • PAGE	DESCRIPTION • PAGE

East-West

"Western sisters" at Nasik • 187	High stairs on Meher Retreat • 212
Not mentioning a man's name • 189	Baba's work on Norina • 213
Baba dressed up as Krishna • 193	Irene and the pills • 216
Voyage out to Cannes • 194	Elizabeth rising early • 217
Seasickness 195	Unity but not uniformity • 231
Norina and the ship captain • 196	Friction and the shoe polish • 234
Mani and the chamberpot • 197	The mahout • 238
Climbing the Eiffel Tower • 201	Katie asked to knit a sweater • 239
Voyage back to India • 202	Games with Baba • 241
Difficult adjustment for the Western women • 208	Visits from Shireenmai • 244

Blue Bus Tours

Tightly packed bus • 265	The Beautiful Stranger • 314
Visit to Chisti's tomb • 277	Love and meditation • 318
Elizabeth's early morning torture • 278	Irene's year of silence • 338
"I am Buddha." • 282	Mani's magic powers • 342
The real chargeman at Jaipur • 286	Chatti Baba bathes Baba • 357
8,000 sadhus and only 8 are real • 288	Swimming lessons at Karwar • 370
Baidul's daughter as "Baba" • 288	Ghost in Lonavla • 373
Baba's work with animals at the zoo • 293	Shireenmai's passing • 374
Soonamasi's alarm clock • 310	Shireenmai's role in Baba's drama • 378

Traveling

Baba might send her away at any time • 382	Gathering stones • 413
Mittu chews Margaret's dress • 383	Going to the movies at 5:00 am • 417
Confusing the cooks in Srinagar • 384	Baba's love of masts • 425
Ravenous in Udaipur • 385	Goher's care for hens and ducks • 428
"Hut" much nicer than the palace • 389	Kitty's feather cushion • 432
Finding the Meherazad property • 390	Mani, the correspondent • 434
Mani's Raipur pudding • 400	Donkin and Mani accidentally touch • 436
The fortunate goat • 401	Staying at Rusipop's • 437
Donkin and the ghorawalla • 403	Telling Baba jokes • 439
Baba gets a "donkey coat" • 407	*Skits for Baba* 442
Early Meherazad • 409	Stay at Mt. Abu • 447

INDEX OF MANI'S STORIES

| DESCRIPTION • PAGE | DESCRIPTION • PAGE |

A New Life

Mani's sympathy for those left behind • *454*	"Master of horses" trains the white horse • *483*
Dr. Ghani's fatigue • *456*	"Happy New Life!" • *485*
Controlling their emotions • *457*	Spinach for breakfast • *486*
Baba improves a cooked stew • *459*	Mani finds a perfect elephant dropping • *488*
New Life's "unfathomable depth" • *462*	"We have to walk on foot." • *492*
Mehera sits on a chair by mistake • *465*	Ferocious weather in the north • *494*
Making puppets • *466*	Todi Singh's family cooks for them • *495*
Mani's cold like Anthea's Guest 470	April Fool's joke on Dr. Goher • *500*
Sarnath gardener who chanted "Ram, Ram, Sita, Ram" • *472*	Apologizing to the proprietor of Goel's Hotel • *502*
New Life caravan procession • *476*	Naosherwan asks Baba a question • *504*
Dr. Nilu and Kaka asking for bhiksha • *477*	The New Life can only be lived • *536*
The 12-door room in Moradabad • *482*	

VOLUME TWO

In the West

Elizabeth's founding of Meher Center • *537*	The kindness of the people in America • *577*
Champagne and a martini on the flight to America • *539*	Soft drinks at Cornell Medical Center • *578*
Children on the flight attracted to Baba • *542*	A letter about the accident • *580*
Sights of New York City • *543*	Lunch on hot dogs in Columbia, SC • *584*
Dinner at the Ceylon India Inn • *544*	Delia's chatting on the ride back • *586*
First glimpses of the Center • *545*	*Vitamins and tonic for Mani 588*
A letter to those back home • *549*	The real meditations • *590*
The fruit juices! The food! • *554*	Sightseeing in New York • *591*
A letter to Jal • *557*	Sightseeing in England • *592*
Shells touched by Baba for the 1995 Youth Sahavas • *559*	Buckingham Palace guard breaks his poise • *594*
Memories of the accident in Prague OK • *565*	Keeping silence at The Rubens Hotel • *596*
A cup of coffee • *568*	London bobby at Madame Tussauds Wax Museum • *597*
The Burlesons • *574*	

INDEX OF MANI'S STORIES

| DESCRIPTION • PAGE | DESCRIPTION • PAGE |

Fiery and Free

Peter's good fortune to die at Baba's feet • 610
Mango mad • 615
Reading aloud to Baba • 617
"The Highest of the High" photo • 620
Brother Beheram's photography • 621
Mani's mushroom "trip" • 630
Correspondence from Satara • 631

Letters to "Elinorkit" • 634
Baba's and Mehera's 1954 Christmas • 640
The flaming tree • 642
Comments on *God Speaks* and others • 644
Baba's second accident in 1956 • 647
Goher's wins a toothbrush contest • 654

Last Twelve Years

Baba blesses baby birds • 660
God-Man's suffering • 672
"Drab, dry, and dusty" Ahmednagar • 677
"Baba is Number 10" • 679
"Why this fly?" • 681
Waves of Supreme Purity • 682
"Always a going forward" • 683
"Nice flower" • 684
Village woman glimpses Baba 688
Baba's teasing the women • 691
"Fast-fast" and Flubber • 693
Dhun's cards on Baba's birthday • 698
People who sang for Baba • 700
"Where does sound go?" • 704
Gifts to Baba • 707
Baba sees through to the love • 711
Mehera's special role • 713
Mani in and out of favor • 716
Mehera trimming Baba's mustache • 718
Peter safe and sound at Baba's feet • 719
How Baba touched photos • 724
Where Baba worked on Fallenfluh • 728
Eruch and Francis discover Baba's strength • 729
Typing fast for Baba • 730

Baba tells Ben Hayman's daughter, "Keep calling." • 733
"Real Giving" • 734
Hidden side to Baba's "gifts" • 736
Baba's arm exercises • 737
Singing "Begin the Beguine" to Eruch • 739
Mani and Eruch on Baba's Silence • 742
The family who forgot Baba didn't "talk" • 745
Baba hiding His Divinity • 747
Difference between a stone and God-Realization • 748
How can you tell a child about marriage? • 749
"Coca-Cola!" "Orange!" • 751
"Waiting for Me, not in vain!" • 755
The tailor's dilemma • 757
The East-West Gathering • 763
Elizabeth's dressing gown 764
The yogi and the fruit 766
The ignored man • 769
The children's play • 776
Baba's baby carriage • 777
"I am the best friend ever." • 778
Jim Reeves • 780
Dr. Goher and Dr. Grant • 783
Intensity of Baba's work, 1968–1969 • 790

INDEX OF MANI'S STORIES

DESCRIPTION • PAGE	DESCRIPTION • PAGE

Eternal Beloved

January 31, 1969 • *803*	"I hear everything. Go on reading." • *830*
"Shut your eyes and count to 20." • *804*	Mani's last birthday embrace • *834*
"Now He was for everybody." • *808*	Mary Bennett visits Meherazad • *834*
Last goodbye at the tomb • *809*	How Mary came to the Great Darshan • *841*
Baba asks Mani to take care of Mehera • *813*	Playing "Begin the Beguine" at the end • *843*
The shepherd watches over his flock • *815*	Trust Baba like a babe in its mother's arms • *847*
Baba tells Joanna Smith "This tree I like." • *822*	Mehera says "Jai Baba" to the men • *847*
Mehera and Mani switch roles • *823*	Mastan's death • *849*
Mani's dream of Baba covered with a towel • *824*	The gong that died • *849*
	The ambulance that died • *853*
Three couplets by Hafiz • *826*	Missing Baba • *855*
Baba listens on a house phone • *828*	

The Great Darshan

Witnessing Baba's presence without His physical form • *858*	Mehera greeting Baba's children • *866*
	Breath of the New Humanity • *869*
The doubting man • *859*	Mandali also feasted in Baba's presence • *873*
The man who received a telegram on his birthday • *862*	Holding on to Baba's damaan • *874*

Continuing On

Dream of Baba "at the mains" • *883*	*"Pack as much as you can in your suitcase." 979*
"What good does 'sorry' do me?" • *899*	
Advice to Pilgrim Centre workers • *900*	*"Love Me more and more" 980*
Talk with "residents" at Ahmednagar Centre • *903*	*Remembering Baba 981*
	Meaning of freedom 982
Samples of her correspondence • *910*	In Meherazad Garden • *985*
"I'm Rachael." • *924*	*Mehera says goodbye by the duck pond 986*
Advice from the parlour • *931*	*Trees of Baba's advent 986*
No one excluded from Baba's love • *933*	*Mani and Goher's scooters 989*
Accept His way 944	*Mani at Baba's Samadhi 990*
Mani's inner voice • *961*	Mehera's shrine • *994*
Speedbreakers 965	Mani's Hindi talks at Amartithi • *1000*
"Baba made the stories." • *974*	Baba's 100th Birthday play • *1007*

DESCRIPTION • PAGE	DESCRIPTION • PAGE
Mehera's reunion • *1013*	Mani's last darshan at the Samadhi • *1045*
A going forward • *1035*	"I am the bird, I am not the cage." • *1055*
The barber's watch • *1038*	
"On the Topic of Suffering" • *1040*	
The dream book • *1042*	

INDEX

This index contains entries for Volumes I and II of *The Joyous Path*. People are indexed under their last names. *Meher Baba* appears as *Irani, Meher Sheriar (Avatar Meher Baba)*. Mani appears as *Irani, Mani Sheriar (Baba's sister)*. Familiar first names direct you to the primary entry. For example, *Eruch* is indexed as *Jessawala, Eruch Beheram*, but you will also find *Eruch. See Jessawala, Eruch Beheram*.

Symbols

7 Names of God 306, 706
7Up 579
82 Family Letters (Mani Irani)
   history of 667–671, 721, 953–954
   Dec 5, 1956 648–652
   Jan 23, 1957 656–657
   Feb 20, 1957 657
   Apr 11, 1957 658
   Jun 28, 1957 664
   Sep 8, 1957 672–673
   Aug 25, 1958 674
   Dec 1, 1958 674–675
   Jan 11, 1959 658–659
   Jun 13, 1959 659, 673
   Sep 15, 1960 670
   Aug 16, 1962 659–660
   Feb 15, 1963 661, 665–666
   Aug 9, 1963 672
   Sep 23–Oct 3, 1963 660–661
   Aug 20, 1964 660
   Jun 1, 1967 675
   Oct 10, 1967 790–791
   Jan 25, 1968 790–791
   Mar 1, 1968 792–793
   Mar 12, 1968 795
   May 12, 1968 791–795
   Sep 9, 1968 795–796
   Nov 1, 1968 796–797
   Jan 26, 1969 798–801
   Mar 14, 1969 802, 805–809
   Aug 26, 1969 869–875
101 Names of God 111, 959
1969 Darshan. *See* Great Darshan
   (Apr–Jun 1969)

A

Abdulla, Abdul Karim (Ramjoo) 116, 644, 646
abhanga (Marathi devotional song) 1046
adab (courtesy at a royal court) 59
Adi. *See* Kotwal, Adi Savak (Savak's son)
Adi Jr. *See* Irani, Adi Sheriar (Baba's brother)
Adi Sr. *See* Irani, Adi Kaikhushru
Adriel, Jean 437, 439
Aga Khan 516
Agast Muni (Hindu saint) 363
Agoos (pet tortoise) 946
Agra 276, 333
agyari (Zoroastrian temple) 28, 75, 77
Ahmednabad 448
Ahmednagar 28, 38, 47, 53, 56, 83, 207, 208,
       301, 367, 373, 392, 414, 417, 652,
       836, 886
   1954 mass darshan 624
   Ahmednagar Baba Centre 821, 903
   "drab, dry, and dusty" 677–679
   Meher Nazar 886
   train station 175
Air India 602
air rifle, Mani's 157, 176
Ajmer 272, 277, 342
Akhtar, Begum 780, 1022
Aloba. *See* Shapurzaman, Ali Akbar
A Love So Amazing (Bili Eaton) 631
Alu. *See* Khambatta, Dr. Alu
Amartithi
   first, on Jan 31 1970 880
   Mani's Hindi talks 1000–1001
   Meherabad Hill covered with people from all
      over the world. 999–1000
   gift of saris from Andra Pradesh 1000–1001
   ambulance that "died" 854
America. *See* United States

Bombay 397, 507, 510–512, 538, 604, 625–626, 432
  Andheri 512
  Ashiana 625, 432
  Bandra 512
  Hanging Gardens 511
  Kandivli 142–143, 442
  Mahim 511
  Manzil-e-Meem 40, 464, 829
  Marve Beach 538, 560
  Taj Mahal Hotel 655
  Tower of Silence
    Sheriarji's body taken there 117
  Vesava Beach 512
  Victoria zoo 511–512
  Vile parle 512
Booth Salvation Army Hospital
  ambulance that "died" 854
  stretcher that bore Baba's body 853–854
Brabazon, Francis 314, 558, 627, 723, 729, 836
  poem about "the Beautiful Stranger" 704
Brahmaputra River 510
Brieseman, Dr. Mel 853–854
Brindaban 276–277
"broken-down furniture" 314, 642–644
Brookgreen Gardens (South Carolina) 556
Buford, Bernard 939
Bruford, John
  sculpture of Meher Baba 939–940
  nicknamed "Aussie Baba" by Mani 940
Buddha Cave (Ellora) 284
Buddha, Lord (Avatar) 276, 283–285, 320, 470, 474–475, 529
"Bujave Nar" arti 966, 1021
Burleson, Beth 574–575
Burleson, Dr. Ned 574–576, 580
Burleson, Julia 574–576, 580, 926
Burleson, Margaret (Julia) 574–575
Byramangala Universal Spiritual Centre 292, 377

C

Caesar's Head, South Carolina 562
Cairo 539, 549
Calcutta 265, 300–301, 347–348, 360
Calicut 365
California 324, 557–559, 561, 580
Cannes 194–204
  Capo di Monte 199
  Villa Caldana 199
Capri (Italian island) 539
Carpenter's Cave. See Buddha Cave (Ellora)
Carr, John Dickson (Carter Dickson) 830
Castasegna (Switzerland) 600

Caucasus 324
Ceylon (Sri Lanka) 265, 309, 326–331, 365
Ceylon India Inn (New York City) 543–545
Chaddar Baba (mast) 296
Champa (donkey) 162–164
Chanda 360
Chanji. See Dadachanji, Feramroz Hormusji (Baba's secretary)
Charteris, Leslie (The Saint series) 636, 830
Chattanooga, Tennessee 563
Chatterji, Dr. S. C. 777
Chatti Baba (mast) 296, 320, 350, 353–357, 367–369
Chick (Edgar Wallace) 417
China 116
Chinnaswami (mast) 296
Chisti, Khwaja Saheb Moinuddin (Perfect Master) 272, 277
Chitali 20
Chopra, Dr. Arvind 1016, 1023–1025, 1039, 1063
Christianity 529
Christie, Agatha 340, 417, 618, 722, 830
Chum (Baba's dog) 168–169
  punished for biting Mani 169, 995
Churchill, Winston 317
Circle, Baba's 633
Cleveland, Tennessee
  Jesus signs 563
Coca-Cola 563, 579, 751–754
Columbia, South Carolina 562
  lunch on hotdogs and tea 585
Complicated Free Life 538
Consuelo. See Sides, Consuelo
Conway, South Carolina 562
Conybeare, Irene 629
Cooper, Mrs. 604–605, 610, 629
Cornell Medical Center 578
Corsica (French island) 199
Cracker (Scottish terrier) 398, 425, 427, 437
Craske, Margaret 150, 200, 202, 231, 240, 340–341, 382–383, 393, 416, 426, 551, 583, 636, 722, 954, 1014, 1020
  "A little of what you fancy does you good." 898
  correspondence from Mani 912
  Dance of Love, The 395
  Ellora guide falls at Baba's feet 285
  finding books for Baba 618
  first visit to Meherabad 190–192
  her dancers meet Baba in 1952 558
  "I do whatever my master tells me." 241
  indifferent to her clothes 383–384
  pumice stone 242

teaches the women
  diving 408–409
  rowing 556
  self-defense 372
  swimming 370–371
Czechoslovakia 300, 302

D

Dadachanji, Arnavaz Nariman xiii, 162, 251, 257, 266, 374, 505, 511, 580, 625, 890, 433, 1027, 1058
Dadachanji, Feramroz Hormusji (Chanji, Baba's secretary) 195, 326, 329
Dadachanji, Nargis (Arnavas' sister) 266
Dadachanji, Nariman 374, 433
  buys Dr. Goher's Rolex watch 655
  Trustee 883, 891
Dadi. *See* Kerawala, Dadi (Eruch's cousin)
Dahm, Helen 243, 262, 992
dak bungalows 267–268
Dal Lake (Srinagar) 400
Dance of Love, The (Margaret Craske) 395
Dara. *See* Irani, Dara Adi (Baba's nephew)
dard (Persian for pain or longing) 844
Dari (Persian venacular) 63, 72, 86, 102, 614, 1024
  "dome" means "bottom" 251
darshan 31, 69. *See also* Great Darshan and Irani, Merwan Sheriar, meetings and public darshans
Darwin. *See* Shaw, Darwin
Dastur, Guloo Kaikobad (Kaikobad's daughter) 992, 1063
Dastur, Jaloo Kaikobad (Kaikobad's daughter) 992
Dastur, Kaikobad 530, 626, 744
Dattatreya (Creator, Sustainer, Destroyer) 821, 989
Daula. *See* Irani, Daula R. (Baidul's daughter)
Daulatmai. *See* Irani, Daulatmai Jehangir (Mehera's mother)
Davis, Velma (Prague nurse) 574
Davy, Herbert (Kitty's brother) 637
Davy, Katherine Laura (Kitty) 193, 199–200, 202, 206–207, 209, 231, 240, 265, 268, 279, 281, 335, 347, 355, 361–362, 371, 382–383, 388, 393, 407, 410–411, 417, 425–427, 451, 507–509, 524–527, 537, 547, 549, 556, 561, 563–564, 580, 631–637, 653, 666–668, 1014, 1020
  100th birthday, song from Mani 954
  bird feathers, collected 432–433
  Love Alone Prevails 620, 631, 667
  roles in Mani's skits 442–447

scared by a "snake" 514–515
Dehra Dun 265, 341, 371, 397–398, 477–480, 492–507, 604–622, 804, 1000
Dehra Ghazzi Khan 334
DeLeon, Delia xi, 142, 200, 437, 439, 551, 561, 584, 593, 597–598, 1020
  Baba's accident 565–566, 569, 573
  "England's National Treasure" 954
  Mani's ploy to stop her chattering 586–587
  Ocean of Love, The 192–193
  "Oh, dear! I mean cowgirl!" 189
Delhi 264, 272, 333, 360, 506–507, 1000,
Delia. *See* DeLeon, Delia
Denmark 300–302
Deolali (near Nasik) 88
Deorukhar, Sushila (Vishnu's cousin) 1009
Deorukhar, Vishnu 153, 392, 464, 530, 649–651
Desai, Dhun 504
Desai, Dr. Meher 1024
Desai, Keki 504
Desai, Mansari 222, 262, 307–308, 338, 355, 534, 583, 992, 1002, 1063
  skit of Mother India 256
Deshmukh, Dr. C. D. 523, 647
de Sousa, Mary (Mani's school friend) 88–89, 91–93
Dhahran (Saudi Arabia) 539
Dhondi (village woman) 689
Dhun. *See* Satha, Dhun (Eruch's cousin)
dhuni (sacred fire) 111, 535
Dina. *See* Talati, Dina
Discourses (Meher Baba) 646
Divali (festival of lights) 326, 530, 956
Dobs, Jess (Prague lab technician) 574
Don. *See* Donkin, Dr. William; Stevens, Don
Donkin, Dr. William (Don) 327, 342, 354, 372, 402, 459, 464, 468, 477, 481, 490, 498–499, 504, 508, 523, 530, 538, 582, 584, 599, 655, 657, 809, 854
  Baba's 1956 accident 651–652
  Donkin and the ghorawalla 403–406
  Vitamins and tonic for Mani 588–589
  Wayfarers, The 436–439
Dorab. *See* Irani, Dorab (Shireen's father)
Dowlamasi. *See* Irani, Dowlamasi Feredoon (Masi, Baba's aunt)
Dreaming of The Beloved (Mani Irani) 66, 80, 83, 883, 948, 986, 1042–1044, 1058
Driver, Faredoon Nowroj (Padri) 78, 412, 476
  set up first pilgrim rooms at Meherabad 1002
  Trustee 883, 891
Dr. Pepper 563
Dubash, Rhoda 928–930
Duce, Charmian 433, 556, 578, 592
Duce, Ivy (Murshida) 433–434, 556–557, 572, 591–592, 644–645, 663, 647, 919

How a Master Works 644
  Mani, contact with 630, 645
Duke Hospital (Durham, North Carolina) 558, 591
Duke in the Suburbs, The (Edgar Wallace) 417

E

East Challacombe 425
East-West Gathering (1962) 108, 639–640, 763–775, 797
  rain sparks a change of clothing 764–765
Eaton, Bili 631–633
  A Love So Amazing 631
Eckhart, Meister (German mystic) 417
Egypt 593
Eiffel Tower 201–202
Elinorina 551. *See also* Patterson, Elizabeth Chapin; Matchabelli, Princess Norina
Elinorkit 634, 638. *See also* Patterson, Elizabeth Chapin; Matchabelli, Norina; and Davy, Katherine Laura (Kitty)
Elizabeth. *See* Patterson, Elizabeth Chapin
Elizabeth II, Queen of England 615
Ella. *See* Winterfeldt, Ella
Ellora Caves 282–285
  Buddha Cave 284
  guide falls at Baba's feet 285
Empire State Building (New York City) 543, 592
Empty Chair, The (Barbara Scott) 868
England 624, 668, 859
Eruch. *See* Jessawala, Eruch Beheram
Europe 204, 668, 859
Evangeline Booth Salvation Army Hospital. *See* Booth Salvation Army Hospital

F

Fallenfluh (Switzerland) 728–729
fal (opening Hafiz' Divan at random) 614, 1041
Family Letters. *See* 82 Family Letters
Ferdoonmasa. *See* Irani, Ferdoonmasa (Baba's uncle)
Ferris, Kate 591–592
Fiery Free Life 538
Filis. *See* Frederick, Filis
films, Baba's work during 417–423. *See also* movies and plays seen by Baba or the women
Finland 300, 302
Florence Hall (Mahabaleshwar) 425–426, 516–523, 622
Florence, South Carolina 545, 550, 562, 591
"Flubber" 694–696
Foreman, Dr. Freny 913

Forest Motor Court (Columbia, South Carolina) 562
Fort Munro (Pakistan) 335
Fort Smith, Arkansas 564
France 300–302
  Cannes 194–204
Francis. *See* Brabazon, Francis
Francis, Saint, of Assisi 417, 620, 958–960
Franklin, North Carolina 562, 584
Frederick, Filis 558, 592, 633, 646
  calls Mani "Granny Long Ears" 637
Free Life 538
Freiny, Freny. *See* Irani, Freiny Rustom; Irani, Freny Sheriar; Narawala, Freiny; and Foreman, Dr. Freny
Frenimasi. *See* Irani, Frenimasi Nowroj (Padri's mother)
"Frivolous Three." *See* Craske, Margaret; Davy, Katherine Laura (Kitty); and DeLeon, Delia
  video of Margaret, Kitty, and Delia 1020
Full Free Life 538

G

Gabriel. *See* Pascal, Gabriel
Gadge Maharaj (Maharashtra saint) 37, 625
Gaimai. *See* Jessawala, Gaimai Beheram (Eruch's mother)
Gajwani, Kishinchand (Bombay Baba-lover singer) 701
Galib (Urdu poet) 702
"Gandalf" plant 953
Gander (Newfoundland and Labrador) 549
Gandipet Dam 274
Ganges River 275–277, 476, 502, 616
Gayley, Estelle (Nonny, Rano's mother) 200, 202, 212, 262, 279, 319
  1939 passing 292
Gayley, Madeleine Estelle (Rano) 195, 201–202, 231, 254, 306, 309, 319, 347, 366, 371, 382–383, 402, 410, 417, 439, 507, 514, 524, 529, 534, 537, 544, 561, 580, 584, 629, 634, 652, 692, 718, 765, 807, 831, 903, 918–919, 930
  Baba, reading to 617–618, 665–666
  Because of Love 327
  biscuit Christmas house 518–519
  Blue Bus Tours 265, 267–268, 279
    map of 4th tour 327–328
    trip back from Bangalore 295–297
  God Speaks, drawing for 645
  Mani, shopping with 925
  Meherabad "very nice, but not for me." 190
  roles in Mani's skits 446
  Trustee 883, 887–888

Geneva (Switzerland) 602
George V, King of England 594
Germany 299–302
Gersoppa Falls. *See* Jog Falls
Ghani, Dr. Abdul (Munsiff) 434, 448, 456, 463, 477
   "God-determined Step" 523
   "Song of the New Life" 460–462, 508, 581
ghorawalla (horseman) 404, 637
Ghose, Aurobindo, Sri 320
Ginde, Dr. Ram 675
Goa (Panjim) 264, 296–298, 325
Godavri River 534
God-Brother (Mani Irani) xix, 23–122, 125, 957–958, 1010, 1036, 1042–1043, 1058, 1067
God-Realization dresses 442–444
Godse, Dr. Vinayak Nilkanth Narayan (Nilu) 447, 463, 478–479, 507, 530, 538, 584, 591–592, 592
   1956 death in Baba's presence 649, 653
God Speaks (Meher Baba) 434, 604, 620, 644–645
Goel's Hotel (Haridwar) 502–503
Goher. *See* Irani, Goher Rustom, Dr.
Gokul 276
Golandoon. *See* Irani, Golandoon Dorab (Shireen's mother)
Golconda Fort 273
Gol (dog) 532
gong that died 849–853
"Gopichand Raja" (mast play) 259–260
Grafton (Satara) 626–644, 650–654
Grant, Dr. K. B. 785–789
Great Darshan (Apr–Jun 1969) 836, 848–849, 852, 857–875, 879
  "a breath of the New Humanity" 870
  announcement 797
  "appointment with God" 858
  first experience of Baba's presence without His physical form 859
  mandali decision to go ahead 857
  Mani's hugs seemingly everywhere 868
  man who doubted Baba 861–862
  man who received a birthday telegram 862
  Mehera's "Jai Baba" began each program 848
  touched by love of Baba's children 867
  "Your old lovers want to see You too." 954
Greenville, South Carolina 562
Gujerat, Gujerati xiii, 63, 96
"Gujerati Arti" 1047
Gulamasi. *See* Jessawala, Gulamasi (Eruch's aunt)
Gulmai. *See* Irani, Gulmai Kaikhushru (Adi Sr.'s mother)
Gulnar. *See* Sukhadwala, Gulnar J. (Baba's niece, Jangu's wife)
Guloo. *See* Dastur, Guloo Kaikobad
Guruprasad (Poona) 69, 497, 680, 757, 793, 835, 840, 858–866, 1018
  Baba's 1951 stay in New Life 518, 658
  Baba's summer residence from 1959 658
  East-West Gathering (1962) 108, 639–640, 764–765
  Great Darshan (Apr–Jun 1969) 857–876
Gustadji. *See* Hansotia, Gustadji
Gyaneshwar (Perfect Master) 519–520
Gylaspy, Dr. 179–180

H

Haefliger, Max 598, 728
  children 599
Hafiz, Shams-ul-Din Muhammad (Perfect Master and poet) 62, 66, 308, 319, 344, 417, 556, 712, 826–828, 959
  "Dance of Life" ghazal 1033–1034
  fal (opening the Divan at random) 614
  taken by Aloba for Mani 1041
Hamirpur 603, 623, 1000
Hansotia, Gustadji 246, 524, 538, 584, 617
Haridwar 476, 477, 492, 499–501, 505
Harry. *See* Kenmore, Dr. Harry
Hathaway, Anne 595
Hayman, Dr. Ben
  Baba tells his daughter to "keep calling" 733
Haynes, Jane 764, 953, 1014, 1038–1039
  common interest with Mani in St. Teresa 959
  Mani's birthday twin 954
  Treasures from the Meher Baba Journal 631
Hedi. *See* Mertens, Hedi
Helen. *See* Dahm, Helen
Henderson, Chick 843
Herbert. *See* Davy, Herbert (Kitty's brother)
"Highest of the High" (Meher Baba) 604
  photo signed by Baba 620–622, 948
Hilla. *See* Kotwal, Hilla (Hilloo, Savak's daughter)
Himalayas 371, 397, 401, 604
Hinduism 529
Hitler, Adoph 317, 325
Hobbit, The (J. R. R. Tolkien) 830
Holland 300–302
Hollywood, California 324, 442, 558, 561
Honolulu, Hawaii 324
hotels, motels, and rest houses
  dak bungalows 267–268
  Forest Motor Court (Columbia, South Carolina) 562
  Goel's Hotel (Haridwar) 502–503
  Hotel Republica (Goa) 297–298

INDEX   1125

Hotel Schweizerhaus (Maloja) 602
Lafayette Manor Hotel 558
Mooreland Heights Tourist Court
 (Murphy, North Carolina) 562
Palace Hotel (Udaipur) 386
Pond Creek Motor Court (Ozarks) 563–564
Poona Club 1012, 1018
Rubens Hotel, The 593, 596
Sims Tourist Court (Waynesboro, Tennessee) 563
Taj Mahal Hotel (Bombay) 655
How a Master Works (Ivy Duce) 631, 644
Hungary 652
Hutchinson, Leslie A. ("Hutch") 844
 his version of "Begin the Beguine" preferred by Baba 844
Hyderabad 272–273, 371, 397, 521–527, 264

I

Illustrated Weekly of India 150, 629
Imampur mosque 532
Indus River 334
Iran 38, 85, 117, 204, 494, 790, 859
Irani, Adi Kaikhushru (Adi Sr.) 531, 538, 561, 583, 584, 791, 800, 820–821
 Baba was master psychologist 997
 tea in Columbia, South Carolina 586
 Trustee 883, 891
 Trust office in family compound 882–887
Irani, Adi Sheriar (Adi Jr., Baba's brother) 13, 15, 25, 103, 111, 116, 376, 752, 780, 1011
 brought gong to Baba 849
 brought Hutchinson recording of "Begin the Beguine" 844
Irani, Amrit Dara 679, 752, 1011, 1062
 marriage to Dara Irani 797, 845
Irani, Aspandiar Rustom (Pendu, Baba's cousin) 36–37, 524, 649, 653
 Trustee 883, 891
Irani, Beheram Sheriar (Baba's brother) 13, 15, 30, 69, 110, 111, 116, 158, 376, 603, 1010
 order to marry 117–118
 photos for the West per Baba 621–622, 725–727
 wedding to Perinmai 140
Irani, Dara Adi (Baba's nephew) 752, 849, 1011, 1062–1063
 marriage to Amrit Kumar 797, 845
Irani, Daula R. (Baidul's daughter) 255, 372
Irani, Daulatmai Jehangir (Mehera's mother) 48
Irani, Dorab (Shireen's father) 8

Irani, Dowlamasi Feredoon (Masi, Baba's aunt) 9, 32–34, 551, 580, 894
 cook in Meherabad ashram 32
Irani, Ferdoonmasa (Baba's uncle) 9, 32–35, 894
Irani, Freiny Rustom (Mehera's sister) 127, 136, 189
Irani, Frenimasi Nowroj (Padri's mother) 78–79
Irani, Freny Sheriar (Baba's sister) 13, 25
Irani, Goher Rustom, Dr. 206, 398, 410, 416, 447, 451, 468, 485, 503, 506, 524, 529, 537, 544, 549, 561, 574, 578, 580, 584, 605, 609, 612, 629, 634, 680, 691, 721, 782, 792, 807, 829, 838, 851, 853, 880, 890, 896, 936, 948–950, 1015–1016, 1019–1026, 1035–1037, 1041–1059, 1062
 April Fool's joke on 500
 Baba, helpless in caring for 783–789, 803
 Baba's 1952 accident 650–654
 Baba's gestures, reading 638–640
 Dr. Grant, consultation with 783–789
 encouraged Heather Nadel to write about Mani xiii
 hens and ducks, care of 428–431
 joins the women permanently 427
 link between men and women mandali 867
 movie taken by 922
 needed "Flubber" 695–696
 roles in Mani's skits 442–447
 scooter named "Ducky" 989
 typical day at Meherazad 662–667
 "wins" a toothbrush contest 654–655
Irani, Golandoon Dorab (Shireen's mother) 8, 19–20, 38–39
Irani, Gulmai Kaikhushru (Adi Sr.'s mother) 269, 715, 830
Irani, Jal Sheriar (Baba's brother) 13, 15, 110, 116–117, 376, 395, 448, 557, 777
Irani, Jambumama (Baba's Iranian uncle) 85
Irani, Jamshed Dara (Baba's grandnephew) 1063
Irani, Jamshed Sheriar (Baba's brother) 9, 32, 32–34
 death celebrated with sweets 33–34
 Mani, love of 33
Irani, Jehangir Hormusji (Mehera's father) 182
Irani, Jehangir Rustom (Jangu, Mehera's nephew) 1025
Irani, Kaikhushru Masa (Small Khorshed's father) 50–51, 177
Irani, Katie Rustom xiii, 205, 239–240, 269–270, 302, 371, 426, 443, 552, 580, 583, 752, 829, 976, 1027, 1057, 1062
 traveling on the Blue Bus 265–266
Irani, Kharmanmasi 149, 254, 326, 338, 355

1126 INDEX

Irani, Khodadadkaka (Sheriar's brother, Baba's uncle) 38
Irani, Khorshed Jamshed (Big) 81–83, 136, 145
   dying at Baba's feet 138–139
Irani, Khorshed Kaikhushru (Small) xiii, 44, 48, 50, 102, 129, 145, 146, 149, 182, 189, 194, 278, 310, 426, 551, 580, 919, 1057, 1062
   lived in Trust Compound in later years 928
Irani, Mani Sheriar (Baba's sister). *See also* 82 Family Letters; Blue Bus Tours; New Life; and Great Darshan (1969)
   "Act II" (after Baba's passing) 829
   Baba, continuing to do what He would want 856
   Baba-lovers begin visiting 879–882
   time when young ones would come to Him 835–843
   Agoos (pet tortoise) 946
   Babajan, visits to 78–80, 81–83
   Baba, relationship with xvii
      "Baba does His own work" 890
      Baba's 1956 accident 647–654
         glimpse of an angelic boy 650–651
      Baba's gestures
         Mani also able to talk in 599
         gesture project 639–640
         "Mani is matchless, after her is Eruch." 639, 646
         primary reader of 638–640
      Baba's presence greets them at the Center 545–547
      early ashram days 144–172
      gift of necklace 137
      grief at His passing 802–809, 855
         Eruch's metaphor of the shepherd 815
         "...now He was for everybody" 808
         "You made us close our eyes and then You slipped away." 804
      "Highest of the High" photo signed by Baba 948
      "Hmm! So now you know!" 738
      "I didn't come to Baba; Baba came to me!" 4
      invitation to join Baba 119–122
      last birthday embrace from 834
      "lesson-games" from 40, 56
      "Look after the family... for My sake." 1010–1012
      "Mani is very intellectual." 646–647, 891
      "My true sister in work" 674, 1049
      "No one, but no one, has a God-Brother" 100–105
      on call during Baba's last illness 792
      one ambition to be with Him 4, 89, 103–104, 114–115
      on His birthday, flowers on their parents' graves 378
      only visit Him on school holidays 45, 86
      only wants to be "His perfect slave" 949–950
      orders
         "Begin the Beguine" taught to Eruch 739–741
         displeasing Him over a painting 716–719
         eat anything on flight to America 539
         films in early mornings 417–423
         "little" and "big" orders 101–102, 110, 121, 127, 132–133, 155, 172
         Mehera, be with 149–150
         most embarassing order 503
         ploy to give gift to Dr. Gylaspy 180
         silence in England 596–598
         skipping rope story 125–127
         questions, no room for 680
         "Will you look after Mehera?" 813
      reading books aloud 416–417, 613–614, 661, 665
         "I always listen" 830–834
         Nero Wolfe with 12 voices 618
      Real freedom 984
      shaped the Baba-world's idea of how to love and serve Him 960
      "She's so very fortunate." 26
      "suitcase" from past lives 979–980
      "The path to God is single file." 952
      "took God seriously and life lightly" 960
      "To us, being with Baba was everything – and we had it." 875
      "waves of purity" 682
      "When Love is present, the path to the Truth is joyous." xii
   birthdays
      age 4 40–41
      age 13 77–78
      age 14 125
      age 50 (and last birthday embrace) 834
      "by special appointment" 25–26
      Jane Haynes, shared a birthday with 954
   books
      Dreaming of The Beloved 66, 80, 83, 883, 948, 986, 1042–1044, 1058
      favorites read
         Lord of the Rings, The 953
         Rumpole, St. Teresa, Georgette Heyer 948
      God-Brother xix, 23–122, 125, 957–958, 1010, 1036, 1042–1043, 1058, 1067

INDEX 1127

Britain, special feeling for 594
Burlesons, relationship with 574–576, 926
Chairman, Avatar Meher Baba Trust 63, 752, 882–893
  fax, discovery of 918
  jokes and squabbling with Eruch 893–897
  liked the "small things" 890
  Mani's desk 888–889
  Mani's parlour 931–934
  meals and snacks 926–931
  a "bump" for coffee 910
  birthdays 930
    jokes told 929
    teatime (and play) 934–936
    tea with bank officials 892
    "The Lunch Club" 928–931
  reservations for first pilgrim rooms 1002–1006
  residents, advice for 897–909, 1005–1006
    "diet" your wants 904
    real work is work on you 900–901
  skills as a manager 884, 891, 898
  statements, marveled about balances 892
  telephone, use of 920
  Trustee 883–885
childhood and school years 86–93
  Baba, early visits to as a child 43, 44, 45, 47, 52, 86
  Baba, flying a kite with 56
  Baba, letters to and from 94–100
  Baba, Shirenmai's letter about Mani's longing 103
  Baba, tiny crown and pair of sandals made for 49, 979
  Baba, wanted to be with when he broke His silence 96
  convent school 43
    "How could they do that to Baba?" 89
    "My brother is Christ!" 91–93
    nuns, love of 87
  homework and exams 70–71
  Masaji, friendship with 36–37, 50–52, 394
  Mehera, letter to 43–44
  "Night and day, Mani remembers You." 100
  parents had different points of view 62
  parents' suffering 26–31, 113–114
  Sheriar, special relationship with 64–65
cooking 415
  learned in Aurangabad 393
  pudding in Raipur 400
correspondence and typing 434–435, 523
  after Baba's passing 910–918
  article for the *Illustrated Weekly of India* 629

Baba comes first, even before His work 730–732
Baba news, sent to the West 632–637
Baba's orders, transmission of 635
Bili Eaton, letters to 631–632
copyrights for Baba's books 644–647
Dr. Donkin's manuscript 436
Duce, Ivy (Murshida), letters to 434, 630
fast typing 731–733
intimate letters from her veranda desk 953–956
Kitty, typing and shorthand lessons from 201
Mehera's death notice, ahead of time 957
"open-air office" 669, 670, 686
Satara, increasing role in 631–637
shells touched by Baba sent to 1995 Youth Sahavas 559–561
Stevens, Don 645–646
Trust minutes, handwritten 956–957
Western family 434–435, 435–436, 549–552, 557–559, 580–583, 653–654
Dehra Dun, daily life in 612
diaries and notebooks
  1932 Mehera's daily activities 150
  1937 Cannes 198–202
  1938 September 259–260
  1938 October 7 262–265
  1938 Meherabad 220–223, 227–230
  1938–1942 Blue Bus Tours 270–271
    preparation 258–263, 266
    1st: Dec 1938–May 1939 272–288
    2nd: Aug 1939–May 1940 288–300
    3rd: July 1940 300–315
    4th: Nov 1940–July 1941 327–365
    5th: Sept–Nov 1941 367–371
    6th: Feb–Dec 1942 371–374
  1940–1941 Baba's orders 303–310
  1949–1952 New Life
    Oct–Nov 1949: beginning 455–460, 463–465
    Nov–Dec 1949: Benares 465–469
    Dec 1949: Sarnath 470–481
    Dec 1949–Jan 1950: Moradabad 482–492
    Jan–Jun 1950: Dehra Dun 493–507
    Jun–Oct 1950 : Satara 507–510
    Aug–Sept 1950: Bombay 1950 510–512
    Oct 1950–Mar 1951: Mahabaleshwar 512–519
    Mar–Apr 1951: Poona 518–519
    Mar–Apr 1951: Mahabaleshwar 520–521
    May–Nov 1951: Hyderabad 521–527
    Oct 1951–Feb 1952: Manonash 529–536

1128 INDEX

1952 America, trip to
   flight to the West 538–539
   arrival in New York 542–543
   Meher Center 553–554
   drive to the West, 562–564
   trip back to Myrtle Beach 583–587
   Youpon Dunes 587–591
   New York departure, 591–592
   London 593
   Switzerland and Italy 599–602
1953 Dehra Dun 604, 622
1953 dog training book 606–607, 629
1954–1955 622–627
1956 648
Baba's informal talks 302–310, 318–321
images in 266, 271, 299, 302, 398, 415, 501, 528
"inner voice" 961–965
drawings and crafts 86, 125, 135, 138, 160–161, 232, 266, 428
   Baba and Mehera, pencil portraits of 159–161
   Baba, embroidered poem for 174
   basket-making 607, 612
   brooch for Mehera 152, 979
   doodles 5, 125, 160–161, 187, 258, 382, 453, 537, 603, 631, 656, 802, 857, 879
   "Goher's whistle fun" 457
   knitting 398
   Mehera, helping with projects 151–152
   New Life, things to sell 505
   origami crane or nun 896
   puppets 451–452, 466–469
   sewing and knitting 397–398, 612
   symbolic scenes 160–161
dreams
   Baba is "at the mains" 883
   "Babajan, oh, don't go!" 83–84
   Baba lying under a towel gesturing, "This is only make-believe." 824–826
   tree that loved like a person 642
   garlanding Baba from head to foot 1047
   God's Court: "I have always loved You." 80, 104
   mango tree with Mary and Mehera's face 987–988
   naked God on a cloud 105
   red goldfish, kissed by 65–66
   "We were all dressed up and going to a great celebration." 1066
dressing up and dressing down 997–998
health
   Baba prescribed her medicines 398–399, 589–591
   begging for a cup of coffee 568–572

   "Begum" scooter 989, 1046, 1055
   cancer 896–897, 988–989, 1044–1048, 1056
   Chum, bitten by 169, 995
   cold like "Anthea's Guest" 470
   food poisoning 506
   hair lice 950–951
   mental shock at Baba's accident 567–568
   operations 175–186, 526–528, 936, 1037–1038, 1055
   Satara mushroom "trip" 630
   skin condition 119, 129–130, 177–181, 398–399
   snuff taken to ward off colds 483
   whiplash, Baba gave her His own neckbrace 892
languages 63, 72, 80, 86–87
later years
   blazing candle "about to go out" 996
   farewell ghazal from Hafiz' Divan 1041
   knew her time was coming 949
   "On the Topic of Suffering" 1040–1041, 1058
   prayers and arti in Poona hospital with the "voice of an angel" 1047–1048
   resigned to His will 1048
   Samadhi, last darshan at 1045
lies, telling 91–92
mango-mad 615–617
"Mani's cupboard" 968–970
Mehera, relationship with 134, 171, 206
   Baba, Mehera's reunion with 943–944, 1013–1034
   close support of 880–882
   connected from "way back" 941
   continued garlanding Baba's room in Mehera's absence 939
   "friendly squabbles" with 406–407, 943
   hid her own grief in Mehera's presence 813–815
   loss of Mehera : "You don't get over it; but you get through it." 1035–1036
   Mehera's last namaste 986
   Mehera's presence still in their room 944–945
"Miss Friendly" 934–937
   Burleson family 574–576
   dog owners in Mussoorie 605
   Great Darshan, at the 868
   Mysore nurses 178–181
   Prague hospital staff 574
   Trust vistors at tea time 935–937
   Western "sisters" 556, 631

music and songs 159, 323, 462
    "25th February" 10–12
    Baba's musicwalla 973–974
    for Rustom and Sorab 1011
    harmonium 72, 159
    "In the dark hour of separation..." 881
    "Kitty's 100th birthday" 954
    "Meher Raj" arti tune 157
    "My beloved Brother, You are God..." 1069
    sitar 71–72, 150, 154, 410
        classic learned from a record 158
    "The Glory of Love" for Mehera's birthday 1037, 1059
Narayan Maharaj, fondness for 80
Nasik ashram 127–143
    modest dress 147
    "right into the fire" 127–128
New Life
    Baba tied her turban 475, 892
    chosen to go with Baba 452
    "our companion...(but) more God than ever!" 494
    plans 498
    thoughts on 536
Perin, friendship with 118
Peter (Mani's cocker spaniel) 604–612, 628, 650, 610, 641, 663, 665, 667–668, 719–724, 953, 936
photography 133, 135, 138, 162–163, 269, 281, 333, 427
    Baba and Mehera 161–162, 921–924
    Baba's face in the Umar tree 818
    "children's album" at Meherazad 937
    Cracker with Baba 426
    Kodak Brownie camera 161–162, 269, 281, 1004
    Mani, photos of 899–900, 951
movies
    Baba films, preserving 923–924
    Baba, home movies of 661
    Baba's body at Meherazad 841
    Goher's film of Mani 923
    Great Darshan 860
    Mary Bennett 839–843
    mugging for the camera 186
    Peter, photos of 605, 607, 609
plays and entertainments 70, 251–257, 269, 291–292
    African cannibals 254
    Cannes skits, singing, and dancing 200–201
    Dastoorji and old Parsi lady 254
    deck of cards 251
    Edgar Wallace skit 634
    Heavenly skit for Baba's 100th birthday 1007–1009
    Hitler, Mussolini, and Chamberlain 254

    humorous nonsense 442
    "I'm Rachel" 924
    Indian movie story 136
    Mani's toys 935, 970–972
    matchbox trains 70
    Mirabai and the Rana 252
    movies, based on 136
    plays by "Mani & Co" 442–447
    puppet shows 451–452
    Radha and Krishna 252
    shadow hand puppets 457, 970, 985
    shadow play behind sheet 255
poems
    "An episode In Dehra Dun 1953" 616
    a "NOT" letter 917
    "A True Story" (Blue Bus) 379–381
    "At the Lotus Feet" 172–173
    "I do not know when or how I go..." 1052
    "Mangoes" in Dehra Dun 615–616
    "Shri Meher Baba, I love you..." 95
    "To His Disciples BABA SAYS" 423–424
    "You have no idea how much He loves me..." 1054
reunion with Baba (Aug 19, 1996) 1048–1067
    Heather's account 1055–1067
    Meheru's account 1050–1054
    pyre's blue smoke drew sadhus 1064
    "Night and day, Mani remembers You." 1067
shopping in the bazaar 925–926
    Christmas shopping with Jesus' sister 926
"speed-breakers" 965–968, 981–982
Irani, Mehera Jehangir (Baba's Beloved) 9, 48, 102, 119–121, 129, 194, 262, 266–268, 278, 305, 316, 322, 382, 398, 402, 412, 439, 447, 450, 487, 504–506, 529, 537, 549–552, 561–563, 580, 584, 612, 655, 680, 691, 764, 782, 792
Baba-lovers, visiting with 880–881
Baba, relationship with
    1956 accident 650–655
        Baba knew that he would not be able to walk as before 651
        concern for Baba's suffering after 658
    Baba lets her win 407
    "Baba was so sporting." 997
    flowers offered to Him 938, 966–967, 986, 996
    gift of necklace 137
    greets men for the first time on Jan 31, 1968 847–848, 866
    grief at His passing 802–823
        Baba's face on tree by her window 817–823
        "Be brave!" 803, 852
        longing to be with Him 881–882

INDEX

"Oh Baba...Come back to me, sweet love."
   1032
His Beloved, special role as 713–719, 1028
   "highest, purest, most spiritual
      relationship" 977
   "In my love, first comes Mehera..." 674
loving and serving Him 151, 666
Meherazad everyday activities 662–667,
   685
mustache, trimming 718
New Life
   meeting him at the end 532
   worked as a servant with others 459
   orders from
      Blue Bus, secluded on 268–269
      doctors allowed to touch her after
         accident 582
      men, not to see or hear a man's name or
         voice 153–154, 175–176, 189–192
      somewhat relaxed in 1940s 433
      words, not to read 154–155
   reunion with Baba 1013–1034
      "a fulfillment and not an end" 1035
   May 20 "Mehera's Day" 1045
birthday celebrations
   1938 275
   1942 374
   1949 480
   1951 535
   1954 640–641
   1955 627
   1968 752, 797, 845
crafts
   Baba, robe and crown for 138
   Baba's hair, ornaments from 151–152
   Baba's New life satchel, embroidered 469
   basket-making 607, 612
   New Life, made things to sell 505
   puppets 468
   "snake" painted for Kitty 516
Grafton (Satara), enjoyed years in 628
Great Darshan, each program began with her
      "Jai Baba" 848
health
   aphasia, but never forgot Baba's name or the
      prayers 1021
   heart-shaped tubercular brain tumour
      1015–1017
   injured in 1952 accident 565–568, 573,
      578, 581, 1014
   no headaches after 576
Kitty, piano lessons from 200
Mani, relationship with 134, 182, 717
   assisting with costumes for skits 252
   connected from "way back" 941

first meeting 41–42
"friendly squabbles" with 406–407, 943
stories about 49–50
suggested convent school 86
Mary Bennett, amazed by 838–840
Mastan (Baba's favorite dog) 437, 607, 663,
      667, 715, 719
   dies from grief at Baba's passing 849
Meherabad, early days 146–152
Meherazad
   designed their home 437–438
   first visit to 392
   gardening 410
   movie taken by 922
   Sheba (Mehera's Arabian horse) 604,
      608–609, 612, 628–629, 664, 953
   swimming 339–340, 394
   teas with female Baba-lovers 880, 952–953
Irani, Meherdil Sohrab (Baba's grandnephew)
   1063
Irani, Meheru Rustom (Mehera's niece) xiii, 382,
      388, 393, 397, 402, 426, 439, 442, 451,
      468, 487, 505–506, 511, 529, 537, 539,
      541–544, 549, 561, 573–574, 578–580,
      584, 599, 618, 629, 634, 647–648, 680,
      692, 715, 807, 851, 898, 936, 950,
      1020, 1027, 1035, 1062
   Baba's 1956 accident 650–654
   Blue Bus, child on 266
   health 526
   joined the women permanently 374
   Mani, attended school with 88
   Mani's skits, roles in 447
   "Mani was never shy to use words." 917
   remembering Mani 1050–1054
Irani, Merwan Sheriar (Avatar Meher Baba).
      See also 82 Family Letters; Blue Bus
      Tours; mast ashrams; masts; New Life;
      Great Darshan; movies and plays seen
      by Baba or the women; ships Baba
      sailed on
   "Act II" (after Baba's passing)
      first Amartithi celebrated 880
      visiting Baba-lovers tell their stories 880
   alphabet board, given up 625
   Avatarhood, public declaration 603
   Babajan, unveiling by 15–17
   beautiful voice 12–14, 84–85
   birthday celebrations 172, 637
      1894 10
      1920s 52
      1927 57
      1937 107–108
      1938 207
      1938 (Parsi calendar) 273

1939 259
1942 346
1943 375
1950 499
1952 535
1954 624–625
1955 634
1969 message 801
1969 (Parsi calendar)
    Baba to be very strong after this 810
1994 (100th birthday) 1007–1010
1996 1042
cards and cables 699–700
Dhun, cards from 700
embraces women mandali only on a birthday or His birthday 666
books read to 613, 617–620
    Anthea's Guest (Mrs. Alfred Sidgwick) 470
    Carr, John Dickson (Carter Dickson) 830
    Charteris, Leslie (*The Saint* series) 636, 830
    Christie, Agatha (Poirot and Miss Marple) 340, 417, 618, 722, 830
    "Go on reading...I always listen." 832–834
    Oppenheim, E. Phillips 417
    Orczy, Baroness (*Scarlet Pimpernel*) 830
    Queen, Ellery 618, 636
    spiritual topics 417, 620, 830
    Stout, Rex (Nero Wolfe) 618, 722, 830–831, 840
        "couldn't keep up with Baba" 832
        Red Box, The (last book read) 831–832
    Tolkien, J. R. R. 618
        Hobbit, The 830
        Lord of the Rings, The 830
    Wallace, Edgar 417, 617, 618
        Chick 417
        Duke in the Suburbs, The 417
        Murder Book of Mr. J. G. Reeder, The 417, 634
    Wodehouse, P. G. (inscribed book for Baba) 618, 722, 830, 840
Dehra Dun, daily life in 612–614
divinity 11–15
    actions were models for a larger plan 834–843
    compassion and forgiveness 54–55
    difficulty hiding 747–748
    L-shaped room, suffering in 16–19, 519, 1011
    provides before the need is known 841–843, 843–847
    spiritual work during films 417–423
    sound, significance of 704–706

    take him as best friend if can't take him as God 779
family 32–39
    father, praise for 6
    father's langugages "a gift from God" 67
    His mother was "purest crystal" 110, 378
    Jamshed's death, sweets at 34
    under His direct orders 32, 111
Fiery Free Life 603–655
games 410, 426
    badminton, spellicans, gilli danda 155–157
    cheating at 156
    dropping the game 241–242
    hide and seek in Kandivli 142
    Mehera, letting her win 407
gestures 638–640
    "acceptance" and "giving" at darshans 735
    East-West Gathering film 639–640
    gesture project 639–640
    "giving" in His arm exercises 738
    His two eyes, for Meherabad and Meherazad 392
    life goes on, like a rolling wave 1035
    Mani, "matchless" in reading 599, 633, 646–647, 742
    ring finger, for His children who are "gems" 977
    "So many" will come 170, 999
    so natural and graceful 343
    "talking" with babies 185
    "Welcome to My World" 781–783
    "yakh" (ice) 703
    yogis, description of 170–171
health 509, 520, 523, 559
    1952 accident in Prague, Oklahoma 565–568, 573, 576, 580–583
        flowers for "the gentleman at the hospital" 578
        injuries 581–582
    1956 accident in Satara 428, 647–654
        "a blessing for the universe and a curse for Baba" 654
        gradual decline after 656
        previous "narrow shave" 648
    baby carriage, exercise with 777–778
    both strong and weak 729–730
    cold air, allergic to 686
    "deep wound" in his cheek 350
    Dr. Grant as Baba's "patient" 785–789
    in public vs. in private 675
    summer heat, problem of 658
    tracoma (eye infection) 505–506
"hot lectures" 270, 275, 344–346
"household Baba" (human side) 680–681

humor 268–269, 272–273, 361–366, 449, 697, 723, 773
  amused by story about hot dogs and tea 584
  "broken-down furniture" 314
  coat that didn't fit 759–763
  favorite Tommy joke 441–442
  "Flubber" 696
  jokes, asking for 439–442
  "Mysore has become an eyesore." 187
  skits, loved mistakes in 256
  teasing 691–693
  "Those I love, I take everything from them." 280–281
"ideal boy" 335
love vs. meditation 318–321
Mani, relationship with
  asked Upasni for a sister 25
  Family Letters at His wish 669
  praises her intelligence 646-647
  present just after her birth 3, 25–26
masts, work with 253, 317, 347–365, 425–426, 449, 480, 507, 529, 534
  "Gopichand Raja" play put on by the masts 259–260
  tours ended with 1956 accident 658
  Wayfarers, The (Dr. William Donkin) 436–437
meetings and public darshans
  1953, 1954 Andhra 603–604, 624
  1953 Dehra Dun 622
  1954, 1956 Sakori 624, 627
  1954 Ahmednagar 621, 624
  1954 Hamirpur 623
  1954 Pandharpur 625
  1955 Bombay 626
  1955 Meherazad 627
  1956 Poona 627
  1962 East-West Gathering 639–640, 763–775
  1968 December, Meherazad 755, 797
  1969 Great Darshan 797, 836, 848–849, 852, 857–875, 879, 954
  Guruprasad, summer darshans at 658–659
music 700–706
  All India Radio or Voice of America 685
  "Begin the Beguine" 292, 739–741
    Leslie A. Hutchinson record after Baba's passing 806–807, 843–847
  Begum Aktar 780
  dholak (drum) 464
  Jim Reeves 780–783
  Mary Bennett 840
  qawwali on the radio 661, 663
  record collection 973
  young people's songs 834–840

New Life 448. *See also* New Life
  announcement 452, 453
  cooking, helping with 459–460
  Dr. Nath's, begging at 468–469
  "God-determined Step" 523–525
  Kumbh Mela, bowed down to sadhus 501–502
  Manonash (annihilation of the mind) 529–536
    dhuni on Jan 31, 1952 535
  message to all disciples East and West 508
  models of world religions 529
  Old Life, one day stepping back 512
  phases 456, 480, 508, 538
  Poona, seclusion sites in 519
  "this New Life is endless..." 514–515
  "will go on living by itself" 536
orders
  1940–1941 orders to the women 303–310
  1968 prayers 791
  Beheram and Perin's marriage 118
  clothes, patching or mending 149
  Daulatmai repeated God's name 49
  ducks and hens, Goher's care for 430–431
  eggplant, not to eat 250
  Elizabeth's flask of coffee 281
  examples of 221–224
  family under His direct orders 32, 111
  feasting and fasting 202
  Jambumama not to leave the room 85
  jokes, telling Him 439
  marriage of Arnavaz and Nariman 433
  New Life 453–454, 461, 464
  no naps in daytime 226
  Norina and the ship captain 196–197
  "not doing" 132
  oranges at the East-West Gathering 768
  Perinmai, love Baba first 142
  prayers, reciting of 791
  silence broken by alarm clock 310
  Wayfarers, The, Donkin to write 436
  women to write Baba's name 71
passing (dropping His body, Jan 31, 1969) 802–809
  1969 last weeks 797–801
  "Begin the Beguine" played at end 806–807, 843–847
  Booth Hospital ambulance that died 841, 845, 853–854
  God-Man drops His body, unlike ordinary persons 850
  gong that died 849–853
  Hafiz couplets brought to His bedroom 826–828
  He listens, even though we can't see Him 828–830

interred in tomb (Samadhi) 805–807,
    809–812
Mehera and Mani, last meetings with 803
"Today is the day of my crucifixion." 803
Zoroastrian birthday, interred on 809–812
personality 302–310
"Beautiful Stranger" 314–315, 542, 704
Baba blesses the babies 183–186
forgiveness like an ocean wave 54–55
generosity
    Baba's arm exercises 737–739
    ignored man received even more 769
    Real Giving unseen 733–736
    unique ways of giving and receiving
        707–713
His pace, hard to keep up with 411
Mysore hospital staff attracted to Him
    183–186
promises 139–140
weaknesses, subtle use of 128–129
pets and animals 165–169, 301
    Begum (small horse) 516–517
    Bhooti (Tibetan mastiff) 437, 531, 626
        "guardian of Meherazad" 657
    Blue Bus: parrot, monkey, dog, goldfish 266
    Champa (donkey) 162–164
    Chum (Baba's dog) 168–169
        punished for biting Mani 169, 995
    Cracker (Scottish terrier) 398, 425, 427,
        437
    geese 230
    goat 135
    goat in Kulu Valley 401
    Gol (dog) 532
    hens and ducks 428
    Kippy (Boston terrier) 212–213
    Lucky (monkey) 307–308
    Mastan (Baba's favorite dog) 437, 607, 663,
        667, 715, 719, 849
        dies from grief at Baba's passing 849
    Mittu (parrot) 383, 398, 953
    New Life caravan: camel, cattle, donkeys,
        white horse 475, 475–477, 483–486,
        489–490
    parrots, ugly babies 165–167
    Pegu (Siamese cat) 757
    Peter (Mani's cocker spaniel) 604–612,
        628, 650, 610, 641, 663, 665, 667–668,
        719–724, 953, 936
    Raja (English bull) 499
    Sheba (Mehera's Arabian horse) 604,
        608–609, 612, 628–629, 664, 953
    Sukoo and Tukoo (donkeys) 486, 490, 492
    Tippu, and Gol (dogs) 531
    Typhoon (wire-haired terrier) 398, 416

white horse trained by horse master
    483–484
zoo visits 291, 293–295, 511–512,
photos
    "Highest of the High" signed photos
        620–622
    touched photos sent to His lovers 621–622,
        724–727
Pirojamami asks for "murti" 37
prayers
    "Beloved God" 966, 1047
    "Master's Prayer" 604, 620, 791, 966
    "Repentance Prayer" 791, 966, 1047
    sound and value of 704–706
publications and messages
    "Baba Explains" 559
    Circle, article for *The Awakener* 633
    Discourses 646
    God Speaks 434, 604, 644–645
        began dictation in Aug 1953 620
        "Highest of the High" 604, 620
    Listen Humanity 646
quotes
    "All rites, rituals and ceremonies of all
        religions of the world are hereby
        consumed in the flames." 536
    "Always a going forward, never a going
        backward." 683
    "Coming, coming, coming--came! I am tired
        of the Illusion Game." 796
    "Even a slight movement of My finger" 294
    "I am Buddha" 282–285
    "If you have that love for Me that St. Francis
        had for Jesus, not only will you realize
        Me, but you will please Me." 889
    "...Living for Me is difficult, because it is
        dying every moment." 134
    "Men unknowingly suffer for God, and God
        knowingly suffers for man." 652
    "Opposition is a help..." 330
    "The whole world will come to know I am
        God in human form." 644
    "...This is the home that I love the best
        because it was given to Me and built for
        Me with such love." 548
    "Those who live with me feel more of my
        humanity than my divinity. Those
        whom I permit to come
        and see me for a while see more of my
        divinity than my humanity." 675
    "To love me for what I may give you is not
        loving Me at all..." 801
    "...Waiting for You, not in vain" 755
    "...Wouldn't equal one hour of My silence."
        112

INDEX

"You will see My children, My lovers...they are gems." 977
seclusion work 428, 670–671, 799–801
   40-day Manonash seclusion 535
   100-day seclusion before New Life 514–521
   1920s in water tank 55
   1934 Fallenfluh (Switzerland) 728
   1940 August 316–317
   1941 August 367
   1947 on Seclusion Hill 412
   1949 Great Seclusion 450–451
   1968 climax of Universal Work 790–798
   1968, July 30: Work complete 100% to Baba's satisfaction 796, 806
   body weight affected by 763
   burden of 664–665, 672–676, 726, 729, 784–790, 795
   Universal Work 657, 1002
silence 96, 672
   Eruch disbelieved that Baba would break it 742–747
   His silent giving to the world 676
   Mani and Eruch reading Baba's gestures 742–745
   Shireenmai challenges Baba 112
"simple sermons" 691, 719, 748–751
toddy shop, work in 23–24
travels. *See also* Blue Bus Tours, New Life
   Aurangabad 393
   Australia 647, 673
   Cannes 194
   Europe 135, 647
   Florence Hall & Mahabaleshwar 376, 396–397, 425–426, 506, 511–521, 622
   India 1943–1946 396
   Jubilee Hills (Hyderabad) 408
   Kandivli (Bombay) 142
   Kulu Valley 401
   Lahore 382
   Mt. Abu 447–450
   Raipur 400
   Satara 427
   Simla 406
   Srinagar, Kashmir 400
   Udaipur 385
   United States (America) 537–592, 624, 635, 647, 668, 673–674
   with name "in seclusion" 288
   World War II, talk about 258–261, 291–292, 308–309, 316–317, 321, 372–373
   Chatti Baba's role in 353–357
Zoroaster, dressed as 108–109, 230
Irani, Naggu Rustom (Meheru's sister) 252, 266, 580

Irani, Naja Rustom (Baba's cousin) 36–37, 48, 102, 119–121, 129, 146, 189, 194, 200, 278, 410, 413, 416, 443, 498, 529, 580, 629, 634, 652, 664, 666, 680, 691, 697, 722, 752, 792, 807
   also died on May 20th 1030
   dressed as Santa on Christmas 641
   "He's very shy." 182–186
   ordered to wear a new costume every day 633
Irani, Peelamasi Masaji (Shireen's sister) 36–37
Irani, Perinmai Beheram (Baba's sister-in-law) 30, 394, 559, 1017
   Baba, orders from 142, 1010
   Beheram, marriage to 140–141
   Mehera, first meeting 140–141
Irani, Pilamai Hormuzd (Goher and Katie's aunt) 252
Irani, Pirojamami Rustom (Baba's aunt) 37
Irani, Piroja Moondegar (Baba's aunt) 8–9, 118
Irani, R. B. (Baidul) 289–290, 350, 367, 448, 490, 524, 617, 791
Irani, Rustom and Sohrab (Baba's twin nephews) xiv, 1030, 1062–1063
   Mani's songs for 1011
   Meher Kawwals 1018
   their aunt "Manifui" x
Irani, Rustom Jehangir (Rusipop, Goher and Katie's father) 414, 437, 829
Irani, Rustom Kaikhushru (Adi Sr.'s brother) "Meher Raj" arti 158
Irani, Rustom Khodadad 73
Irani, Rustommama (Shireen's brother) 37, 71, 136, 257
Irani, Rustom Masa (Masaji, Baba's uncle) 36–37, 51–52, 394
Irani, Sarosh Kaikhushru 306, 392, 417, 538, 561, 565–566, 580, 752
   Trustee 882–883, 891
   forced mandali to take Fridays off 898, 977
Irani, Sheriar Beheram (Sheroo, Baba's nephew) 1012, 1035
Irani, Sheriarji Moondegar (Baba's father) 3, 103, 1010–1011
   Baba, relationship with
      God, search for 5–7
      knew who his son was 10, 12
      many languages, knowledge of 66–67
      "matchless" 114
      orders from 111–112
   Beheram's wife, selected 118
   "Bobo" to his children; "Shorog" to Shireen 62
   employment 13–14, 24
   marriage 7–8

passing at age 79
   grave, flowers on 378
   memorial on Meherabad Hill 376–377
   mukti (liberation) at death 116–117
personality
   complement to Shireenmai 61–63
   "in the world but not of it" 14
   scolded Mani by blessing her 62-63
   taught Mani how to pray 65
   toddy shop partner, betrayed by 67–70
   "Yezdan" on his lips 29, 64
Irani, Shireen Adi (Baba's niece) 849
Irani, Shireenmai Sheriar (Baba's mother) 3, 128, 294–295, 333, 1010–1011
   Baba, relationship with 106–108, 295
      giving Baba up 23
   Belle of Poona 13–15
   children 4, 9, 13–15
      excellent mother 61–62
      giving Mani a coat 292
      giving up Mani 119
   dreams
      goddesses in the well 17–19, 1010
      river of humanity 9–11
   her pillow rested beneath Baba's head on the stretcher 996
   marriage 7–9
   "Memo" to her children; "Shireennog" to Sheriar 62
   passing and memorial on Meherabad Hill 375–377
      grave, flowers on 378
   personality 13–15, 30–31, 74, 109–110
   taught cooking to Perinmai 394
   visits to ashram 243–250, 374–375
   Zoroastrian opposition 26–31
Irani, Silla (Pilamai's daughter) 252
Irani, Soonamasi Kaikhushru (Small Khorshed's mother) 48, 146, 194, 310–314
   gatekeeper on Meherabad Hill 153–154
Irani, Sultoon R. (Baidul's wife) 255–256, 367, 372
Irani, Villoo Sarosh 752, 837
Iran (Persia) 5, 10, 204
Irene. See Billo, Irene; Conybeare, Irene
Irwin, Phil 685
Islam 529
Italy 199, 299
   Baba's women visit 600–602
Ivy. See Duce, Ivy (Murshida)

J

Jabalpur (Jubbulpore) 248, 253–254, 272, 274
   river touched by Baba 727
Jaffna 352
Jaipur 272, 286–288, 325, 332, 360
Jakkal, Anna (Anna 104) 498
Jal. See Irani, Jal Sheriar (Baba's brother)
Jaloo. See Dastur, Jaloo Kaikabad
Jambumama. See Irani, Jambumama (Baba's Iranian uncle)
Jamshed. See Irani, Jamshed Sheriar (Baba's brother); Irani, Jamshed Dara (Baba's grandnephew)
Jane. See Haynes, Jane
Jangu. See Irani, Jehangir Rustom (Jangu, Mehera's nephew); Sukhadwala, Jehangir (Jangu, Gulnar's husband)
Japan 317
Jaunpur 479–480
Jean. See Adriel, Jean
Jeanne. See Shaw, Jeanne
Jehangir. See Irani, Jehangir Hormusji (Mehera's father)
Jessawala, Beheram (Pappa, Eruch's father) 561, 566, 576, 583, 592
   also known as "Pistol" 363, 895
Jessawala, Eruch Beheram xii, xiii, 269, 278, 310, 350–352, 391, 401, 468, 476, 497, 524, 653, 722, 727–729, 807–808, 838, 849, 882, 890, 903, 919, 976, 993, 1049, 1061
   Baba's frequent driver 649
   Baba's gestures, reading 639
   Baba's perfect adab manners 59
   Baba's silence, disbelieving Baba would break it 742–747
   Baba's wishes, we continue to follow 856
   "Baba was too compassionate!" 997
   "Begin the Beguine"
      reminds Mani to play per Baba's order 845
      taught by Mani 739–741, 893
   Mandali Hall stories 974
   Mani, goodbye hug for 897
   Mehera and Mani, Baba asked him to look after 814–817, 894–897
   "now is not the time to start thinking of ourselves..." 841
   shows Mani the shepherd 815–817
   "There are as many paths to Baba as there are Baba-lovers." 1005
   thermos for Elizabeth 281–283
   Trust work 883, 887, 891
      "Chechoo-mummy" to Mani 893

purpose of Meherabad pilgrimage 1003–1004
table on the veranda 887
"This is Office here." 895–896
"What's the matter with you people? Don't you ever talk to each other?" 898
"Your Brother had this same habit..." 896
"You're just a Loni girl!" 33, 894
visit to potter in Pimpalgaon 1041
"You have kept your appointment with God." 858
Jessawala, Gaimai Beheram (Eruch's mother) 248, 262, 275, 310, 343, 624
  black sari given to Perinmai 377–378
  saw golden hands above Shireenmai 375–376
Jessawala, Gulamasi (Eruch's aunt) 310–314
Jessawala, Manu Beheram (Eruch's sister) xiii, 248, 377, 1020, 1057
Jessawala, Meheru (Eruch's sister) 222, 228
Jessawala, Meherwan Beheram (Eruch's brother) xiii, 310
Jesus Christ, Lord (Avatar) 88–89, 182, 318, 345, 347, 533, 678–679
  burial in Kashmir 400–401
  Jesus on barber's watch kept watch over Mani 1039
Jigar (mystic poet) 674–675, 702
Jog (Gersoppa) Falls 296–297
jokes, dictionary of 440
Jonah Falls 300
Jubbulpore. *See* Jabalpur
Jubilee Hills (Hyderabad) 371, 408, 522
Judson, Janet 1053
Judson, Ted
  "The Lord of the Dance" at Mani's cremation 1053
Jyotia. *See* Roy, Jyotia

K

Kabir (Perfect Master and poet) 70, 152, 345, 417, 620
  "Nothing in me is mine..." 1048
Kaikhushru Masa. *See* Irani, Kaikhushru Masa (Small Khorshed's father)
Kaikobad. *See* Dastur, Kaikobad
Kaka. *See* Baria, A.S.
Kakaria, Meherjee 437, 538, 568, 599, 1018
  Trustee 883
Kalchuri, Bhau xiii, 302, 375–376, 667, 903, 1062
  Trustee 887–888, 891, 919
Kalchuri, Raj (Bhau's daughter-in-law) 929

Kalchuri, Rama (Bhau's wife) 929
  sugarcane juice extractor, cleaned 926
Kandivli (near Bombay) 142–143, 442
Kandy 327, 331
Karachi 602
Karim Baba (mast) 348–350
Karnataka 296
Karwar 265, 298, 324, 367
Kashi 276
Kashmir 143, 384, 397, 400, 422
Katie. *See* Irani, Katie Rustom
Keats, John 1035
Keki. *See* Narawala, Keki
Kenmore, Dr. Harry 829, 831
Kerawala, Dadi (Eruch's cousin) 658
Khambatta, Dr. Alu 521, 580
  Mani's crushing burden 889
Khandoba Hill 412, 534
Kharas, Minoo 140, 861
Khare, Dr. 465–467, 476
Kharmanmasi. *See* Irani, Kharmanmasi
Khodadadkaka. *See* Irani, Khodadadkaka (Sheriar's brother, Baba's uncle)
Khorshed (Big). *See* Irani, Khorshed Jamshed
Khorshed (Small). *See* Irani, Khorshed Kaikhushru
Khujaguda (Hyderabad) 529–531
Khuldabad ("Valley of the Saints") 395, 531
Kippy (Boston Terrier) 212–213
Kitty. *See* Davy, Katherine Laura
Kloten airport (Zurich) 599
Kokla Mast 360
Kolhapur 458, 625
Koran 509
Kotwal, Adi (Savak's son) 321
Kotwal, Hilla (Hilloo, Savak's daughter) 266, 321
Kotwal, Najoo (Savak's daughter) xiii, 251, 257, 321
  child on the Blue Bus 266, 321–323
  Mani, letters and calls from 323
  "Typing meant Mani and Mani meant typing." 322
Kotwal, Nergiz Savak (Savak's wife) 321, 376
Kotwal, Savak 321
Krishna, Lord (Avatar) 207, 276–277, 320, 344, 364, 468, 512, 678–679
Kulu Valley 397, 401, 402–403
Kumar, Mataji (Kumar's mother) 504
Kumar, Shatrughan (Kumar) 493, 499, 679, 797
Kumar, Subadhra (Amrit's mother) 493, 499, 797
Kumbh Mela 476, 499

L

L-shaped room (Baba-House, Poona) 16–19, 519, 1011
Lahore 327, 333, 382, 396
Lake Como (Italy) 601
Lake Maggiore (Italy and Switzerland) 601
Laurens, South Carolina 562
Links, The (Bangalore) 291–292, 296
Listen Humanity (Meher Baba) 646
Locarno (Switzerland) 599–601
Lombard, Carole 723
Lonavla 265, 272, 373, 507
London 356, 592–598
    Buckingham Palace 593–594
    Fleet Street 595
    Kew Gardens 595
    Madame Tussauds Wax Museum 597
    Richmond Park 595
    Rubens Hotel 593, 596
    Thames River 595
    Theatre Royal Drury Lane 595
    Tower of London 595
    Trafalgar Square 593
Long Island, New York 542, 549
Loni (village near Poona) 33
"Loni Girl" 33, 894
Lord Meher (Bhau Kalchuri) 302, 375–376
"Lord of the Dance, The" 1053
Lord of the Rings, The (J. R. R. Tolkien) 953
Lorelai 336
Love Alone Prevails (Kitty Davy) 620, 631, 667
Love Personified (Lawrence Reiter) 1022
Lucknow 360, 481, 512
Lucky (monkey) 307–308
Lukes, Sparky 556

M

MacMurray, Fred 695
Madeira 324
Madras 360, 512
Mahabaleshwar 376, 396–397, 425–426, 506, 511–521, 622
    Arthur's Seat 624
    Florence Hall 425–426, 516–521, 520, 622
Maharani of Baroda. *See* Shantadevi, Maharani of Baroda
malaria 384
Maloja (Switzerland) 600–601
Mandi 402
mangoes 615–617
Mani. *See* Irani, Mani Sheriar (Baba's sister)
Manjri Mafi 494, 499
Manmad 363
Manonash (annihilation of the mind) 524–525, 529–536
"Manonash" cabin 743, 802
Mansari. *See* Desai, Mansari
Manu. *See* Jessawala, Manu Beheram (Eruch's sister)
Marble Palace (Calcutta) 301
Marble Rocks (near Jabalpur) 275
Margaret. *See* Craske, Margaret
Marks, Fred
    found Hutchinson record of "Begin the Beguine" 844
Marple, Miss 417
Marrich, Shelley 1051, 1057
Marseilles 199
Martin, Mary 595
Mary. *See* de Sousa, Mary (Mani's school friend); Backett, Will and Mary
Mary (Mother of Jesus) 88–89, 715
    seen by Mani in mango tree 987
Masaji. *See* Irani, Rustom Masa (Baba's uncle)
Masi. *See* Irani, Dowlamasi Feredoon (Masi, Baba's aunt)
Mastan (Baba's favorite dog) 437, 607, 663, 667, 715, 719
    died from grief at Baba's passing 849
mast ashrams
    Ajmer 347
    Bangalore 291–292, 347, 353
        mast hotel 296
    Jabalpur 347
    Mahabaleshwar 425, 624
    Meherabad 260, 299, 317, 347, 353
    Rahuri 187
    Ranchi 347, 348
"Master's Prayer" 604, 620, 704, 791, 966, 1021, 1047
masts (God-Intoxicated) 317, 337, 347–361
    7th plane majzoob in Bombay 705–706
    Baba's five favorites 353
    Chaddar Baba 296
    Chatti Baba 296, 320, 350, 353–357, 367–369
    Chinnaswami 296
    Karim Baba 348–350
    Kokla Mast 360
    Mohammed (Mohommed) 274, 350, 357–359
    Nilkanth from Rishikesh 624
    Phulwala (flower mast) 296, 350
    Ramshish 296
    Shariat Khan 296
    Tippu Bava 351
Wayfarers, The (Dr. William Donkin) 436–437

INDEX

Matchabelli, Princess Norina 192, 195, 202, 213–215, 231–238, 255, 269, 289, 308, 326, 330, 355, 362, 412, 427, 439, 452, 468, 537, 551, 634, 668
   health 558
   Jesus play 255
   Mani embarrasses her with chamber pot 197
   Meher Spiritual Center 436
   ship's captain and 196
   steals Delia's jokes 440–441
Mathura 276–277
Max. *See* Haefliger, Max
Maya, the principle of ignorance 673
McLoyd, Mrs. 604–605, 618
Mehera. *See* Irani, Mehera Jehangir (Baba's Beloved)
Meherabad 43–44, 145–174, 187, 204, 300, 316, 344, 396, 534, 858, 886
   1942, use as soldier camp 371
   ashram established 45
   Baba's Cabin 168, 807, 845, 853, 995–997
      stretcher that bore Baba's body 853, 995
   Baba's *gaadi* 58, 170, 998–1002
   Cage Room 348–349
   Dharmshala, Old 52
   dhuni (sacred fire) 111
   East Room 145, 808, 999
   hospital quarters 349, 367
   Mani's shrine 1050, 1065–1068
   Meher Ashram school for boys 614
   Mehera's shrine 994–995, 1029
   Meher Pilgrim Centre 210, 1002–1009
      Baba, photographs of 1004–1005, 1006–1007
      rules 1002
   Meher Retreat 207, 324, 452
   Museum 808
   Post Office 47, 48
   Prem Ashram 55, 147
   Sabha Mandap 1029, 1062
   Samadhi (tomb) of Avatar Meher Baba 805–812, 845, 853
      "gates would be open" 880
      mural restoration project 891, 992–993
      portico 880
      women's arti 990–991, 998
   Soonamasi's handbell 153
   Study Hall 210
   Tin Shed 220, 225, 226
   Water Tank 55, 145
   Western "sisters" arrive 189, 208–220
   West Room 147
Mehera-Meher (David Fenster) 804–805
Meherazad 397, 531–536, 858
   1956 accident, return after 657
   1960s, typical day in 662–667
   "an 'oasis' in the midst of nowhere" 659
   Baba-lovers visit 880–881
   Baba's bedroom 662, 664–665, 666, 681, 694, 831, 938–940
      bust by John Bruford 939–940
      Mehera's remembrance 938
      "television window" 681, 840
   Baba's lift chair 685–686
   Baba's room in the cottage 416
   Baba's wheelchair 1021
   dining room 662–667, 693–694, 952–953
   electricity installed before needed 836
   Eruch's (Manonash) cabin 743, 802
   finding the property 390
   Fridays were catch-up days 886
   gong 849–853
   gulmohr tree by the gates 988
   Mandali Hall 1047
      Baba, memories recounted 657
      Baba's time with the men 663–664
      brass hand bells 721
      Mani's jokes in 978–979
      Mani's stories in 974–984
         keep your connection with Him strong 980
         "You are looking in us for His humanity and we are looking in you for His Divinity." 976
      verandah 880
   mango tree on the approach road 987–988
   "Mani's cupboard" 968–970
   Mani's "sofa chair" 948
   Mani's toy cupboard 970–972
   Mani's veranda desk 669–670, 686, 953–958
      intimate letters written there 954
   Mehera-Mani's room 946–948
   Mehera's garden 399, 410, 414, 416, 657, 661, 667, 686, 985–989
      Baba says, "Nice flower." 687
      "Garden of Allah" per Baba 985
      umar tree with Baba's image 817–823, 986
         Baba said, "This tree I like." 822
         sacred to Dattatreya (Creator, Sustainer, Destroyer) 821, 989
         spider web repaired broken piece 823
   Meher Free Dispensary 882
   naming 392
   natural world 657–661
      trees (Mani's "old friends") 410
   new house
      housewarming 437–438
      stones used in foundation 413–415
   passageway 950–952
   Seclusion (Tembi) Hill 412–413, 529, 532–533

INDEX 1139

Swanee (small van) 1062–1063
women's first stay at 392, 409–412
women's typical evening 666–667
Meher Baba. *See* Irani, Merwan Sheriar
    (Avatar Meher Baba)
Meher Baba Journal 221, 222, 365
Meher-Center-on-the-Lakes 435–436
"Meher Chalisa" (Keshav Nigam) 959, 973
Meherdil. *See* Irani, Meherdil Sohrab (Baba's grandnephew)
Meherjee. *See* Kakaria, Meherjee
Meher Mount (Ojai, California) 559
Mehernaz. *See* Sukhadwala, Mehernaz (Baba's grandniece)
Meher Nazar (Ahmednagar) 886
"Meher Raj" arti 158
Meher Retreat (Nasik) 187
Meher Spiritual Center (Myrtle Beach) 435–436, 537–560, 668
    Baba's future plans for 556
    Baba's House 547, 551, 553
    Barn 553
    beach 555
    Gater Lake 553
    Guest House 551, 553, 556
        breakfast with Baba 555
    Long Lake 553
    Mani and Mehera's last visit 591
    Mani, contact with 631
    public day 556–557
Meheru. *See* Irani, Meheru Rustom (Mehera's niece); Jessawala, Meheru (Eruch's sister)
Meherwan. *See* Jessawala, Meherwan Beheram (Eruch's brother)
Memphis, Tennessee 563, 584
Merog (family nickname for Baba) 38
Mertens, Hedi 262, 598–600
Merwan. *See* Irani, Merwan Sheriar (Avatar Meher Baba)
Mini Taj. *See* Bibi Ka Maqbara
Minoo. *See* Kharas, Minoo
Minta. *See* Toledano, Minta (Delia's sister)
Mirabai (devotee of Krishna) 1022
Miraj 507
Mississippi River 563
Mistry, Roda xiii, 1057
Mittu (parrot) 383, 398, 953
Mohammed (Avatar) 678–679
Mohammed (Mohommed Mast) 274, 350, 357–359, 1059
moholla (neighborhood) 72–75, 83, 130, 159
Mohommad Gaznavi King 227
Monteagle, Tennessee 584

Mooreland Heights Tourist Court (Murphy, North Carolina) 562
Moorty, Dr. G. S. N. 647, 767
Moradabad 482–492
Mortimer, John (Rumpole series) 948
motels. *See* hotels, motels, and rest houses
Motichoor 499–501
Moucka (man near Baba's Oklahoma accident site) 567
movies and plays seen by Baba or the women
    Absent-Minded Professor, The (movie) 695
    All About Eve (movie) 524
    Annie Get Your Gun (movie) 524
    Dr. Ehrlich's Magic Bullet (movie) 364
    Flaming Feather (movie) 556
    Gone with the Wind (movie) 625
    Gopal Krishna (movie) 298
    King and I, The (musical) 592
    Paradine Case, The (movie) 524
    September Affair (movie) 524
    South Pacific (musical) 595
    Sweet Madness (comedy) 593
    Wake Up and Dream! (movie) 420–422
    Where's Charley? (Broadway show) 592
    White Tower, The (movie) 524
Mt. Abu 447–450
Mt. Everest 615
Mt. Vesuvius 539
Mulog (Sheriar's business partner) 67–70
Multan 333
Murder Book of Mr. J. G. Reeder, The (Edgar Wallace) 417
    Reeder played by Rano 634
Murphy, North Carolina 562, 584
Mussolini, Benito 37, 325
Mussoorie 493, 604–605
Myna. *See* Shelke, Myna Sadashiv (Mani's friend in Toka)
Myrtle Beach, South Carolina 555
    Baba's initials and someday "Meher Beach" 538
    drive-in cinema 555
    Florida Oceanarium 556
    Kiddieland 556
    Lafayette Manor Hotel 558
    ocean touched by Baba 727
    Youpon Dunes 580, 584
        Baba's stay at Elizabeth's home 587–591
Mysore 175, 187
    Dassera procession 292
    Nurse Rose brings the babies 184–186
    zoo 293–295

N

Nadel, Erico 1060
Nadel, Heather x, 956
Nadine. *See* Tolstoy, Countess Nadine
Naggu. *See* Irani, Naggu Rustom (Meheru's sister)
Nagpur 360, 710
Naja. *See* Irani, Naja Rustom (Baba's cousin)
Najibabad 480, 491
Najoo. *See* Kotwal, Najoo (Savak's daughter)
Nalavala, Naosherwan 504–505
Naldurg 522–523
Nanhi Dunya (Little World school for the deaf and dumb) 499
Naples (Italy) 539
Narawala, Freiny 504, 507
Narawala, Keki 493, 499
Narayan Maharaj (Perfect Master) 80
  in Mani's dream 105
Nargis, Nergiz. *See* Dadachanji, Nargis (Arnavas' sister); Kotwal, Nergiz Savak (Savak's wife)
Nariman. *See* Dadachanji, Nariman
Narmada River 275
Nasik 43, 44, 88, 108, 112, 126, 507
Nath, Dr. Siddheshwar 465–467, 470, 476
Natu, Bal xiii, 903, 976, 1041, 1045
  "Mani's letters had life." 917
  passing 885
  Trustee 885–886, 887, 888
Nero Wolfe. *See* Wolfe, Nero; Stout, Rex
New Life (1949-1952)
  public announcement 453
  lack of privacy for the women 488
  "Song of the New Life" 460–462, 508, 581
  Plans I, II, and III 498, 506
  Arrangementwalas 506
  Oct–Nov 1949: training period in Belgaum 455, 458
  Nov–Dec 1949: Benares 465
  Dec 1949: Sarnath 470
    caravan with the animals 475–477, 491
    men in loincloths in underground passage 475
  Dec 1949: Moradabad 482–485
  Jan 1950: "Happy New Life" in Moradabad 485
  Jan–Jun 1950: Dehra Dun 493
  Apr–May 1950: Mahabaleshwar 520–521
  Jun–Aug 1950: Satara 507
  Aug–Oct 1950: Bombay 510
  Oct 1950–Mar 1951: Mahabaleshwar
    Oct 16, 1950 (step back into Old Life) 512
  Mar–Apr 1951: Poona 518–519
  May–Nov 1951: Hyderabad 522–527
    "God-determined Step" of Annihilation 522–523
  Oct–Nov 1951: Aurangabad & Khuldabad 529–532
  Nov 1951–Jan 1952: Pimpalgaon (Manonash) 531–536
  Jan 31, 1952: *dhuni* consuming "rites, rituals, and ceremonies" 535
New York City 543–545
  Broadway 543
  Ceylon India Inn 543–545
  Cloisters, The 592
  Empire State Building 543, 592
  George Washington Bridge 592
  Junior League Club 592
  Natural History Museum 592
  Penn Station 591
  Planetarium 592
  Radio City Music Hall 550, 592
  St. James' Theatre 592
Nigam, Keshav
  "Meher Chalisa" 959, 973
Nilkanth (mast from Rishikesh) 624
Nilu, Dr. *See* Godse, Dr. Vinayak Nilkanth Narayan
Nonny. *See* Gayley, Estelle (Nonny, Rano's mother)
Norina. *See* Matchabelli, Princess Norina
Notre Dame (Paris) 201

O

Ocean of Love, The (Delia DeLeon) 192–193
Ojai, California 559
oodi (sacred ash) 111
Ootacamand (hill station) 179–180
Oppenheim, E. Phillips 417
Orczy, Baroness (*Scarlet Pimpernel*) 830
Oxford (England) 595

P

Padri. *See* Driver, Faredoon Nowroj (Padri)
Pakistan 859
Palace Hotel (Udaipur) 386
Palm Beach (Cannes) 200
Panama 557
Panchgani 207, 265, 353, 367, 376, 396, 521, 1012
Panday, Bhaiya 992
Pandharpur 625
Pandu Lena caves (Nasik) 273
Panjim. *See* Goa

Pappa. *See* Jessawala, Beheram (Eruch's father)
"Paradoxes of Prayer" 932
Paris 201–202, 299–302
   1937 World's Fair 201
Parvardigar Prayer. *See* "Master's Prayer"
Parwar, Valu 146, 194, 204, 229, 382, 410, 415, 449
   planted Meherabad trees 987
Pasarni 397
Pascal, Gabriel 552, 558
Patil. *See* Shelke, Sadashiv G.
Patterson, Elizabeth Chapin 202, 212, 231, 262, 268–269, 278–282, 287–288, 306, 308–309, 326, 355, 359–361, 412, 427, 439, 443, 452, 537–539, 542, 544–549, 550–552, 554, 561, 580, 631–637, 664, 765–766, 891, 954
   accident May 24, 1952 565–567, 581
   circulars from Baba 653
   difficulty getting up early 217–219
   history of the Family Letters 668–669
   Meher Spiritual Center 436
   thermos for Elizabeth 281–282
Pavlova, Anna 30
Peelamasi. *See* Irani, Peelamasi Masaji (Shireen's sister)
Pegu (Siamese cat) 757
Pendu. *See* Irani, Aspandiar Rustom (Baba's cousin)
Perin. *See* Irani, Perinmai Beheram (Baba's sister-in-law)
Persia (Iran) 5, 10, 204
Peter (Mani's cocker spaniel) 604–612, 628, 650, 663, 665, 667–668, 936
   as puppy, slept on Baba's lap 724
   death and future human lives 610
   dressed as a reindeer 641
   helped raise Mastan and chipmunks 607–608, 953
   "safe and sound at My feet" 719–724
Phulwala (flower mast) 296, 350
Pilamai. *See* Irani, Pilamai Hormuzd (Goher & Katie's aunt)
Pimpalgaon 392, 530–536
   visit to a potter 1041
Pirojamasi (Dr. Alu Khambatta's aunt) 511
Piroja, Pirojamami. *See* Irani, Piroja Moondegar (Baba's aunt); Irani, Pirojamami Rustom (Baba's aunt)
Pistol. *See* Jessawala, Beheram (Pappa, Eruch's father)
Poirot, Hercule 417, 831
Poland 300–302
Pond Creek Motor Court (Ozarks) 563–564

Poona 458, 510, 518–519, 604, 649. *See also* Guruprasad
   Baba House (House-with-the-Well) 41, 83–85, 1010, 1018
      L-shaped room 16–19, 519, 1011
      Zoroastrian wishing well 60
   Babajan's shrine 1045
   Badshah restaurant 1018
   Bhigwan 522
   Bindra House (Jessawala family home) 624, 1012, 1018
   Bombay Dyeing 1019
   Chattersingh's temple and tomb 519
   Covent of Jesus and Mary 43, 86–93
   Deccan College 15
   Empress Gardens 510, 1018
   Ganeshkhind 658
   Hadapsar 510
   Inlak's Hospital 1038–1039, 1046
   Jangle Maharaj cave 519
   Kashmir House 1019
   Kirkee 510
   "Lal Deval" (Red Temple Synagogue) 1018
   Medinova Diagnostic Centre 1015–1016
   New Life seclusion sites 519
   orthopedic surgeon 652
   Parsi cemetary 519
   Parvarti 522
   Poona Club 1012, 1018
   Poona School & Home for the Blind
      their candles lit Mehera's bedside 1019
   Pumpkin House 3, 16, 25
   Sassoon Hospital 3, 25
   Silver Oaks 654–655
   Sizzler, Ashok, and Sagar Plaza 1017
   St. Vincent's School 13
   summer retreat for Mehera, Mani, Goher, and Meheru 1012, 1017–1021, 1042
Prague, Oklahoma 564–584
Prem Basera (Aurangabad) 393
Primrose Hill Estate, Kandy 331
puppets 451–452, 466–469
Puri 360
P.W.D. ("Irrigation") Bungalow (Ahmednagar) 207

Q

qawwali (devotional songs) 56, 396, 663, 666, 685, 700–703, 712, 770, 969, 974
Queen, Ellery 618, 636
Quetta 265, 333, 336–341, 829
Qwaal, Pyaru 140

R

"Rachel" 924
Radha (Beloved of Krishna) 715
Rahuri 187
Raipur 397, 400
Raja (English bull) 499
Rajasthan 447
Rakhni 336
Ramakrishna, Paramahamsa (Perfect Master) 301, 348–350
Ramjoo. *See* Abdulla, Abdul Karim
Ramnad 360
Ramshish (mast) 296
Ranchi 300, 303–304, 347–349, 353–354, 358
Rano. *See* Gayley, Madeleine Estelle
Ratanfui 490
Reader's Digest 667
Red Box, The (Rex Stout) 831–832
Reeves, Jim 780–783
    "There's a Heartache Following Me" (Baba's favorite) 781–783
    "Welcome to My World" 639, 781, 1060
"Repentance Prayer" 791, 966, 1047
restaurants
    Andermatt restaurant (Zurich) 599
    Badshah restaurant (Poona) 1018
    Bethea's Restaurant (Monteagle, Tenneessee) 584
    Ceylon India Inn 543–545
    Columbia drug store (South Carolina) 585–586
    Hotel Schweizerhaus (Maloja) 602
    Junior League Club (New York City) 592
    Palace Hotel (Udaipur) 386
    Sizzler, Ashok, and Sagar Plaza (Poona) 1017
    White House Cafe (Searcy, Tennessee) 563
Rhoda, Roda. *See* Dubash, Rhoda; Mistry, Roda
Rishikesh 341, 371–373, 499, 505
Rock City (Chattanooga, Tennessee) 563
Rome (Italy) 549
Rosewood (Satara) 650–651
Roy, Jyotia 140
Ruano. *See* Bogislav, Ruano
Rubens Hotel, The (London) 593, 596
Ruby Falls (Chattanooga, Tennessee) 563
Rumi (Persian poet) 417
Rumpole series (John Mortimer) 948
Rusipop. *See* Irani, Rustom Jehangir (Rusipop, Goher and Katie's father)
Russia 317
Rustom. *See* Irani, Rustom Kaikhushru; Irani, Rustom Khodadad; Irani, Rustom Masa; Irani, Rustom and Sorab
Rustommama. *See* Irani, Rustommama (Shireen's brother)

S

Sadashiv. *See* Shelke, Sadashiv G. (Patil)
sadhus, types of 501
Sai Baba (Perfect Master) 710–711
Saint, The series (Leslie Charteris) 636, 830
Sakori 16, 20, 624
Salvation Army Hospital. *See* Booth Salvation Army Hospital
samadhi (meditation state) 320
Samadhi (tomb) of Avatar Meher Baba 805–812, 845, 853, 880, 891, 990–993, 998
Sanchi 272, 278
San Francisco, California 561
Sarnath 276, 470, 470–481
Sarosh. *See* Irani, Sarosh Kaikhushru
Sarosh Cinema 417
Sarwar (child on the Blue Bus) 266
Satara 397, 425, 427–428, 506–510, 511, 624, 644
    Baba's 1956 accident 649–654
    Civil Hospital 651
    Grafton 626–644, 650–654
    Jal Villa 625, 642–643
    Mutha's Bungalow 507
    Rosewood 651–652
Satha, Dhun 777
    Baba loved her cards and letters 698–700
Savak. *See* Kotwal, Savak
Savannah, Tennessee 563
Scarlet Pimpernel (Baroness Orczy) 830
Scarsdale, New York 591
Scott, Barbara Bamberger 868
Searcy, Arkansas 563
Seclusion (Tembi) Hill 412–413, 529, 532–533
"Seclusion, Great" 450–451
Secunderabad 408
Shahnameh (Persian epic) 3, 62, 66
Shams-e-Tabriz (Perfect Master and poet) 417
Shannon (Ireland) 549
Shantadevi, Maharani of Baroda 519, 757, 767
Shapurzaman, Ali Akbar (Aloba) xiii, 614, 837, 976
    took a *fal* from Hafiz' Divan for Mani 1041
Shariat Khan (mast) 296
Shaw, Darwin 632
Shaw, Jeanne 558, 632
Shaw, Leatrice and Renae 558, 632
Sheba (Mehera's Arabian horse) 604, 608–609, 612, 628–629, 664, 953
Shelke, Myna Sadashiv (Mani's friend in Toka) 114–115
Shelke, Sadashiv G. (Patil) 83, 114
Shelly House 199
Sheriar. *See* Irani, Sheriarji Moondegar (Baba's father)

Sheroo. *See* Irani, Sheriar Beheram
    (Sheroo, Baba's nephew)
Shimoga 296
ships Baba sailed on
    R.M.S *Ausonia* 119–121
    S.S. *Rajputana* 345
    S.S. *Strathnaver* 194, 198
Shireenmai, Shireen. *See* Irani, Shireenmai
    Sheriar (Baba's mother); Irani, Shireen
    Adi (Baba's niece)
Shivaji (Maharashtrian warrior) 428
Sholapur 272, 522, 531
shows. *See* movies and plays seen by Baba or the
    women
Sicily 324
Sides, Consuelo and Alfred 201
Silla. *See* Irani, Silla (Pilamai's daughter)
Simab, Nazir Ahmad 702
Simla 397, 406
Sims Tourist Court (Waynesboro, Tennessee)
    563
Singh, Todi 493–498
Sirur 456
Sita (Beloved of Krishna) 715
Smith, Joanna 822
Sohrab. *See* Irani, Rustom and Sorab
    (Baba's twin nephews)
Song Celestial, The (Sir Edwin Arnold) 619, 830
"Song of the New Life" 460–462, 508, 581
Soonamasi. *See* Irani, Soonamasi Kaikhushru
    (Small Khorshed's mother)
Sparky. *See* Lukes, Sparky
Sri Lanka. *See* Ceylon
Srinagar 384, 400
Stevens, Don 627
    film of Baba in the crypt 842–843
    Mani, work with 645–647
St. Joseph (Jesus' father) 14
Stout, Rex (Nero Wolfe) 618, 722, 830–831, 840
    "couldn't keep up with Baba" 832
    Red Box, The (last book read to Baba) 831–832
Stratford-on-Avon 595
Streza (Italy) 601
Subhadhra. *See* Kumar, Subhadhra
    (Amrit's mother)
Sudam and Asha. *See* Wagh, Sudam and Asha
    (Khorshed's caregivers)
Suez Canal 198
Sufism Reoriented 557
Sufis, Sufism 320
Sukhadwala, Gulnar J. (Baba's niece, Jangu's
    wife) 559, 1011–1012, 1017–1023,
    1060, 1062
Sukhadwala, Jehangir (Jangu, Gulnar's husband)
    923, 1011, 1017, 1063

Sukhadwala, Mehernaz (Baba's grandniece) 1020
Sukoo and Tukoo (donkeys) 486, 490, 492
Sultoon. *See* Irani, Sultoon R. (Baidul's wife)
"Sultoon's sister". *See* Irani, R. B. (Baidul)
Sumpter (South Carolina) 562
Supa 455
Sushila. *See* Deorukhar, Sushila (Vishnu's cousin)
Switzerland 116, 624

T

Taj Mahal (Agra) 276–277, 333
Taj Mahal Hotel (Bombay) 655
Talati, Dina 136
Tales from the New Life (Don Stevens, et. al.)
    457, 459, 486, 489
Tembi Hill. *See* Seclusion (Tembi) Hill
Teresa, Saint, of Avilla 417, 620, 958–960
Tex toothbrush contest 654
Theologia Germanica 637
"There's a Heartache Following Me" 781
"Three Incredible Weeks" (Sept 1954) 624
Tibet 510
Time magazine 665
Tippu Bava (mast) 351
Tippu (dog) 531
Toka 43, 44, 114, 532, 534
Toledano, Minta (Delia's sister) 443, 595
Tolkien, J. R. R. 618, 953
    Hobbit, The 830
    Lord of the Rings, The 953
Tolstoy, Countess Nadine 231–238, 289, 304,
    338, 355, 362
Tolstoy, Count Leo
    What Men Live By 390
Tommy, jokes about 440
Townshend, Peter 851
Treasures from the Meher Baba Journals
    (Jane Haynes, ed.) 631
Tukaram (Hindu saint) 959
Turkey 299
Twins (Baba's twin nephews). *See* Irani, Rustom
    and Sorab
Typhoon (wire-haired terrier) 398, 416

U

Udaipur 365, 385
Udwada, Sacred Fire Temple 111
United States (America) 135, 204, 537–592, 624,
    635, 647, 668, 673–674, 790, 859
    kindness experienced by Mani 577–579
Upanishads, the 705
Upasni Maharaj (Perfect Master) 19, 78, 81,
    369–370

Shireenmai's "wonderful garland of sandals" 20
threw stone at Merwan 16
Usman Lake 529
Uttar Pradesh 325

V

"Valley of the Saints". *See* Khuldabad "Valley of the Saints"
Valu. *See* Parwar, Valu
Varanasi. *See* Benares
Vedas, the (Hindu scriptures) 705
Vengurla 425
Veyangoda 327
Victoria, Queen of England 594
Vieillard, Anita de Caro 200, 598, 600
Viloo. *See* Irani, Viloo Sarosh
Vishever Golden Temple 276
Vishnu. *See* Deorukhar, Vishnu
Vivekananda, Swami 348

W

Wagh, Sudam and Asha (Khorshed's caregivers) 928
Wallace, Edgar 417, 722, 830
 Chick 417
 Duke in the Suburbs, The 417
 Murder Book of Mr. J. G. Reeder, The 417
 Mr. Reeder played by Rano 634
Waltair 360
Wayfarers, The (Dr. William Donkin) 436–437
Waynesboro, Tennessee 563
"Welcome to My World" 639, 781–783, 1060
White House Cafe (Searcy, Tennessee) 563
Williams, Beryl 632–633, 725
Winterfeldt, Ella 592
Wodehouse, P. G. 722, 830, 840
 inscribes a book to Baba "To the Greatest Humanist in the world" 618

Wodin (artist) 72
Wolfe, Nero 618, 722, 830–832, 840, 928, 948.
 See also Stout, Rex
Wolkin, Adele 558, 592, 633
World War I 147
World War II 258–261, 291–292, 299–302, 308–309, 316–317, 321, 372–373

X

Xavier, St. Francis 298

Y

yakh (ice) 703
Young, Loretta 584
Youpon Dunes (Myrtle Beach, South Carolina) 580, 584, 587–591
Youth Sahavas (1995) 559

Z

Zar-Zari-Zar Bakhsh (Perfect Master) 395
Zend–Avesta (Zoroastrian holy book) 65, 509
zoos 291, 293–295, 511–512
Zoroaster 106, 475
 Shireenmai asks Baba to dress as Him 108–109
Zoroastrians 529, 594
 "All the Zoroastrians will come to Me." 31
 Avatar, no concept of 106
 calendar 810, 834
 customs 4, 32
 opposition to Baba's family 26–30
 Tower of Silence 117
Zurich, Switzerland 599

ABOUT THE AUTHOR

Heather Nadel was born in 1950 in San Francisco, California, USA. An English Literature major in college, she first heard of Avatar Meher Baba in 1969. In 1974, Heather and her husband Eric were drawn to stay near Meher Baba's Samadhi and to be near Baba's Beloved Mehera and His other close mandali. They moved to India and Meherabad became their lifelong home.

Heather had the good fortune over the years at Meherabad and Meherazad to spend time in close contact with Mehera, Mani, Padri, Eruch, and others of Baba's mandali. Under their caring tutelage she became deeply involved in the activities at Meher Baba's home.

Heather worked in close association with Mani at the Trust Office for many years. Her abilities were put to good use by Mani in correspondence, work with Trust-related documents, and in the preparation of the two books Mani wrote, *God-Brother* and *Dreaming of The Beloved*.

After Mani passed away in 1996, drawing from their more than twenty-year working relationship, Heather began to compile materials and to work on a book about the story of Mani's life with Baba. That labor of love has become *The Joyous Path*.